CHINA

CHINA

Black R.

Red R.

NORTH
VIETNAM

● Dien Bien Phu

◉ **Hanoi**

● Haiphong

A N N A M E S E   C O R D I L L E R A

L A O S

Mekong R.

◉ **Vientiane**

Mekong R.

Gulf
of
Tonkin

HAINAN

17°
**DEMILITARIZED
ZONE**

Con Thien ● Gio Linh ●
QUANG ● Quang Tri
TRI ● **Hue**
Khe Sanh ● THUA
THIEN
A Shau
Valley
QUANG
NAM

Da nang ●

**I
CORPS**

QUANG
TIN

QUANG
NGAI

T H A I L A N D

Mekong R.

● **Dak To**
● Kontum
● Pleiku

BINH
DINH

C A M B O D I A

Tonle Sap

CARDAMOM MTS.

Gulf
of
Thailand

**SOUTH
VIETNAM**

● Ban Me Thuot

Dalat ◉

● Loc Ninh
IRON
TRIANGLE
ZONE
● Phuoc
Binh
ZONE
D

● **Phnom Penh**

Tay Ninh ●

● Bien
Hoa

Saigon ◉

● Vung
Tau

**III
CORPS**

Long ● My Tho ●
Xuyen ● ● Ben
Vinh ● Long Tre
● Can Tho

Mekong Delta

South
China
Sea

PHU
QUOC

N

MILES

0   50   100   150

**IV
CORPS**

**II
CORPS**

THE ROAD FROM WAR

Vietnam 1965–1970

THE

ROAD FROM WAR

Vietnam 1965-1970

by *Robert Shaplen*

HARPER & ROW, PUBLISHERS

 NEW YORK AND EVANSTON

1817

This book is dedicated to all
my Vietnamese and American friends
who have believed in, and fought for,
revolution with freedom.

Contents

Introduction   ix

1. *March 20, 1965*—Saigon   1

2. *April 24, 1965*—Saigon   10

3. *November 13, 1965*—Saigon   20

4. *March 12, 1966*—Saigon   32

5. *April 16, 1966*—Saigon   48

6. *June 4, 1966*—Saigon   61

7. *August 20, 1966*—Saigon   74

8. *October 1, 1966*—Saigon   83

9. *December 17, 1966*—Below The D.M.Z.   90

10. *February 18, 1967*—Saigon   121

11. *June 17, 1967*—Saigon   131

12. *October 7, 1967*—Saigon   151

Contents

13. *January 20, 1968*—Saigon 170

14. *March 2, 1968*—Saigon 188

15. *March 23, 1968*—Saigon 206

16. *June 29, 1968*—Saigon 216

17. *November 16, 1968*—Paris 235

18. *January 13, 1969*—Saigon 247

19. *April 12, 1969*—Saigon 262

20. *July 12, 1969*—Paris 285

21. *September 21, 1969*—Saigon 303

22. *January 31, 1970*—Saigon 325

Postscript: June, 1970—Indo-China 348

Index 355

Introduction

Whatever the outcome of the war in Vietnam, including the manner and method of American withdrawal, the long conflict has beyond any doubt written one of the most tragic chapters in American history, and surely in Vietnamese history, too. The tragedy exceeds the terrible death toll alone—at least between seven and eight hundred thousand Vietnamese to date, in the North and the South, and close to forty-five thousand Americans—and a total wounded of more than two million on all sides. The war has not only done much to destroy Vietnamese society; it has divided and embittered American society more than any other war we have fought since the Civil War.

This much is obvious.

What seem to me less obvious are the whys and wherefores of the conflict, the reasons it began, among the Vietnamese themselves, and the reasons that prompted our overinvolvement. It is easy to say, in hindsight, that we had no business to be in Vietnam at all, and that what happened there after World War II, and particularly after the defeat and withdrawal of the French in 1954, did not concern us, certainly not to the point of the military commitment we made. I disapprove of the extent of that commitment, including its belated extension in the spring of 1970 to Cambodia; but I believe that Vietnam did initially concern us politically, and still does, and that our justified political concern warranted an advisory and even a limited military involvement, though one that should have been confined to low-level counter-insurgency action with some air support, and to economic aid. However, any form of military or non-military assistance to the various Saigon governments should have been extended only under the condition that the Vietnamese seriously undertake political reforms. These reforms came far too slowly, if at all, and we could have done far more than we did to encourage them. In fact, by condoning reaction, or inaction, we frequently discouraged reform.

Our association with Vietnam began in 1945 and increased after 1954, and increased again after 1961 and after 1965, but our policy was never, from the outset, properly conceived or developed, and we were quickly led astray by our confusion of purpose and by our inability to formulate and implement programs that might have helped the Vietnamese become aware of their potentialities. As things turned out, I believe we retarded rather than advanced the natural development of the Vietnamese revolution in the South, a revolution that might or might not have been able to follow a path independent of the revolutionary struggle in North Vietnam dominated by the Communists. In this sense, we probably could have achieved more by doing less. Having made the mistakes we did, dating back to our support of the French between 1946 and 1954, the tragic consequences that prompted our own subsequent overengagement may have been inevitable. We were perhaps compulsively bound to come a cropper somewhere, and that somewhere was Vietnam. And if we have not been defeated militarily in Vietnam, we have been defeated morally and politically, and have been responsible for much of the death and destruction that have occurred.

Furthermore, I still fear that we have learned very little from our Vietnam experience. The divisiveness the war has caused in the United States has limited and confounded our capacity to determine what our goals in the world should be, and what our responsibilities are to respond, or not to respond, to highly complicated situations embracing both revolutionary and reactionary possibilities. We are, at the moment, groping through guilt to find a path short of neo-isolationism that will enable us to play a role commensurate with our power but that will also acknowledge our inability to control events that are uncontrollable, or that are best left to their own unfolding. Short of a nuclear holocaust, this process of anguished reappraisal will, I think, take many years, for Vietnam has created in us a new shock of recognition, one that has tempered but not yet eliminated our sense of *hubris.* The self-criticism we are engaging in has healthy but also unhealthy and distorting characteristics. It will take time to develop a new spirit of pride and confidence, and to reach an awareness of what our purpose and our goals are, both at home and abroad.

In an earlier book, *The Lost Revolution* (1965), I tried to set down what happened in Vietnam between 1945 and 1965, and to explain as best I could the meaning behind events over those two turbulent decades. The thesis of that book was that by our miscomprehension and mishandling of those events we forfeited any chance there might have been to guide a nationalist revolution away from Communism. It is fashionable nowadays to say that nationalism, like liberalism, is an outworn and meaningless concept. I disagree, and the more sanguine peaceful developments in Southeast Asia, as well as some of the more radical and violent ones, tend, I think, to substantiate that conclusion. In a later book, *Time out of Hand* (1969), I sought to analyze and evaluate some of those developments in the Southeast Asian area, particularly in Indonesia.

All of the twenty-two articles in this book—twenty written from Vietnam and two from Paris after the peace talks began—appeared in *The New Yorker* under the dates of issue as listed, covering almost five years. I have reduced them, in total length, by about a fourth for purposes of book publication, but I have not edited them otherwise. They thus represent one man's evolving thoughts and appraisals of a highly complex situation over half a decade, and whatever contradictions or changes of opinion they demonstrate will, I hope, be regarded by the reader as the product of my own experience and learning process. Thus the book is not meant to be one of historical summary or reinterpretation, but of history as it unfolded. In editing the articles, I have eliminated repetitive material wherever it seemed advisable to do so, but not to the point of removing what seemed important to include within shifting contexts. In so doing, I have tried to relate what was happening today to what happened yesterday and might happen tomorrow.

The opinions and judgments expressed are all my own, including what the reader may regard as changes of attitude or tone. I have considered my chief function to be one of interpretive reportage, but, subjectively, frustration, like hope, is a double-edged sword, and no man can observe a tragedy such as Vietnam without becoming part of it and suffering its anguish.

As before, I want to express my deep thanks to all those Vietnamese and American friends who helped so unstintingly over the years. And once again my special thanks go to William Shawn, the editor and guiding force of *The New Yorker,* who has given me both total opportunity and freedom to write about Vietnam as I saw and felt about it. My appreciation for their editorial guidance and advice is also extended to William Knapp, of *The New Yorker,* to Miss Genevieve Young, of Harper & Row, and to my wife, June Herman Shaplen, who has lived through these years with me.

Saigon
May, 1970

THE ROAD FROM WAR

Vietnam 1965–1970

1. Saigon

~~~~~~

March 20, 1965

The determination of the United States to maintain pressure on North Vietnam by bombing selected targets, first in the lower part of the country and then, if necessary, farther north, has served to stiffen the Saigon government's backbone, but skepticism is growing here about just how effective the bombings will be in persuading the Hanoi government to call off the infiltration of South Vietnam and the subversion of its people. Because of this, and also because the Saigon government is beset by the usual political imponderables, there is a good deal of confusion here about the aims and the likely outcome of this protracted and many-faceted conflict. Since no one expects South Vietnam's troubles to be resolved very soon—most people foresee two or three more years of war—the bombings and also the arrival of two battalions of American Marines to guard the northern air base of Danang, with more Marines reportedly coming to guard other bases, have somewhat paradoxically had the effect of strengthening not the offensive but the defensive posture and mood. Many South Vietnamese feel that if the bombings continue to be restricted to the less important targets and are carried out only sporadically, they will encourage the North Vietnamese to step up the attack in the South. In the crucial central plateau and coastal areas, the Vietcong—increasingly reinforced by officers and troops from the North but still very much a southern revolutionary force in its own right—have already been moving toward what looks like a showdown, reminiscent of the showdown against the French in 1953. The possibility looms that more and more of the countryside will fall to the Communists and that the South Vietnamese and the Americans will be reduced to holding less territory, but retaining the important provincial and district towns, as well as such major cities as Saigon and Danang.

If, on the other hand, the bombing attacks are extended to targets farther north in North Vietnam—important bridges and railheads, roads leading into China, and factories and other installations relatively close to Hanoi and Haiphong, including the Red River Delta dikes—the possibility of direct Chinese involvement, and the certainty of an increase in material help from both China and Russia, might have the same effect, hardening the resolve of Hanoi neither to give up nor to go to the conference table. Either way, of course, the bombing represents a calculated risk, and one that will have obvious repercussions in a number of important capitals, in terms not only of diplomacy but of public opinion, which is inevitably turning against us throughout the Afro-Asian world. Yet despite these handicaps and these dangers, there is a certain sense of gratification among both Americans and South Vietnamese that a first step, at least, has been taken. The feeling is that not only has the war on the ground been going so badly that something new had to be devised to rally resistance—as the American air attacks against the Vietcong boosted morale here—but also that if the North Vietnamese are sufficiently hurt by the bombings, they just might welcome the opportunity to halt hostilities. They could then trade with the South for rice, achieve a better balance in their relations with Russia and with China, and consolidate their strength for the next big move.

The move, in due time, would surely come. Few Vietnamese here are ingenuous enough to believe that even a new Southeast Asia agreement, with "teeth" in it—presumably American ones—would convince the Communists that they should renounce their long-term objective of reunifying Vietnam to their own advantage. In this respect, the situation today is far more complex than the one in 1954, when, following the Geneva settlement, almost a million refugees, most of them Catholics, came down from the North and an estimated hundred thousand Communist fighters and Communist sympathizers moved up from the South. The Communist apparatus in the South now is much larger and more effective than it was then, and no matter what terms might be agreed upon, one could hardly expect that all the hard-core Vietcong forces could be got out, that all the guerrillas would turn in their arms, or that the National Liberation Front, North Vietnam's supposedly "independent" agency in South Vietnam, which it insists that the Saigon government must deal with, could or would be broken up. The best that could be hoped for, it is thought, would be a new kind of cold war, in which a reoriented Communist campaign of subversion would be faced by a group of governments strong enough to contain it in most respects—political, military, and economic. South Vietnam, in other words, would be part of an independent bloc of Southeast Asian states, of the sort envisioned by Prince Norodom Sihanouk, of Cambodia. This is pretty much of a long-shot gamble, most realistic observers admit—one that would have to depend ultimately on an agreement between the United States and China.

If South Vietnam is to have any chance of fulfilling this hopeful prognosis, it will need a strong national government with sufficient popular support and with the ability to contain all the disparate South Vietnamese elements that, wittingly or unwittingly, have been tearing the country apart in the year and a half since the overthrow of Ngo Dinh Diem and his family oligarchy. Whoever has been most responsible for this chaos—and observers tend to blame the Americans as much as the Vietnamese for failing to come up with any sound plan for dealing with the situation after the coup against Diem, which the Americans supported—everyone agrees that the disintegration caused by the series of repeated coups cannot be allowed to continue if South Vietnam is to reach an eventual conference table intact. At the moment, for the first time in months, there appears to be some slight promise of stability, but, Vietnam being Vietnam, this could be shattered overnight if certain elements got out of hand or if the group of generals who still sit on top of the civilian government start engaging in another power struggle.

The most disruptive figures of the recent past have now managed either to eliminate each other or to defeat themselves; the three top-ranking generals—Nguyen Khanh, Duong Van Minh, and Tran Thien Khiem—who were bitterly fighting for control six months ago are all out of the country, in diplomatic posts. "We have our own three sputniks," one Vietnamese editor says. Some of the other important generals who were part of the first junta after Diem's assassination are out of uniform and are quietly engaged in the export-import business here; in the late afternoon they can be seen sipping coffee in cafés on Tu Do, the main street. But among the score of generals on the Armed Forces Council there are new candidates for power, and despite a pledge by all of them that they will devote themselves to fighting the war and allow the potentially efficient government of Prime Minister Phan Huy Quat to run the nation without interference, several of these officers are already skirmishing for the role of strong man just vacated by General Khanh. The most important of them, and therefore the man regarded as the worst potential troublemaker, is General Nguyen Chanh Thi, who commands the northernmost corps of the South Vietnamese Army. Part of the danger he represents derives from the fact that he is closely associated with the leaders of the Buddhist movement, who are now conducting a curious campaign for peace while privately saying that they will support the full prosecution of the war, including the American bombings of North Vietnam, if their efforts to bring the Hanoi and Saigon governments together fail.

The Americans here, who first loved Khanh, because he was a firm leader, and then hated him, because he didn't love them back, and also because he kept plotting and maneuvering to enhance his own position, have their fingers crossed in the hope of warding off any move by Thi or anyone else that might upset the applecart. But the fact remains that, in spite of the government's potential strength, a vacuum exists, and vacuums are likely to be filled even more quickly in Vietnam than they are elsewhere. Another man who may try to fill this one is Colonel Pham Ngoc Thao, who led the unsuccessful coup against Khanh on February 19th—a failure that nonetheless served as a catalyst when the generals saw Khanh on the run and took advantage of the situation to vote him out of office and out of the country. American officials think that even without Thao's coup Khanh would eventually have been forced out as commander-in-chief and head of the Armed Forces Council, but in view of Khanh's great capacity for bluff and maneuver, other people believe that this was by no means certain. At any rate, Thao is still in the country, in hiding, and if he can remain undetected, *his* capacity for gathering armed support and making another attempt is not to be underestimated, either. General Thi has had a squad of gunmen out looking for him, but Thao has a lot of friends. Some people think the government would be safer if it lifted the price on Thao's head and amnestied him, so that he could "surface."

In all respects, Thao is one of the most remarkable Vietnamese around, being a conspiratorial revolutionary figure straight out of a Malraux novel and, at the same time, a highly sophisticated and politically astute man, whose talents, if only they were properly channelled, could profitably be used right now. He comes from an educated Vietnamese Catholic family that held French citizenship but was strongly anti-French. After attending good French schools in Saigon, Thao himself renounced his French citizenship in 1942 and went to work in 1947 for the Vietminh as an independent resistance leader in the South. By 1949, he was in charge of the entire Vietminh espionage apparatus around Saigon and also had the job of organizing guerrilla companies in the countryside. Soon thereafter, he broke with the Vietminh, though he was still in touch with its leaders in the South. By 1956, Thao had begun to ally himself to Diem, and he was soon working in various Army units as a propagandist for the government-created Can Lao Party. Next, he became a trouble-shooter for Diem in the provinces, and was named Chief of Kien Hoa Province, where, by using his intimate knowledge of Vietminh tactics to win the support of the peasant population and organize resistance against the Vietcong, he distinguished himself as a counter-insurgency leader. But, like so many others, he then turned against Diem, and when the coup took place, Thao led the tank assault on Diem's palace. Afterward, because the generals who took over were afraid of Thao and other officers who, like him, had done the real job of creating the coup machinery, he was sent off to the United States, where he pursued military studies at Fort Leavenworth. When Khanh seized power, Thao returned to Saigon to become his press attaché, and then was, in effect, sent into exile again, as a result of the intrigues and contests of strength between Khanh and various other generals, particularly General Khiem; before long, Khiem was named Ambassador to the United States, and Thao became his aide. Late last year, Thao was summoned back by Khanh, ostensibly for consultation. Actually, Khanh planned to arrest him, but Thao found this out in time to go underground. Finally, last month, he pulled his coup.

The coup failed because of tactical mistakes, but Thao had considerable support behind him. Many of the officers involved were Catholics, and the coup was described as a Catholic coup, but in fact Thao had also consulted the two leading Buddhist leaders in the country, Thich Tri Quang and Thich Tam Chau beforehand. Though they did not give him open support, it is conceivable that they had no strong objections to seeing Khanh overthrown; over a period of a year, the Buddhists and Khanh had used each other from time to time in their separate and joint drives for power, but they had also fought each other. Since Thao now has the sympathy of some Buddhists, a similar marriage of convenience, typical in this country of shifting alliances, could come to exist between them, too.

The current Buddhist campaign for peace is regarded by most observers who have followed the ups and downs of the political-religious movement in the last two years as a tactical maneuver by Buddhist leaders to reëstablish their somewhat diminished control over the nominally Buddhist masses, who mostly do not practice their faith. The Vietnamese Buddhists are basically not nearly as pacific as the Buddhists elsewhere in Southeast Asia, and they are using the peace issue primarily as a political weapon; one reason they are playing it up now is the existence of an opposition peace movement, which was patently inspired by the Vietcong. It is a foregone conclusion that the Buddhists, who have some differences on tactics but none on essential strategy, either will keep up their offensive maneuvers, calculated to control the government in power, or else will demonstrate against it and bring it down, as they did with the regime of Premier Tran Van Huong, which preceded Phan Huy Quat's. At the moment, guided by the militant views of Thich Tri Quang, they are quietly gaining control of most of the pagodas in Saigon, purging the monks who do not go along with them, and maintaining a tight vertical chain of command, down to the block level in the city. It is always difficult to gauge the sincerity of the Buddhists here, but they seem to be dominated by motives of self-preservation and of aggrandizement of their new political role. Many people here still think that, whatever they say, they are fundamentally xenophobic—especially anti-American—and that they are anxious to make an accommodation with the Communist North, hoping then to be left in peace in a neutralized South.

The Catholics, though they are ordinarily less given to demonstrations than the Buddhists, are also to be reckoned with; they feel that they have been shunted aside by the Quat government, and resent the fact that the Catholics who helped lead last month's coup have not been amnestied. The Army is still another source of uneasiness; there are some strong Buddhists, like General Thi, but there are also many officers and men, Catholic or neutral, who resent the attempts of the Buddhists to seek political power, and these elements could become rebellious. In this touchy situation, Prime Minister Quat and his Cabinet are treading cautiously—too cautiously, some would say—in the hope of keeping peace among all the factions and creating some semblance of orderly government. Quat, a long-time nationalist who served as Minister of National Defense under the French-sponsored regime of the former Emperor, Bao Dai, joined the political opposition to Diem but managed to stay out of jail. He is a quiet, urbane northerner, and he has his own small brain trust composed mostly of fellow-northerners or men from central Vietnam; he has already been accused of selecting too many northerners to fill administrative posts—a charge he has countered with the comment that he can't find enough able southerners willing to work with him. In any event, he has so far made a fairly good impression on most Vietnamese, as well as on the Americans. One of his first declared tasks is to control the prices of rice, sugar, water, and electricity, and this is not easy to do in a long-established climate of corruption. If he is allowed to go his own way for two or three months, particularly by the Buddhists and the generals, he has a chance of clearing up the messy situation. At the moment, practically everyone seems to realize that an even keel is an absolute necessity, but whether the keel will remain even is doubtful. Chaos feeds upon itself, and anarchy has become endemic in Vietnam. "In a way, after all the pent-up years under the French and under Diem, we are like children letting off steam," one Vietnamese political observer said the other day. "Maybe there will have to be another half-dozen coups before we settle down—even though we know we can't afford them."

That the Vietnamese can't afford more coups is being dramatically demonstrated right now on the plateau north of Saigon—a region stretching across the country from the Laotian border to Qui Nhon, on the coast. Here the Communists have been trying to cut South Vietnam in two, and while government reinforcements have so far stopped them, they are bound to keep trying in the weeks ahead. Attacking in battalion strength, the Vietcong have cut in several places the coastal road leading from the southern port of Nhatrang to Danang, and have done the same on a strategic east-west road, though they haven't been able to hold their positions there. Most military men admit that if it had not been for attacks by Vietnamese Skyraiders and American B-57s, the government would probably have suffered a disastrous defeat in the past fortnight. As it is, this plateau battle still promises to be the most crucial of the war.

What the Communists are apparently seeking to do is to create a "liberated area" in the central coastal province of Binh Dinh, a historic cradle of Vietnamese revolutionary activity, and to make it a link between smaller zones of Vietcong control to the north and south. It is significant that in this campaign, despite the influx of North Vietnamese units discussed in the recent American White Paper, the southern hard-core and regional forces are leading the battle, and the northerners are playing the role of what the North Vietnamese call "participating observers." Indeed, part of Hanoi's purpose in sending men into the South is to get them accustomed to American-Vietnamese fighting techniques and to give them the experience of living under aerial attack—by bombs, by napalm, and by a nasty new device called the "lazy dog," a canister contrivance that explodes thirty feet above the ground and sends several thousand finlike pieces of metal shooting off at high speed in all directions. One disturbing aspect of the continuing crisis in the highlands is the tactics being used by the Vietcong in pushing large numbers of refugees from the embattled areas into coastal cities still controlled by the government, where they are causing serious feeding and housing problems. The Communists also infiltrate with these refugees and create a fifth column in the towns. It seems astonishing that, in a war that has been going on for so many years, so little should have been done either by the South Vietnamese government or by the Americans both to take better care of the refugees and to counter this sort of subversion.

In sum, in this Year of the Snake, infiltration from the North and increased attack and subversion by the Vietcong all over the South have brought the war to a new pitch of intensity. American and Vietnamese planes may continue to avert disaster, but guerrillas, like snakes, are hard to eliminate, and ultimately they must be dealt with on the ground. Ambassador Maxwell Taylor said to Prime Minister Quat the other day, in a moment of euphoria, "Your government will be the victory government in South Vietnam." American optimism out here has been severely jolted in the past, and there are signs, despite the new position of firmness, that it may be jolted again. Even partial victory, through negotiation, seems far off. The struggle in Vietnam, one way or another, is bound to go on for a long time.

2.   # Saigon

~·~

April 24, 1965

Early one recent morning in the town of Phu Cat, in the coastal province of Binh Dinh, some two hundred miles north of Saigon, I climbed aboard an American Army helicopter that was about to accompany a so-called Eagle Flight—in this case a flight of six helicopters, each with an American pilot and co-pilot, each with American machine gunners guarding the two doors, and each carrying six Vietnamese soldiers, whose mission was to attack and destroy a fortified Vietcong village fifteen minutes' flying time away. Shortly before we reached the objective, two American Skyraiders strafed and bombed the village, which lay in a shallow valley below a long range of hills, and sank a small junk in a nearby river, and then, as we approached the site, two more helicopters, which were carrying rockets and were known as gunships, made another attack on the village and on the designated landing zone— a field about two hundred yards away. As the troop-carrying ships approached the field, the pilots found that dozens of short tree trunks had been driven into the soil to prevent just such a landing, but they managed to ease the helicopters in among the stumps, and they set down, debouched their troops, and took off in the remarkable time of ten seconds, which is thirteen seconds less than it takes a shell from a mortar—a weapon that the Vietcong now have in considerable supply—to reach its target.

While the pair of gunships and the helicopter that I was in hovered overhead, to provide protection and to attack any Vietcong flushed from their hiding places, the three dozen government soldiers and a young American lieutenant who was serving as their adviser dispersed through the village, which consisted of twenty houses and was surrounded by a moat filled with sharpened bamboo spikes two and three feet high—punji sticks, they are called. The Vietcong had apparently fled, and there was no sign of activity, but eight bodies were found in ditches and beside foxholes. After carefully searching the houses, the troops set fire to all twenty of them. Then, deploying through the fields, they found seven women and children cowering in canals and took them prisoner. The whole operation lasted a little less than an hour, and then the helicopters landed again, picked up the troops, and flew back to Phu Cat, arriving with their fuel tanks almost empty. The prisoners, frightened and weeping, were immediately questioned by Vietnamese interrogators, who sought information about the men of the village and the movements of the Vietcong contingents in the area. I was told the seven would be free to settle in one of the government-held villages, but, as I subsequently found out, they were sent to a refugee camp.

Eagle Flights are perhaps the best example of the improved mobility provided by the growing participation of American aircraft in the war. Early in February, for example, when the Vietcong made a night attack on the American barracks at Pleiku—an action that proved to be a small Pearl Harbor, in that it precipitated our air attacks against North Vietnam—fast-pursuing Eagle Flight troops caught up with the fleeing terrorists at dawn and, with the help of reserves brought in by helicopter, killed twenty-seven of them. There is little question that the combination of fast troop movements and aerial assaults against enemy troop concentrations and bases within South Vietnam—especially quick retaliatory strikes by jet bombers—has forced the Vietcong to alter their basic plan, which was designed to give them victory this year. This plan, which was conceived in mid-1964 as the beginning of the third, or all-out, stage in the Communists' long-term strategy, was predicated on the continuing instability of the Saigon government and on the seem-

ing demoralization of government troops, and it provided for a series of assaults on the central coastal plains, the establishment of
enclaves along the shore to receive new, Chinese-made Soviet-style
weapons brought in by sea, and the use of forces up to regimental
size to cut the country in two, leaving the southern delta, which is
already mostly held by the Vietcong, as the lower jaw of a vise in
which to grip Saigon, while the other jaw was, of course, the central
plateau. Then the mountainous, northern region just above the plateau and just below North Vietnam would be isolated and attacked.

Until a month or two ago, it looked as if this plan might succeed.
In February, both regular and local elements of the Vietcong, bol-
stered by infiltrators from North Vietnam, had moved boldly onto
the plains of the two most important coastal provinces then held by
the government, Binh Dinh and Phu Yen, and had completely disrupted earlier pacification efforts there. Since then, our air attacks
have driven the Vietcong back into the mountains or have forced
them to lie low in villages and swamps near the coast; any assaults
they now make in the open are likely to be costly. The arrival last
week of three thousand more American Marines in the northern-
corps area, bringing the total Marine force in South Vietnam to
about eight thousand men, or half a reinforced division, with air
and missile support, has probably forestalled any immediate Vietcong plans to launch a major attack in the region around the northern port of Danang. These troops constitute the first sizable
American ground units to be used for offensive as well as defensive
action in South Vietnam, and sooner or later they will undoubtedly
tangle with the Vietcong; in fact, nothing rules out their use as
direct combat forces on Eagle Flight actions, and in an emergency
they may be airlifted to areas at some distance from their base.

The combination of this influx of Marines, of the succession of
government victories, of the evolving pattern of bombings aimed at
destroying North Vietnam's communication and transportation
systems, and, finally, of President Johnson's speech at Johns Hop-
kins University on April 7th has brought the war into new focus
here. The President's speech, with its promise of future long-term
aid for North as well as South Vietnam, got an odd reaction: it was
officially praised by Prime Minister Phan Huy Quat and Foreign
Minister Tran Van Do, but an undertone of official worry was de-
tectable, prompted by the fear that the United States had gone too

far in opening the path to negotiations, even though American spokesmen made it clear that while we were ready to hold "unconditional discussions" of the situation, we would not "negotiate" until we were satisfied that aggression had ceased.

South Vietnam's role in its own defense is still far from successful. Politically, despite much talk about stability, the situation is by no means stable, and militarily, despite the turn for the better, the picture is still pretty dark. Not only do the Communists currently control almost two-thirds of the country—including big chunks of new territory gobbled up where they are now consolidating their political position and regrouping their military strength—but there is every indication that in about a month, when the rainy season starts in the South and it becomes harder for planes to fly, there may be a new Vietcong offensive, possibly aimed simultaneously at provincial and district capitals in the highlands and major towns along the coast, which will tax to the utmost the government's ability to resist with the forces it has available. Government plans call for augmenting troop strength this year by a hundred and sixty thousand men, for a total of seven hundred thousand, but though the number of volunteers is increasing, many of the regular government battalions in the nine Army divisions are still some twenty-five per cent under strength as a result of desertions and combat losses, and conscription is still necessary. The requirement of new manpower for the important secondary elements—the Regional (or provincial) Forces and the Popular (or local) Forces, whose joint ranks were decimated in battle during the Vietcong offensives last year and early this year—is not proceeding nearly as fast as either the government or the Americans would like.

Despite the government's new offensive spirit, its forces are not gaining much real ground, because, as most experts are quick to point out, the major roads that have been recaptured are still easy to cut off, and mere mobility and the application of special techniques are not enough in themselves to turn the tide. For example, the use of chemical sprays to kill rice crops in Vietcong-controlled areas, of defoliation sprays and fire bombs to rout the Vietcong out of their forest bases, and of tear-and-nausea gas to flush them from caves does little toward actually winning the war here; in fact, even when such measures are preceded by warnings to the population— as is done in the case of the sprays, and when napalm and ordinary bombs are used in what are now called "bomb-free" zones—their value is doubtful when set against the basic need "to win the hearts and minds of the people," a phrase that, however shopworn it has become, remains the key to the situation. The conflict in South Vietnam is as much a political and social one as a military one, and the effect of certain military measures may be just the opposite of the effect desired, and may be far from making people love us, even if for the moment, out of fear of being killed, some of them renounce the Vietcong and come over to our side.

Any kind of warfare is grotesque, and in a war as messy and fluid as this one, in which the elements of hide-and-seek play a large part, the civilian population is bound to suffer greatly. Escalation breeds further escalation, and notwithstanding the President's speech, if the continuing attacks against North Vietnam fail to achieve the desired result, it is considered very likely that additional American troops will be committed as fighting units in South Vietnam, and that the United States will assume greater operational control of the war through the formal establishment of a joint command. Such a greater involvement obviously would be an admission of the failure of the four-year-old American advisory system, whereby American officers in the field both train the Vietnamese and serve as consultants to them down to the battalion, and sometimes company, level in the Army and down to the administrative districts that are the paramilitary subdivisions of the country's forty-four provinces.

The chief reasons cited for the failure of the South Vietnamese forces to do better than they have up to now, even with American advisers, are lack of leadership and lack of motivation. Those who have watched the situation for some time tend to emphasize the fact that there is a big difference between courage and leadership, and between morale and motivation. The individual Vietnamese soldier is brave and can be aggressive, if he is imaginatively inspired and properly led, but too many of the senior officers and most of the junior officers prefer fighting the easy way, going out on an action in the morning and returning for dinner and a relatively comfortable bed in camp or in a village where, under the Vietnamese system, the families of all troops, officers and men alike, will be waiting for them, having followed the unit about from place to place. The Americans have for several years been urging the regular forces to stay out on patrol and fight at night, but such urging has been unsuccessful, except among a few elements, such as the Special Forces, with whom American advisers have a much more coöperative relationship. It is significant that these troops, usually operating in squads or platoons but sometimes in companies, have in the past two years done a really good job of cutting the various mountain, valley, and riverbed trails along the Laos border and on the central Annamite mountain range, over which the Vietcong infiltrate men and supplies from the North.

While the greater American involvement has strengthened the South Vietnamese tactically—that is, in matters having to do with communication and transportation, as well as in aerial-combat assistance—it has also increased their reliance on American helicopters and other new techniques and forms of assistance. Morale, so low last year, has undoubtedly been lifted in recent weeks, chiefly as a result of the new display of American air power; attack planes are being encouraged to buzz Vietnamese troops during actions to enhance their confidence, and the South Vietnamese greet the news of air strikes with almost childlike glee. Significantly, though, the troops still show no desire to remain in the woods and swamps, set traps for the enemy, clobber him, and then pursue him relentlessly, nor is there any willingness to settle down in strange villages and protect the villagers and get steady intelligence from them—"from girl friends in place of wives, if need be," as one American senior officer has bluntly put it.

This matter of motivation is essentially a Vietnamese problem— something that the Americans can do very little about, although they keep trying. The problem has to do with many subtle aspects of Vietnamese life—with the French orientation of the Army, with a whole system of rewards and punishments that reflect political and family influence in the structure of the Vietnamese officer corps and civilian administration, and with lack of confidence resulting from the countless shifts of government over the past two years. In the last month, even as the military situation has slowly improved, there has been constant talk in Saigon of another coup and of fresh rivalries among the generals on the Armed Forces Council—a body that continues to inhibit the freedom of action of the well-meaning but still tentative and not altogether popular government of Prime Minister Quat.

It seems to be impossible for Vietnamese groups and factions to work together, and jealousies and power plays tend to be self-perpetuating. The impact of the kind of skirmishing that is now going on again is naturally felt throughout the countryside, where it inevitably disrupts the war effort by provoking fresh uncertainties among both military and civilian leaders. Each time there is fresh talk of a coup, things grind to a halt in the provinces, because province chiefs tend to cling to the funds allotted them by the Saigon government out of fear that a new government will accuse them of waste, or, even worse, of malfeasance. Almost always when a new government takes over, new province chiefs are appointed, and in the last year and a half most provinces have had four or five different chiefs—a state of affairs that makes any kind of continuity of operation impossible. As one astute Vietnamese officer I know puts it, "If the civilians don't trust their leaders, and if the troops don't trust their officers, how can you fight?" And right now, no one has much faith in the staying power of the present government.*

In trying to cope with a military situation that involves so many fluctuating psychological and emotional factors as well as political and social ones, the American advisers, who are selected from the top ten per cent of the United States officer corps, are subject to countless doses of frustration and exasperation. Sooner or later, either their patience wears thin or they succumb to the temptation of believing that they are accomplishing more than they really are. Mainly because they spend only a year here, the Americans cannot possibly comprehend all the intricacies of Vietnamese history and

---

*On May 20th, Colonel Pham Ngoc Thao, who had been in hiding since the "failure" of his coup in February that had nevertheless led to the ouster of General Nguyen Khanh's strong-man government, tried another coup, or was trapped into trying it by some of the generals seeking to eliminate him and his supporters. Though Thao escaped again, most of his followers were arrested. In the ensuing chaos, Prime Minister Quat turned to the generals to "mediate" matters, but instead they forced his resignation and took over themselves. Defense Minister General Nguyen Van Thieu became the head of a new National Leadership Committee of ten officers, and Air Marshal Nguyen Cao Ky became Premier. Once again, government by civilians had proved unsuccessful. In July, 1965, Thao was captured near Saigon and brutally strangled to death on the orders of some members of the new ruling junta who were afraid he would make another attempt to overthrow them. To my mind, Thao's loss to Vietnam was a tragic one; whatever his motivations to seize power and in spite of his sometimes devious ways, he was a true social revolutionary figure who believed that the only way to save Vietnam from Communism was to introduce a form of "humanitarian Socialism."

culture that put personal and bureaucratic stumbling blocks in the way of efficient military action. Vietnam, of course, is not the first place where the United States has had an advisory military role, but the rules of the game here have made the role unprecedentedly subtle and complex. In Korea, it was far more direct. There was a true joint command, and not only was there more American decision-making but, as one adviser assured me, "the Koreans were more persuadable than the Vietnamese." Other advisers have pointed out that the same was true of the Greeks, who had American advisers with them during their war against Communist guerrillas in 1948 and 1949. "There were no American helicopters or bombers in Greece, but we gave the Greeks some good Missouri mules," one adviser recalled. "I spent six months in the field with a mountain division, climbing around and lugging howitzers on muleback. We chased the guerrillas night and day, and never lost contact with them, as the troops here do. In Greece, too, we were able to force political reforms. And there were other factors that helped turn the tide. When the borders with the neighboring Communist satellites were sealed and no more military assistance came in, victory over the local Communists became possible. We never have been able to seal the borders here, so men and supplies are still coming in from the North."

Both in Korea and in Greece, Americans and their counterparts showed a great readiness to adapt themselves to each other's ways. Nothing like this has happened in Vietnam, and the trouble can perhaps be attributed to the Americans as much as to the Vietnamese. There are many military experts who feel that, starting in 1954, when there were a few hundred advisers here, and increasing after 1961, when their number rose into the thousands, we tried to re-create the shattered South Vietnamese Army in our own image, as an American-style organization. This approach extended not only to administration but to ways of fighting; many Vietnamese junior and senior officers were sent to American war colleges for training, and for the most part were given courses in conventional warfare, scarcely suited to the type of guerrilla war being waged here. This, combined with the previous French influence, explains the predilection of many Vietnamese commanders for committing their forces in large numbers to so-called "sweep actions," in which whole battalions, and even regiments, are flown by American helicopters to areas where the Vietcong, according to intelligence reports, are in control; the very size of such operations defeats their purpose, for the time it takes to mount them almost always gives the Communists a chance to escape.

The ability to deal with the Vietnamese situation at its grass roots, first militarily and then politically and socially, is basic to the problem of winning the war, and it will be just as important in winning any peace. Millions of words have been written and spoken about pacification programs and psychological warfare and the like, but very little has actually been done, partly because more and more of the country has been coming under Communist control. I have talked with a handful of Vietnamese, and with a handful of Americans, who firmly believe that the only way to reach the people is to start not from the top but from the bottom—that is, from the twelve thousand hamlets of the country. In the opinion of this group, the hamlets need to be reorganized so that the men who speak and fight for them are truly representative of them, rather than of government officialdom and higher military echelons. According to a Vietnamese official I know in a key province, this would require the formation of a real "People's Force," consisting of local partisans who would be responsible only to the province chief, who would become the military as well as the civilian head of his province.

"In many respects, I think we should look upon the war as lost, and we should consider ourselves the true guerrillas," this Vietnamese official says. "The Communists have sown many seeds in the last ten years, but if we do things right we can still reap the harvest. We must think in terms of a social revolution, the way the Communists pretend to think—and in terms of true social justice in the villages and hamlets. Up to now, despite all the talk, there has never been any real village democracy or any real land reform. The members of the hamlet militia have protected the government's hamlet chief, and if the Vietcong killed him, they have run away or deserted to the enemy. If a village is liberated by the government, the landlords, who were the first to flee, are always the last to come back, and then they collect all the back rent they can. There must be a true village democracy. One way we can start, I think, is to establish small village governments-in-exile among the refugees from the Communist areas. When we can get these people back to their villages, let them take over as the heads of new coöperative village councils. There is not enough arable land for everyone, but what there is should be distributed to those who till it, while those who protected and supported the Vietcong should be sent to virgin lands in the central highlands, where they can raise new crops and create new homes, working with the mountain tribes. Perhaps in a generation or so, they will be able to integrate themselves and the mountain people into the national society. To do all this, we will need the help of the United States in mechanizing agriculture and in other ways, just as we need your help now, logistically, to fight the war, but, in all vital respects, it must be a Vietnamese fight."

There are a few quietly conceived and quietly functioning American-backed programs in South Vietnam where ideas like these are being slowly introduced today. They are based on the injection of native elements—often refugees from the same village—into areas that the Vietcong now control. A well-armed platoon of these "black commandos," in Vietcong-style black pajamas, not only seeks out and fights the enemy but then remains in a recaptured village and works with the people, helping them tend their crops, dig wells, and so on. These programs, which are outside the major war effort, are making some headway. The question is: Will there be time for them to expand to the point where they have a real impact? Most impartial observers of the Vietnamese scene who have watched the slow process of erosion and retrogression for a long time are convinced that if the answer is no the battle here will be lost, whether in war or under conditions of armed peace, and such bold schemes as those outlined by President Johnson will never have a chance.

3. Saigon

~~~~~~

November 13, 1965

Saigon today is a city at war not only with the Vietcong but with itself. I have been here a number of times in the last four years, most recently last spring, and each time there has been a difference in tone and atmosphere, mainly an increase in tension. In no other period, however, has there been such a startling transformation as the one that has taken place in the last six months. When I left Saigon, in April, the American buildup was just beginning. The city, already raw and frenzied, awaited the heavy influx of American forces with confidence and with scarcely concealed greed. Now, with a hundred and fifty thousand American troops in Vietnam and fifty thousand more due to come, it is a thoroughgoing boom town. But, unlike the rest-and-recreation towns I remember from the Second World War—Sydney, to name one—which were quite a distance from the fighting, Saigon is surrounded by the war and, in effect, is part of it.

Quite often, battles are fought only a few miles away, and across the Saigon River artillery and flares are heard and seen practically every night, while the skies by day are fuller than ever with screaming or sonic-booming jet fighters and bombers, roaring cargo planes, and sputtering helicopters—sky noises that mix cacophonously with the din of traffic. In the morning, at noon, and in the evening, the streets, many of them chopped up and unrepaired, are practically impassable. The smell of exhaust from the hordes of motorbikes, cars, trucks, and buses fills the air, along with the odor of uncollected garbage and of sheer human swarm. Restaurants where it was once possible to eat a leisurely meal and conduct a quiet conversation are now bursting with boisterous soldiers, and after five o'clock the bars are as crowded as New York subway cars in the rush hour. The Vietcong have been sabotaging the overburdened power lines, and in the evening large sections of the city are blacked out. Every day, there are accounts in the newspapers of raids on brothels and of the arrest of Americans and Vietnamese as a result of fights in bars and other public places, and, all in all, Saigon is scarcely restful.

The overblown condition of the capital has a more serious aspect, too, which has to do with the nature of the war—a war that contains a great many subtle and subtly conflicting social, psychological, and economic elements as well as military and political ones. For the Vietcong, it has always been primarily a war of subversion and attrition. In past years, the campaign of subversion was concentrated in the countryside, where the principal objective of the Communists was to win over the peasantry. To a considerable extent, they succeeded in doing this, but now, what with the deterrent force of American air power, which has blunted their military offensive and upset their political balance, the Vietcong have begun to lose ground in the villages. Partly because of the pressure to which they have been subjected in the countryside, they are now paying more attention to the subversion of the cities, and especially of Saigon. The situation is ripe for such tactics, because the capital, in addition to its physical wounds, is suffering from a severe inflation. The cost of living here is officially said to have risen forty or fifty per cent this year, and according to some unofficial estimates it has doubled. Thanks to an emergency import program, which has brought in a hundred thousand tons of rice from Thailand and two hundred thousand tons from America, there is no shortage of this basic commodity, but the price of rice remains high, and some economic experts say that it won't go down unless the United States floods Vietnam with rice and other necessities. Aside from the masses of the poor, those who suffer most from high prices are civil servants with fixed incomes.

The government, with American help, has made some efforts to curb inflation, but these have so far proved unavailing, and in terms of Vietnamese piastres on the black market the value of the dollar, as well as the price of gold, gyrates from day to day. There are still far too many piastres around, and costs keep rising—construction costs are up to about two hundred per cent over last year, and some rents have increased fivefold in a matter of weeks—but, money glut or no money glut, the government has been unable to devise a workable taxation scheme, and virtually no income taxes are collected. Bribery and corruption are widespread, among other places on the waterfront, where the Vietcong, taking advantage of a confused labor situation and a transport bottleneck, are siphoning off or surreptitiously purchasing undetermined quantities of incoming goods, including some war matériel. There has also been a sharp rise in juvenile delinquency. Saigon's troubles have been compounded by an influx of refugees from the battle areas, most of whom are living in shacks or in abandoned warehouses on the fringes of town. In the last year or so, the city's population has risen from two million to two and a half million. Never have the contrasts between rich and poor seemed to me so sharp. I have seen a number of fine private homes, with high walls around them, going up in what are considered Vietcong-infested neighborhoods, only yards away from dilapidated huts and from dumps being scavenged by skinny youngsters and bony old men and women. The rich grow richer, and the ordinary people have been ignored; until a lot more has been done to restore the balance, the situation will remain explosive.

These grave economic and social conditions have furnished the Vietcong with an opportunity to cause trouble, and squads of Communist propagandists, saboteurs, and terrorists are infiltrating the city in growing numbers; it is even said that the equivalent of a Vietcong battalion of Saigon youth has been taken out, trained, and then sent back here to lie low, with hidden arms, awaiting orders. Such reports, whether true or false, naturally contribute to the tension of a people who are dreadfully tired of the war and have so little confidence in their government that they are not at all sure they want to go on fighting to defend it. The Vietcong propagandists have, of course, taken advantage of this mood, and they constantly refer to the misery suffered by the masses as a result of the high cost of living. The Americans are blamed for it, and are cast more and more in the role of plundering successors to the colonial French. In actuality, resentment is rising on the part of many nationalist-minded Vietnamese not so much against the Americans as against fellow-Vietnamese who are getting richer because of the American presence in the country; there is a wide range of such persons—from building contractors to prostitutes, who can earn four or five times as much in a month as a province chief or a Cabinet member. Prostitutes aside, a new privileged class is emerging, not only in Saigon but elsewhere in the nation—an American-financed class that complements the old French-educated class, which still dominates the government and much of the country's economic life. The peasants resent both classes, which is one reason they still turn to the Vietcong.

The Vietcong called for a Hate America Month, starting on October 15th. A general strike that was supposed to take place throughout the country that day didn't materialize, and some analysts believe that the Communists were simply using it as a scare technique and a means to bargaining in the future with some of the pro-government or neutral or self-seeking labor leaders. The National Liberation Front radio is still calling for acts of terror ("One American killed for every city block"), citing the continued use by the Americans of tear gas and crop-destroying chemical sprays, together with the bombing of civilians, as justification for reprisals, and, incidentally, making great capital out of the demonstrations in the United States against American policy in Vietnam and particularly against the use of such weapons. The Communists' anti-American propaganda drive is bound to continue, and the Americans here are not taking the threats of terror lightly. The weeks and months ahead are apt to be difficult ones, with the possibility of riots and insurrection spurred by inflation as the war moves on into a new phase.

There is little doubt here that the new phase has already begun, but there is considerable argument about what it portends and what effect, if any, it will have on the chances for negotiation. The past few months of the monsoon season have certainly proved to the Vietcong that they run a severe risk whenever they employ more than a battalion, or even two companies, in an operation. The series of summer and early-fall battles in the central and northern coastal provinces, plus a few in the Mekong River Delta, to the south, have clearly demonstrated the ability of American and Vietnamese ground elements to beat back the enemy in any engagement involving as many as four hundred Vietcong. However, except in the Battle of Chu Lai Peninsula, in August, when American Marines trapped and killed more than six hundred hard-core Vietcong troops bottled up in a stronghold, what has also been proved—so far, at least—is the continuing failure of large-scale attacks to catch and destroy many Vietcong; most victories, in fact, have been the result of repulsed enemy attacks. The strategy and tactics of the Vietcong in a whole series of more recent battles, including big ones in the last week of October—at Plei Me, in the highlands, and in Phu Yen Province on the coast—were obviously based on the need to keep open their lines of communication and supply eastward from Laos, southward across the Seventeenth Parallel, and westward from the sea. In view of the current preponderance of American force and firepower, it seems certain that the Vietcong will never be able to cut the country in two, as they had hoped to do this summer, from the Laos border across the central highlands to the ocean, but their capacity for maintaining an astonishing mobility in the jungle and for mounting major destructive efforts from time to time remains undiminished.

The latest estimates of Vietcong strength—at least eighty thousand hard-core troops, a hundred and twenty thousand regional and local guerrillas, and some thirty thousand generally unarmed political cadres, adding up to two hundred and thirty thousand men—show about a twelve-per-cent increase in the past several months, even though approximately twelve thousand Vietcong have been killed so far this year. It is estimated that at least a thousand hard-core soldiers and cadres are still infiltrating the country each month from North Vietnam—a figure that is expected to more than double during the coming dry season in the highlands, and that denotes a growing North Vietnamese influence within the Vietcong ranks. For its part, the Saigon government now has six hundred thousand men under arms, including two hundred and fifty thousand in the Regular Army. When the hundred and fifty thousand Americans are taken into account, the over-all anti-Communist force maintains a ratio to the Communist force of a little more than three to one. The argument that new mobility and firepower make it unnecessary to have the classic ten-to-one superiority over a guerrilla force in order to defeat it cannot yet be said to have proved itself, even though there has been a general improvement in the military situation, with something between three and five times as many guerrillas as government soldiers being killed each month, and with the ratio of Vietcong defectors to government deserters having now swung heavily in the government's favor.

Over all, the Vietcong hold just about as much of the country (around two-thirds) as they did when I was here in April, and although they have lost control over some segments of the population —notably seven hundred thousand refugees who have fled to government-held cities—they still dominate half or more of South Vietnam's fifteen or sixteen million. In such key provinces as Binh Dinh and Quang Ngai, on the northern coast, and Kontum, in the highlands, the situation is not much better than it was in the spring, and in some areas it is worse. In a number of vital places—including the Chu Lai Peninsula, where they were badly beaten in the August battle—the Communists waited until the American and Vietnamese troops left and then moved back to regain control of the area. In the Delta, the government's position has improved somewhat, though the Vietcong still hold most of the ground and most of the people there, too; the plain fact is that there are not enough Vietnamese or American troops to clear and then hold all important areas, let alone lesser ones. Some of them can be blocked off for a time, but sooner or later the Vietcong filter back in and reëstablish their domination of the villages. To hold as well as clear, a million more troops would be needed.

It has been correctly said, then, that what has been achieved in South Vietnam over the past summer is simply the denial of a major victory to the Vietcong. In itself, that is no small achievement. It does not mean, however, that victory for the Vietnamese government is anywhere in sight, either militarily or politically or socially. The highest-ranking Americans here, both in the Embassy and in the Army, agree that there is still a very long way to go, and that to propound any other view, as some influential Americans are doing at home, is not merely erroneous but dangerous. It is also considered dangerous to underestimate the ability of the Vietcong to adjust themselves to the new military situation, perhaps by returning to a phase of guerrilla warfare that combines political action and subversion with hit-and-run military thrusts and the occasional battalion-size attack to gain a major victory for morale purposes. In the months ahead, the Vietcong's chief objective will undoubtedly be to control as large a proportion of the rice-growing regions as possible during the harvest season, so that they can gather rice to store in their hinterland and underground sanctuaries. It will be virtually impossible to stop them from achieving at least part of their aim, and the degree to which American troops and, more important, Vietnamese forces are able to keep the Communists on the run, deny them rice, and spread what is now called "a mantle of security" over key areas in pivotal provinces will be the real indication of progress made.

Relating the military and political position of the Vietcong today to the possibilities of negotiation is extremely difficult, and analyzing these possibilities is further complicated by the unclear relationship that exists among the National Liberation Front, Hanoi, and Peking. That there are differences, reflecting not only traditional Vietnamese fears of China but fundamental disagreement over Communist aims and strategy in Southeast Asia, is becoming apparent. There have been some recent signs of a willingness on the part of the Liberation Front to enter into preliminary discussions, possibly without insisting on the prior withdrawal of American forces but only on a suspension of bombing attacks against North Vietnam. It is too soon to determine the sincerity of these soundings, but it is reasonable to assume that any attempt by the Liberation Front to start conversations with the Americans and the Saigon government now has two essential aims: first, to preclude the sending of any more American troops to Vietnam and to prepare the way for a withdrawal of some already here, and, second, to avoid further damage to the Communist apparatus in South Vietnam, which has been subjected to incalculable stresses as a result of the unexpected might of the American effort. Some middle-rung southern Liberation Front leaders also seem to resent the fact that northerners may come to dominate the movement (this is apparently due in part to the difficulty the southerners are now having in recruiting cadres of their own), but in the final analysis the decision to call a halt or not to call a halt to the fighting will undoubtedly be made by a handful of men around Ho Chi Minh in Hanoi, including the men who are the chief links to the Liberation Front down here.

So far, North Vietnam has held up remarkably well under the impact of the bombings, and its vastly improved anti-aircraft facilities, including the Russian ground-to-air missiles, now pose a real menace; there are an estimated five thousand anti-aircraft weapons in North Vietnam today, some capable of reaching up to eighty thousand feet, compared with only fifteen hundred six months ago. I have been told that despite the great damage that our bombers have done to roads and bridges, an astonishing series of piecemeal repairs has kept the supply of goods coming in from China and flowing into South Vietnam, and that though the people require more exhortation than before, their morale remains reasonably good. There is enough to eat, though it includes such things as manioc and corn instead of rice, and people aren't happy about the substitutions. (One interesting by-product of this situation is that young men seem to volunteer for the Army because they know they will get fed better in uniform.)

Hanoi is clearly digging in for a long war, but despite the proclaimed determination of the North Vietnamese to stick it out indefinitely, if necessary, it is apparent that North Vietnam might welcome a respite, and that efforts to seek one might be made before the Americans take the calculated risk, which is still being considered, of bombing such targets as the port of Haiphong, the dikes of the Red River Delta, and even Hanoi itself. I have also been told that the Chinese would definitely enter the war if Hanoi should be bombed, and, according to my informant, Hanoi expects this to happen any day. What Peking would do if only Haiphong should be bombed or blockaded—the port is more vital than ever now, because both railways running north from Hanoi have repeatedly been knocked out of service by air strikes—or if a number of industrial targets should be hit, or if just some of the dikes should be damaged or destroyed, is less clear. What *is* clear is Peking's desire to have the Vietcong and the Liberation Front continue fighting. After the Communist debacle in Indonesia, Peking's shaky prestige in Asia is more than ever riding on victory in Vietnam.

Very little that is concrete has yet been accomplished either by the five-month-old South Vietnamese government of Premier Nguyen Cao Ky or by the Americans in the way of getting a program rolling that could seriously challenge the Communists' rural revolutionary appeal and arouse the fundamental nationalism among the mass of the people. Once again, as so many times before in Vietnam, the Americans have been inclined to put all their eggs in one basket and to regard the flamboyant General Ky—he still commands the Vietnamese Air Force—as the hero of the moment, the man who might lead the nation out of the political and bureaucratic wilderness and provide the sort of leadership that Vietnam so desperately needs. They admit that the General, who is only thirty-five, is immature in many respects, that he represents the old bourgeois French-trained class, and that he has made mistakes, but they say "he is learning all the time and has some good people with him," which is true, though the "good people"— notably a group of young Cabinet members running the Rural Reconstruction, Psychological Warfare, and Economics Ministries—have not yet done much more than make promises and plan projects.

Everyone here talks about the need for time, and it is true that, in the most critical political sense, there isn't much time. Or, to put it differently, there are two kinds of time. There is the time needed for the long-term program of building up the country's rural areas —a program that everyone acknowledges is the key to victory, and that includes, as one high-ranking American general has summed it up, the gradual expansion of military security in the hamlets and villages and districts, and then the gradual working out of projects for education, health, land reform, and other economic benefits, all to be done in the spirit of "social justice," which the peasants have never enjoyed but presumably yearn for. This program, it is thought, will cover a three-to-five-year period. The other kind of time is far more immediate; it is needed for dealing with extremely hard political realities and with something that is now finally regarded by at least a handful of Americans here as an American as well as a Vietnamese responsibility—the job of seeking out and fostering the kind of leadership in Vietnam that not only can achieve stability at the top but can function dynamically and daringly in the countryside, employing truly revolutionary social techniques in order to convince the peasants that there is a meaningful alternative to Communism.

Despite an apparent stability within the ten-man directorate of generals that rules the country, there remains a considerable degree of internal division and animosity. So far, the generals have simply hung together because they have realized that if they countenanced any more plots or coups, they would hang separately. But this adhesive, being negative rather than positive, shows increasing signs of deterioration. Two basic power blocs exist: one headed by General Nguyen Van Thieu, the chief of the directorate, and the other headed by General Nguyen Chanh Thi, the commander of the I Corps, which is the country's northernmost corps, with headquarters in Danang. General Ky is in the middle, which means that in comparison with Thieu and Thi he is powerless, despite his Air Force command. Though Ky is taking trips around the country in an intensive effort to make contact with the people, he still has no popular base of support, whereas Thi, who comes from peasant stock, seems able to keep in touch with the common folk automatically. Thi, though, is both opportunistic and unpredictable; a man of strong Buddhist leanings, he has in the past coöperated closely with Thich Tri Quang, the Buddhist leader in the northern part of the country, who is suspected of being neutralist. The religious issue still runs deep in Vietnam, and the principal aim of Thi and Tri Quang is to unseat General Thieu, a moderate Catholic, and the other Catholics in the government, together with a group of generals who have aligned themselves with Thieu. There are other rumblings and rivalries below the surface, and, all in all, Vietnam is still caught up in power struggles.

On the American side, there are also many problems, most of them a result of the almost unbelievable proliferation of the American bureaucracy here in the last few months. As a result, the lines of authority are unclear, and there is growing competition among such agencies as the United States Operations Mission, which is the economic and social-aid body; the Joint United States Public Affairs Office, which is in charge of psychological warfare and public information; the different Embassy sections, especially the political and economic ones; the Central Intelligence Agency and other intelligence-gathering organizations; and the various Army elements, which have their internal conflicts and struggles as well. All these groups make separate approaches to the Vietnamese, who, naturally, are confused about whom to deal with when and about what, and who, to achieve their own ends, are perfectly willing to play one American organization or individual off against another.

It is the hope of Ambassador Henry Cabot Lodge that the new special liaison office, headed by Major General Edward G. Lansdale (retired), will be able to make some sense of this bureaucratic muddle. Lansdale, with a group of about a dozen counter-insurgency experts in various fields whom he has worked with for many years, is currently establishing liaison with all the American agencies and directly with the Vietnamese, primarily on the rural-resurgence and reconstruction programs that are the political and social keys in the fight against the Vietcong. Many experienced observers believe that the Lansdale approach is the one that stands the best, and perhaps the only, chance of success today. It consists, in the simplest sense, of the creation of a new political *modus operandi* among the ordinary people in the country. This means working from the bottom up, on a broad horizontal basis, in the hamlets, villages, and districts, and not—in the traditional Vietnamese way, which is also the traditional American way—from the top down, with everything funnelled vertically from the central government in Saigon through the old French and mandarin bureaucracy in the country's provinces to the districts, villages, and hamlets below. Today, this downward movement must also filter through the cumbersome and politics-ridden South Vietnamese Army command structure, built around four corps and ten divisions and the training centers. In addition, the downward movement often collides with the prerogatives of the province chiefs, nearly all of whom are Army men themselves, and who theoretically, if not always in practice, control the district chiefs in their provinces and maintain some operational control over provincial and local troops.

Only through a shakeup of this divided and corrupt and all but moribund administrative organization of the country, most observers believe, can a truly counter-revolutionary appeal be made to the peasants, who, after so many years of dictatorial and corrupt colonial rule, are deeply suspicious of all forms of government. Blending effective grass-roots measures with the programs being worked out by the central government—programs for civic action and pacification by the regional and popular forces and undertaken by the Rural Reconstruction and Psychological Warfare Ministries —is an extremely difficult and touchy procedure, particularly since both the Vietnamese and the Americans have already set in motion half a dozen separate schemes for creating cadres to deal with these multiple political, social, economic, and psychological-warfare matters. It is highly debatable whether, in view of the fragmentation that exists at all levels of Vietnamese society today, these overlapping and sometimes conflicting programs can be pulled together and given a popular appeal, but that is the task that Lansdale and his men are concerned with.

The next three months in Vietnam will surely determine the shape of things to come, and the degree to which the United States is willing and able to inject itself, however belatedly, into the most vital non-military, or paramilitary, aspects of this confused war. The challenge is unlike any other challenge that America has faced in the postwar period—or, probably, in its entire foreign experience. For Vietnam, the challenge is equally revolutionary. It remains to be seen whether somehow, late as it is, the true nationalists can recapture the revolution from the Communists after twenty years of bitter and futile strife.

4. Saigon

~~~~~~

March 12, 1966

The objective of creating "a social revolution," to build "a better material life" and establish "democracy in the rural areas"—the rather well-worn phrases enunciated by the leaders of South Vietnam after meeting in Honolulu last month with President Johnson —may be impossible to achieve at such a late hour in this tormented, and by now cynical, country, but it at least represents a new awareness on the part of both the South Vietnamese and the Americans of fundamental revolutionary dynamics.There is, however, an odd contrast between the grandiose statements issued at Honolulu, which had such a strong Johnsonian ring as to amount almost to a call for a Great Vietnamese Society, and the more restrained announcements that have been made here of plans for what is being called "rural construction and development"—a term that has in this context replaced the previously all-embracing term "pacification." The latter term now denotes, specifically, military campaigns to clear out the Vietcong.

Earlier Vietnamese reform programs were always too broad in concept and too centralized in their administration, and were constantly caught up in webs of personal and bureaucratic conflict reaching from Saigon down into the provinces. Perhaps the biggest mistake was a failure to establish effective coördination between the military and the civic-action aspects of these plans; they invariably collapsed because of a lack of sustained security measures in the villages and hamlets. Direct participation by the peasants was never spontaneous and seldom became more than halfhearted, mainly because of the fear of Vietcong reprisals. During the early sixties, there was the Strategic Hamlet Program, directed by Ngo Dinh Nhu, the brother of Ngo Dinh Diem. The program's chief aim was to establish and maintain political control by creating what amounted to private paramilitary forces, and its main accomplishment was to extend the grip of the Ngo family. The programs of the shaky regimes that succeeded them, though they were also motivated primarily by the urge for political self-preservation, were inhibited at the start by military conditions of near-collapse and later on by the lack of both a coherent philosophy of government and a grasp of counter-revolutionary techniques. The attempts at rural reform between late 1963 and mid-1965 were, at best, sporadic ameliorative measures, vitiated not only by power contests among civilian and military officials but by corruption as well.

As a result of the huge and still increasing American involvement in Vietnam, plus inflation, the problem of corruption is worse than ever; as for the contests for political strength and influence, if they are not as open or as violent as they once were, they continue to simmer. Yet, for the first time, there seems to be both an attempt at genuine self-diagnosis by the Vietnamese and an acceptance by the Americans of fuller responsibility for guiding as well as for financing the reform program. The problems that remain include social integration, the still unresolved bureaucratic confusion within both the Vietnamese and the American hierarchies, a paucity of Vietnamese civilian leadership at the top and of trained cadres below, and the sheer pressure of the war. On top of all this is the general uncertainty about what course the war will take, whether the fighting will increase or slow down. This involves, in turn, the enemy's immediate purposes and tactics and his long-term objectives and strategy, which are bound to shift according to whether the government makes or fails to make headway in its efforts to convince peasants that it not only can protect them but can offer them a better way of life than the Vietcong.

The Americans are still determined that the bulk of what Senator

Mike Mansfield, in his recent report on Vietnam, calls "social engineering" be undertaken by the Vietnamese themselves, the role of the United States being confined to offers of advice and donations of material help. An attempt is being made to coördinate our overlapping lines of policy and administration by placing them all in the able hands of Deputy Ambassador William Porter. Porter's task, which is not an easy one, is to settle the jurisdictional disputes that have continued among the various American agencies engaged in the effort—most notably the Army, the State Department's Agency for International Development, and the Central Intelligence Agency. The retired Air Force major general and counter-insurgency expert Edward G. Lansdale, who is now serving in our Embassy in Saigon, continues to work behind the scenes at establishing liaison between individual Americans and Vietnamese. As the program proceeds, more and more of it is expected to come under the direction of A.I.D., but at the moment this agency lacks sufficient manpower in the provinces, having fewer than two hundred economic advisers there compared to a thousand representing the Army at the sector, or provincial-headquarters, level, not to mention another thousand or so working for the Army at subsector, or district, levels. The feeling in the American Embassy, however, is that construction should be essentially a civilian undertaking, with the military much less in evidence.

It is not so simple for the Vietnamese to deëmphasize the role of *their* military. The lack of competent civilian officials, primarily a legacy of the colonial past, and the fact that the country is ruled by a military Directory probably mean that construction will continue to be carried out by military men for some time. Premier Nguyen Cao Ky, whose political stature was rather disproportionately elevated as a result of President Johnson's trip to Honolulu to meet him and his fellow-members of the ruling junta, continues to make a good impression on the Americans here, despite his fondness for Pop Art showmanship. The sight of Ky and his wife dropping in on embattled villages dressed in "His" and "Hers" black flying suits has had a comic-strip quality. But Ky, nevertheless, is aware of the danger that he will seem to the Vietnamese too much of an American protégé. "We realize that during eighty years of French control and ten years of Diem, a small minority profited but never the common people of Vietnam," he told me. "To get ourselves accepted by the people takes time."

It may take more time than Ky realizes, for among the Vietnamese there remains a strong disinclination to support a military
government indefinitely, and among leading Buddhists and Catholics, as well as in the press and various political groups, pressure to
bring in more civilians is again rising, though it has not yet become
the emotional issue it was a year or two ago. Ky's announced long-
range plans for the preparation of a new constitution and for a
referendum on it, followed by free elections, have not yet had much
of an impact. What may turn out to be more important than the
legal introduction of democratic forms is the application at the
local level of measures that, for the first time, really promise to
combine collective social and political activities with insurgency
and counter-insurgency methods not altogether unlike those employed so successfully by the Vietcong. The old military aphorism
"Know your enemy" is at last beginning to be fully understood and
accepted here. Whether it can be widely applied in both rural and
urban areas—the importance of the cities as an insurgency battleground having grown in the last year, with the influx of refugees—
will be the true test of the construction program. One danger that
is already apparent is that the plan will become too mechanical in
its implementation, too heavily dependent on blueprints and
schedules handed down from the top. Where the Communists work
horizontally through cells in hamlets, villages, and districts, and tie
their program together in nine military regions or zones, which
receive orders both from Hanoi and from the National Liberation
Front, the government's structure is still a vertical one, working
down from the central focus of power in Saigon, through the province chiefs, to the chiefs of the districts and villages.

The present setup in Saigon imparts a peculiar vagueness to the
system, consisting, as it does, of a ten-man Directory and an executive branch, the latter presided over by Prime Minister Ky, who is
himself a Directory member. Sitting on the Directory, which is
headed by Chief of State Nguyen Van Thieu, are the four Army
corps commanders—who are, in fact, the most powerful men in the
country. Theoretically, their job is to mold policy and then pass it
on to Ky to carry out. In their individual capacities as "government
delegates" as well as Army chiefs, they are in the position of being
able to do what they wish, in the manner of warlords, irrespective
of what Ky may order. This means, among other things, that province chiefs are being shifted about according to the whims of these

four men; not all the whims, unfortunately, are in tune with the national construction effort, since they appear sometimes to be motivated primarily by self-protection and self-aggrandizement. An American friend of mine who has been here since 1955 says, "There is probably no other solution now but to go on trying. However, the longer we stick with the non-military construction task, the more difficult it will be to avoid concerning ourselves directly with Vietnamese political problems, and particularly with those related to such things as a man's being removed from his job because he is too effective, or because he is beginning to look too much like a natural leader, or—what is even more dangerous—because he seems too much a pet of the Americans."

Late in February, just such a situation arose in the important central province of Binh Dinh, which includes one of four priority areas in the 1966 national construction program. These four areas —the three others are a group of villages around the northern base of Danang, most of the western Delta province of An Giang, and Saigon and parts of six surrounding provinces—have been accorded priority both because they are of strategic importance and because the government wants to prove that it can effectively introduce and pursue its new construction program under varied conditions. Each of these areas presents a different set of problems, involving such factors as the religious and political backgrounds of the population, the presence or imminent presence of Vietcong or North Vietnamese forces, the economic situation (including the number of refugees from bombed hinterland zones), and the availability of rice. The Vietnamese and the Americans have agreed that Binh Dinh—a cradle of revolutionary activity, where the Vietcong have always been strong—is in many respects the most important of the four priority regions. It is the one where the greatest progress has been made with the new construction techniques. This has mainly been due to the effective work done over the past year by Colonel Le Truong Tuong, the province chief, and a dedicated deputy, Major Nguyen Be. Despite their accomplishments, Colonel Tuong and Major Be have just been eased out of their jobs, to the dismay of American provincial advisers, who claim that the construction effort will be set back at least six months in consequence. The removal of the two men was demanded by Major General Vinh Loc, the commander of the II Corps, which includes Binh Dinh and most of the surrounding plateau area. Here was a clear case of a powerful commander exerting pressure to achieve his own ends, which were said to include the bringing in of a cousin as the new province chief.

The program that Tuong and Be created is built, as are such programs elsewhere in the country, around Rural Construction Units of fifty-nine men each. Each R.C.U. is theoretically made up of an armed People's Action Team of thirty-nine men, a Civil Affairs Team, and a Propaganda and Maneuver Team. The leader of the unit is the platoon chief of the People's Action Team, who has two assistants—one for security and one for political work. Under the security man are three squads of twelve men each, whose main job is to protect the hamlet or hamlets they are working in—usually one or two at a time for a period of three or four months. The political man directs the two remaining teams—Civil Affairs, and Propaganda and Maneuver. The first consists of an investigating cell, whose task is to interview all the people in each hamlet the team works in and make a preliminary effort to classify the population, politically and otherwise; an administrative cell, including hamlet chiefs, which takes a census of the land and other properties and starts organizing the population for hamlet and village-council elections; and an action cell, which is in charge of taking any necessary steps to deal with elements harassing the hamlet. The Propaganda and Maneuver Team also has three cells, one for "maneuver," or acquainting itself with local sentiment and trying to get the people to work together; one for civic action; and one for propaganda. Essentially, this group's job is to organize political courses in the hamlet, by age and other groups; to disseminate propaganda; and to get self-help and repair projects started—on schools, bridges, dams, and so on.

Binh Dinh, which has a population of nine hundred thousand, including some one hundred thousand refugees from neighboring provinces, was occupied almost solidly by the Vietminh—the anti-French predecessors of the Vietcong—between 1945 and 1955. When the Communists withdrew to the North after the French war, they left cadres behind them in the hamlets and villages, and these people create the vital protective screen for the Vietcong. In Binh Dinh, as elsewhere, construction starts only after the extermination and pacification efforts against main-force Vietcong units and guerrilla bands have been completed, first by the Americans and their Korean allies in this province, and then by the government troops. Following this, the Rural Construction Units, spearheaded by the People's Action Team, come in and begin their work, in coöperation with local Popular Force contingents that patrol village perimeters, and with newly established local self-defense forces, including young boys and girls and elderly men and women.

Two years ago, when the P.A.T.s were originally formed, they were known as Advance People's Action groups. Directed by Vietnamese after being organized and trained by the United States Central Intelligence Agency, they were, specifically, guerrilla outfits of six men each who, dressed in black pajamas, like those worn by the Vietcong, surreptitiously entered a Vietcong-controlled hamlet, usually at night, engaged in direct armed counter-insurgency action against the Communists; and followed this up, once the Vietcong were dispersed, by staying on the scene and helping the people harvest their rice and repair whatever damage had been done. Some counter-insurgency experts among the Americans feel that this method of operation should have been retained. Even though the P.A.T. members are now selected from specific hamlets and villages, then taken off for the ten-week training course at Vung Tau, on the coast near Saigon, and sent back where they came from, they still bear a government stigma when they return, and the peasants of Vietnam are understandably mistrustful of any representative of the central government. If the Vietcong are to be defeated at their own game, many counter-insurgency experts maintain, the effort to recapture small areas from the Communists must be based on infiltration from within. Secret campaigns against Vietcong agents right in their own hamlets—dangerous work, for even though there are only a handful of Vietcong in many hamlets, the handful control the population—would confront the Communists with opposition based on their own agitprop methods. Once the people of a hamlet—preferably a hamlet where the harsh taxation and conscription methods of the Communists had aroused resentment—were persuaded that they could obtain more benefits from a friendly government than from the Vietcong, the government would be in a stronger position to furnish meaningful economic assistance.

To find out how the present program was working, I visited a number of places in Binh Dinh. I went first, by helicopter, to a village consisting of three hamlets in the middle of the province, just west of the main north-south highway, where a P.A.T., its members dressed in jungle camouflage suits dyed purple, had been operating for three months. The hamlet in which the team was working the day we were there had a population of ninety-seven families—four hundred and thirty individuals—and the P.A.T. chief proudly showed us a preliminary census map his men had made, on which ten houses belonging to "Vietcong sympathizers"—families with relatives now in the Vietcong—were colored red, fifteen houses of families with relatives in North Vietnam were colored yellow and several houses belonging to families of "doubtful" loyalties were also marked. The hamlet had been considered insecure from the spring of 1963 until the spring of 1965, when government troops conducted a campaign against the Vietcong in the area. Now, with the P.A.T. there, and some Popular Forces nearby, it was regarded as secure, but the population, though it seemed to appreciate the presence of the P.A.T., was well aware that it was still in danger, especially since the team was scheduled to move on soon to another village area. At least a fairly good start had been made on construction; the houses had been cleaned up, the fields were being worked, and everyone appeared busy.

My next stop was the village of Hoai An, nearer to the Phu Cu pass. Hoai An, still in a secondary phase of pacification, was little more than a fort protected by some Regional and Popular Forces, and, surrounded as it was by the Vietcong, it served as a clear illustration of the fact that it would be a long time before all or even most of Binh Dinh was sufficiently pacified to benefit from a permanent construction program. The same was true of Bong Son, an isolated airstrip at the northern end of the province, just south of where the 1st Airborne Cavalry Division and the American Marines were soon to start their sweeps in the An Lao and the Dam Quan Valleys. When I flew back up to Bong Son ten days later with Prime Minister Ky, the pressure on the area had been relieved somewhat, but the enormous job of completing the pacification, to say nothing of beginning construction work, remained apparent. In one village, we saw a twelve-foot-high white concrete Vietcong war memorial in the central square. Government troops had been here twice in the past three years but had not been able to stay. "We'll stay this time," Ky said grimly, but within a week bitter fighting had resumed in the

Dam Quan Valley, and it was obvious that convincing demonstrations of the government's strength and real proof of its intention to remain would be needed in order to win the "hearts and minds" of these war-weary people.

The contrast between one community and another was further emphasized when I visited two hamlets only a few miles west of Phuoc Hai, near Qui Nhon, the capital of Binh Dinh, in the south. In one, called Tho Nghia, which had been rated "insecure" a month before, considerable progress had been made by a P.A.T. that was working in coöperation with some Popular Force elements and a locally organized self-defense group. This group included a middle-aged woman who was sitting under a canopy holding a wooden pole to which two blocks were loosely attached; she was part of the warning system, she explained; if there was any report of Vietcong guerrillas around, she would sound her primitive klaxon. There was one big project in Tho Nghia in which the whole population was engaged, and that was the building of a new dam before the dry season began. In the past, a dam in the same spot had been washed out each year by the spring floods, and an outside contractor had been summoned to erect a new one, at a cost to the villagers of forty thousand piastres—about six hundred dollars. This year, the P.A.T. had persuaded the villagers to build a new dam themselves, with P.A.T. assistance.

The problem of the over-all impact of Americans on Vietnam is one that has many subtle aspects. In bureaucratic terms, a small group of Americans initially had a great deal to do with helping the Vietnamese untangle the administrative maze that had grown up during earlier reform efforts. Until recently, there were no fewer than thirty-nine different sorts of groups engaged in one form or another of rural construction and development. The first corrective steps were taken as far back as March, 1964, when the Advance People's Action groups, the predecessors of the P.A.T.s, were created and were put through a course at Vung Tau. In mid-1965, it was decided to combine a political course with the paramilitary course these people were getting, and it was then that the P.A.T. concept came into being. In addition to the P.A.T.s, twenty thousand members of which have now been trained, there pass through Vung Tau members of all the other mixed and overlapping groups of the past and present, for training or retraining. Elsewhere, in a large house on the outskirts of Saigon, there are trained what may turn out to be the most important groups of all, the Census/Grievance and Aspiration experts, who deal painstakingly with the long-term aspects of moral rejuvenation in the countryside. The members of this select group are mostly men over forty—former village or district officials or professional people, such as schoolteachers. They are specially chosen by the province chiefs and are sent to Saigon for a fifteen-day course, after which they return to their provinces as instructors themselves, selecting individual hamlet agents and giving them a repeat version of the basic fifteen-day course in preparation for their first assignment, which is to make a highly detailed blueprint of their respective hamlets. These reports are an extension of the census map work originally undertaken by members of the P.A.T. to pinpoint households with members in the Vietcong and so on. Next, the Census/Grievance and Aspiration workers ascertain what the people of a hamlet want and what their complaints are. The emphasis is on the common desires of the hamlet citizens rather than on individual gripes. To cite two recent cases, one hamlet reported that it had no drinking water available within a radius of five kilometres, and another said that its pagoda, taken over as a headquarters five years ago by the regular Army, had never been replaced; in both cases, as soon as the reports of the census agents were received, the province chief, with the help of his A.I.D. representative, took action to correct the situation.

I was far less impressed by what I saw being done up north, particularly around the big base of Danang, than I had been in Binh Dinh. The Danang section is in the area of I Corps, which consists of five provinces, with a population of approximately two and a half million. Only about a quarter of the area is regarded as secure, the rest being about evenly divided between territory controlled outright by the Vietcong and zones where, although hard-core Vietcong elements have been cleared out, at least temporarily, local guerrillas are still active. Much of this region, that is, is still being fought over, and the Communists, since they have more troops in the north than they have ever had before, are quite capable of attacking again in strength. One of the major difficulties in the north is a lack of sufficient manpower, especially in the area south of Danang, where the Vietnamese have been unable to create enough of a Popular Force or other local militia to be of help in defending the population. Most of the young men in a nine-village region that, up to late last year, had been under Vietcong control for a solid decade have either gone over to the Vietcong or fled with their families to Danang, where they can get good pay working for the Americans or can otherwise make money out of them. As a result, in this particular region the American Marines are tied down by the pacification-and-construction campaign, which keeps them from going out and pursuing the enemy.

Not long after the Marines arrived in Vietnam last spring, they became involved in pacification and construction in a village called Lei Me. Starting with the provision of medical aid for the local population, the program quickly grew and soon included assistance to the village in building or repairing roads and bridges, schools, wells, and latrines, and also in constructing showers, which the villagers had never seen before. Success at Lei Me inspired Major General Lewis W. Walt, the Marine division commander, and a tough fighting man with a heroic combat record, who had become sold on rural development, to create a joint council of high-ranking Vietnamese and Americans, both military and nonmilitary. This council, which has the backing of Lieutenant General Nguyen Chanh Thi, the I Corps commander, now meets regularly in Danang to discuss and formulate pacification-and-construction policy. Since, of the four corps commanders, Thi is the most independent, the council often serves as a convenient instrument for helping him run his corps area as he sees fit—in conjunction with the Americans when he sees fit to consult them. As a fervent nationalist, Thi still exhibits a sporadic aloofness toward American assistance and is firmly on record against any "Americanization" of Vietnam. Recently, he ordered all the commercial signs in English in Danang taken down, and reminded the Vietnamese there to remember their national identity.

Thi has promised to strengthen his own local forces, even if he has to bring volunteers or conscripts in from outside, but meanwhile the Marines have to hold the ground, especially in the touchy nine-village area. In five of the villages, grouped together to the west, only two of twenty-one hamlets are secure; the Marines are guarding two sides of the nine-village area, and mixed elements of local forces and some P.A.T. and miscellaneous special groups are at work in the remaining hamlets. The most troublesome village in the area has been Cam Ne. Government troops took the place in September, and between then and late December the Vietcong counterattacked three times, the Marines being forced at one point to come to the rescue of a battered Regional Forces platoon. Now, at Thi's orders, Cam Ne is being levelled to the ground, except for its fruit trees, and trenches and tunnels from which the Vietcong had fought are being filled in. The population, which has been heavily indoctrinated by the Vietcong, is being moved to an area close to a nearby road. When I visited the village, the Marines were handing out clothing supplied by the Catholic Relief Services, and the various Vietnamese elements in the village, including some P.A.T. members, were trying to get the villagers to coöperate in moving their homes and belongings. I saw few smiling faces. Along the road itself there were, in keeping with Marine policy, numerous signs in English advertising laundries and similar services, most of which, I learned, had been set up with the help of the Marines and their equipment. In several huts, Vietnamese were selling soft drinks and American canned goods and rations, all of them bought on the black market or stolen.

My next stop, farther south, was the village of An Trach, where another Marine company was based. An Trach was considered to be eighty per cent pro-Vietcong last September, when the Marines first got there, and at least half of the two hundred and fifty families were still regarded as Vietcong sympathizers when I arrived. So far, the Marines have established a medical program, operated by their own orderlies; have fixed up the damaged school building; have built a playground; and have distributed some bulgur wheat and other foods to the people. A ten-man P.A.T. in the village had just been reinforced by the addition of fifteen more cadre members, but it was obvious that the P.A.T. leader and the Marine captain had not yet established any rapport, and apparently neither knew quite what the other was doing. This situation was attributable largely to translation difficulties, which frequently all but nullify the good intentions of both South Vietnamese and Americans; there simply are not enough good translators, and very little has been done to correct the situation. The interpreter in An Trach turned out to be my former busboy at the Continental Palace Hotel in Saigon, a pleasant young man of nineteen who had been drafted, given a one-month crash course in English to bolster his busboy lingo, and assigned to the Marines. He was clearly incapable, through no fault of his own, of occupying the delicate position of liaison man between the Marine captain and the P.A.T. leader. Finally, my own interpreter was able to make it clear to the captain, for the first time, that the P.A.T. leader wanted some food from the Americans, not for his own team, as the captain had supposed, but to pay off informers who were willing to give him some data on the Vietcong. The P.A.T. chief told us that there was no use appointing a village council yet, because the Vietcong would simply assassinate its members. All in all, the government presence in An Trach, which was still being subjected to sniper fire and perimeter ambushes, was little more than a holding operation, and one that would have been impossible without the Marines.

The Marines, as General Walt acknowledged, simply did not yet have enough over-all strength themselves to do more than hold on to key village areas beyond the Danang and Chu Lai air base perimeters—the defense of these still being their primary task—and to conduct patrols in and around those areas, as they were doing day and night. Even now, they were spread so thin in some places that the Vietcong had been able to infiltrate and conduct counter-thrusts against hamlets, keeping the Marines off balance and delaying construction measures. One Marine experiment was bringing rather special results. Because of his part in establishing the joint American-Vietnamese council, General Walt was able to persuade General Thi to go along with him in creating a Combined Action Group, consisting of an integrated company of Marines and Popular Forces. The experiment, which was begun several months ago at Phu Bai, the communications base near Hué, north of Danang, has proved so successful that it is now being carried out around Danang as well, and, I was told, would soon be extended southward into the nine-village area, and eventually farther south into Quang Nam. At Phu Bai, which was my next stop after Danang, the joint squads, each of them led by an American sergeant, were conducting regular day and night patrols, during which the Americans and the Vietnamese used each other's weapons and communicated with each other by means of hand signals—though they had also, under stress, begun to learn each other's language. As a result of these joint patrols, the Vietcong network in four villages around Phu Bai has been measurably damaged, though the Communists still slip in eight or ten armed agents at a time to collect food and taxes from the population and nothing as advanced as a Census/Grievance and Aspiration unit can yet function safely. Road traffic in this area has picked up noticeably, and hamlet markets now attract buyers and sellers from as far off as two kilometres, which may not sound like much but is a lot compared with what the safe-travel radius was six months ago.

If the Marine area in the north continues to present all kinds of construction difficulties, an equally hazardous and perhaps even more crucial area is the one forming a broad ring around Saigon and Cholon, the immediately adjacent city of several hundred thousand Chinese. This includes all or part of six provinces, and it constitutes the largest of the priority areas in the government's 1966 construction-and-development program. The province of Gia Dinh, which contains both Saigon and Cholon, constitutes a separate Central Military Region, while part of another province, in the the Saigon River delta, is designated as the Rung Sat Special Zone, and comes under the supervision of the Navy. Within the Central Military Region, the Special Zone, and the rest of the six provinces, less than a third of the hamlets are now candidates for construction programs. The situation varies greatly throughout the area; several of the six provinces are under at least partial Vietcong control, particularly at night. The worst of the six is Hau Nghia, southwest of Saigon, where approximately eighty per cent of the population either is controlled directly by the Communists or is under their influence. The former province chief, who was recently replaced, commented ruefully, "There are two hundred and twenty thousand people in Hau Nghia, and two hundred thousand of them are ruled by the Vietcong, which made me a hamlet chief, not a province chief." In Hau Nghia, where it is unsafe to ride around in a jeep even in the daytime, less than half the hamlets—there are three hundred all told—are scheduled for construction; only twenty-eight, even today, have chiefs. Among the latter, only about half feel safe enough to spend the night in their hamlets. The Vietcong not only have maintained their pressure throughout this crucial area but have increased it, sometimes with hit-and-run attacks and small-scale offensives but mostly with assassination, sabotage, and propaganda actions and incidents.

The Communists have directed many of their attacks against the

National Police, the military police, and the auxiliary field, or local, police—forces that are the key to the government's pacification efforts in this region. The principal job of the police is to institute what are called "population and resources control measures," designed to try to keep the Vietcong from obtaining the supplies they want—mostly food, medicines, cement, small machines, and electrical parts—and to maintain a constant check on population movements in and out of the Saigon-Cholon area. It is obviously impossible to control the more than two million people who live in the two cities, and the war-swollen population gives the Vietcong an opportunity to infiltrate propaganda agents and terror squads almost at will. Considerable progress has been made by the various police groups in establishing checkpoints on the roads, where people, cars, and motorbikes are regularly searched—but it remains just about impossible, even with house-to-house checks and a wide use of identity cards, to determine who is and who is not a Vietcong activist or sympathizer. Control of incoming and outgoing goods is theoretically easier to maintain, but the opportunies to move things in and out of Saigon are manifold, thanks largely to a system of palm-greasing whereby the Vietcong and the government both collect taxes on the carriers of commodities. Anyone in Saigon can buy two phials of penicillin in any drugstore, and can keep going from one drugstore to the next all over the city, collecting countless phials for delivery to the Vietcong. The biggest problem in resources control is in Cholon, for the Vietnamese police have scant knowledge of what is going on among the Chinese population. "We haven't the slightest idea of what's what there, or who's who," one veteran American official admitted to me. "I'm afraid a lot of the people we pick up are with or for the Vietcong, but we can't prove it so we have to release them."

The fact is, that despite the improved police methods, the Vietcong are still able to move freely through the metropolitan area, to control the waterways and many of the roads around the city, to reduce incoming supplies (and thereby increase inflation), and, in general, to keep their terror and propaganda activities going at a great rate. Within Saigon-Cholon, Communists are extremely active in at least three of the combined cities' eight wards, or precincts. In these wards, there have been cases of Vietcong agents' getting up at public meetings or in theatres and making speeches;

the Communists also regularly attack police posts in these wards with bombs or grenades. No one underestimates the dangers of insurrection here. The question remains: Would the Vietcong risk such a step, which could lead to a bloodbath and repression by sheer force?

Today, out of nearly sixteen thousand hamlets in the whole of South Vietnam (including those abandoned but still listed), some thirty-eight hundred are listed, in the earlier terminology, as "pacified," but it has been estimated that as many as half of these are still under some degree of Vietcong penetration or influence. The 1966 program prepared by Major General Nguyen Duc Thang, the dynamic Minister of Construction and Development, calls for two thousand additional hamlets to be either constructed or "consolidated." Half of these represent hamlets to be brought under construction-and-development programs for the first time; the other half are hamlets where programs are already under way, and in these the programs will now be reappraised and developed further. The two thousand hamlets will contain only twenty-three per cent of the country's population, which indicates how low the government is setting its sights because of the Vietcong's current control of the countryside. There remains a dire shortage of cadres, among other things. Under the Vung Tau and Census/Grievance training programs, about twenty-five thousand cadre members have now been trained or retrained; it is hoped that by the end of the year forty thousand will be available. To extend a construction-and-development scheme throughout Vietnam would probably require another hundred thousand, and nobody at this point will even hazard a guess at where they could come from in this manpower-short country. Nevertheless, whether there is a cease-fire soon or the war is prolonged indefinitely, this is the challenge that the United States and South Vietnam will presumably have to face. An accepted estimate here is that it would take ten years.

5. # Saigon

~~~~~~

April 16, 1966

The disturbances of the past month in South Vietnam, though reminiscent in many ways of various other crises in the past three years, are more serious in their effect on the whole American position here. They emphasize, greatly to our disadvantage, the differences between the political and tactical approach to the war taken by the Communists and that taken by the South Vietnamese and by us. To the Communists, the conflict has always been primarily a political one, and the workings of their military machine and their organizational apparatus have been carefully synchronized to achieve clearly defined political goals. We and the South Vietnamese, on the other hand, have consistently tended to separate the war's military aspects from its political ones, or, at best, have made only sporadic and cut-and-dried—rather than constant and flexible—attempts to adjust one to the other. Suddenly, as a result, the Vietcong and the North Vietnamese have come perilously close to winning the war politically by helping to foment a state of insurrection in the major cities, taking advantage of a new move by the Buddhists to assert themselves, and of a fresh power conflict among the ten generals who compose the ruling Directory. The present state of chaos is attributable chiefly to the manner in which the generals' squabble was allowed to start and then allowed to get out of control, and their inconclusive and confusing efforts to establish a legal basis for constitutional and legislative government in the country have done nothing to resolve that chaos.

In the private opinion of many officials and observers here, whether Vietnamese or American, the errors of omission and commission in the last few weeks may very well, in the light of the failure to create any real stability in the government since the overthrow of the Diem regime, in November, 1963, prove irreparable, for deep regional cleavages that have always existed in Vietnam may now produce a new civil conflict within the larger civil war. Most of these observers also believe that the recent mistakes were largely the result of poor or insufficient advice from the Americans to the inexperienced South Vietnamese generals and, especially, to Premier Nguyen Cao Ky. Last year at this time, the big American military buildup had just started, and by the fall it was apparent that a swift and efficient use of American strength had narrowly averted a complete Communist military victory. This year, though we are in a far stronger military position at the beginning of a new monsoon season—meaning a new and more intensive fighting season for the Vietcong—we are also faced with the far more difficult problem of stemming the Communists' political offensive. To a certain extent, this offensive has already proved successful; as the political conflict has mounted, the war itself—in which the Americans initiated some two dozen separate major actions of their own last month—has seemed far away, almost in another country, along with a third war, being waged somewhere else by the South Vietnamese. Meanwhile, in the countryside, a revolutionary new construction-and-development program that was just beginning to get under way has been halted by the confusion and uncertainty. All this has inevitably had its psychological impact. In fact, in many years here I have never seen the morale of both the South Vietnamese and the Americans descend so close to a state of panic.

The present crisis, like the preceding ones, may be said to have occurred principally because the masses of South Vietnamese peasants and workers have lacked any significant non-Communist—let alone anti-Communist—political foundation. It cannot be claimed that the Buddhist *bonzes*, or priests, have a mass following, though their most radical and ambitious leader, Thich Tri Quang, has tried hard to create one. Tri Quang, who has played a very important role in the current disturbances, as he did in earlier ones, has, if any-thing, lost some of his appeal among the generally backsliding Bud-dhists of central Vietnam, which has always been his area of strength, and from which, in the summer of 1963, he mounted the protest campaign that triggered the successful military coup against Diem. This time, in setting forth new demands for a civilian government, Tri Quang and his supporters in the cities of Hué and Danang were motivated largely by resentment at what they re-garded as the undue exaltation, at the Honolulu Conference in early February, of the military regime headed by Ky and Chief of State Nguyen Van Thieu. Ironically, President Johnson and his aides ar-ranged that conference in order to stress social and economic re-form and to persuade Ky and Thieu to broaden the base of their government. In Vietnamese eyes, it had no such results. To be sure, a more realistic rural construction program emerged, and, late in February, the Cabinet that works under the Directory was enlarged from seventeen to twenty-six members, including some more civil-ians and also some more southerners, to answer criticism that there were too many northerners in the government. What was more important, though, was that the generals, and particularly the flam-boyant Ky, saw themselves as having been given the President's personal seal of approval. As a result, they became more reluctant than ever to surrender power. The enlarging of the Cabinet was totally inadequate to satisfy the Buddhists and the other dissident groups, who justifiably complained that there were still no clear plans for providing a new constitution or for holding elections to set up a national legislature.

In early March, there took place a succession of events that should be set down in order. In Hué and Danang, Tri Quang and a small group of prominent lay Buddhists who were eager to set up a so-called Buddhist Force, as the precursor of an actual political party, began to shape a new attack against the government. At first, they concentrated on denouncing Chief of State Thieu (largely be-cause he is a Catholic) and General Nguyen Huu Co, the Deputy Prime Minister, who is also Minister of Defense, and they made the most of the government's obvious weak points—inflation, and the failure to move toward valid democratic processes. The precise aims of the often purposely obscurantist Tri Quang, who played a large role in the overthrow of Diem, were a matter of debate. Apart from trying to further his apparent ambition to become, if not Prime Minister, the *éminence grise* of a neutralist Buddhist nation, Tri Quang has more often than not followed a line parallel to that of the Communists. In the opinion of a particularly astute and knowledgeable Vietnamese friend of mine—a disillusioned former adherent of Ho Chi Minh—Tri Quang is not a Communist himself but has labored, and still labors, under the delusion that he can outsmart the Communists. This friend cites the historic flexibility of the Buddhist community in Indo-China, as elsewhere in Asia. He traced their recent history back to 1930, when they were crushed by the French during an uprising, only to surface again in 1936 during the Popular Front period. In 1940, they were crushed once more, but by 1945 they had again become a decisive factor in the North. As early as 1936, the Communists successfully began infiltrating the pagodas, placing their agents in them and later using them as privileged sanctuaries, as hiding places for documents and weapons. My friend commented, "The Communists will always be able to exploit the *bonzes*, but the *bonzes* will never be able to exploit the Communists. In the case of Tri Quang, they may use him to their advantage but then they will ruthlessly discard him."

Whether or not this proves to be so, other events certainly played into the hands of the Vietcong as Tri Quang and his aides began pushing their most recent anti-government campaign in central Vietnam. The most important of these events was the coming to a head of inner conflicts within the Directory—whose stability, most observers feel, the Americans had tended greatly to overestimate simply because it had managed to endure for nine months without a coup. Honolulu was the ultimate expression of this wish fulfillment. What Honolulu actually did, many now feel, was to spur Ky on to be brave and bold and to make a bid to enhance his own authority. In fact, he had less power than most of the other generals on the Directory, even though the Air Force, which he still commands, had previously served as an effective coup deterrent. Ky suddenly decided to take steps against the so-called warlords—the four top generals who run the four corps areas in the country and are also "chief government" delegates in their regions—that is, heads of the civilian as well as the military apparatus. As Directory members themselves, the four warlords were both making policy in Saigon and implementing it in their regions in their own way, regardless of what Ky, as Prime Minister, was telling them to do. The system was indeed a creaky one, and in theory Ky was justified in wanting to end it. The trouble was, as everyone now agrees, he didn't properly prepare his ground, and he picked the wrong time, the wrong place, and the wrong warlord. In the first instance, the tasks to which the Directory at this time should properly have been devoting itself, if it wished to ward off disturbances by the Buddhists and others, were the creation of some kind of constitutional framework for the country and a more realistic program to combat the twin problems of inflation and corruption. In connection with these, Ky's order to execute a Chinese speculator, Ta Vinh, at just this time was widely criticized—by, among others, the Americans —both because it was unduly harsh and because it was bound to incense South Vietnam's million or so economically influential Chinese; the execution, it was felt, would discourage their economic coöperation with the government and encourage fifth-column elements among them while doing nothing to solve the problem of corruption. As for Ky's choice of place for a showdown, he elected to assert his strength in the I Corps area, comprising the country's northernmost region, where the people have always been independent-minded and where for some time there had been signs of anti-Americanism. For his wrong man, Ky picked the commander of this area, General Nguyen Chanh Thi.

Thi, who is in his early forties, has been the subject of almost as much debate as Tri Quang. There are those who regard him as a born leader and those who maintain that he is only a colorful demagogue. He has been called pro-Communist, neutralist, anti-Communist, pro-American, and anti-American. Some say that he is one of the best soldiers in Vietnam; others claim that his military reputation is greatly exaggerated. As is often so in this country, there are elements of truth in practically all the allegations. Thi is a highly emotional man of peasant stock, without any political background or political sophistication, and he has shown himself on previous occasions to be both unpredictable and opportunistic. In 1960, he led an unsuccessful coup against Diem and then fled to Cambodia, where he may have come under temporary, and probably not significant leftist influence. In 1964, he took an important part in the coup that brought General Nguyen Khanh to power, and in 1965, working with Ky and other officers, he helped overthrow Khanh. A Buddhist, he was formerly close to Tri Quang, but in the past year the two men claimed to have had a falling out, though it is widely believed that their differences were not as great as they declared, and that they maintained some contact. In the past year, while maintaining a posture of ardent nationalism, Thi first appeared to veer in the direction of the Americans, coöperating closely with the United States Marines stationed in his area. Since the recent disturbances, he has appeared to move back into a pro-Tri Quang and anti-American position. His colleagues in the Directory, who regarded him as something of a dangerous lone wolf, capable of attempting a coup of his own, may accordingly have decided to attack him as the major warlord instead of going after two other corps commanders who, for one reason or another, primarily corruption, might have been more vulnerable—General Dang Van Quang, of the IV Corps area, in the Mekong Delta, and General Vinh Loc, who heads the II Corps area, on the high plateau just south of General Thi's area.

One of the dangers that Ky apparently overlooked was the political strength of the Vietcong in the I Corps area, which in recent months had been heavily infiltrated by North Vietnamese. Another was the increasing anti-American sentiment there, which extended to some members of General Thi's own staff. Late in February, word of how these staff officers felt was relayed privately by a Vietnamese in Danang to an official of the American Embassy, and he passed the word along to his superiors in Saigon, but subsequent events indicate that the warning made little or no impression. In any case, on March 3rd Premier Ky flew to Danang and confronted Thi privately. He accused him of acting like "a feudal lord," of placing his own people in office without considering the wishes of the central government, of trying to curry favor with civilian politicians by appointing them to posts normally reserved for military men, and of playing the civilians and the military off against each other. Next, Ky repeated some of his accusations in front of Thi's staff. Thi angrily demanded, "Shall we listen to this little man from Saigon?" but his officers remained oddly quiet, either out of fear that Ky had more strength behind him than they had supposed or, more likely, out of a desire to bring matters to a head, since they would have liked nothing better than to be independent of both Saigon and the Americans. Though a showdown was obviously in the making, the Americans, in the crucial next five days, did nothing to avert it, displaying a tendency—fairly evident here in the last few years—to back away from a Vietnamese crisis rather than meet it.

On March 9th, Ky informed Ambassador Henry Cabot Lodge that the Directory was in session and that the subject of dismissing Thi —who had flown to Saigon—was being discussed. Ambassador Lodge asked Ky if he had prepared his ground carefully and if he had considered the consequences. Ky replied to both questions in the affirmative, saying that, among other things, Tri Quang had expressed himself as unconcerned over the prospect of Thi's ouster and had said he would do nothing to oppose it. At three o'clock on the afternoon of March 10th, Ky told Lodge that Thi had been fired. Thi, it developed, had agreed to accept the dismissal with good grace when he was promised that he would be allowed to return to Danang to settle his affairs and to take a sick leave before being given another post. Lodge has since privately maintained that he raised warning flags at the time of the firing. Opinion in the Embassy and throughout the American community is that Ky received no firm advice against firing Thi, but that, rather, the official American position was to go along with the action, and even encourage it, in the interests of the ever-elusive "stability."

The firing of Thi presented the Buddhists with just the issue they had been needing to step up their anti-government campaign, and it was immediately apparent that if Tri Quang had told Ky he would raise no objection to it, he had led Ky up the garden path. Support for Thi welled up in the north, starting with a demonstration by high-school students in Hué on March 12th. That same day, Tri Quang, who had been travelling back and forth between Hué and Saigon, met with forty Buddhist leaders in the Vien Hoa Dao, the Buddhist Institute of Secular Affairs, in Saigon, and there a new declaration was prepared. It included a demand that immediate steps be taken to create a civilian government. The following day, the thirteenth, the Buddhist machine went into high gear. Students were ordered to continue demonstrations—against Generals Co and Thieu as well as against Ky. In Danang, the shops closed and the dockworkers went on strike. Thi soon became more of a pretext for demonstrations than an object of support, with student demonstrators using his name as a rallying cry. On March 14th, a general strike was called. The demonstrations rapidly spread southward down the coast, into the highlands of the II Corps area, and, ultimately, to Saigon itself. In several cities, including Hué, Danang, and Dalat, demonstrators seized government radio stations and issued a steady stream of inflammatory broadcasts. By the second week after Thi's ouster, anti-Americanism had become an important factor. Communist agents were fully prepared to stimulate it and, in general, create as much dissension as possible. Tri Quang, when it was suggested to him that the effect of the disturbances might be a complete American withdrawal from central Vietnam, replied, "If the Americans do leave, I will have achieved passively what the Vietcong have been unable to do by killing and suffering."

While the Buddhist and Communist campaigns continued, separately at first and then along a single path, another crisis was developing within the ranks of the military. Generals Thieu and Co invited Thi to accompany them on March 11th from Saigon to Danang, where he would formally turn over the leadership of the I Corps to his successor, General Nguyen Van Chuan. At the last minute, though, Thieu and Co had second thoughts about letting Thi go north. Early on the morning of the eleventh, at the Saigon airport, where the three had gone together, he was surrounded, on Co's orders, by soldiers with drawn guns. Thi began shouting, "Shoot me! Go ahead and shoot me, but not in the back!" Then, tearing off his shirt, he cried, "I curse the moment I left my pistol behind! If I had it, I would shoot myself right now!" Thoroughly humiliated, he was taken into custody and conducted to Joint General Staff Headquarters, near the airfield.

By March 16th, however, the other generals wanted to use Thi to help quiet the disturbances that they themselves had stimulated, so that day he was put on a plane and rushed north. Once there, amazingly under the circumstances, he did attempt to do the job requested of him, calling upon the demonstrators in Danang to disperse and the strikers to go back to work. In Hué, at a huge rally held on March 17th on the banks of the Perfume River, he received an ovation, which was followed by shouts of abuse against Generals Co and Thieu. Within a few days, Thi ceased to play the role of peacemaker. He was now obviously on the side of the demonstrators, and although he did not formally align himself with the so-called Struggle Force to Achieve the Revolution—the group running the demonstrations in the area—he privately consulted with both its student and its Buddhist leaders, including Tri Quang. It quickly became apparent that most of the soldiers of the I Corps, and also Dr. Nguyen Van Man, the new Mayor of Danang, who had been appointed by Thi, backed the movement, which was beginning to espouse outright separatism for the region.

By now, the crisis involved a tangle of highly emotional issues, complicated by conflicting personalities, by differences between Buddhist moderates and Buddhist radicals, by special demands from Catholics and other religious groups, and by the whole confused question of government reform. Generals Thieu and Ky were busy seeing delegations of religious leaders and politicians and trying to work out a formula for the calling of a council to draft a constitution and plan some sort of elections. The moderate Buddhists, headed by Thich Tam Chau, and based mainly in Saigon, seemed willing to go along with the government's apparently sincere attempts to find solutions, and so did the Catholics and, to a lesser extent, some of the sect leaders. But tension was still high, and fresh disputes were easily touched off. On March 19th, when Ky made a speech attacking "troublemakers," the demonstrators in central Vietnam, assuming that Ky's accusation referred to them, stepped up their attacks on him and his "American advisers."

Thi, though he had made his sentiments in favor of the demonstrators very plain, was living suspended in a kind of limbo, and his successor, General Chuan, was doing a precarious balancing act, in which he implied that he was not opposed to the aims of the demonstrators, either, but was hoping that the disturbances would die down, so he would not have to take any action in the government's name. On the night of March 31st, the first big Saigon demonstration took place; there, in the central market, pictures of Generals Thieu, Co, and Ky appeared, with demands for their execution. After this, General Pham Xuan Chieu, the Secretary-General of the Directory, flew north to see Thi and ask him to come back to Saigon —a repetition of a summons that Thi had received a week earlier and had ignored. In Hué, Chieu was seized by student demonstrators and forced to ride in a pedicab to the Hué radio station, where he made a speech saying that he agreed with the aims of the demon-

strators but not with their speeches, and that he believed the government ought to have more popular support. Chieu was held by the
demonstrators until the morning of April 2nd, and then was permitted to return to Saigon. Thi still refused to go there.

In Saigon, that same morning, after a Buddhist student demonstration was broken up by tear gas at 2 A.M., the Directory and the
Armed Forces Council, consisting of some sixty officers, held a joint
meeting and made three decisions: to take "very energetic and
strong measures to maintain security for the people, especially the
poor people"; to convene a national political convention, "with the
participation of various groups, religions, and all strata of the population," that would lay the groundwork for drafting a constitution;
and to make clear the nation's gratitude for the "impartiality and
disinterestedness" of various unnamed allies. At four o'clock that
afternoon, the Directory and the Armed Forces Council held a mass
press conference. Premier Ky, dressed in his air marshal's uniform,
made an impressive, moderate statement outlining the decisions
taken and the reasons for them. He denied that the generals wanted
to "cling to power," and said he himself would resign if his resignation would "restore stability"; he denounced the increasingly shrill
tone and the growing violence of the demonstrations as "quite inhu-
man and dangerous," especially in their effect on the economy; and
he warned against the rising anti-Americanism, declaring it to be
inspired by the Communists. "They center their attacks on the
Americans because the United States is our strongest ally," he said.
"If we believe their propaganda, and think that we are guilty, we
then fall into their trap."

It was a good speech, and everything would have been fine if Ky
had stopped right there, and not stayed on for a question-and-
answer period. Having just said that the government was "determined to exterminate" subversive elements, he now made the
mistake of declaring, in answer to a question, that Danang was
controlled by Communist rebels and that action would be taken
"very soon to liberate it." He accused Danang's Mayor, Dr. Man, of
having supported the rebels and said that either the Mayor would
be shot or the government would quit. Now a showdown was inevitable, inasmuch as Ky had, in effect, announced publicly that the
government was ready to invade Danang. Secret plans had in fact
been made to airlift some South Vietnamese Marine and paratroop

battalions up north and to move them, under cover of darkness, into Danang and Hué. Having been alerted, the already separatist military forces around the two cities, to say nothing of the Buddhist and student demonstrators, were more furious than ever and began preparations to combat the "invasion." On Monday night, several South Vietnamese battalions were transported to Danang in American planes, but after landing they remained at the airfield. General Thi now openly lined himself up with the dissidents, declaring that if the government troops moved into town he would "go into the streets and tell the people to stand up and fight."

April

On Tuesday, the fifth, Ky flew to Danang and made a complete retreat. Speaking over the radio, he confessed that he had been wrong in calling Danang Communist-controlled, announced that Mayor Man—whose successor he had already named—would keep his job, and declared that the recently arrived troops would remain at the airfield only until they could be flown back south. Barricades had been erected on the roads leading into town, and it was virtually certain that if Ky's troops had tried to enter Danang, South Vietnamese troops would have opened fire on each other.

In Saigon, while American M.P.s stood by to keep Americans out of the fracas, local troops and police moved quickly to break up demonstrations with tear gas—a challenge that the demonstrators sought to meet by placing small plastic bags over their heads, giving them the odd appearance of spacemen. In the following days, as the demonstrations became steadly more anti-American in tone, the government continued its discussions with the various religious and political groups, trying to evolve a means of establishing a civilian system, but little progress was made. When Premier Ky promised to hold general elections "within four to six months," the Buddhists rejected the promise as too vague, and the moderate and the radical factions joined forces to announce the formation of a new Committee of Force headed by Thich Thien Minh, Tri Quang's chief lieutenant, who declared, "We are determined to go to the bitter end even if it means bloodshed." For the moment, however, the new committee called on the demonstrators to stop their activities, apparently out of fear that Vietcong agents and their hired hoodlums were taking over the street demonstrations, as they had during the 1964 disturbances that toppled the regime of General Khanh. The Catholics, while condemning the growing violence, made it clear that they agreed with the Buddhists on the need to establish a new civilian government as soon as possible. In central Vietnam, General Chuan asked to be relieved as I Corps commander, and other Army officers demanded the resignation of the government and remained in such open dissidence that several hundred American civilians were evacuated from Danang.

Almost everyone agreed that Ky's own future had been gravely jeopardized. Whether or not he had been egged on by his fellow-generals, he had lost tremendous face as a result of his impetuosity in firing Thi in the first place. He had made another blunder, it appeared, in waiting too long to take action against the demonstrations. If Ky and his fellow-generals had been firmer at the outset of the crisis, if they had announced definite plans for civilian rule and had come up with some kind of interim compromise, such as the addition of civilians to the Directory, and if, meanwhile, they had moved subtly and carefully to reduce the power of all the corps commanders, much of the trouble might have been avoided. But things in Vietnam never seem to happen as rationally as this. If, as many people here believe, the United States is now faced with the prospect of having to deal with a new alignment, Washington and our Saigon Embassy will have to start all over again on the task of building up relationships. "Maybe then, for once, we won't put all our eggs in one basket and start babbling about 'stability,'" one official here says.

The weakening of the social and political fabric and the rise of separatism and xenophobia are serious in themselves. Still more serious, the observers point out, is the possibility that these developments and sentiments will lead to compromises that would bring into the government individuals who are willing, or even anxious, to negotiate with the Vietcong and the National Liberation Front on almost any terms. It would be foolish to think that such men don't exist. In fact, in a revealing moment of despair recently, one of the highest-ranking leaders of the present government remarked to a friend that he didn't know who among the twenty-six members of the present Cabinet "might be Communists." This is not to say that negotiations including the Liberation Front will not at some point become unavoidable. But to approach that point through the sort of weakening process that has been taking place would open the way to defeat at the negotiating table before the negotiations began.

In the last analysis, though successful military operations are continuing, the initiative on the political front seems to rest with the Communists and their witting or unwitting Buddhist allies, headed by Tri Quang. As one veteran Vietnamese political observer says, "Either the Communists will maintain the present pace of insurrectional activity or—what seems more likely—they will figure they have gone as far as they can for the moment. They will then simply regard what has happened in the past month as a successful rehearsal for next time. That could be a month or two months from now, or maybe more, but, in view of their ability to attack and retreat and then attack again, the moment will surely come. The prospect is not one that we Vietnamese who have been fighting Communism for a long time—or you Americans, either—can look forward to cheerfully."

6. Saigon

~~~~~~

June 4, 1966

About a week before the sudden, secret movement of Vietnamese Marines to Danang on May 15th to restore the Saigon government's authority in the rebellious northern city, I had a long talk with Thich Tri Quang, the Buddhist monk who is the master strategist of the campaign against the rule of Premier Nguyen Cao Ky and his fellow-generals. We met at Tri Quang's headquarters, in the lovely, tree-shaded Tu Dam Pagoda in the university city of Hué, north of Danang, which has become the headquarters of the Struggle Force to Achieve the Revolution—the body, composed of students, workers, peasants, and an undetermined number of dissident officers and troops, that has led the recent anti-government rebellion, under the guidance of Tri Quang and his fellow-monks. I remarked to Tri Quang that the situation in Hué and Danang was then seemingly quiet, and a broad, white-toothed smile flashed over his highly mobile face. "Yes, you are right—*seemingly,*" he said. If there was any further trouble, he added, it would not be the fault of the Struggle Force and the Buddhists, who, largely on his advice, had recently called off planned demonstrations throughout the country in order to test the good faith of the government in pledging that it would hold elections for a constituent assembly by mid-September—elections in which the Buddhists hoped to emerge as South Vietnam's dominant political force. Then, with another bright smile, Tri Quang quoted an old Vietnamese proverb: "The tree wanted to keep still, but the wind didn't want to stop."

The tree was, of course, Tri Quang and his followers, and while there is reason to doubt that they wanted to keep still, there is no denying that the wind—Premier Ky and the other generals of the ten-man Directory—didn't want to stop. Whatever justification the generals have come up with for bringing troops into Danang "to maintain security and order," the opinion of most non-Vietnamese here is that the move was unwarranted at this time, even as a calculated power play, and that it certainly wasn't worth the risk of causing more trouble and dissension. Now the threat of chaos is looming darker than ever, and the consensus here is that the situation has not been so grave since the fall of the Diem regime, in November, 1963. It is grave to the point where, with the country again on the brink of a civil war within a civil war, and the Americans carrying virtually alone the burden of the war against the Vietcong and the North Vietnamese, there is growing doubt whether the process of disintegration can be reversed, even if the elections are held on schedule—which at the moment also seems unlikely. As one American official has said, "It is important, of course, for the Vietnamese to establish orderly governmental institutions, and it is important for us and the rest of the world to be able to deal with such institutions. But elections will solve nothing if these people can't learn to develop some lasting community of interests."

Never before in recent years have I seen so much dissension and confusion here, so much behind-the-scenes maneuvering for power or for survival. One might like to think that this is the unavoidable result of a nation's attempt to give birth to a representative form of government while prosecuting a cruel war against powerful enemies within and without, but there is more to the situation than that. The sour atmosphere in Saigon and elsewhere contains an ominous mixture of vengefulness and despair: people are tired; politicians are not only berating one another but—in a couple of cases, resulting from intraparty feuds—assassinating one another; and more than one Army unit, its leader having grown disillusioned and bitter, has in effect stopped fighting the Vietcong. Under these circumstances, it may indeed be—as so many observers maintain that it is—the wrong time to seek to impose Western-style democratic forms on a country that has never had a real national government of its own, its traditional way of life having been based on a system of village autonomy, whether under a Vietnamese emperor, a Chinese overlord, or a French colonial governor. On the other hand, it may be argued that this is South Vietnam's last chance to forge some kind of national unity, imperfect though it is bound to be. At any rate, the machinery for establishing a new system of government has, for better or worse, been set in motion, and while it may be delayed, it probably cannot now be stopped, except by the total chaos and collapse that might follow another coup.

The Americans, unfortunately, were caught totally unprepared for the latest turn of events. In early April, when Premier Ky made his first, abortive effort to "liberate" Danang, he rather rashly told the world in advance, at a press conference, what he was going to do, and then he not only took the Americans into his confidence on the details but persuaded them to lend him some transport planes for ferrying his troops and tanks north. This time, he and his fellow-generals, acting on their own, made their dramatic move at a moment when the two highest-ranking Americans, Ambassador Henry Cabot Lodge and General William C. Westmoreland, were out of the country. The result was panic among the Americans on the scene —a panic that was only increased by instant orders from the White House for the Americans in Saigon to lie low and keep mum. By May 20th, when Ambassador Lodge returned from Washington, things were thoroughly out of hand. The only official American comment had been a plea that Secretary of State Dean Rusk made to the Vietnamese to set aside their "lesser issues" and get on with the tasks of forming a government, prosecuting the war, and rebuilding the country. For the Buddhists, the causes of their rebellion were anything but "lesser issues." In their view, the main issue was the misuse of military authority, and, for the first time, they appealed directly to the Americans for help—through Tri Quang, who asked President Johnson to prevail upon Ky's government to cease its attacks on the three Danang pagodas. The President seemed disinclined to do anything more than urge the embattled parties to get together, for he echoed Secretary Rusk's remarks and then suggested that a junior American diplomatic officer, our able young consul in Danang, be accepted by the two sides in the role of a broker—as opposed to that of a presiding arbiter—in any mediation efforts designed to bring about a cease-fire and obtain an amnesty for the rebels.

When I spoke with Tri Quang in the Tu Dam Pagoda, he left me in no doubt of how he felt about American responsibility, or irresponsibility. Having declared that things would stay quiet only if the election process went off smoothly, honestly, and on schedule, he added that he hardly expected this to happen, especially if the Americans did nothing to restrain Ky and his troops at this preëlection moment. He advised me "to find out more about the causes of instability in Saigon," where, he told me, the government, in its attempts to cling to power, was "trying to create dissension among different strata of the population and trying to buy off those groups it couldn't play off against one another." Alternately smiling and grim, he said, "We are taking precautions to deal with the situation that may arise if our conditions for the election are not met. In that case, not only will the central government be opposed by the Vietnamese people but the Americans, too, will be opposed, in the same way the French were. If the Americans do not back the idea of a constituent assembly, all Americans will be seen as colonialists, and the population will turn against them as well as against Ky."

Already there are many indications that Tri Quang was right, and the current hostility toward Americans, whether it has been artificially stimulated or not, is adding immeasurably to our difficulties. The ironic thing is that we are being accused of something that, for good or ill, we have not done; namely, interfering directly in Vietnamese affairs. An increasing number of people here, including other Allied diplomats and various chagrined American officials, feel that we should have involved ourselves much more actively, not just in the recurring crises of the Ky government but in the other crises of the past three years. In that time, it is thought, any one of several revolving-door governments might have been preserved if it had been more actively supported and guided by the United States, which repeatedly chose to remain aloof or to confine itself to polite coaching from the sidelines. This opinion is not unanimous, however. A while ago, I had a long conversation with a high-ranking American diplomat here who is a staunch defender of our policy of non-interference. "Our policy, of course, has both strengths and weaknesses," he said. "First of all, we ardently desire to avoid anything that smacks of colonialism. If our leverage were to be used brutally, it might achieve more in a given situation, but it would also really make us look like colonialists and would thus be the opposite of productive in the long run. Our continued restraint allows us to speak with complete frankness to the Vietnamese and lets them do the same to us. It's not that we don't try to adjust ourselves to their crisis mentality but that we prefer to reason, to use Anglo-Saxon logic, not to use our leverage too openly. Despite the erosion of the Vietnamese body politic, it seems to endure, and for us the key element is not Vietnamese politics *per se.* It is our effort to prosecute the war, both militarily and socioeconomically. Until the Vietnamese wrangling interferes with the war effort, it doesn't really affect what we're doing here."

Most observers would find it hard to deny that the "wrangling," which is certainly a euphemism for what has been going on in the last two weeks, has now affected the whole American effort so powerfully that this effort is in great danger of being subverted, or even of being summarily stopped. The American jets that had to quit the Danang air base when it was brought under rebel mortar attack last week could be seen as a portent. Whether this ominous situation could have been avoided by more timely American diplomatic intervention is a question that historians will have to settle, but most of the Vietnamese I know feel strongly that it could have, and should have, and they also maintain that the Vietnamese leaders, for all their bravado, want counsel so firm as to amount to an actual partnership in making decisions.

The decision-making undertaken by the Vietnamese themselves has of late been more than usually erratic. The recent series of events, following on those of March and April when Ky dismissed Lieutenant General Nguyen Chanh Thi, the independent-minded commander of the turbulent I Corps area, began with the Buddhists pressing their offensive against Ky and his fellow-officers of the Directory. As they continued their demonstrations, they issued anything but subtle warnings of "a civil war that will take tens of thousands of lives and cause the total collapse of national unity." It subsequently became apparent that the Buddhists had been preparing their campaign to overthrow Ky and the generals for some time, and, in fact, that the ouster of General Thi had interfered with their plans by forcing them to alter their strategy and openly embrace Thi's cause. The Americans, believing in an orderly but not necessarily swift transition to civilian rule, are said to have suggested to Ky in mid-April that he be firm and take the risk of seizing Danang by force and imposing an economic blockade on Hué, but Ky backed down at the last minute. This was probably the high point of American "involvement" in the crisis, and it may be presumed that the Embassy expected to be told in advance about any further repressive action that Ky decided to take. As events progressed toward a new showdown, and the Unified Buddhist Church officially identified itself with the anti-government agitations, Ky called a three-day congress of political, religious, and professional leaders, in accordance with earlier Buddhist demands. On April 14th, the Directory Chairman and Chief of State, Lieutenant General Nguyen Van Thieu, read to the congress a decree establishing an Electoral Council to prepare the machinery for the election of a constituent assembly in from three to five months. As it turned out, the response of the congress, which the military junta had hoped would be a moderate one, was close to the extremist Buddhist position, even though the Buddhists had largely boycotted the meeting; in consequence, the government was forced to back down still further and bow to other Buddhist demands, including clemency for all arrested demonstrators and a guarantee that there would be no more arrests.

Instead of concentrating on personal attacks against Ky and other members of the junta, the Buddhists now seemed to feel that they could attain their ends earlier and more easily by making Ky stick to the election schedule they had virtually forced down his throat. Tri Quang left Saigon for the north, and began pushing the new line in a series of speeches—most notably one at the Dieu De Pagoda in Hué on April 18th—employing all his demagogic skill. Having asserted that Vietnam was being "oppressed by both the Communists and the Americans," he indicated that the Vietnamese could best achieve their goal of ruling themselves without interference by playing along with Ky instead of by trying to overthrow him. He warned his listeners that Ky and Thieu, with the support of the Americans, would try to renege on their election pledge, and said that it was the solemn duty of the Buddhists to "make them keep their promises," so as to avoid another "betrayal." "We know that they may send their troops or armored cars here at any time they want by means of the foreigners' airplanes, and we know that they will not hesitate to betray us, but we are not afraid," he said in the Dieu De speech. "We cannot just demonstrate against this government, and go from this government to another government, to be betrayed again and again."

From this moment on, the Buddhists carefully maintained the position that they were acting "in good faith" and that everything depended on the government's proving *its* good faith—specifically, by sticking to the election calendar. Tri Quang emphasized this point when I spoke with him. "We could have gone further in April, but we want the credit for establishing the assembly," he told me. "Once we have a constituent assembly and it adopts a constitution, it can turn itself into a pro-tem legislative assembly and can choose a new chief of state, who will have prestige because he will represent the popular will. This leader can then select a Cabinet. Once you have a constitution, the goverment is obliged to work in accordance with it."

In the contest of "good faith" that followed, Tri Quang and his Buddhists, whatever ulterior motives they may have had, put on a better performance than the Ky Directory. At the same time, as Tri Quang himself had made clear, they were preparing for any eventuality. Their preparations, not all of which Tri Quang directly controlled, included the bolstering of the Struggle Force in Hué and Danang and the formation of a so-called Death Volunteers Association of two or three thousand students, several hundred of whom obtained weapons either on their own or by turning up for short periods of training at nearby Vietnamese Army camps. A careful liaison system was established between Hué and Danang, and the university students in both cities resumed the strikes they had begun several weeks earlier, during which they devoted themselves to holding rallies and "seminars." The various elements of the opposition—religious, military, and civilian—were carefully coördinated under the over-all direction of Tri Quang and his aides, his principal lieutenant being the Buddhist monk Thich Thien Minh, who operated mostly out of Saigon. The nominal leader of the Struggle Force was Buu Ton, a medical student in Hué, but it was apparent that he was taking orders from others. In addition, there was increasing evidence that Vietcong agents were infiltrating the movement, despite its avowed anti-Communist position. In fact, the propaganda broadcasts of the Communist-run National Liberation Front have constantly encouraged the movement.

In a number of interviews, including the one with me, Tri Quang spoke out more ardently and more frequently against both Communism and neutralism than ever before. Perhaps he was indeed unaware of the extent of the Communist infiltration of the Struggle Force, even though, as early as Ky's abortive first "liberation" of Danang, Vietcong agitators had helped the rebel elements build roadblocks and perform other insurrectional tasks, and even though captured Vietcong instructions to their cadres in the Danang area, which I later saw, revealed in detail the degree to which the Vietcong had taken advantage of the situation. Both in Hué and in Danang, the Struggle Force used local radio stations to broadcast propaganda that was both anti-government and anti-American. Certain military units—elements of the 1st South Vietnamese Division that were stationed around Hué, and elements of the Quang Nam Special Sector Command that were stationed south of Danang, along with some individual Ranger units and other contingents—openly identified themselves with the Struggle Force. So, despite the protestations of "good faith" all around, a potential, or even an actual, state of insurrection existed. General Thi, who was living in a private villa in Hué, aligned himself with the opposition officers and troops, which included most of his former I Corps staff members, and he kept in touch with Tri Quang. However, he also tried to tone down the anti-American clamor, and he quietly coöperated with General Ton That Dinh, the new I Corps commander, who was making earnest efforts to reëstablish harmony.

Ky's choice of Dinh as a replacement for General Nguyen Van Chuan, Thi's initial successor, was an odd one. Back in August, 1963, Dinh, though he was himself a Buddhist, had led an attack ordered by Diem's brother Ngo Dinh Nhu, against pagodas in Saigon, yet a few months later he had played an important, if somewhat reluctant, role in the coup against Diem. Now Tri Quang promised Dinh his support, and he even offered no objection when Dinh proposed to get rid of certain officers at corps headquarters who were considered politically unreliable and who happened to be Buddhists, though he counselled Dinh to go slow in this. Dinh ran the I Corps for only a month, but in that time he succeeded in calming things down, at least on the surface. He took personal command of the Danang garrison, meanwhile permitting the Mayor of Danang, Nguyen Van Man, whom Ky had previously threatened to shoot, to stay in office and perform his routine administrative tasks, and he cracked down to some extent on the Vietcong infiltrators, arresting three in Hué and reportedly having them shot, rounding up a number of suspects in Danang, and collecting two hundred illegal weapons.

Although Dinh was making headway in bringing Danang back under government control, he was obviously going too slow to suit Premier Ky and the junta, who did not altogether trust him anyway. Also, it was at just about this time that Ky began demonstrating that, in the language of Tri Quang's proverb, he "didn't want to stop" his efforts to curb the Buddhists and their adherents. On May 7th, at an impromptu but not entirely unplanned press conference in the city of Can Tho, in the Mekong Delta, Ky told reporters that he expected to stay in office "at least for another year," despite the coming election, which he indicated would be only a first step, to be followed the next year by the election of a legislative assembly, which would then choose a new government. Ky spoke of his "destiny," and the implication was that he envisioned for himself, and perhaps for some of his friends in the Directory, a role not unlike that assumed by Chung Hee Park, the President of Korea, and his mentor, Kim Chong-pil, who together, following their successful coup in 1961, ran the revolutionary government in Korea for a year and a half and had things well in hand before they permitted elections, which merely "legalized" their rule.

While the Electoral Council in Saigon was diligently at work on preparations for bringing together a constituent assembly, Tri Quang maintained his policy of forbearance, despite Premier Ky's provocative statements. The monk made more speeches up north, urging his audiences to forgo demonstrations in the interests of obtaining "a democratic structure," and repeatedly declaring, "We are making a revolution, not a *coup d'état.*" It had been suspected in some quarters that Tri Quang's control over the masses of central Vietnam was far from complete, and now Struggle Force groups in certain cities and villages confirmed the suspicion by continuing their agitation, while farther south, in the town of Dalat—where four students and three government soldiers had been killed during demonstrations late in April—fresh trouble started when student sitdowns forced city shops and a large vegetable coöperative to close. On May 8th, Ky sent to Dalat, as its new commander, an ardent anti-Buddhist lieutenant colonel named Nguyen Ngoc Bich, and Bich cracked down on the demonstrators, arresting two hundred of them.

In the days that followed, Ky and the Directory were preparing for a new showdown, just as the Buddhists were. Perhaps most important, Buddhist chaplains were openly telling troops in the central highlands and around Hué and Danang that if things got worse the Army might be called upon to suspend the fight against the Vietcong and support the Struggle Force. Furthermore, Ky knew, from what Ambassador Lodge had said to him before going back to the United States, that we believed in a policy of firmness and felt that the government had a right to reëstablish its authority in the Hué-Danang area. Ky is reported to have consulted a fortune-teller, in the Oriental fashion, a day or so before he made his new move in Danang, and is reported to have been told that if he could pull it off and remain in power for four days afterward, he would be out of the woods. So he went ahead. Because the Vietnamese revere their past heroes, both the operation in early April and the movement of troops to Danang on the morning of May 15th were given the name Dinh Bo Linh, after a tenth-century Vietnamese patriot who, as one of a dozen warlords, succeeded in destroying his rivals and bringing about a brief period of national unity. In his effort to emulate Dinh Bo Linh and reëstablish unity, not to mention his own authority, Ky dispatched two battalions to Danang and then two more, and he also cracked down on the Buddhist Youth Association in Saigon and on the left-wing instigators of a textile walkout there that had led to a brief tieup of the port and had threatened for a while to turn into a dangerous general strike.

Throughout the drama—which reached its climax on May 23rd, when the three main pagodas in Danang surrendered, as did a force of about four hundred rebel troops, at least fifty of whose comrades had been killed—a subplot was being worked out on the same stage. It involved some of the same cast, the principal actors being the Buddhists. One of the most astute students of Vietnam, Professor Paul Mus of Yale, has pointed out that Buddhism in Vietnam has never been a truly vital force except when it was fighting for its own survival—which is what it was doing when it led the revolt against Diem. Ordinarily, Mus noted in a recent article, "Confucian behaviorism—directed, staid behaviorism—is enough for all problems. But . . . when there is trouble, when the will of heaven is not known and [the community] is in the state of interregnum, Buddhism comes to the fore . . . as an alternative when the temperament of history and the world change." Having made the point that "the pattern of indignation is Buddhist rather than Confucian," Mus recalled that "when the Diem regime fired on the Vietnamese and killed many young boys and girls, the Vietnamese became indignant, and at that moment, they were Buddhists." In all their activities since the fall of Diem, including the role they played in overthrowing three governments and their attack on this one, the Buddhists, as they see it, have been fighting to survive rather than to seize political power. Now, however, they have shown themselves ready to enter the political arena. This largely accounts for Tri Quang's public emergence in recent weeks. Meanwhile, he has been playing a more typical leading role in the subordinate drama.

This involves, first of all, the efforts of Tri Quang's Mahayana Buddhists, who are influenced by Chinese Buddhism and are Vietnam's principal Buddhist sect, to consolidate their influence in the south, where the less highly organized Theravada Buddhists, influenced by the Buddhism of Laos, Cambodia, and Thailand, are concentrated. Vietnam is unlike every other Southeast Asian country in that its two Buddhist groups have managed to get along fairly well; in fact, they have joined forces in what is officially known as the Unified Buddhist Church. Even so, Tri Quang's personal influence on the Buddhists in the south has never been as great as he would like. To enhance it, he has taken advantage of the confusion of the last few weeks to move in on a new, informal alliance of southern Buddhists, elements of the Hoa Hao and Cao Dai religious sects, certain southern Catholics, certain labor groups, and certain important military leaders, past and present. The acknowledged leader of this disparate group is former General Tran Van Don, who, along with four close associates, was retired from the Army in early 1964 in the aftermath of the post-Diem coup led by General Nguyen Khanh. Don is still held in high esteem, especially by many junior officers. Furthermore, he is a southerner; as such, he is regarded as a potential man of the hour, conceivably capable of achieving the much desired national unity that Ky, a northerner, cannot produce. It is no longer any secret in Saigon that Don has become the center of a new cabal. Tri Quang has astutely moved in on the situation, and is believed to have been in touch with one of Don's closest allies, former General Mai Huu Xuan. A few days before Ky made his new move against Danang, I saw Don in Saigon. He made no effort to hide what was going on, but modestly maintained that he himself, if he were to play any role, would wish to do what he could to unify the Army and get it out of politics.

Toward the end of last week, Ky was obviously preoccupied with the need to stabilize the situation in any way possible. Rather than risk more bloodshed by invading Hué, he intensified the government's economic blockade of the city, cutting off all shipments of food up the coastal highway. Then, on the twenty-seventh, he went north to the American base at Chu Lai for what he subsequently described as an amicable confrontation with Thi. Ky now had even more reason to attempt to achieve some sort of truce, for the American Library in Hué had been burned the day before and demonstrations in the city were continuing. There undoubtedly will be more of the same, in Saigon as well as Hué, for the two Vietnamese factions in the continuing conflict are on an unmistakable collision course, and lasting compromise seems impossible. On the twenty-seventh in Saigon, demonstrations took place all over town; at seven in the morning, in the square outside my hotel window, about two hundred young priests in orange robes, parading with banners that called on the government to resign and denounced its American backers, were interrupted by police throwing tear-gas grenades. Earlier in the week, there had been two further indications that the differences between Ky and the Buddhists were irreconcilable. First, Ky told a military-civilian council, which he and Thieu had summoned in an effort to pacify the dissidents—and which the Buddhists and their allies had, predictably, boycotted—that order would have to be not only established but maintained if the elections were to be held. Next, Tran Quang Thuan, the Buddhist representative on the Electoral Council, quit, along with an associate—an act implying that even if the election should come off as scheduled, the Buddhists would boycott it as long as it was held under Ky's auspices.

Despite Tri Quang's repeated anti-Communist and anti-neutralist declarations, most observers remain skeptical about his intentions. That he is a sincere and devout religionist cannot be doubted, nor can it be doubted that he is basically a pacifist, who profoundly hopes to see the war ended—though he *has* made some strong statements about South Vietnam's having to go on fighting until the Communists are willing to negotiate on fair and equal terms. It is probable that in looking ahead to such negotiations he sees the emerging Buddhists, having by now not only survived but become a political force, leading the way toward some sort of neutralist solution for the nation. Though the preparations for the election have been slowed down, or perhaps temporarily halted, his stated primary goal is still to have it held as soon as possible.

Ky and Thieu and the other generals of the Directory, despite their attempts to smooth things over, are adamant in their determination to force the rebel elements to the wall, including an estimated ten to twenty thousand dissident anti-government armed forces in the I Corps area alone. The Danang episode is bound to have heightened the resistance, both open and latent. As for the war against the Vietcong, there is every indication that it will increase in tempo in the monsoon months ahead. The longer the Vietcong war and the South Vietnamese political war rage concurrently, the greater the opportunity the Buddhists will have to become the champions of a negotiated settlement along neutralist lines. Perhaps this is what Tri Quang had in mind when I asked him if he thought the chances for peace looked any brighter. He dismissed the question brusquely: "When we want to talk about peace, we will call you."

7. Saigon

August 20, 1966

In the coming elections for a national constituent assembly, to be held on September 11th, South Vietnam is facing one of the most decisive crises in its turbulent history. The most obvious and important question is whether the means can be established for creating a legal and freely chosen government—something that South Vietnam has not had at any time since it became a separate nation, in 1954. Few people would argue that the elections held under the regime of Ngo Dinh Diem—a referendum in 1955 that resulted in Diem's overwhelming defeat of former Emperor Bao Dai for the title of Chief of State; a Presidential election in 1961, which Diem won just as overwhelmingly; and three elections for rubber-stamp national assemblies—were in any sense free, since Diem never adhered to the constitution he adopted and never allowed any political opposition. (The real turning point of feeling against Diem came as early as 1956, when he refused to hold scheduled village elections.) The elections next month here are regarded as a necessary step toward the establishment of a government with a *bona fides* that none of the many governments since Diem's have possessed—a government that can continue to wage war or proceed to make peace, by negotiating with Hanoi and perhaps with the National Liberation Front of South Vietnam.

What principally remains to be cleared up is the question of the real intentions of the military leaders who control the Directory now in power—notably Chief of State Nguyen Van Thieu and Premier Nguyen Cao Ky, who, somewhat unconvincingly, professes to want to go back to running the Air Force. Other questions that are being asked are: Will the Vietnamese Army engineer the election of enough pro-military candidates to enable the generals to maintain their power under the guise of legitimacy, no matter what kind of constitution the new assembly prepares? Will there be a large enough popular vote in the secure areas of South Vietnam, to which the elections are limited, to warrant a claim that they have been truly representative—particularly since the Buddhist leaders whose rebellion was crushed in May have called for a boycott? Will a "loyal opposition," even if it is elected as a minority element, be able to play a role of any significance in the democratic process supposedly being set in motion? And will that process, given the political fragmentation that has existed in Vietnam for so many years, and the current bitterness over the country's serious economic situation, operate smoothly, or is it destined to end in another succession of coups?

At the moment, the mood in this noisy and ever more crowded and dirty war capital, and elsewhere in the country as well, can be described as, at best, one of restrained skepticism. The prospect of the elections has aroused little enthusiasm, but the government is now doing its best to engender some. The Vietnamese feel much more concern about the prices they must pay for food than about their political future, and while the various fiscal measures, including devaluation, that were taken two months ago are just beginning to show some slight effect, the prices of all essential commodities, including rice and pork, are still approximately seventy per cent higher than they were a year ago, and they were already too high then. Furthermore, while military personnel and civil servants have received recent salary increases ranging from twenty to thirty per cent, the cost of living remains far out of line with the pay of most government employees, and civilians, including both white-collar and blue-collar workers, who did not benefit from the official wage raises, are having a still harder time making ends meet. Financial scandals that have revealed corruption on a vast scale—some of it involving the American bases, not to mention individual

Americans—have brought about a further deterioration of the moral and social climate. All in all, the picture is not a pretty one, and the consensus of many Vietnamese and American officials is that the elections might better have been postponed until some greater degree of equilibrium had been created.

Ironically, the elections were scheduled for such an early date as a result of clamorous demands for them by the very groups and individuals that, for reasons ranging from political and revolutionary conviction to sheer anger and pique, are now snubbing them. These objectors include not only the militant Buddhists of the Struggle Force led by Thich Tri Quang, who has been conducting a prolonged, if modified, hunger strike in a Saigon clinic, but also a number of minority elements among the Catholics and the Hoa Hao and Cao Dai religious sects, and a good many prominent politicians as well as politically conscious citizens who disapprove of the repressive actions of the government in recent months. Opposed to these nay-saying elements are a handful of old-time nationalist leaders who, although they share much of the discontent, feel that they should make the best of the opportunity now being given them to create some semblance of political opposition and, at the same time, to get a constitution written and a governmental framework for the future constructed. The Americans are determined to do what they can to make the elections a success, not only because of their Western democratic heritage and their eagerness to deal on legal terms with a duly constituted Vietnamese government but because of the bearing that successful elections here would have on this year's congressional elections in the United States and on support for President Johnson's Vietnam policy generally. This policy has been increasingly criticized here as well as at home for having condoned Premier Ky's repressive acts against the Buddhists.

This spring, for better or worse, many of the current malcontents supported the Struggle Force in its unsuccessful aim of compelling the resignation of the Directory leaders and establishing a temporary civilian-led government pending elections for a legislative as well as a constituent assembly. Those who supported the Struggle Force did so mostly out of legitimate convictions, seeing it as the only functioning mass movement in the country. It may be true, as some people here now maintain, that after the crackdown Ky and his military associates should have pursued their investigation further and sought specifically to arrest all the Communist agents who were working in and with the Struggle Force, including some who were almost certainly masquerading in yellow Buddhist robes. However, the government instead carried out a wholesale roundup of all dissidents and suspected dissidents, among them five or six hundred officers and noncommissioned officers and several thousand ordinary soldiers, mostly of the 1st Division and of the Quang Nam Province Special Sector Command, in the northern part of the country. Also arrested were about two hundred students in Hué and Danang and about two hundred more in Saigon, and an undetermined number of Buddhist monks and their pagoda followers. These people—perhaps four or five thousand in all—are still in jail, in Hué, Danang, or Saigon, or on Phu Quoc Island, most of them without having had any charges brought against them.

The man who directed the crackdown and has been chiefly responsible for following up on it is Colonel Nguyen Ngoc Loan, and he is in a powerful position, for he heads both the National Police and the Military Security Service. Loan—whom the Americans have nicknamed Laughing Larry, because he has a nervous giggle —is a former classmate and a close friend of Premier Ky's. He has played a considerable role in manipulating the choice of military candidates in the elections, and thus has alienated additional potential voters. Still other potential voters, especially the better-educated ones, and a number of potential candidates as well, have lost whatever interest they may have had in the elections because they feel that the constitutional process has been emasculated. This segment of the electorate has made a number of charges, including one that the Directory disregarded the Electoral Council's recommendation of allowing the voters to vote for individual candidates and decreed instead that (with some exceptions, based on geography and population) voting should be done by slates, with seats to be awarded by proportional representation—a procedure that, it is alleged, will help the government win seats. It is also charged that the Directory, in setting strict and highly specific requirements both for candidates and for voters, did so in such a way as to promote the selection of government or government-supported candidates, and that an article in the election decree barring candidates who "have been directly or indirectly working for the Communists, or pro-Communist neutralists, or have been involved in activities advantageous to the Communists" is far too loose. Under the last stipulation, just about anyone with liberal ideas, including the belief that someday, when negotiations are conducted, the National Liberation Front will have to be represented, can be barred by the local review boards, which canvass the candidates.

The possibility remains that a truly independent or a suddenly rebellious constituent assembly could vote to turn itself into a legislative assembly—as Tri Quang, among others, once suggested. It could then vote for a Chief of State and perhaps for a Premier, depending on the kind of constitution it had written. How the Directory would react if the assembly did this is conjectural, but the chances are that the generals would not take it lying down. In fact, there are a number of Vietnamese—and some Americans as well—who are predicting a new political explosion on just this matter. The candidates for the constituent assembly—approximately six hundred and thirty are running for a hundred and eight seats—can be broken down into four groups: outright military and pro-government men; an undetermined number who are running purely to gain prestige; a small group of truly independent-minded men, who could be the core of a loyal opposition; and (probably a majority) men who are running because they believe that there won't be another election, and that they could remain as legislators for several years and hold the balance of power in any government. This last group could well lead a rebellion within the constituent assembly to keep it going and turn it into a legislative body. One experienced American observer has said of the situation, "It's a guessing game right now. Anything can happen. I hope we can avoid a blowup, but I wouldn't want to bet on it."

At the opposite end of the spectrum from this national election, another electoral process is slowly going on—one that may eventually prove more significant for South Vietnam. This is taking place in the country's hamlets, which are its smallest administrative units. Under the rural Revolutionary Development Program, which is still in its infancy, about two hundred elections have so far been held for hamlet chiefs and hamlet councils in "pacified" areas—that is, areas that have been cleared of Vietcong by government troops and are currently being protected by regional and local troops and by People's Action Teams, which are the offensive combat arm of the fifty-nine-man Revolutionary Development Units.

Ultimately, it is hoped, a combination of respected central authority and enthusiastic local self-government can be achieved at the district and provincial levels so that the interests of the common people will be served both administratively and politically. It would be illusory to expect anything like this to happen soon. Nevertheless, the hamlet elections are a start, and, of the two hundred so far held, about half, in the opinion of American experts working with the Vietnamese on the program, have been successful; that is to say, they have instilled in the people of the hamlets a real sense of participation in the process of government. The lack of success in the other half is attributable to the fact that the hamlet officials were in effect shoved or promoted into office by a Revolutionary Development Unit without ever quite grasping what they were supposed to do or represent.

At present, there are some twenty-six thousand members of Revolutionary Development Units working in government-controlled areas, but only a few units have accomplished much. The Regional and Popular Forces are still controlled by the Defense Ministry and are moved around by division and corps commanders at will, which almost invariably means that they cannot perform their prescribed task of affording protection to the hamlets and villages where the Revolutionary Development Units are assigned. Furthermore, district chiefs have frequently given the People's Action Teams routine guard duty and other jobs apart from their assigned functions. "Despite our big military operations, we are not yet even beginning to keep the Vietcong out of the hamlets and the villages," one American with five years' experience of working in the countryside says. "The National Police system, except for some contingents of special field police, is almost totally ineffective at this. Militarily, we are still fighting a completely different war from the Vietcong. We are being mesmerized by big battles and are missing what's happening underneath, where, through terror and through the utilization of all local resources, including people, the Vietcong are still ruling the roost. Convoys and outposts are still being regularly attacked and hamlet and village officials assassinated. We have a big edge in firepower and in many other resources, but *they* still have the people, and they use the people for their cause. You don't need a regiment to fight a wicked hamlet chief; it takes only thirty seconds to slit a throat."

This American estimates that thirty-five per cent of the South Vietnamese population, including city dwellers, now wants to see the government and the Americans win the war, twenty per cent is still thoroughly pro-Vietcong, and the remaining forty-five per cent is in the middle. Most of the people in the middle would welcome government control, but on their own terms; they still don't trust the Saigon government, and that is why the national election means so little to them. "These are the war-weary people in no man's land, and how much you influence them depends on how successfully you can inspirit them the next time you get a chance to try," this man says. "We can't afford to make the kind of mistakes we are still making. The present development concepts are O.K.; it's their implementation and followup that have to be improved. It's one thing to treat a sick patient by getting his fever down and another thing to get the bugs out of his system. The Vietcong 'bugs' are still around in places we have supposedly cleared, and they keep flaring up."

Even though the number of Vietcong and Vietcong sympathizers surrendering under the government's Chieu Hoi (Open Arms) program is increasing, word is brought out by many individuals that more people would like to come over to the government side but don't because they are afraid they won't be accorded the equality that they enjoy with the Vietcong. Significantly, even those village people who now want the government to win the war believe that the Vietcong will win it in the long run. The reasons for this feeling are deeply rooted in the nature of this brutal and seemingly endless war, which is being fought more and more on two levels—the level that the Americans now dominate by their tremendous technology and mobility, and the level that the Vietcong still dominate by their continuing sway over the people. The Vietcong and the more than sixty North Vietnamese battalions now fighting with them are being subjected to heavy punishment by the immense American air and ground attacks. Prisoners' reports on the suffering undergone by Communist troops as a result of bombings and other actions that are keeping them on the run and depriving them of food make it clear that they are faced with increasing difficulties. And as more North Vietnamese soldiers are called in to fill the ranks of the Vietcong, and as more northern political cadres take over, there are signs of growing friction between the South Vietnamese Communists, together with their non-Communist partisans of the National

Liberation Front, and the North Vietnamese "invaders." One such sign is the fact that the People's Revolutionary Party cadres, who, though they are South Vietnamese, are closely tied to the Lao Dong Communist Party of North Vietnam, are openly taking control of the National Liberation Front, down to the level of hamlet cells. But despite the difficulties facing the Communists both in the South and in the North, there is no reason to suppose that either group is thinking of giving up; if anything, the diehard revolutionaries who have been fighting in the South since 1958—many of whom fought the French before that—seem more rigid in their thinking and more firmly set in their determination to go on fighting than some of their North Vietnamese colleagues.

In purely military terms, the Communists have been suffering some severe defeats, though they have been making the Americans and the Vietnamese-government troops pay for them in dead and wounded. General William C. Westmoreland's "spoiling" tactics, whereby the mobile Americans, acting on intelligence from their own long-range patrols, have prevented the North Vietnamese and the Vietcong from getting into position for large battles by striking them first, have worked well. The over-all military picture, even so, has not changed greatly in the last few months, yet it is worth noting that the North Vietnamese are still looking for their first big victory in South Vietnam. Some of the United States generals feel that they have now definitely prevented the Communists from entering Phase 3 of their long-term strategy—that of full-scale counter-offensives, involving large units and conventional engagement of the enemy. Militarily, the Communists can't win, these generals say, but they admit that a political victory remains possible. A political victory for the Communists, however, can also be a military victory for them if one assumes that the Vietcong have the ability to return to Phase 1—guerrilla warfare based on terror, assassination, sabotage, and constant infiltration.

If the Communists do revert to Phase 1, this can be expected to continue during or after a period of negotiations, and the war in Vietnam is thus likely to go on indefinitely. The issue then will be between the Vietcong's resolve to win, and their continuing ability to deal with the people in the countryside, and the resolve of the Americans and whatever Vietnamese government is in power to contend with the Communists on what will be essentially Communist terms—a marathon social, economic, and political contest to win over the hamlets and the villages. Not long ago, Lieutenant General Van Tien Dung, Chief of Staff of the North Vietnamese Army, and apparently a rising figure in the Hanoi hierarchy, wrote an article in which he declared that, despite "new difficulties and trials" caused by the Americans' military might, "the United States imperialists' fundamental weaknesses in the political field profoundly affect and weaken their military position." The General noted that the Americans "can never turn our rear into theirs," and went on to say, "Military superiority originates from the global interaction of all the political as well as pure military factors, from subjective as well as objective factors. . . . We can fight year after year, generation after generation." Then, striking at the core of the American-Vietnamese problem, General Dung said, "If he [the enemy] withdraws from a number of posts so as to have more mobile forces, he will not be able to hold control over the people, and the areas he occupies will shrink. If he tries to widen these areas, he will spread his forces even more thinly and his mobile forces will get smaller. Whenever he wants to occupy a position or to capture a new one, he has to solve complex problems: occupation, combat troops, pacification troops, artillery support, transport and supply, and so forth. . . . That is why, willy-nilly, the Americans and their puppets remain caught in the traditional dilemma of all aggressive wars against the developing people's war."

There is much in this analysis that is hard to contradict. If the General is proved wrong, it will be by years of patient effort on all fronts of the war rather than just on the military one. Politically, the holding of elections now, on both the national and the hamlet level, represents two small elements in that effort. It is widely believed here that, while the Americans will continue to help South Vietnam in various ways—the less obtrusive the better—the real challenge is to get the Vietnamese people to realize what their own government, as opposed to the Americans or any other outsiders, can do for them.

8.   # Saigon

~·~

October 1, 1966

The new spirit of optimism in South Vietnam produced by the election of the Constituent Assembly on September 11th may serve as
a much needed tonic for a nation whose mood in recent years has
typically been one of frustration and despair. Nevertheless, in the
opinion of certain Vietnamese who have come to view all new developments here with skepticism, the establishment of the Assembly must be regarded as, at best, a challenge and an opportunity
rather than an accomplishment in itself. To be sure, as an exercise
in organization and promotion the vote was impressive, particularly in the midst of a war and in the face of Vietcong threats and
harassment; even though there may have been a certain amount of
exaggeration, as is widely suspected, in the government claim that
eighty-one per cent of the registered voters cast ballots, and even
though the voting was limited to the fifty-five per cent of the country that is under government control, it was still without doubt the
fairest election ever held in South Vietnam. The quiet and orderly
manner in which men and women (many dressed in their best
clothes) went to the polls was clearly an expression of their desire,
or at least their willingness, to take part in the democratic process.
The skeptics point out, however, that so far the process has more

form than content and that the Constituent Assembly, which is supposed to write a new constitution in six months, could actually aggravate rather than ameliorate the uncertainties that plague this country.

Judged by its hundred and seventeen members, it is difficult to predict how the Assembly will operate. Aside from about half a dozen nationally known figures, most of them elected in Saigon or in the adjoining province of Gia Dinh, the members of the new body are generally unknown outside their own communities. The average age of the delegates is less than forty—quite young anywhere, and very young in a nation where lawmaking and the conduct of government have traditionally been carried out by older men. Among the delegates, there are—in addition to nine representatives of tribal areas—twenty-three professors and teachers (including the Assembly's one woman), twenty-two businessmen, twenty active or retired military men, eighteen civil servants, eight farmers or small landowners, seven doctors or pharmacists, five lawyers, three judges, one journalist, and one labor leader. It might have been expected that in an election for a conclave designated to draw up a constitution more lawyers and judges would be chosen, but in fact the constitution was scarcely an issue in itself, and there was very little talk about it during the campaign. For the most part, the candidates discussed matters that had greater political appeal, such as food shortages and the rising cost of living, local security in battle areas, and the hopes for peace. The election of only twenty of the sixty-four military men who ran was less than might have been expected, but, even so, it has been generally acknowledged that the Directory that now runs the government in Saigon—ten generals and ten carefully chosen civilians—will control at least half of the Assembly. Thus, the Directory will presumably be able to get whatever kind of constitution it wants, since it has the power to pass on the one the Assembly presents—it can revise it, reject it, or even propose a substitute—and can be overridden only by a two-thirds vote of the whole Assembly.

According to present law, the Assembly is to be dissolved after a constitution has been adopted, a second election being scheduled for next year, to choose a legislative assembly and whatever sort of executive—probably a president—the new constitution prescribes. It is hoped that the delegates, having learned something from the chaotic experience of the last three years, will take their responsibilities seriously and work harmoniously together, both to write a constitution and to form the two or three major parties that have been constantly called for since the fall of Diem but have yet to be created, because of the jealousies and conflicting ambitions besetting some of the individuals who might be expected to form them. Much will depend on the sort of leadership provided by four of the elected delegates. These four, who are among the few veteran politicians in the Assembly, are Dr. Phan Quang Dan, a politician with some national following who has recently been active in provincial affairs in Gia Dinh; Dr. Dang Van Sung, who publishes *Chinh Luan,* a major Saigon newspaper; Dr. Phan Khac Suu, who was Chief of State during two of the post-Diem regimes; and Tran Van Van, who was head of the Council of Notables and now heads the Army-Civilian Advisory Council, a rather ineffective group set up by the present administration. Although the dozen candidates who ran on a platform of southern separatism were all defeated, forty-four of the individual delegates are southerners, forming the largest single regional bloc, and this gives Dr. Suu and Van, both southerners, something of an edge in the competition. Dr. Sung is seeking to create a broader coalition—one that would include members of the Hoa Hao and Cao Dai religious sects, as well as Buddhists and Catholics, and members of the two old-line nationalist parties, the Vietnam Quoc Dan Dang and the Revolutionary Dai Viet. If Dr. Sung succeeds in forming his independent bloc, he hopes to use it to achieve a temporary balance of power in the Assembly.

The trend at the moment is away from religious sectarianism. The Buddhists' boycott of the election was no more effective than the Vietcong's threats to attack voters—about thirty-five Buddhists running independently were elected, and violence was at a minimum—and now a number of Buddhist leaders are said to be considering giving up their anti-government campaign, which culminated in the severe crackdown on them last May. They can hardly hope to achieve much by continuing to demand that Chief of State General Nguyen Van Thieu and Premier Nguyen Cao Ky— or, anyway, one of them—must resign as the price of Buddhist coöperation in an interim government, for it now seems obvious to nearly everyone that this government will stay in office until a new one is chosen legally. Whatever course the Buddhists adopt will be determined in large part by Thich Tri Quang, the extremist monk and leader of the anti-government movement in central Vietnam, who has just stopped his three-month-long hunger strike. Until his superiors ordered him to start eating again, he was apparently prepared to continue his fast until he died—a demonstration of defiance that would undoubtedly have led to a period of national mourning, with obvious political significance. A thousand Buddhists, including both clerical and lay leaders, are still in jail as a result of last spring's disorders, and their release, with a collective pardon, would also have to be part of any reconciliation between the Buddhists and the government. In any event, the future of the Buddhists as a political force is obscure at the moment, and the Catholics, who have not tried to form a Catholic party as such, are remaining quiet. If both the religious and the military leaders can at least stay in the background for the time being, there may be some hope that the civilian politicians, including those just elected, can begin to develop a certain amount of genuine interest in national institutions of self-government among the peasants.

While the election did show that a surprisingly large number of people cared enough about the future of their nation to go to the polls, their doing so scarcely amounted to a demonstration of nationalist fervor. It is generally agreed that willingness to support a central government must be inculcated, for a start, in the people of the hamlets and villages, and the question of how to do this will play an important part in the constitutional discussions that are about to begin. While most of the delegates now engaged in preparing drafts agree that the constitution should provide for a strong executive, there is also considerable support for providing a constitutional guarantee of local elections. All past elections in Vietnam, including the most recent one, were ordered by decree, and they have always been called or postponed according to the whim of the national executive. Dr. Dan, among others, believes that the villages should have some degree of fiscal as well as administrative autonomy, and that after the village electoral and administrative procedures have been established they should gradually be extended to the provincial level, so that province chiefs and other provincial officials would ultimately be elected by the people rather than appointed by the central government, as they are now. All the experts who are working on the constitution agree that it should include positive guarantees of fundamental human rights, including habeas corpus, freedom of religion and of the press, freedom of assembly, and the right to work, to own property, and to obtain an education. There is less agreement about the matter of checks and balances, though there is a general desire to establish firm legal bulwarks against the threat of dictatorship. Everyone grants the desirability of protecting the independence of the judiciary, but how to let the legislature maintain some control over the executive without impeding it unduly is clearly a subject that will call for a good deal of debate.

With the formation of the Constituent Assembly as a first step toward establishing a civilian government, the Directory may be said to have entered a kind of interregnum. While there is no overt dissension among the generals who dominate it, their relations do show signs of strain. The two men principally concerned are Chief of State Thieu and Premier Ky, who have been engaged in an elaborate pas de deux in which each has from time to time affirmed and then denied any desire to stay on as either first or second man in whatever government the new constitution establishes. Ky, in particular, has played an astonishingly coquettish game with the press concerning his availability. At the celebration of his thirty-sixth birthday, a fortnight ago, he declared that he might allow himself to be drafted, especially if General Thieu meant what he said a few days before about not wanting to become the chief executive. Then, a week later, ostensibly at the suggestion of his wife, Ky indicated he wanted to return to the Air Force. Of course, one can scarcely regard the flamboyant Ky as the indispensable man, and as for Thieu, a much less colorful personality, he seems to lack the popular appeal necessary for political success. All in all, there is a sad dearth of potential candidates for chief executive among both civilians and military men, and as one Vietnamese observer of the many coups and counter-coups of the last three years has said, "The trouble is we've eaten up all our young."

In the long run, the public contest between Ky and Thieu may be far less significant than an undercover struggle currently going on among some of the other generals on the Directory. The most vulnerable, at the moment, are General Nguyen Huu Co, a Deputy Premier and the Minister of Defense; General Vinh Loc, the head of the II Corps, in the highlands; and General Dang Van Quang, the head of the IV Corps, in the Delta. Loc and Quang rule their areas like warlords, almost without reference to Saigon, and, according to reports, enjoy the benefits that traditionally accompany that kind of rule. A newly important figure is General Nguyen Ngoc Loan, who is chief of both the National Police and the Military Security Service. Loan, just promoted from colonel, is now one of the most powerful men in the country; he is a protégé of Ky's, and in any contest he can be counted on to remain in the Premier's corner.

In addition to straight power politics, the current struggle among the generals involves the role of the French in Vietnam today. The French here—there are about fifteen hundred of them left, and another fifteen hundred persons of mixed blood—are trying desperately to maintain as much of an economic and cultural position as they can in their former Southeast Asian possession. According to Vietnamese financial sources, they have spent large amounts to buy friendship and information, and it is an open secret that French business concerns—along with other foreign companies, including some American ones—have been paying taxes to the Vietcong in order to be able to go on operating. The French still have four major rubber plantations in Vietnam, each of which represents an investment of at least a hundred million piastres, or about a million dollars at the unofficial rate of exchange; loss of these investments would be a financial disaster for a number of French banks. The Vietnamese government annually collects between thirty and forty million piastres in taxes from each of the plantations, and while this is a drop in the bucket compared to American aid, the plantations are a potentially important tax source if one looks ahead to the end of war and the withdrawal of American financial support; furthermore, rubber is a major Vietnamese export in ordinary times. The government is thus in something of a quandary; while it resents what Ky calls a "disruptive" French influence on Vietnamese politics, it also wants to keep the French economic influence alive.

As political matters have taken over the center of the stage in recent weeks, it has sometimes seemed as if the war were going on in another country. This has been especially true in Saigon, where American troops were kept off the streets in the days immediately before and during the election; the city hasn't been so quiet in a year or more, and the relative calm is still being maintained, for a permanent limit has been placed on the number of troops allowed in town at any one time. The city has become a much more orderly place in various ways. For one thing, the collection of garbage, which for a time seemed to have been abandoned entirely, has been resumed on a regular basis. There are still plenty of reminders of the war, of course—especially economic ones. The prices of most commodities, including such essentials as rice and pork, remain high, and financial experts are now saying that the stringent financial measures taken several months ago—particularly the devaluation of the piastre—proved to be an overdose of reform, drying up the money market and stopping all speculative investment, so that in many areas of business, including shipping and the export-import trade, all but the largest firms are in serious trouble.

Even though the Vietcong failed to sabotage the election to any large extent, they have certainly not been inactive. In areas not far from Saigon, their presence is very apparent at night, when the skies are filled with flares and tracers and the flash and boom of artillery. Considerable numbers of enemy troops are known to be concentrated around the capital, and the authorities here anticipate a fresh attempt to cut off the city's food supplies. Although Hanoi is claiming general success throughout the country on the basis of the fact that the Vietcong have kept the Americans running after them all summer, the Communists have failed to achieve any major military victories during the rainy season, which is when they usually make their hardest strikes. The rainy season will last a month and a half longer, and some large-scale battles are still expected, chiefly in the area near Danang, where there are known to be heavy concentrations of North Vietnamese troops; in and around the Demilitarized Zone; and in the highlands near the Cambodian border. Activity in the Delta region, south of Saigon, also seems to be picking up, and the expectation is that American troops will soon be engaged there, for the first time. The ever heavier bombardment of the North shows no sign of forcing Hanoi to yield, and, indeed, those who know the North Vietnamese best say that, short of the total obliteration of their country, air assaults alone will never bring them to heel. The same experts predict an intensive dry-season campaign by the Americans and the South Vietnamese, followed by another monsoon period of on-again, off-again fighting. The Communist strategy, it would appear, is still one of continuing the war until finally, for political reasons, the United States is ready to quit.

9. Below the D.M.Z.

December 17, 1966

At seven o'clock on the morning of May 17, 1966, following a three-hour truck ride and a nighttime march from Vinh Linh, on the North Vietnamese coast, a group of two hundred North Vietnamese soldiers waded across a shallow section of the Ben Hai River, which divides North Vietnam and South Vietnam just below the Seventeenth Parallel, and proceeded in a single column along a jungle trail through the lower half of the six-mile-deep Demilitarized Zone, in the province of Quang Tri. Under the 1954 Geneva agreements that ended the Indo-China War, the Demilitarized Zone, or the D.M.Z., as it is generally known, was created as a buffer area to reduce the chances of "any incidents which might result in the resumption of hostilities." No troops are supposed to move in or across the D.M.Z., but it is unlikely that any of the two hundred North Vietnamese—fifty of them officers and the rest mostly young and recent draftees—gave any thought that morning to the fact that they were violating the Geneva agreements. Their thoughts, as some of them subsequently wrote in their diaries, were of their wives or girl friends left behind in the North and of the dangerous mission that lay ahead. This was to reconnoitre four districts in central and eastern Quang Tri, an area about which the soldiers

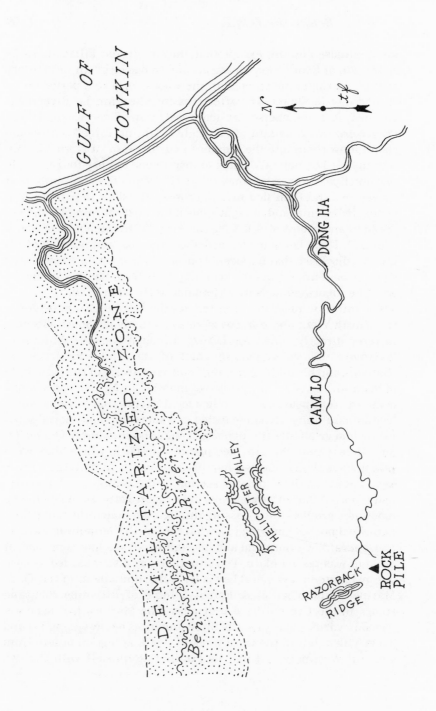

knew almost nothing except that they might be killed there by American or South Vietnamese ground troops or by air or artillery strikes. As the group stopped in the woods for a rest period on its second day in Quang Tri, after crossing the Cam Lo River near Highway 9, its members were addressed by an officer who told them they were the vanguard of "a mighty fighting force" that would soon follow them into the province and "liberate" it from "the imperialists." The pep talk failed to inspire one twenty-four-year-old private first class, who lingered at the rear of the column as it moved on, and then fled into the forest. He slept that night in a concealed ravine, and at eight o'clock the next morning he surrendered to an outpost of A.R.V.N., the Army of the Republic of South Vietnam. Upon being questioned about the size and position of his unit, he disclosed that its specific purpose was to explore routes and suitable base areas for a forthcoming invasion of South Vietnam by what he identified as North Vietnamese Division 324B.

The information of this deserter was the first important evidence that North Vietnamese troops were about to invade South Vietnam in force directly across the D.M.Z., although General William C. Westmoreland, commander-in-chief of the American forces in Vietnam, and his intelligence staff had been aware of the possibility of such an invasion for about two months. In March, reports had come in from peasants and other local agents that various North Vietnamese units, some identified and some not, had moved separately and gradually through the D.M.Z. and into lower Quang Tri and Thua Thien, the province just to the south, where they were said to have then coalesced into two regiments. In mid-April, three local agents in the populated section of the D.M.Z. near the coast had reported that some elements of Division 324B—probably reconnaissance groups—were passing through the Zone into South Vietnam. Without yet knowing just what the North Vietnamese were up to, General Westmoreland and his staff could see that some sort of buildup was taking place. The situation was also regarded as serious by Lieutenant General Lewis W. Walt, commander of the Third Marine Amphibious Task Force—a force of fifty-nine thousand troops in the five northern provinces. The Marines had been engaged in various battles in the three provinces below Quang Tri and Thua Thien, but in the third week of April, acting on orders from General Westmoreland that he familiarize himself with the two northernmost provinces, General Walt dispatched a battalion commanded by Lieutenant Colonel Van Bell to Khe Sanh, a town in the western part of Quang Tri, only four miles from the Laotian border, where there was an American Army Special Forces camp of a dozen American officers and a mixed force of three hundred Vietnamese and Bru tribesmen. Colonel Bell, a tough officer of the old school, known throughout the Marine Corps as Dingdong Bell, spent a week patrolling the Khe Sanh area, searching for a thousand North Vietnamese soldiers that another local agent had reported on, but the battalion found nothing, so the information was discounted. Bell then marched his men thirty miles along Highway 9 to Dong Ha, in the eastern part of Quang Tri, and though fifty of his troops succumbed to the heat, which rose to 125 degrees, and had to be lifted out by helicopter, he ran into no trouble with the enemy and, much to his disgust, "didn't even fire a shot in anger."

On May 1st, the day that Bell and his battalion arrived at Dong Ha, General Westmoreland went up there to talk over the situation with him and with a small group of Americans who were stationed there. This was a detachment of a hundred and thirty Air Force radar specialists, who were manning radar facilities—the northernmost in South Vietnam—to assist in the bombing of targets in North Vietnam. Dong Ha is a town of eight thousand people, a number of whom were known to be pro-Vietcong. The Air Force men stayed alongside an old French airstrip, and though there was a small A.R.V.N. detachment in the area, the Americans were pretty much off by themselves. One evening at dusk, a company of Vietcong walked down the runway as far as a minefield that the Air Force men had laid outside their headquarters. "They just looked at us for half an hour or so and then left," Major Lawrence Cummings, the commanding officer, said later. "It was weird and scary. My guess is that the Vietcong simply wanted to study our installations for the mockups they keep, and figured they could knock us off whenever they wanted to." The detachment did receive three mortar barrages in its first few months at Dong Ha, but the only damage was the destruction of a frozen-meat storage box. The detachment was never attacked directly by the Vietcong, though six Air Force men on a reconnoitring mission in a jeep were killed one day when they ran into a Vietcong ambush.

After interviewing some of the Air Force forward observers, and after he had received the report of Colonel Bell, whose battalion was moved back south, General Westmoreland flew to General Walt's headquarters in Danang on the afternoon of May 1st. Despite Colonel Bell's report, both generals were pretty certain that trouble was brewing in the D.M.Z. In fact, as far back as the Honolulu Conference, in February, General Westmoreland, on being asked what he would do if he were General Vo Nguyen Giap, the commander-in-chief of the North Vietnamese Army, had said he would strike into Quang Tri and Thua Thien Provinces to seek a quick victory. By early June, the evidence that the North Vietnamese were studying Quang Tri in preparation for an invasion was judged sufficient for contingency plans to be drawn up in the Saigon war rooms. Until this time, the D.M.Z. had been used only sporadically as an infiltration route for small groups of Communist soldiers, while most of the North Vietnamese infiltrators had come south by two other known routes. One of these was through the coastal waters, giving the North Vietnamese access to numberless places along the South Vietnamese coast in the Mekong Delta. This was the main route of infiltration in the early nineteen-sixties, when southern Communists who had been sent north in 1954, after the French surrender in the Indo-China War, had begun trickling back in 1958 and 1959 as the guerrilla war in the South picked up again. In the last two years, the water route has been quite effectively cut off by United States Navy and Coast Guard patrols and by motorized junks of the South Vietnamese Navy. Since early 1965, therefore, the principal infiltration route from the North has been the Ho Chi Minh Trail—an elaborate network stretching southward from bases in North Vietnam, past a way station in the northern part of the D.M.Z., then down through the southwestern corner of the D.M.Z. into the northwestern corner of South Vietnam and on into Laos, where part of the route has been widened to carry trucks, then dwindling into hidden jungle foot trails, which reach back eastward into South Vietnam at a number of points, mostly in the central highlands.

American intelligence experts who were evaluating the movements of North Vietnamese elements in the D.M.Z. last spring took heavily into account the fact that the steady bombings of North Vietnam and the Ho Chi Minh Trail were hurting the Communists; some estimates of the bombing damage indicated that the effectiveness of the long supply-and-infiltration line into South Vietnam had been reduced by as much as fifty per cent. Furthermore, the bombing of the trail was having a decided effect on morale; units now arrived in South Vietnam after arduous trips of as long as three months and were said by captured prisoners to be sorely depleted both by the bombings and by illness—mostly malaria and dysentery. Besides all this, it was thought, the North Vietnamese had two more reasons for trying to find an easier way to get reinforcements and supplies south. First, they had not achieved a single major victory since they began sending their own troops in large numbers into South Vietnam last year. Indeed, they had been routed several times —most notably in the Ia Drang Valley, near the Cambodian border, in November, 1965, when the 1st Cavalry Division (Airmobile) beat them back and killed more than fifteen hundred North Vietnamese soldiers. Second, some of the sanctuaries and supply bases of the Vietcong forces, into whose ranks northerners were increasingly being introduced as replacements, were under heavy and steady aerial bombardment—in some cases by B-52s from Guam—and these bombing attacks were being followed up by ground sweeps by American troops. While the Communists had by no means been defeated in the highlands, or around Saigon or in the Mekong Delta (where they still had large bodies of troops), they were undeniably being kept off balance by what General Westmoreland called "spoiler" tactics. Obviously, the American intelligence experts figured, they were looking for an alternative battleground.

And there was another reason—perhaps the most compelling one of all—for Quang Tri and Thua Thien to be considered a logical invasion area. The North Vietnamese had surely been encouraged by the political disturbances in the northern provinces in March and May, when it seemed for a time that a separatist movement, considerably infiltrated by Communist agents, would succeed in taking over. After the Saigon government of Premier Nguyen Cao Ky managed to put down the rebellious Struggle Force and curb the militant Buddhists who supported it, divisiveness and bitterness lingered on, and the usefulness of A.R.V.N. troops in the northern region, some of whom had openly sided with the rebels, was called into question. It was also held to be significant that the provinces of Quang Tri and Thua Thien were removed in March from the jurisdiction of Communist Region Five, whose headquarters are at

Mang Xim, in the mountainous Do Xa area northeast of the highlands in South Vietnam, and placed under that of Region Four,
which is the area just north of the D.M.Z. in North Vietnam. This,
as the analysts saw it, underscored the intention of Hanoi leaders
to invade Quang Tri and Thua Thien, and perhaps to incorporate
them into North Vietnam as a condition of any peace negotiations.

Indeed, some American military officers were surprised that the
attempt to cross over the D.M.Z., which offered the advantage of
short supply lines, had not occurred sooner. One reason the North
Vietnamese had moved so slowly there, and thus attenuated the
advantage they might have derived from the political unrest of
early spring, was that they insisted on methodically "preparing the
battlefield." In Communist terms, this entails careful reconnaissance to establish advance logistical bases and then the gradual
movement of supplies into them. In the case of Quang Tri, which
—except for one area, near the coast—is particularly low on food,
the preparation meant establishing hidden supply depots in the
thick forests of the province. Weapons and ammunition would be
carried in by the invading force itself, but the North Vietnamese
Army leaders apparently planned that food, especially rice, should
be obtained in South Vietnam. This job had been assigned to the
Vietcong 6th Regiment, operating primarily in the Ba Long Valley
of Quang Tri and in Thua Thien Province. But the 6th had run into
trouble. In February, the Vietcong had been badly mauled along the
coast by the A.R.V.N. 2nd Regiment, and, besides, the Marines and
the A.R.V.N. forces had been conducting such efficient rice-protec-
tion campaigns—Golden Fleece campaigns, they were called—that
the Communists were forced to risk fighting in the lowlands on the
Americans' terms in order to obtain food, and even then were generally unsuccessful.

Whether or not the North Vietnamese knew the full extent of
their Vietcong allies' failure to collect and store rice, they were
determined to go ahead with the invasion of South Vietnam across
the D.M.Z., and on May 28th, following a month of reconnaissance,
Division 324B began to move. The division, with a strength vari-
ously estimated at from nine to twelve thousand men, was composed of three regiments, the 90th, the 812th, and the 803rd, which
were given the code names of rivers, and during the month of June

the regiments were infiltrated into South Vietnam by battalions. Each soldier was well armed with a Chinese-made Russian-type AK rifle, fifty to a hundred rounds of ammunition, and some grenades; heavier weapons included mortars, various types of Russian and Chinese submachine guns, and anti-tank guns and rockets. Each man's supplies further consisted of two khaki, green, or purple uniforms, a canteen, a canvas bag, a raincoat, a pair of rubber sandals, a pair of boots, a hammock, a blanket, a mosquito net, some halazone water-purification tablets, some quinine tablets, some vitamin pills, a small can of chicken or shrimp, a kilogram and a half of salt, and seven kilograms of rice. According to information obtained later from prisoners and from captured documents, food, especially rice, was in very short supply, and several of the battalions had to be pressed into service as transport units, going back and forth a number of times to bring more rice down from North Vietnam before crossing the Ben Hai River for good.

The diary of one captured soldier contained the following entries:

19 June 66—Today we were in the woods near the Demilitarized Zone. This afternoon we were ordered to move husked rice to the other side of the Ben Hai River; however, we waited until nightfall, but the rice had not arrived. We had to return to our position.

20 June 66—Early in the morning we were ordered to take our empty rucksacks and rush to the woods to pick up rice. This occurred before we had eaten. Each of us had two balls of pressed rice. We received rice at 0800 hours and moved southward immediately. Arrived at the northern bank of the Ben Hai River at 1200 hours. This section of the river is about twenty metres wide and the current flows swiftly through a gorge. Heavy foliage covered both sides of the river. We waded knee-deep across the river and at 1210 hours we set foot on South Vietnam soil. We then quietly walked through mountainous and heavily forested areas while [American] aircraft buzzed crazily overhead. However, it was quite a rough route, going up and down; there weren't any level sections of more than a hundred metres. At 1400 hours we arrived at the rice depot and turned in the rice. We then began our return trip to our unit. . . .

This particular soldier and his unit lugged rice and ammunition for three more days before crossing the southern boundary of the D.M.Z. into the Cam Lo area of Quang Tri.

By this time, General Westmoreland and his intelligence aides, back in Saigon, were putting together a good deal of information about the invasion. Early in June, local agents had provided them with four specific reports on Division 324B's movements through the D.M.Z., and they also had reports of aerial observations of trucks and troops moving into the eastern part of the Zone. In addition, infra-red aerial photographs, which record emissions of light from the ground even through a thick jungle canopy, had begun to detect nighttime fires in the forests, indicating troop encampments. In the last week of June, General Westmoreland ordered General Walt's Marines to conduct extensive reconnaissance missions to determine the scope of the infiltration. "I didn't want to react too quickly, and I wanted to be sure we had enough intelligence to guide us," General Westmoreland recalled recently. "At the time, though I had nearly two hundred and fifty thousand troops in the country, I was still operating on a shoestring, maneuvering battalions all over the place. I had to have more intelligence on what was going on up north, and there was no better way to get it than by sending in reconnaissance elements in force."

Shortly before dusk on July 1st, this reconnaissance effort began when a group of about a dozen heavily armed Marines, their faces smeared black with grease, boarded two CH-46 Sea Knight helicopters at Dong Ha and flew some ten miles northwestward to a point north of Cam Lo, in the foothills near a junction of two incoming trails two miles below the D.M.Z. The helicopters faked two landings and then set the Marines down in a patch of six-foot elephant grass. "We intended to stay forty-eight hours, find out what we could, and, if possible, capture a prisoner," Captain Terry Terrebonne, the commander of the group, who at the time was still a lieutenant, said not long ago. "As it turned out, we were on the ground only an hour and twenty-three minutes. Nineteen minutes after we landed, we spotted about fifty N.V.A."—that is, soldiers of the North Vietnamese Army—"coming over a ridge. They were wearing green uniforms with camouflage leaves pinned on their backs, and they were carrying automatic weapons. They saw us moving and began an enveloping action, so we started back toward our landing zone, since we were outnumbered. When some of them started running at us, we regrouped in a tight defensive perimeter and I called for gunships"—those helicopters armed with rockets and machine guns—"and for artillery, both of which had been preplanned. We put in some Willie Peter"—white phosphorus—"to help direct the gunships. The first plane on the scene was a gunship piloted by Captain Buck Buchanan, who had been on his way back

to Dong Ha when he intercepted our message. By this time, the
N.V.A. were only fifty yards away. They were holding their fire,
which showed good discipline. Ten minutes later, two A-4 Skyhawks and another gunship arrived. They sprayed the area with
heavy fire, and received automatic-weapons fire in return. Two CH-
46s were right behind them, and they came down and lifted us off."

On July 4th, Terrebonne's reconnaissance party landed near what
was called the Rockpile, an extremely steep conical promontory,
seven hundred feet high and covered with heavy foliage, nine miles
west of Cam Lo. On this occasion, they managed to stay on the
ground twenty-four hours, and, for the first time, they saw well-
fortified enemy positions, including mortar pits, trench lines, and
fighting holes. The morning after they landed, they spotted twelve
N.V.A. and—after calling in artillery, which drove the Communists
into an open field as they tried to escape into the jungle beyond—
killed all twelve. "At this point," Terrebonne said, "we figured that
we were going to be spotted on any insertion we made, but we still
wanted that prisoner." As things turned out, Terrebonne's men
never did get a prisoner, but over a two-week period they spotted
more than three hundred and fifty N.V.A. troops and substantiated
the fact that the North Vietnamese were in Quang Tri in considerable strength. On July 10th, the Terrebonne team killed an N.V.A.
battalion commander, a company commander, and an adjutant
messenger, and seized documents that provided the first written
proof of the presence of Division 324B and also stated its mission
to be the capture of key areas of Quang Tri, ultimately including the
provincial capital.

Five days earlier, on July 5th, A.R.V.N. troops near the Rockpile
had captured a private who stated that he belonged to the 812th
Regiment of Division 324B and that all three regiments of the division had entered South Vietnam. On July 9th, a lieutenant who was
an assistant company commander of the 812th Regiment surrendered to A.R.V.N. troops near the Rockpile. He gave the most useful
information yet, including positions and designations of the compo-
nents of Division 324B, their specific objectives in Quang Tri, and
their over-all mission, which was to destroy all A.R.V.N. troops in
the province. Other N.V.A. and Vietcong forces, in both Quang Tri
and Thua Thien, had the mission of destroying A.R.V.N. reinforcements that might try to move north, he said, and he added that

another N.V.A. division was poised to move east from Laos along Highway 9 to help 324B, which was to act as a transport-and-supply unit after additional divisions from North Vietnam had passed through Quang Tri and moved farther down into South Vietnam. The lieutenant, who obviously had no stomach for the war, volunteered the further information that most of the North Vietnamese people were tired of the fighting and wanted it to end, although they still had enough to eat and, except for bombings, were not suffering undue hardships. All the young men taken for military service, he said, had no choice about coming south. They received anywhere from two to nine months' training, including at least five days of intensive political indoctrination, in which they were admonished not to talk if captured and were given even sterner warnings against South Vietnamese Chieu Hoi (Open Arms) appeals to surrender; if they did surrender, they were told, they would be killed by A.R.V.N. or American troops.

On the third of July, when the reconnaissance missions had been under way three days, General Westmoreland flew up to Dong Ha and over the D.M.Z. area with Admiral Ulysses Grant Sharp, the commander-in-chief of the joint services in the Pacific, who has his headquarters at Honolulu. "I knew by now that it was just a matter of time before we had to respond in force to the North Vietnamese threat," General Westmoreland has said since. "On the eleventh of July, I got in touch in Saigon with General Cao Van Vien, the chief of staff of the Vietnamese Army, and General Vien and I decided to go to Danang and Hué the next day to talk to our area commanders. I was now convinced that the better part of 324B had moved across the D.M.Z. We already had made our final logistical arrangements, which included resurfacing the airstrip at Dong Ha with aluminum matting and arranging for General Walt to get ashore all the supplies he would need for a quick and effective response to the North Vietnamese action. Much of this, of course, had already been planned at our war-games sessions in Saigon. We knew what we had, and we knew what we were able to do with it. On the twelfth of July, in Hué, I told General Walt to move up whatever troops he required to Dong Ha and the area beyond and around it, and I promised to try to get him a Special Landing Force of Marines from the Seventh Fleet and whatever other help he might need. We arranged for B-52 air strikes to begin the next day."

In addition to the helicopter-borne reconnaissance troops that were making constant contacts with North Vietnamese troops, an infantry battalion that was to conduct some patrols on foot and an eight-gun howitzer battery had been sent to Dong Ha on July 7th. Now that General Walt had his orders, additional battalions were ready to move on July 15th. Operation Hastings, as the response to the North Vietnamese thrust across the D.M.Z. had been named, was about to begin.

The province of Quang Tri, which has a population of two hundred and eighty thousand, begins in the west at the Laotian border in mountains; these drop off eastward into foothills and then into a piedmont plateau, which is separated from the sea by a stretch of low paddy land and finally by a sandy coastal area. The mountains, which make up roughly half the province, are covered by almost impenetrable jungle—a three-ply growth that consists of thick brush topped by a canopy of deciduous trees that grow as high as thirty feet and by a second canopy of trees that grow as high as a hundred feet. Barring some thirteen thousand Montagnards of the Bru tribe, the western jungle area is uninhabited except for a few isolated spots such as Khe Sanh, and most of this region has been under loose Communist control for ten years. In the central plateau area, the soil is red and rich and is suitable for the raising of fruits and vegetables, but there are not many people there, either, and most of this region, too, has been under Vietcong control for many years. The paddy section contains three-quarters of Quang Tri's population and has been in government hands on and off since 1954, but never constantly. The coastal area, consisting of white sandy plains, is unproductive except for some fishing villages.

The tactical plan of N.V.A. Division 324B was to come into Quang Tri along five basic trails. The two most important of these enter the province from the D.M.Z. at points northeast and northwest of the Rockpile, which lies in the center of the province about seven miles below the D.M.Z. boundary. The two trails converge at a point some four miles below the boundary. East of the Rockpile are the Thon Son Lam area, then the Cam Lo area, then the Dong Ha area, and then the paddy fields and the sandy coast. South of the Rockpile is the district of Ca Lu, and then farther southeast is the Ba Long Valley, a Vietcong stronghold. The initial mission of 324B was to come in and take control of all these places in preparation for a move on the provincial capital, the city of Quang Tri, which lies eight miles southeast of Dong Ha. The mission of the 90th Regiment of the division was to act as a blocking force north of Highway 9 in the area between Thon Son Lam and Cam Lo. The 803rd Regiment was to be to the west, and the 812th Regiment was to go south of Highway 9 and take over the Ba Long Valley. A vital part of the North Vietnamese plan was the capture of the Rockpile, for it commands the whole surrounding area, including a mountain ridge just to the northwest, known as the Razorback, and a longer ridge, farther to the northwest, along the top of which runs one of the major trails from the D.M.Z.

The combined American and South Vietnamese forces responding to this North Vietnamese attack in Operation Hastings consisted of seven battalions of American Marines and five South Vietnamese infantry and airborne battalions, supported by seven batteries of American artillery and the resources of the 1st Marine Air Wing, including A-4 Skyhawks, F-4 Phantom bombers, helicopters, and C-130 Hercules transports. The area of operations was divided into three zones, with the South Vietnamese operating in the east and south-central parts of Quang Tri Province and the Americans in a large triangular area in the middle. The South Vietnamese force on the ground totalled about three thousand men, and the Americans, whose battalions were somewhat undermanned because of rotation and battle injuries, totalled about eight thousand, including artillery and other support elements. The basic strength of a United States Marine division, which is larger than an Army division, is between twenty and twenty-one thousand men, organized in three infantry regiments and one artillery regiment. The smallest fighting unit is the squad, composed of the squad leader, three fire teams of four men each, and a grenadier, who carries an M-79 grenade launcher; there are three such squads to each fighting platoon. Attached to each division are separate engineer, shore-party, medical, motor-transport, tank, anti-tank, amphibious-tractor, and reconnaissance battalions. The firepower of a Marine infantry battalion is probably greater than that of any unit of similar size in the history of warfare. Its basic weapon is the powerful M-14 automatic rifle, which fires a 7.62 millimetre cartridge. Additional weapons include flamethrowers, M-60 machine guns, M-76 and M-79 grenade launchers, 60- and 81-millimetre mortars, 90- and

106-millimetre recoilless rifles, and pistols. The artillery batteries have 4.2-inch mortars, 105- and 155-millimetre guns, and eight-inch howitzers.

The Marine force engaged in the battle, called Task Force Delta, was under the direction of Brigadier General Lowell E. English, a fifty-one-year-old combat veteran of the Second World War battles of Guadalcanal, Bougainville, Guam, and Iwo Jima, and of the Korean War. As assistant commander of the Marine 3rd Division, General English established forward division headquarters at Cam Lo and Dong Ha. The commander of the division, Major General Wood B. Kyle, remained at the principal division headquarters, at Phu Bai, forty-five miles to the south. General English's battle plan, approved by Generals Kyle and Walt and Westmoreland, was brilliantly conceived to take the enemy by surprise on his key trails and behind his own lines and to smash and destroy him before he had a chance to regain his balance and his momentum.

The action began at eight o'clock on the morning of July 15th, when the 3rd Battalion of the 4th Regiment of the 3rd Division was dropped by CH-46 Sea Knight helicopters, which look like huge mechanized grasshoppers, into the Son Ngan Valley, five miles northeast of the Rockpile and only about a mile below the D.M.Z. The first wave of helicopters, each carrying twelve men of the 2nd Platoon of Kilo Company, landed without opposition, and the troops quickly began to deploy through the jungle. The second wave received some sniper fire about a hundred yards from its landing zone. During the third wave, three of the helicopters crashed; two of them locked rotors as they landed and caught fire, and the third hit some trees while trying to avoid the other two. Fortunately, no men were killed, but the helicopters were unsalvageable and were later destroyed. From then on, the Son Ngan Valley was called Helicopter Valley by the Marines. The mission of Three/Four, as the battalion is referred to in military shorthand, was to establish a blocking position across the suspected trail lines of 324B. An hour and a half after the initial landing of Three/Four, the 2nd Battalion of the 4th Regiment (Two/Four) was landed at the other end of Helicopter Valley, about three miles northeast of the spot where Three/Four had set down. Its mission was to move toward Three/-Four, link up with it, and then begin search-and-destroy operations against 324B, whose divisional command post was thought to be in the area. According to an account given later by Lieutenant Colonel Arnold E. Bench, the battalion commander of Two/Four, "Our first objective was Hill 208, overlooking Three/Four's position, but we made very slow progress, because of the heat and the seven-foot-high elephant grass we encountered, which the aerial reconnaissance had underestimated, and it took us until midafternoon to cover less than two miles. About four o'clock, just after we had stopped for the day and begun to set up our nighttime perimeter and to requisition supplies, I got a radio call from Lieutenant Colonel Vale"—this was S. A. Vale, the commander of Three/Four—"who said he had come under heavy fire and was in trouble. I told him of our terrain problems and suggested we start out toward him at dawn, to which both he and General English agreed."

Three/Four had indeed run into trouble, and its ordeal was to last three days. As soon as its platoons had been assembled after landing, it started moving south toward its blocking-position objective along a trail that ran beside a stream. "All along the way, we saw hundreds of firing holes, only two or three feet apart, on the surrounding slopes," Captain Robert J. Modrzejewski, the commander of Kilo Company, has recalled. "They looked as if they had been scooped out by machines. We were receiving steady sniper fire from the brush, and we killed two of the snipers. Underneath the jungle canopy we found a complete two-hundred-bed hospital in a bamboo building about thirty yards long and twenty yards wide. One man was guarding it, and we shot him. Inside we found twelve hundred pounds of medical supplies. Nearby was a cache of two hundred and fifty thousand rounds of small-arms ammunition, being guarded by three men. We shot them, too. Lieutenant [David] Richwine's 2nd Platoon, which found the arms, got into a two-hour fire fight a half mile farther on and killed at least ten N.V.A. In midafternoon, we made our first attempt to cross the Son Ngan, at a point where it was twenty feet wide, but we got caught in a crossfire and couldn't do it. We had three men killed and five wounded. While Richwine's platoon was searching for another crossing spot, the men heard voices in the brush and quickly set up an ambush. That got us ten more N.V.A., at the cost of only two men wounded. During the afternoon, we spotted an N.V.A. photographer just across the river —he had cameras dribbling all over him—and we nailed him. After three unsuccessful attempts to cross the river under fire, we decided to stay where we were for the night, on a knoll about two hundred yards from the river. We set up our perimeter defense, had C rations for chow, and about seven-thirty the show really started. It began when a huge North Vietnamese—he must have been six feet three—came walking up the trail just like it was Sunday. We shot him, and almost immediately the N.V.A. opened up with machine guns and small arms. This lasted three hours, and we figured there was about an enemy company in the area. It was so dark we couldn't see our hands in front of our faces, so we threw out trip flares and called for a flare plane overhead. We could hear and smell and occasionally see the N.V.A. after that. When the firing stopped, we heard them dragging the bodies of their dead away, but in the morning, at the first light, we found twenty-five bodies, some of them only five yards away, stacked on top of each other."

On the second day, Three/Four made two more unsuccessful attempts to cross the Son Ngan. The Marines kept hearing voices in the brush and, after dropping back, called for air and artillery strikes. Some of the bombs and shells hit targets only a hundred yards away from the Marines, and the concussions were shattering. That night, Kilo Company engaged in a four-hour fire fight, often at pistol and bayonet range. The next morning, the Marines counted seventy-nine N.V.A. bodies. At one point during the night, the Marines heard the N.V.A. rolling something up a small hill. They threw grenades at the object, and in the morning they discovered they had killed two N.V.A. manning a .30-calibre Chinese machine gun on wheels. The N.V.A. troops tried to confuse the Marines during the night by shouting English phrases, like "Pull on back!" and once, when a Marine yelled "Are you all right, Doc?" to another Marine, a North Vietnamese a few feet away in the brush mimicked him, shouting the same question—"You all right, Doc?"

By July 17th, two days after Operation Hastings had made direct contact with the N.V.A., Colonel Bench's Two/Four had managed to effect a tenuous link with Three/Four in Helicopter Valley, and the two battalions established a rough dual perimeter for the third night, which proved relatively quiet. In view of the heavy resistance that had been encountered, General English decided on July 18th to disengage the two battalions and move them out through the eastern end of the valley, where Two/Four had landed, and then have them move back up toward the valley by way of some high ground to the south, where he suspected that the North Vietnamese had their main positions and a command post. Another battalion that had been sent to help Three/Four—the 2nd Battalion of the 1st Regiment of the Marine 1st Division, which had lost twelve men when a helicopter was shot down the first night—was patrolling to the south, and General English now brought in some fresh troops, the 3rd Battalion of the 5th Regiment of the 1st Division, which constituted a Special Landing Force. Three/Five was transported by helicopter from aboard the U.S.S. *Princeton,* offshore, and was given the mission of sweeping two valleys in the center of the Marine area of operations, thus providing protection to the south. The 1st Battalion of the 3rd Regiment of the 1st Division was also brought in, and One/Three patrolled north of Helicopter Valley.

Shortly after noon on July 18th, Three/Four began moving, behind Two/Four, out of its original landing zone in Helicopter Valley, first heading west and then swinging around east. Bringing up the rear was Kilo Company's 1st Platoon, led by a twenty-six-year-old sergeant named John J. McGinty. "We stayed behind to protect the engineers blowing the ammo dump we found," McGinty has recalled. "After the explosions, we heard some voices, but it wasn't until the tail end of the platoon started up the river that we started getting mortar fire, followed by automatic-weapons fire from all sides. This time, they were blowing bugles, and we could see them waving flags. We managed to get all our three fire squads across the river near the landing zone by about two o'clock, but then the squad on my left flank—I had the other two with me—started taking heavy casualties. Charlie"—another name for the N.V.A.—"moved in in waves with small arms right behind the mortars, and we estimated we were being attacked by a thousand men. We just couldn't kill them fast enough. My squads were cut off from each other, and together we were cut off from the rest of the company. I had some of my men in the high grass, where our machine-gunners had to get up on their knees to shoot, which exposed them. Charlie never overran us, but he got one or two of his squads between us. By around three o'clock, we had begun getting air and artillery support. This fight lasted three and a half hours, and by the end of it eight of my men were dead and the platoon had twenty-two casualties out of the thirty-two men we had started out with at noon."

In midafternoon, Captain Modrzejewski—he is generally known in the outfit as Captain Ski—asked for reinforcements, because he had only about one platoon still functioning. Help arrived shortly after four o'clock, when a platoon of Three/Four's Lima Company managed to fight its way back and give McGinty's platoon some supporting fire. The Marines were able to evacuate their wounded during a lull, but they left their dead behind, temporarily, when the firing started up again. Captain Modrzejewski afterward recounted, "We were getting mortars right in the landing zone, and the bombs and napalm were dropping only fifty yards away from us. At one point, the N.V.A. were trying to get the ammo out of those three wrecked helicopters that were still sitting there. Napalm got about twenty of them, and then another forty, in the middle of the landing zone. I remember one kid shouting, 'Here come some more Marines!' But they weren't Marines at all—they were N.V.A. And when they saw us, they ducked into the river on our flank. All we could see was their heads and their rifles above water—it was like shooting pumpkins. The firing continued sporadically until dawn, and when it was over we figured we had killed more than five hundred. Our company was down from a hundred and thirty to eighty, and I had kids who were hit in five or six places."

This long fight was the biggest of Operation Hastings, and also the bloodiest. On the morning of July 19th, India Company came across Lieutenant Robert Wilson, the Kilo Company forward air observer, who had been seen to fall during the battle of the previous day and had been presumed dead. He was found stumbling through a stream. He had plugged a big hole in his chest with a sock and wrapped a binocular strap around it. He was also suffering from numerous mortar and shrapnel wounds, and had been twice left as a corpse by the North Vietnamese. At one point, struggling to his feet after the Communists had passed him by, he had been shot in the arm by one of the Marine helicopter rocket gunships, whose crew thought he was a North Vietnamese. He was partly paralyzed, but despite that and a collapsed lung and multiple other injuries, he survived and recovered. For that day and night in the jungles of Quang Tri he was awarded three Purple Hearts.

After the ordeal that Three/Four had been through, some of its elements were evacuated for rest and for replacement of losses, but the battalion remained in the field. With Colonel Bench's Two/Four, it moved back up toward Helicopter Valley from the south, in accordance with General English's plan. Most of the action during the following days was concentrated in two areas—in Helicopter Valley and around the Rockpile. During this period, Colonel Bench experienced what he afterward described as one of the most amazing episodes in his career as a soldier. "I was on a slope of the valley that gave me an unusual view of the whole battlefield," he said. "A fire fight was going on below me in a relatively open area. Two of my companies were engaged, and I could see both of them, as well as a third one, which was behind me. I was able to control the whole operation by arm signals, and as I stood there moving my arms I could see North Vietnamese and Marines firing and falling."

Two/Four fought and then patrolled in Helicopter Valley for a total of ten days, during which one of its companies was badly mortared one night; it accounted for fifty-six N.V.A. confirmed killed and sixty-eight probables. Colonel "Dingdong" Bell's One/One Battalion, which by now had been dropped in to the South, stayed nine days, killing thirty-five North Vietnamese and claiming a hundred and fifty probables. This battalion also captured five of the fourteen prisoners taken, all told, in Hastings. Colonel Vale's Three/Four battalion killed two hundred and seventy-nine enemy soldiers in all, claimed four hundred and thirty-two probables, and suffered the severest Marine casualties—more than twenty killed and nearly two hundred wounded. Two/One, which was in a blocking position below Helicopter Valley, made several contacts with enemy forces trying to flee westward. The other battalion that fought in the area south of Helicopter Valley—Three/Five, the one that had been brought in as a Special Landing Force from the sea—made two heavy contacts. The first was with a company-size unit of North Vietnamese at one of a number of sizable hills that rise out of this jungle area; after this action, the battalion captured eight hundred enemy packs, ten thousand rounds of ammunition, and clothing and equipment for five hundred men, and it also destroyed three battalion-size command posts. Two days later—the ninth day of Operation Hastings—Three/Five tangled with an enemy force of battalion strength. Much of this action took place during a heavy rainstorm, and the jungle was so dense that the wounded could not be removed by helicopter until temporary landing zones had been blasted out by explosives or cleared with chain saws lowered on cables. A prisoner captured during this fight gave information indicating that Division 324B, particularly the 90th Regiment and elements of the 812th alongside it, had been fragmented as a result of the Marines' enveloping tactics, and that these elements had begun to move back to the D.M.Z. along the trails over which they had come into Quang Tri. On the basis of this information, General English shifted some of his units to pursue the stragglers, and General Westmoreland called for B-52 bombers to strike the battle area and also the D.M.Z.

While General English was enveloping the 90th Regiment of Division 324B from the rear in Helicopter Valley, he also had troops engaged in a corollary offensive—the occupation of the Rockpile. The summit of the promontory is a narrow ledge no more than a few feet wide. After fifty-pound bombs and napalm were dropped on top of the Rockpile to knock out a small flat area, Lieutenant James Hart and twelve specially trained parachute reconnaissance men, plus a demolition team, were dropped on the promontory on July 16th by two helicopters, which hovered above it while they jumped down. Most of the men made a jump of six or eight feet but just as Hart was jumping wind currents lifted the helicopter, and he fell thirty feet; he was stunned and temporarily paralyzed. Within half an hour of landing on top of the Rockpile, Hart's team sighted thirty-eight N.V.A. moving through the valley below and called for artillery, which killed them all. The team remained on top of the Rockpile for two weeks, during which it was regularly supplied with food. It was able to spot more North Vietnamese moving along the trails that converged near the Rockpile, often making its observations with Starlight scopes, which can detect movement through darkness. As a result of their watches, artillery and air attacks were called in, and the North Vietnamese were unable to maneuver down along the trails from the D.M.Z., as they had planned. In fact, all the signs showed they were withdrawing.

Marine operations officers formally terminated Operation Hastings at noon on August 3rd, after a break of several days in the action. General English has calculated that at one time or another the seven Marine battalions he deployed in Hastings engaged all or parts of six or seven battalions of N.V.A. Division 324B. The A. R.V.N. elements made fewer contacts, but they helped as blocking forces. A.R.V.N. had its own name for the operation—Lam Son 289.

(Lam Son means Blue-green Mountain in Vietnamese and is also the name of a famous fighting king in Vietnamese history.) The South Vietnamese contributed two task forces—three infantry battalions to the east of the Marines' tactical zone and three airborne battalions to the south of it. The task force on the east made one important contact on July 18th, during which it killed thirteen N.V.A. and lost twelve of its own men. This contact was with another North Vietnamese division, 341, which was known to be based in the northeast corner of the D.M.Z. and to have been assigned to make patrols of its own in Quang Tri and to serve as a source of replacements for the dead and wounded of 324B. The A.R.V.N. airborne task force, in a two-pronged drive from the eastern and western ends of its southern tactical zone, killed fifty-six N.V.A. and lost twenty men.

Although the battle of the north was by no means over, it was now apparent that by striking swiftly as soon as they had obtained sufficient intelligence the Marines had thrown the North Vietnamese off balance and off schedule. Air mobility, together with the Marines' own tactical air and artillery support, some 175-millimetre Army guns, and the five- and eight-inch guns of destroyers and cruisers in the Seventh Fleet offshore, provided a combination of firepower and surprise that staggered the North Vietnamese, who nevertheless fought in their own dogged way with notable valor, discipline, and skill. In fact, man for man, on the ground, the troops more often than not were engaged in even combat. It was American air and artillery support that made the difference and that largely accounted for the total of eight hundred and eighty-two North Vietnamese definitely known to have been killed; the Marines suffered less than a fourth as many casualties. In addition, more than eight hundred North Vietnamese were listed as probably killed, most of them by air and artillery strikes. Operations and intelligence officers have estimated that at least thirty per cent of the remainder of Division 324B, whose strength was finally put at between eleven and twelve thousand, were wounded, and that twenty per cent were immobilized by malaria and other illnesses.

General English has said, "The use of the tactic of vertical envelopment—of dropping in units where we thought we had located the enemy—was a calculated risk, but it caught him off guard, because he never expected it, especially in this rough terrain, which, in my opinion, was worse than Guadalcanal or Bougainville. I was a battalion commander at Iwo Jima, and I didn't get anywhere near the support I was able to give these Marines here." Each evening, helicopters supplied the battalions in the field with fresh ammunition and water. Between July 15th and August 3rd, the day Hastings ended, some seventy helicopters made more than twelve thousand sorties, lifting more than seventeen thousand troops about and delivering thirteen hundred tons of cargo. During this period, twelve hundred tons of ordnance—bombs, napalm, rockets, and other forms of ammunition—were either fired or dropped by helicopter into the battle zones, and fighter-bombers based at Danang and Chu Lai, south of Danang, made more than twelve hundred sorties. During some of these attacks—particularly at night or in poor weather—targets were hit by radar control, the bombs being dropped when buttons were pushed in Dong Ha. In some respects, the most amazing job was that performed by the lumbering, awkward-looking C-130 transport planes, which during the Hastings period flew ten and a half million pounds of cargo from Danang into Dong Ha, which at the outset had only a small dirt airstrip. Everything had to be brought in by air—ammunition, food, barbed wire, and other equipment and supplies of all sorts, including fuel for the helicopters and for the 0-1Es, the small observation planes that act as spotters for artillery and air support. Over the battle period, C-130s brought in four hundred thousand gallons of fuel, carrying most of it in their wings and, upon arriving at Dong Ha, pumping it out into rubber bladders called T.A.F.D.S.s—for Tactical Air Fuel-Dispensing System—each of which has a capacity of ten thousand gallons.

Immediately after the official termination of Operation Hastings on August 3rd, the Marines began Operation Prairie, which was destined to go on a lot longer than Hastings. At the outset, only one battalion—Bench's Two/Four—and some artillery and reconnaissance units were left at Dong Ha, though two other battalions were on eight-hour alert. The mission of the reconnaissance units was to explore the trail areas for any signs of reinfiltration and thus provide early warning of any new large-scale invasion effort. Soon, in the D.M.Z. and on the far side of it, there were indications that 324B or some other unit was making far more extensive efforts than before to prepare for an invasion and, at the same time, to protect itself from B-52 and other heavy bombing attacks. The North Vietnamese were constructing, among other things, deep and well-covered bunkers and heavy trenches with bays for automatic weapons, footbridges and cables across rivers and streams, supply-storage areas, and thousands of foxholes. This activity was spotted by forward air-control planes of the Air Force and the Marines operating out of Dong Ha and by spotter planes of the 20th Tactical Air Force Support Squadron, which had as its principal assignment the detection of suitable targets in North Vietnam. Spotting from the air is a science in itself. The pilots learn what to look for, including changes on the ground between missions. "I'd been watching a trail just north of the Ben Hai for several days," Captain John R. Hanna, one of the spotter-plane pilots, has recalled. "It ran along a river, and there was a little loop that zigged off the river and then rejoined it. One day, I noticed that some new branches had been laid across the loop. I called in attacks and got twenty-five secondary explosions, indicating a pretty big ammunition dump. We got another dump after we spotted some fresh truck tracks leading into a clump of trees."

It was conjectured at Marine headquarters in Danang and at General Westmoreland's headquarters in Saigon that the North Vietnamese might be digging in extensively out of fear that they themselves might be invaded through the D.M.Z. The North Vietnamese were undoubtedly aware of this possibility, and they had seen a preview of what it might be like when the Marine Special Landing Force came in from the sea during Operation Hastings. By the first week of August, American intelligence officers had fairly firm information that, in addition to those parts of 324B within the D.M.Z. or still to the south of it, two other divisions were in or around the D.M.Z. area—the 341st, to the east, and the 304th, just beyond the D.M.Z., in a staging area in North Vietnam.

Between August 3rd and August 8th, there was practically no contact in Operation Prairie. On the sixth, a four-man "recon" unit with the code name of Groucho Marx was dropped by helicopter on a hill north of the Rockpile and about four miles below the D.M.Z. For two days and two nights, the four Marines heard voices in the valley below and saw some campfire smoke, but that was all. Then, on the morning of the eighth, fifteen North Vietnamese soldiers were seen moving toward the recon unit's hill. The Marines, assuming that they had been spotted, asked to be flown out. Instead, six CH-46s brought in a forty-man platoon of Colonel Bench's Two/-Four battalion and set it down on an adjacent hill. The platoon patrolled toward the recon unit and found some fresh trails, fighting holes, and booby traps, but it looked as if the North Vietnamese forces had fled. Colonel Alexander Cereghino, the commander of the Marine 4th Regiment, then ordered in helicopters to remove all elements. The first two CH-46s, each with six men aboard, drew automatic-weapons fire as they lifted away, and then the fire became so intense that the other helicopters had to be waved off. There were thirty-two Marines remaining on the ground, and they pulled into a tight perimeter on a densely wooded piece of high ground and braced themselves for an attack. All during the early afternoon, the Marines and the North Vietnamese exchanged heavy fire, and at five-thirty about three hundred N.V.A. made the expected charge. The Marines managed to throw them back, but they suffered substantial casualties, including the platoon lieutenant—the only officer present—who was killed. Artillery fire could not reach in close enough to relieve the pressure on the Marine lines. Three attempts to bring in ammunition by helicopter failed; two helicopters were driven off by fire, and one dropped its package in a creek bed some distance away from the Marine position.

Finally, a smaller, faster Huey helicopter landed Captain Howard V. Lee, the commander of Echo Company, with three of his Marines and some ammunition. Captain Lee took charge, and during the next three hours the Marines repulsed several more North Vietnamese attacks. By midnight, however, the situation was desperate. Ammunition was again running out. Near midnight, a helicopter piloted by Major Wayne Hazelbacker was hit by heavy rifle fire as it approached with fresh ammunition, but it managed to set down. Captain Lee took into his fighting force the four crew members, two of whom had been slightly wounded, and removed the helicopter's machine guns in order to use them on the ground. The Marines returned fire all night, with the help of parachute flares dropped from planes. At dawn on August 9th, Captain Lee, wounded and severely weakened by loss of blood, relinquished command to Major Hazelbacker, who called for napalm strikes on the enemy positions. Shortly after that, reinforcements arrived from Dong Ha, landing behind a smoke screen. The North Vietnamese then withdrew, and a check of the area showed fifty-three enemy dead, including a company commander; it was estimated that a hundred more N.V.A. had been killed by the air and artillery strikes and their bodies dragged off. Marine losses were described as "moderate."

The Groucho Marx battle, as it came to be called, proved that Division 324B was again present in considerable strength south of the D.M.Z., and for the rest of August contact with the North Vietnamese was fairly regular. On August 17th, at a bridge on Highway 9 just west of Cam Lo, half of one of Bench's companies came under heavy fire from N.V.A. troops in concrete bunkers, protected by sheet iron, in surrounding meadows and on rocky hillocks. For the first time in the campaign, tanks were brought in, and they fired point-blank into the bunkers. The battle lasted nearly three hours, and ninety-seven dead N.V.A. were counted afterward. Bench then took his battalion up into the vicinity of Razorback Ridge, north of the Rockpile, and engaged in more heavy fighting over a three-day period, during which, with air and artillery support, the battalion killed a hundred and seventy N.V.A.; a score of its own men were killed, and nearly a hundred wounded. In this fight, the battalion had the help of one of the most devastating arsenals that the Americans possess in Vietnam—a converted old C-47 armed with a variety of weapons and known as Puff, the Magic Dragon, which is capable of delivering six thousand rounds of fire per minute. That is equal to the firepower of about five Marine rifle companies. During the fight around Razorback Ridge, an N.V.A. sergeant who defected to Two/Four confirmed what was becoming apparent—that 324B had begun a new invasion of Quang Tri, again with the aim of capturing the Rockpile and the areas to the east, particularly Cam Lo and Dong Ha. A few days later, 324B launched a heavy attack at four o'clock in the morning on the Marine and Army artillery positions around Cam Lo. N.V.A. soldiers with demolition charges strapped to their bodies hurled themselves at barbed-wire fences surrounding the positions, and at daylight Marines pulled seventy-nine bodies off the wire.

Having failed to take the Rockpile and knock out the American artillery, the North Vietnamese were once more off balance, and there followed a lull in the fighting until September 7th, when a new enemy movement in battalion force was detected in another area—the Con Thien district, due north of Cam Lo and just below the D.M.Z. Bench's battalion was now lifted by helicopter to the Con Thien area, and made a vertical assault on the N.V.A. positions there, which included elaborate trenches that ran more than a thousand yards right into the D.M.Z. Bench almost immediately came across a completely fortified village laced with trenches and fireholes and full of signs that read "Death to All Americans." Since this was relatively flat hedgerow country, tanks were again sent in to fire straight into the trenches. The village and some fortified hamlets nearby were destroyed and burned. Colonel Cereghino waited two days to see if the N.V.A. would attack again, and when there were fresh stirrings he brought in a Special Landing Force composed of the 1st Battalion of the 26th Regiment of the Marine 5th Division. Between the seventeenth and the nineteenth of September, three of One/Twenty-six's companies conducted a coördinated attack, under a rolling barrage of supporting artillery, to envelop and destroy an N.V.A. force concealed in bunkers and tunnels.

General English and Colonel Cereghino next decided to mount an attack on the long ridge that lies behind Razorback Ridge, north of the Rockpile. In mid-September, the 1st Battalion of the 4th Regiment of the 3rd Division was dropped into the area and attempted to attack the ridge through its southern ravines. A company of One/Four led by Captain Daniel K. McMahon, Jr., encountered an N.V.A. force the size of a battalion, and engaged in a violent three-day fight between September 16th and 18th, during which, with the help of artillery and air strikes, the company was credited with a hundred and seventy-two enemy killed and two hundred and ten probably killed. This was the largest single encounter to date in Operation Prairie.

The task of assaulting the ridge from its eastern end and advancing straight up to its summit was then given to Three/Four, which had borne a heavy share of the cost of clearing the enemy out of Helicopter Valley during Operation Hastings. On September 22nd, Three/Four, now under the command of Lieutenant Colonel William Masterpool, began an ascent that culminated in fights to gain control of two heights known to the Marines as Hills 400 and 484. As Masterpool's first two companies set out to mount the ridge line, each man carried only his rifle and ammunition, two canteens, a poncho, and, in his uniform pockets, two socks filled with cans of

C rations—no pack. At the base of the ridge was a six-foot growth of heavy brush, which rose straight up to a canopy of mixed bamboo and deciduous trees so thick that hardly any light came through, and the trees of a heavier layer, rising above the middle canopy, were sometimes as much as eight feet in diameter. The Marines had to hack their way through with machetes or wait for chunks of jungle to be burned or blasted out by napalm or bombs.

Masterpool's plan of attack was to make as much progress as he could each day on the ground, then stop before dusk and call for radar-controlled bombing attacks and artillery fire, which were directed to the rear as well as the front and sides of the battalion. Masterpool has compared his method of pushing slowly ahead step by step to the action of a ball-point pen. The idea, as he has explained it, was to probe slowly with the tip of the pen and then, when contact was made, retract the point into the pen's larger sleeve; that is, as soon as contact was made, supporting fire, including napalm, was directed onto the enemy positions. This method of attack was slower than a steady assault but was calculated to save Marine lives, and, by and large, that was what it did throughout the battle, with alternating companies serving as the point of the pen. What the Marines were confronting, as they had suspected, was the N.V.A.'s main line of resistance. Camouflaged bunkers covered with heavy logs and sometimes with steel plates were strong enough to sustain even the heaviest artillery strikes or naval gunfire. The best weapons against them were tanks, firing from nearby hills, but then the N.V.A. had to be dug out with grenades, machine guns, and rifles. "The weather was all right for the first five days," Masterpool said later. "But then there was a lot of rain or a steady fog and haze, so logistics became a problem. We could move only a short distance at a time, build our emergency-landing zones, and put out some colored smoke, so the helicopters could grope their way in with ammo and water and evacuate the wounded. We had to shift our supply priorities each day, depending on what we needed most for the next day."

Captain Roger Ryman, the commander of Lima Company, who took one part of Hill 400, picked up the story: "As we got closer to 400, moving along some of the lower hills in front of it, we saw more and more enemy positions, including enough huts in the ravines to harbor a regiment, and piles and piles of ammunition. N.V.A. bodies lying about and hastily dug graves were signs that we were moving in right behind them. Invariably, they'd pick just the right piece of terrain, where it was so narrow that we couldn't maneuver on the flanks, and they'd dig in and wait for us in the bottleneck. Sometimes they'd let the point man go by and then let us have it. Once, I heard a sudden snigger when one of our men slipped. The sound gave away a concealed enemy position a few feet away, and started a fire fight. The N.V.A. was damn clever. We'd walk the artillery in —that is, direct it fifty yards at a time toward us, sensing by sound where it was dropping. Then we'd pull back, opening the artillery sheath, and call for saturated firing in the area. But the N.V.A. would guess what we were doing, and when we pulled back they'd quickly follow us into the safety zone between us and where the shells were dropping. And when the shelling stopped, they'd start shooting again." Sergeant Arthur Downey, one of the platoon leaders, said afterward, "Every time a point moved up, the stuff was so thick you couldn't tell who was firing, Charlie or us. They had everything—mortars, mines, and heavy weapons—and they had ladders in the trees for spotters to climb up and direct the fire." Downey went back and forth, dragging off his wounded and directing the fighting at the same time, and somehow suffered nothing worse than light shrapnel wounds. Eventually, on the fifth day of the battle, the battalion got a foothold on Hill 400, which is L-shaped, and they managed to take the rest of it the following day.

The fight for Hill 484 then began, and it turned out to be two fights, because what the Marines named the Fake, a third hill, between 400 and 484, and which wasn't on their maps, had to be taken first. The same ball-point-pen tactics were adopted, with companies alternating as the point of the pen, while supporting fire was furnished from Hill 400 and, when it was taken, from the Fake. On October 5th, with the help of fire from eight-inch howitzers on the Army's artillery plateau west of Cam Lo, Captain Robert Handrahan's Mike Company took Hill 484, and the N.V.A. began to flee back to the D.M.Z. along the ridge-line trail and through the deep jungle beyond it. On that last day of the battle, Captain J. J. Carroll, who had taken over Kilo Company from Captain Modrzejewski after the earlier Helicopter Valley battle, was on Hill 400 directing fire toward Hill 484 when a misdirected Marine tank barrage from several hundred yards away struck his position, killing him and two other men, and wounding ten. Carroll, a former Notre Dame football player, had described the action in capturing Hill 400 after the N.V.A. counterattacks as "the high point of my career." He was killed exactly a month after he arrived in Vietnam.

In the four months so far that Operation Prairie has been going on, more than twelve hundred N.V.A. dead have been counted; sixteen hundred more have been listed as probably killed—again, as during Hastings, mostly by artillery and air strikes. The Marines, who at one time or another have had eleven different battalions in action in Prairie, have lost approximately an eighth as many as the known enemy dead—a more favorable ratio than that of Hastings. Since October 6th, when the main elements of Division 324B withdrew, there have been no major contacts with the N.V.A. General English, however, has said, "I'm sure of one thing. Although we've definitely killed more than two thousand in Hastings and Prairie combined, and probably a lot more, they haven't quit." The Communists have certainly been more careful during Prairie; only eight prisoners have been captured so far, and far fewer documents have been taken than during Hastings. Throughout both Hastings and Prairie, the N.V.A. seems to have had trouble coördinating its activities with those of Vietcong troops in Quang Tri. This was primarily the result of the Marines' having upset 324B's timetable, but there are those who believe that the lack of liaison and coördination may also be attributed to resentment on the part of the hard-core Vietcong against the manner in which the N.V.A. came into Quang Tri and gave orders to Vietcong leaders who had been running their own show for a long time.

Evidence that the North Vietnamese have not given up the idea of making a frontal attack into Quang Tri—either another full-fledged invasion effort or a quick thrust in search of one dramatic victory—has been seen in a recent fresh buildup within the D.M.Z. Though 324B took a severe beating in Hastings and Prairie, the N.V.A. is perfectly capable of building the division up to strength again with draftees or by inserting elements of other divisions. Four or five other divisions are known to be in staging areas north of the D.M.Z., and any one or any combination of these could be used for another attack. Most probably, it will come through the mountainous western side and into Quang Tri by way of Khe Sanh. Strategically, the key to the control of the whole province is still the

Rockpile and the ridges around it, and the North Vietnamese undoubtedly understand this just as thoroughly as do the Americans, who now hold the area.

To men who have the responsibility of evaluating Operations Hastings and Prairie—in many respects the most significant actions of the war to date—and of relating the two actions to the current over-all military situation in Vietnam, it seems apparent that Hanoi is still determined to wear out the Americans' patience. American casualties, though so far they are not large in comparison with those of other major wars, are mounting—more than six thousand Americans have now been killed in the war in Vietnam—and they are bound to go up somewhat more rapidly in the future, because of the increased number of American troops being deployed in the interior and because of the very nature of the war, which is one of fluidity and sudden, bursting violence. There are still not enough American troops here to hold and defend all the areas that have been taken and at the same time keep chasing after both the North Vietnamese and the Vietcong forces. At present, there are 350,000 American soldiers in the country, plus 52,000 so-called "friendly foreign forces," who are primarily Koreans. A.R.V.N. forces total 285,000, and there are 284,000 Regional and Popular Vietnamese troops, plus about 130,000 police. The enemy strength in South Vietnam is figured at 279,200. Of the hundred and eighty Communist battalions, the N.V.A. has approximately half; the rest are Vietcong main- or local-force elements, and about a third of the main-force battalions are in the Delta area. The Communists not only have maintained their high infiltration rate from the North but have managed to step up their local recruiting.

The job that the Americans initially set for themselves in Vietnam, at the invitation of the Vietnamese, was to reorganize and advise the Vietnamese armed forces. From 1962 to 1965, this was attempted, and proved impossible, because advice was not enough —the Vietnamese, for the most part, paid no attention to it or merely gave it lip service. Since mid-1965, the Americans have been directly and increasingly engaged in the war themselves. By upsetting the Communists' timetable—hitting them before they were ready and then keeping them on the run—the Americans and the Koreans, with some help from A.R.V.N., have been winning notable victories not only in the D.M.Z. area but also in Kontum, Tay Ninh, and Binh Dinh, and, to a lesser degree, elsewhere on the coast.

As a consequence of these campaigns, the Communists are being forced to regroup and to refashion both their strategy and their tactics, searching for any weak spots where they might possibly achieve some success. Though seemingly dedicated in the past year to so-called Phase 3 operations—that is, in Communist terms, to an all-out offensive—the enemy has by no means given up guerrilla activity, and the expectation is that American forces will continue to encounter all kinds of warfare, from terrorist raids on outposts to attacks by regular units ranging from platoons to divisions. Under these conditions, General Westmoreland will require many more troops than he has now if he is to contain and punish the enemy as well as chase him around and keep him off balance. There is no one in South Vietnam, least of all General Westmoreland himself, who believes that the job can be finished within a fixed time limit—whether six months or a year or two years. In Vietnam, no time limits are being set on anything.

10. Saigon

~-

February 18, 1967

For the Vietnamese, Tet, the New Year period, which has just
begun, is traditionally a time when accounts are settled, reapprais-
als made, and new plans adopted. As the Year of the Horse—it was
a plodding one—gives way to the Year of the Goat, symbolizing
positive action, there is a distinct stir in the air, an awareness that
important events and determinations lie ahead. One of the more
notable manifestations is a new attitude of national pride among
the Vietnamese. This is something the Americans have been hoping
for for a long time, but among its effects has been a growing abra-
siveness in the relations between Americans and Vietnamese.
Given the overwhelming impact of the American intervention
here, an increase in anti-Americanism was probably unavoidable.
Much of the continuing inflation is caused by the influx of American soldiers, whose heavy spending floods the economy with Vietnamese piastres, and a good deal of public and private corruption
is caused by the tremendous flow of American goods, some of which
find their way from ships and barges and warehouses in the harbor
into the hands of profiteers on the black market and also into the
hands of the Vietcong.

The burgeoning anti-American sentiment, which is chiefly an
urban manifestation, has its roots in a natural resentment against

the privileged position of the Americans here. The other day, after a Vietnamese shot himself because an American soldier had wooed away his wife by giving her presents and taking her to places he couldn't afford, the Saigon *Post,* an English-language daily, commented, "The staggering American presence here gives reasonable grounds to assume, with little fear of contradiction, that this is not an isolated case, indeed, that a good many 'combatants' pursue this aspect of what is popularly known as 'the battle for hearts and minds.' . . . It goes without saying that one of the chief attractions of the American lover boy prowling around in this country is the money in his billfold. The G.I. knows it and acts accordingly, laying down the unfortunately workable but fallacious dictum in this inherently xenophobic country that the color of love is the shade of green in the American dollar." Although limits have been placed on the number of American troops in Saigon, there has been a spate of fights in bars and of traffic accidents in the jammed city streets. The American press has been involved in a number of incidents, too. There is growing resentment, for example, over unfavorable stories that have appeared in American newspapers—such as several casting doubt on the ability of the Vietnamese armed forces to take over the pacification aspects of the war in the countryside.

None of this is especially serious, but it all serves to emphasize the fact that the Vietnamese are now saying, in effect, that they won't always do just what the Americans want. There have been many times in the last few years when the Vietnamese were looking desperately for guidance, and didn't get it, but now things have changed. "I am not an American puppet," Premier Nguyen Cao Ky said during his recent trip to Australia and New Zealand. Moreover, it appears that the Vietnamese are beginning to express definite feelings of their own about when and how to negotiate with the enemy. During his trip, Ky said he was ready to sit down and talk with Ho Chi Minh—something he would probably not have said a few months ago—and though he and other high officials have stated over and over again in public that they will not negotiate directly with the Vietcong through their political representatives in the National Liberation Front, there have lately been quiet acknowledgments of the Front's existence and there seems to be at least the beginning of a willingness to include Front representatives among the parties at the conference table.

The possibility that the Vietnamese might negotiate a settlement entirely among themselves, leaving the Americans out, has begun to strike some South Vietnamese as one that might appeal to President Johnson, not to mention Senator Fulbright. Of the South Vietnamese who have adopted this view, some—not including officials in the government—are saying privately that, as a prelude to peace talks, a halt should be called to the bombing of the North, and perhaps the intensity of the bombing in the South should be reduced; but these same individuals warn that the United States must be patient, and they emphatically do not advocate the withdrawal of American troops. This, they say, is something that, along with the problem of what should be done with the very substantial bases that the Americans have built in this country, should be the subject of careful negotiation. In arguing that the bombing of the North should cease, these people claim that it has essentially failed to accomplish its objectives and that it has been responsible for driving the North Vietnamese closer to the Chinese Communists. Those who advanced these arguments in the past were in favor of a much stronger United States role here, a role that might even have included a full and frank occupation of the country until it could be made ready, within a stated number of years, to make a real success of independence. Now, however, the best thing that the United States can do, they feel, is maintain its ground operations and assist the Vietnamese in their pacification and Revolutionary Development campaigns, on the theory that a mobile and expanding operation of this sort—not in any way to be confused with the so-called enclave theory of simply holding on to a few strategic areas—could still do much to create an effective alternative to the Vietcong.

One thing the people of Vietnam want, even more urgently than peace and certainly more urgently than politics, is cheaper rice and more of it. The price of rice, which has been rising steadily, has gone up fifty per cent in the last two months, and the grain is in extremely short supply at any price. Tens of thousands of peasants who once grew rice have been forced to flee to the cities, and thus have become consumers instead of producers. The first of this year's American rice allotments will arrive in the next two months, but will not immediately amount to enough to make much difference. At first, the Vietnamese didn't like the taste of American rice, but, as one official assured me, with a grim smile, "they're getting to like it." They don't like frozen pork, but since there is a serious pork shortage, they're getting used to that, too.

Faced with the difficulty of simply getting enough to eat, the average Vietnamese is not much concerned with political developments, although he is vaguely aware that a constitution is in the process of being completed and that a President and a Vice-President are due to be elected sometime this year. The Constituent Assembly that was elected last September is expected to finish preparing a draft constitution by mid-March. Then the ruling Directory, which is dominated by military men, has a month to make changes in it before it is finally adopted. The Presidential election must be held within six months after that, and the expectation is that it will take place in August or September, and possibly even sooner. Elections for a new National Assembly must then be held within a year.

As of this moment, the draft constitution, though it provides for a strong executive form of government, establishes a number of checks and balances that reflect the desire of the members of the Constituent Assembly to give the legislature a firm restraining role. The restraint would be achieved mainly by establishing the right of the National Assembly—composed of a House of Representatives and a Senate—to remove the Premier or any other member of the Cabinet, by a two-thirds vote, at any time after any such officials have been in office one year. In addition, a special court, composed of representatives, senators, and members of the Supreme Court, would have the right to prepare charges of treason or "high crimes" against the President, the Vice-President, or any other government or military official, and such charges, if they were accepted and approved by two-thirds of the Assembly, could lead, after a trial, to the official's removal from office. Another body, called the Inspectorate, would have the right, on its own or when charged by the Assembly, to investigate any government servant, including the President, for "corruption, speculation, or acts harmful to the national interest." The generals of the Directory will surely try to whittle down these legislative prerogatives during private meetings that are to be held with the constitution drafters later this month. The feeling is that a series of compromises will be reached. Whatever is done, a number of Vietnamese with long and painful political experience, including terms in jail under the French or under the regime of President Ngo Dinh Diem, feel strongly that the preamble must proclaim the permanence of the constitution and make it clear that although the document can be revised and amended, it can't ever be suppressed, as happened under Diem.

In the opinion of almost all impartial observers here, one of the greatest difficulties the country faces in putting a new democratic constitution into effect is getting the Army out of politics. There are no signs at present that this is about to happen, though some steps have been taken to reduce corruption in the military. One such step was the removal, late in January, of General Nguyen Huu Co as Minister of Defense and Deputy Premier, following the earlier removal of General Dang Van Quang as commander of the IV Corps, in the Mekong Delta. No charges were brought against Quang, who was given a new job—the unimportant and rather amorphous one of Minister of Planning and Development. The removal of Co, who was officially charged with having been involved in corruption through his family, took place while he was absent from the country, on a trip to Taiwan. The new deputy chief of staff, General Nguyen Van Vy, who has unjustly been accused of being "pro-French" because he once served in the French Army but who actually has a long record of staunch independence, has been raising a lot of hackles in recent weeks by removing more than a hundred officers from their jobs; some of the officers had close connections with the Directory, but so far, at least, Vy has been permitted to go his own way. His investigations, which are reaching into all four of the Army corps areas, are regarded by the Americans as the healthiest sign to date that there are members of the government who mean what they say about cleaning up the military as well as the civilian establishment.

Local elections are supposed to be held in about a third of South Vietnam's twelve thousand hamlets and twenty-five hundred villages—the ones that are considered secure—sometime between April and June under a decree issued last December by Ky. Some members of the Constituent Assembly have strong reservations about the advisability of holding such elections so soon. These delegates feel that the local elections—for hamlet chiefs and for village councils, which in turn will choose village chiefs—should come after the elections for President and Vice-President and the elections for the National Assembly. Any local elections that are held now, the delegates say, will bear the imprimatur of the present military government, rather than of a newly elected government—in other words, without some political preparation, all the old officials and the government-picked candidates would win easily, the result being that the misuse of authority and influence would be maintained in the hamlets and villages and nothing would change.

One Vietnamese I have known for many years, the nation's top labor leader, Tran Quoc Buu, has summarized the case against holding local elections in the spring this way: "The nationalist forces have no mass base, because the Communists are thirty years ahead of us. We must not fool ourselves into believing that we have eliminated their roots, even when underground tunnels and storage areas are destroyed and people are evacuated from Vietcong villages. The roots have not been pulled up, and they will surely grow again. The Vietcong will see to that, because their organization is still with the people, while ours isn't. Before we hold local elections, we must build our own organization, and this will take time. And we have to give the people some understanding of what it means to elect their own representatives. An election now would mean nothing to them, and any election that means nothing has no value. It may look good in international eyes, but that's all." There are others —both Vietnamese and Americans—who feel that there should be no delay in holding elections. What these people are saying, in effect, is that the Americans and the South Vietnamese are in a race against time with the Vietcong and that such a contest cannot be won by delaying tactics.

Hopes have been expressed that political organization at the grass roots might be stimulated by members of the Revolutionary Development cadre, of whom there are now thirty-three thousand —by the end of this year there will be fifty-five thousand working in the hamlets. No one denies the need for some sort of political activity among the Vietnamese people if the new constitutional structure is to have any meaning. In effect, Vietnam today is a country with no political parties. After the overthrow of Diem, on November 1, 1963, fifty or sixty so-called political parties sprang up, despite attempts to limit their number, and acrimony among these elements, frequently abetted by the generals in power, had much to do with provoking the subsequent coups and counter-coups and with maintaining the supremacy of the military. During the elec-

tions for the Constituent Assembly, most slates were simply combi-
nations of friends or temporary marriages of convenience between
disparate factions. Once the Assembly began to meet, about half a
dozen blocs were formed, but only for purposes of maneuver and
bargaining. A group of southerners led by the late Tran Van Van
held together better than the others, but he was assassinated two
months ago while riding to the Assembly in his car one morning.
There were rumors that the government, which is dominated by
northerners and central Vietnamese, had killed Van because he and
his group were becoming too important, but it is now generally
accepted that the Vietcong shot him in order to disrupt the close
bargaining relationship that was growing up among various regional elements, in and out of the government.

The expectation is that the number of parties will eventually be
limited by law, but the problem is not in writing laws but in getting
politicians to work together—something that hasn't been possible
in Vietnam for twenty years. What is lacking in all the attempts to
form blocs or other arrangements so far is mass appeal. One Vietnamese who is deeply concerned with this problem is labor leader
Tran Quoc Buu. Before his union of peasants was sabotaged by
Diem's brother, Ngo Dinh Nhu, ten years ago, it numbered three
hundred thousand. The membership is back up to two hundred
thousand, including some fifty thousand fishermen, and Buu is now
busy trying to bring in more agricultural workers, including those
on tea and coffee plantations as well as on such rubber plantations
as are still functioning. He feels that the sort of party that is needed
at the outset is a relatively small one, made up of "dedicated, experienced, and able militants," whose purpose is not to engage in
political maneuvers at the top but to organize peasants and workers
at the village level and, generally, "to rally people of prestige and
good will in a campaign of national reconciliation."

Another figure still to be reckoned with in the future of Vietnamese politics is Thich Tri Quang, the Buddhist monk who early
last year lost his gamble to unseat the Directory, his movement
being crushed by Premier Ky and the Army in central Vietnam last
May. After that defeat, Tri Quang spent several weeks in what was
tantamount to hospital arrest. He is now officially in seclusion at
the An Quang Pagoda, in Cholon, the Chinese section of Saigon, but
he has not been idle. A year ago, Tri Quang assumed that he had the

Buddhist masses with him. It turned out that he did not; in particular, he lacked the support of the lay leaders and of the vast numbers of Buddhists who pay at least as much attention to the influential laymen among them as they do to the monks. Tri Quang is a hard man to keep down, though, and recently he has begun another effort to acquire a base of power within the southern group of Theravada Buddhists. He has a keen awareness of political issues, and one issue that is made to order for him is anti-Americanism. A number of people who have spoken with him within the last few weeks have come away shocked by the virulence of his anti-American feelings. He has been quoted as saying,"I am more anti-American than I ever was anti-French."

As rumors about talks on prisoners and chances for peace negotiations floated around the world during the last three weeks, there was no indication in Saigon that the reports had any foundation, yet the mere suggestion that some sort of negotiations could conceivably take place this spring or summer has made the political pot here boil more fiercely than ever. There has, in fact, been an increase lately in private contacts between members of the National Liberation Front and certain persons in the government. Nothing of any significance has resulted, nor is it likely to until both the South Vietnamese and the Americans display more willingness than they have so far to deal formally with the Front. People familiar with the operations of both the Front and the North Vietnamese government are firmly convinced that the relationship between them is as tight as it could possibly be, and express certainty that the Front will do nothing without Hanoi's approval. At the same time, Hanoi and the Front, for purposes of maneuver, are trying harder than ever to make themselves seem separate, and the establishment, in December, of a "permanent" Front representation in Hanoi is apparently part of this game.

There is considerable evidence that the Communists are experiencing growing difficulties as a result of the heavy pressure, military and otherwise, that they have been under during the last year. The rate of infiltration from the North has gone down, though perhaps not as sharply as Secretary of Defense McNamara has indicated. In a document captured last month in the so-called Iron Triangle, the most interesting revelation was the admission, in what was apparently a battalion or regimental political officer's summation of a self-criticism session, that the guerrilla force as a whole had "dropped to a hundred and eighty thousand," while "the requirement of this year is three hundred thousand." The document also disclosed that "the present population in the liberated areas is five million people"—representing a loss of a million "owing to the presence of United States troops." These, as a matter of fact, are the same figures that the Vietnamese government and the Americans have been using.

Nobody here in Saigon can be sure, of course, just how deeply worried the Communists are about the new political atmosphere in South Vietnam. People who pride themselves on avoiding excessive optimism say that, far from being concerned, the Communists are just as convinced as they ever were that if they don't win the war militarily they will surely win it politically. However, some government leaders feel that both Hanoi and the Front are disturbed about their relations with the population in South Vietnam and, for that reason, might welcome the opening of protracted negotiations as a means of delaying or halting important political developments in the South and creating uncertainty and confusion from which they could ultimately benefit.

In any event, the Saigon government has made no attempt to conceal its fears that President Johnson has in effect painted himself into a corner by his eagerness to talk peace. The fears are based on the theory that the Communists, concluding that Mr. Johnson won't be able to say no to any halfway decent offer to negotiate, are likely to come up with a phony one that will put the South Vietnamese out on a dangerous limb. Some Americans in the State Department are apparently convinced that if the North Vietnamese and the Americans can agree on joint reduction of troops in the two Vietnams, the South Vietnamese, with continued American military help for a while and a lot more civilian assistance, can then handle the guerrilla problem. But there are serious doubts on this score among officials of the Saigon government, and also among many Americans on the scene. Consequently, though it is true that a sense of pride and nationalism is rising among the leaders of the country, so that they are more determined than ever before to settle their own fate, as Vietnamese dealing with Vietnamese, the leaders of the present government are decidedly reluctant to undertake negotiations until the constitution has been adopted and elections have been held. While Ky publicly says that he will sit down and talk with Ho Chi Minh if it will serve any useful purpose, he privately says that there is nothing to negotiate right now—though that doesn't mean there won't be something later on this year.

It seems even more likely than before that, whenever the elections are held, Ky will run for President. His trip to Australia and New Zealand and his actions and statements since have made him look very much a candidate. Ky has undoubtedly gained political stature during his time as Premier, and if he is not exactly the common man's image of a democratic leader (he still favors purple scarves and Captain Midnight uniforms), he must be credited with boldness, firmness, and a kind of vitality that, unfortunately, is lacking in almost all the other potential candidates for President. A possible exception is Chief of State General Nguyen Van Thieu, the Directory chairman, who, despite his disclaimers, is also a likely Presidential candidate. Various civilian political leaders have been mentioned as candidates, but unless they can agree among themselves to back one man, which remains highly unlikely, the winner is very likely to be either Ky or Thieu.

11. Saigon

~~~~~~

June 17, 1967

The war here is now in its most crucial stage since the spring and
summer of 1965, when an American counter-offensive averted military disaster and, very probably, a quick Communist takeover. The
present tense situation is not likely to be resolved as quickly, chiefly
because, since 1965, the war has become so much more complicated,
both militarily and politically. A good example of its current complexity was provided by the American and South Vietnamese invasion last month of the southern half of the Demilitarized Zone, near
the Seventeenth Parallel, not long after we had stepped up our
bombing of military targets around Hanoi and Haiphong. The
D.M.Z. invasion, pointing the way, as it seemed to, toward further
escalation, had repercussions that went all the way from the confused local political scene—now further confused by a potentially
explosive Presidential campaign—to distant capitals. When the operation began, on May 18th, the key questions—whether it might be
time to give up the bombing of the North and again attempt to
cajole Hanoi into talking, or whether to carry the fight further in
the air and on the ground in hopes of forcing the North Vietnamese
to their knees—were being debated here more hotly than they had
been in some time. The attack on the D.M.Z. naturally heightened

the debate, and while it was generally felt that the move was justifiable in view of prior violations of the Zone by the North Vietnamese, there remained considerable doubt about the necessity and wisdom of it.

Official opinion, among both Americans and South Vietnamese, has been that to start negotiations now, when a new constitutional government is coming to birth and rural development may be about to get somewhere, would be a mistake, but unofficially there are now probably more fledgling doves than there are hawks in South Vietnam. While political ornithology here may be compared to wandering through an enemy-infested jungle with a gun in one hand and a bird guide in the other, the majority opinion of the Vietnamese seems to be against further enlargement of the war, though most people within Saigon's hazy purview—perhaps three-fifths of the seventeen million population—are resigned to, if they are not in favor of, continuing to prosecute the war in the South. However, everyone knows the fighting must stop at some point. The question is: Whose interests will be best served, and in what way, by calling a halt at what time? The North Vietnamese have recently made it clear that they are psychologically much better prepared for a future phase of what they classify as "fighting *and* negotiating" than are the South Vietnamese and the Americans, who have not done much planning either for negotiations or for the creation of workable peace-keeping machinery.

While there are Americans who believe that we cannot now give up the fight and that we still have a good chance of winning it, others, including some who have been here the longest, feel that even as we get more tied up in large-scale fighting, in shoring up the country economically, and in the intricacies of administering the pacification—or, as it is now known, Revolutionary Development—program in the countryside, our chances of permanently redressing the situation are declining. Many of these same Americans, whose identification with Vietnam has been a passionate one and who have on many previous occasions advocated a more thorough and thoughtful involvement on our part, are now beginning to think it is too late, that too many earlier political opportunities have been irrevocably lost, and that the whole effort has become too big, too preponderantly military, and too costly. Basically, they are tending more and more to agree with Senator Mansfield's analysis, which envisions no foreseeable conclusion to the war and constantly increasing risks of a wider conflict. These people do not advocate withdrawal, but, in addition to cautioning against further escalation, they urge the "de-Americanization" of the war in as many ways as possible and our fuller concentration on economic and social problems, not only here but also elsewhere in Southeast Asia. Many of the more thoughtful Vietnamese, among them those who are staunchly anti-Communist and those who believe in genuine neutrality, also feel this way. While they do not advocate American withdrawal, either, they are increasingly worried by the erosion of Vietnamese identity, a kind of denationalization process caused by the massive American impact.

Behind this predominantly negative mood is the realization that the war, which has now cost eleven thousand American lives, is far from being won militarily—if it ever can be—while the rate of progress in Revolutionary Development is still much too slow. It has been fashionable to separate the military effort from the social-economic-political one; in fact, President Johnson has himself often referred to the latter as "the Other War." The Communists have never separated the two, and it is worth noting that the new American Ambassador, Ellsworth Bunker, made it a point, at one of his first appearances at a weekly meeting of the Mission Council, which is composed of top American officials in Vietnam (including General William C. Westmoreland, our military commander), to say, "I dislike the term 'the Other War.' To me this is all one war." Probably Ambassador Bunker was thinking of this when, ten days later, he announced his decision to place "the civil and military aspects of the Revolutionary Development Program" under "a single management" and "a single chain of command," and to give General Westmoreland the over-all responsibility for running all American programs.

Although rumored for some time, Bunker's announcement came as a shock to many Americans and Vietnamese who have believed it is important to maintain a predominantly civilian image in Revolutionary Development. Under Bunker's reorganization, the functions of the Office of Civil Operations, under the direction of Deputy Ambassador William J. Porter, will be taken over by a new division of Civil Operations and Revolutionary Development Support. In each corps area, there will soon be a brigadier general or a top civilian who will be specifically responsible for pacification, and the former O.C.O. people will report through him to Deputy Ambassador Robert Komer, who is assigned to Westmoreland's headquarters and is responsible to him. Undoubtedly, from a managerial standpoint, this setup will make things simpler, but the new system, its critics maintain, seems equally likely to make Revolutionary Development more mechanistic—another sign of the enveloping bigness of a war in which the individual villager, the man everyone presumably wants to help, is increasingly lost in the shuffle. It seems hard to believe that after so many years and so many experiments in this field of reform, from the old strategic-hamlet program of the Ngo Dinh Diem regime to the present scheme, the problem of simultaneously providing the villagers with economic help and proper protection, as well as that elusive factor, revolutionary motivation, should still be so far from solved. The nub of the Revolutionary Development Program, and its greatest weakness so far, has been security, and a big reason for turning the program over to the Army was the hope that this aspect might be improved. Primarily, security means furnishing protection for the fifty-nine-man Revolutionary Development Teams and for the people of the hamlets in which the teams are working. Until now, the force responsible for providing security has been the regular Vietnamese Army (A.R.V.N.), sixty of whose battalions, or about half its total strength of three hundred and thirty thousand, are specifically assigned to this task.

The Revolutionary Development Teams, while they still lack experienced cadremen and what one expert calls "intellectual guidance," have been far ahead of A.R.V.N. in point of training and *esprit de corps,* but though the members of the teams are all armed, there are obviously not enough to defend the hamlets and at the same time develop them socially and economically. Many observers doubt that A.R.V.N. can ever perform the security job satisfactorily, partly because it doesn't really want to, considering it a demeaning and secondary function, and partly because the villagers have little faith in the good will of the troops, with their record of frequent misbehavior, including mistreatment of women and stealing. The Americans have not, over the thirteen-year period since the French withdrawal in 1954, been able to remold A.R.V.N. into an efficient fighting force with a proper attitude toward what is generically called civic action, so there is no reason to suppose that the job can be accomplished now. Furthermore, the calibre of American advisers, which was excellent in 1962, is not as good today, chiefly because our primary function now is to fight, not advise. Once our present enormous commitment was made, our potential for persuasion, backed up by the threat of withdrawal of money, men, or matériel, was bound to diminish. Of course, many Vietnamese still look to us for leadership. When Westmoreland took over pacification in addition to his military duties, a number of Vietnamese I know commented, in effect, "Now you finally have chosen your de Lattre," referring to the late Marshal Jean de Lattre de Tassigny, who in December, 1950, was appointed both Supreme Commander of the French Expeditionary Forces in Indo-China and French High Commissioner.

The first item on the list for reëvaluation, many experienced American and Vietnamese observers believe, should be the structure of all the nation's armed elements, including not only A.R.V.N. but also the three-hundred-thousand-man Regional and Popular Forces. These observers, among them a number of veteran Vietnamese military men, maintain that it would be far more efficient and far less conducive to corruption if the whole clumsy system of corps and divisions were abolished and the armed forces broken down into mobile battalions, assigned as needed to the country's forty-four provinces, each of which would be governed, for the duration of the war, by a general. Most of the provincial chiefs today are military men, but they are either majors, lieutenant colonels, or colonels, and their honesty and capability vary greatly, as do their regional and national political commitments.

If such a drastic reorganization of the armed forces is unlikely to take place—it would entail a shakeup of the whole military-political structure—there are variants of the plan that stand a better chance of being adopted. One of them would place the Popular Forces under the control of the Revolutionary Development Program, and this would mean combining the former units with the R.D. cadres during what is now thirteen weeks of regular training. According to Major Nguyen Be, the able and articulate head of the big R.D. training camp at Vung Tau, whose six years with the Vietminh, the precursors of the Vietcong, have given him invaluable knowledge of Communist methods, if the Popular Forces were worked into the R.D. training schedule, there would be no need for A.R.V.N. to furnish protection; it could then return to fighting the "big" war, which it prefers to do even though it doesn't always do it well. Be's idea, which a number of Americans, including General Westmoreland, believe has merit, is a radical effort to cope with the harassment of villagers by Communist guerrillas—which is still, of course, the biggest problem of the war.

The Communists no longer regard their form of revolutionary warfare as a three-phase operation, beginning with the guerrilla defensive phase; continuing with the attritional phase, in which they begin to take the offensive; and ending with a counter-offensive phase capped by a Dien Bien Phu type of blow. What they are doing now is combining the various phases in various areas, shifting from one to the other, but operating mostly somewhere between Phase 1 and Phase 2 and between Phase 2 and Phase 3. They can still make big or medium-sized attacks and then break up into smaller units and step up their harassment and terrorist actions, which they carry out with continued effectiveness. If Major Be's plan of combining the Popular Forces and the R.D. cadres is adopted, he and his supporters believe it would greatly diminish the effectiveness of the Vietcong guerrillas and would ultimately tend to shove them, against their will, into the Communist main-force elements. And by denying the Communists the ability to break their large units down into the smaller ones that are used to control their own so-called "combat hamlets and villages," where their basic political-military structure is still concentrated, Be's strategy would further keep the enemy off balance. This would hit hard at the classic Communist strategy, which Ho Chi Minh and his generals practiced so adeptly throughout the long war against the French and still practice now: suck the enemy into battle, draw blood even at the cost of your own, and then, before he has a chance to recover or follow up, disperse and move back to shelter. "If we can make the enemy fight a more conventional war," Be says, "we might be able to fill the village vacuum with our *own* guerrillas."

Unfortunately, we are a long way from fighting the sort of war that Major Be envisions, although we have, by sheer weight of armament and by virtue of our air mobility, kept the Communist main-force elements and their North Vietnamese Army compatriots on the run. This has been particularly true in the vital III Corps area around Saigon, where over the last few months strong American search-and-destroy operations have been conducted in, among other places, Tay Ninh Province. Recent American attacks on such longtime Communist sanctuaries in the III Corps area as Zone C, the Iron Triangle, and the adjacent Zone D have forced the enemy to keep moving. Large amounts of arms and ammunition and food, especially rice, have also been captured, as well as tons of important documents. However, the attacks have not by any means deprived the Communists of all their secret bases in the area. The jungle hideouts, many of which date back to the Vietminh war against the French, and some even to the Japanese war, are so big and so complex that they can't possibly be fully explored even during actions of multiple-division strength. Furthermore, the Vietcong and the North Vietnamese Army forces are able to keep returning to the areas once the Americans have left. Undoubtedly, there are plenty of such networks that haven't even been found and may never be found. Generally speaking, however, the American military feels that the situation in the III Corps area, which includes nine provinces north, east, and west of Saigon, is for the moment under control.

Most Vietnamese and American military observers regard the situation as more serious in the I and II Corps areas, embracing, respectively, the five northernmost provinces and the highlands. In the I Corps area, where there are an estimated sixty-four thousand N.V.A. and Vietcong troops, and across whose borders at least four more N.V.A. divisions are prepared to move from North Vietnam, the Communists show no inclination to give up their aim of pinning down as many U.S. Marines and South Vietnamese as possible. The Marines have suffered considerable casualties in the D.M.Z. campaigns, many of them from surprise mortar and rocket barrages the Communists have thrown from within the D.M.Z., or from coastal hit-and-run assaults on Marine bases at Con Thien, Gio Linh, Dong Ha, and Camp Carroll, the principal Allied artillery base. The mortar and rocket attacks involve the use of the latest Soviet-type 120-millimetre mortars and 140-millimetre rockets, which have ranges of up to thirty miles and are fairly accurate. The violence of the recent major attacks on the ground was typified by one on Khe Sanh that began April 24th, when a Marine patrol stumbled on new enemy fortifications in the mountainous terrain. In the nine days ending May 3rd, during our costly fight to take Hill 881 and other high ground, a hundred and thirty-eight Marines and about a thousand Communists were killed, and a record weight of 3,500,000 pounds of B-52 bombs and 2,750,000 pounds of tactical air-support bombs was dropped in the ultimately successful effort to dislodge the N.V.A.'s 325th Division and drive it back across the D.M.Z. Meanwhile, there has been the big battle within the D.M.Z. itself, which has also cost heavy casualties, and there has been a lot of action farther south in the I Corps area. To the west of Hué, in the hills toward the Laos border at A Shau, the N.V.A. is now busily building new emplacements and a road that seems designed to pour in more support for its forces farther south, around Danang, which has been another longtime Vietcong hideout and the scene of constant fighting.

If a new major Communist assault began, its objectives would undoubtedly be the cities of Pleiku and Kontum, which already have been heavily bombarded by mortar fire, while a secondary objective would be to try to do what the enemy failed to accomplish in 1965—drive across the highlands to the coast and cut the country in two. It is doubtful that the Communists could achieve this today, but they could—if they attacked in strength in the highlands—pin down large numbers of Allied troops. Not long ago, both the progress being made in the II Corps area and the problems that remain were brought home to me during a trip I made there with General Westmoreland. In the area from the Phu My Valley, stretching northward into the An Lao Valley and northeast into other lush valleys, a large American operation, involving elements of the 1st Airmobile Cavalry and the 25th Divisions and the 101st Airborne Brigade, and the 196th Light Infantry Brigade, had been in progress over several weeks. The 1st Cavalry was brought into Binh Dinh in September, 1965, to safeguard the Phu My Valley and the Bong Son Plain, just to the north of it—both areas the Communists have held in the past and which, each time the Americans or South Vietnamese had taken them, had slipped back into enemy hands after the Allies left. Once the 1st Cavalry leaves, as it sooner or later must, the whole Binh Dinh area could easily slip out of the government's hands again, and next time it will be harder to persuade the local people to return to the Saigon side. The cavalrymen claimed to have eliminated forty-five per cent of the guerrilla elements in the area since their arrival, but division officers admitted that the Communists were still infiltrating from the west and getting logistical support from along the coast.

Following our visit to the 1st Cavalry, we continued north by helicopter to the headquarters of Major General William B. Rosson, in command of Operation Oregon, a large combined action by the 101st, the 25th, and the 196th, coördinated with that of the 1st Cavalry to the south. Since Oregon had begun, on April 20th, our officers had claimed seven hundred enemy dead at the cost of fifty-one dead Americans. Oregon consisted of a lowlands and a highlands effort. In the lowlands, where a brigade of the 25th Division was operating, the campaign was designed to root out the Vietcong and to get a major pacification effort started in what had been solid Communist territory for many years. General Rosson described this lowlands region as "a big island of hope." General Westmoreland agreed, but emphasized the difficulties that still lay ahead in bringing permanent peace to the region and persuading the Vietcong to quit—a task that indeed did loom as enormous. The enormity was emphasized when we flew back into the hills, where part of the 101st was trying to root out two regiments of the N.V.A. 3rd Division, breaking them up and pushing them down toward the area of operations of the 1st Cavalry or east into open areas where they could be more readily attacked. The 101st has established the remarkable record in Vietnam of moving twenty-five times in twenty months. With the help of a Special Forces team on the mountains far to the west, among the Montagnard Re tribesmen, the 101st was discovering a number of enemy infiltration routes and, as its briefing officers said, was forcing N.V.A. company- or battalion-size elements to move about in smaller numbers. There were still plenty of enemy soldiers about, though, and one of the battalion officers said, "We feel surrounded out here."

It was quite apparent to me, by the end of the day, that General Westmoreland was taking his new job as pacification chief extremely seriously. It is doubtful if any commander in the history of warfare has ever faced such a complicated combination of tasks as Westmoreland. His energy and his grasp of details constantly impress his staff. He is also highly solicitous about the welfare of his troops. Morale by and large is good in Vietnam, mainly because a soldier knows he has only a year to serve. The food is also a big factor. One of the remarkable changes I have observed since I covered the Pacific and Korean wars is the manner in which front-line troops, within a day or two of being set down in a far-flung outpost, are served hot meals, often flown out by helicopter, instead of having to eat K and C rations for days or weeks on end. This is part of a whole new science of logistics. A major I know, who fought in Korea, said the other day, "One of these days they'll be pumping Muzak down to company level."

The essential problem General Westmoreland still confronts is a twofold one—how to find enough troops to wage battle and to afford protection at the same time. The problem of moving troops around to meet emergencies is enhanced by the fact that, as has been the case all along, two-thirds of a division is still required for what are called control-and-hold (including logistics) operations, leaving only a third for strike, or attack, duty. The war in Vietnam, from the way it looks in Westmoreland's planning rooms, is akin to both a complicated chess game and a session of musical chairs. It is felt at the moment that at least two more American divisions will be needed in Vietnam before the end of the year—some thirty-five thousand troops in addition to the approximately four hundred and sixty-two thousand that are now here.

If there is any "other war" in Vietnam today, it is in the Mekong Delta, the rice bowl of the country, where there are eighty-two thousand Communist troops, about half full-time Vietcong main-force elements, supported by full-time regional guerrillas. The war in this region—the IV Corps area—is still a true guerrilla war, fought for control of the myriad canals and the few major roads, and for the hamlets and villages surrounding them. Frequently, the greatest amount of damage is inflicted by ten or so guerrillas moving in a couple of sampans along a canal at night, with four men firing rifles, two handling larger weapons such as heavy machine guns, and four handling ammunition. They will attack, on a hit-and-run basis, a small hamlet that is in government hands or in no man's land—causing no more than a handful of casualties, perhaps, but doing a great deal of damage to morale.

Estimates of how much of the region is under Allied control vary, but even the most optimistic ones don't claim more than a quarter of the total land space, though this includes much of the arable land. The goverment and the Americans consider ten of the sixteen

Delta provinces as priority areas this year; the others—mostly along the Cambodian border and on the Ca Mau Peninsula, in the far south—will have to wait. More than half of the fifty-four hundred hamlets in the Delta are still outside government control, and many of those considered "safe" are subject to constant attack or harassment, especially at night. The target for 1967 is to pacify two hundred and eighty-seven hamlets in all—a modest ten-per-cent improvement and a figure that, perhaps more than anything else, reveals the difficulty of the Delta problem.

While the Communists are showing signs of having trouble recruiting new guerrillas, their total strength in South Vietnam has not decreased, and is still just under three hundred thousand, including between fifty thousand and sixty thousand North Vietnamese. With some exceptions—notably the movement of full divisions across the D.M.Z.—the North Vietnamese infiltrators are no longer entering South Vietnam in unit strength but are being sent down in groups of a hundred or a hundred and fifty, on arduous marches along the Ho Chi Minh Trail network through Laos, which average four to six months in duration. Recently captured North Vietnamese prisoners, many of whom are in their teens or early twenties and who have received only a few months' training, have reported to interrogators that these infiltration groups are arriving badly depleted, as a result of American bombing and shelling and of malaria, and many groups have lost half their members by the time they reach their destinations in the highlands, at camps on both sides of the Cambodian border, or in the key bases the Communists still hold in their jungle redoubts of the I and II Corps areas.

Not long ago, I read through a large sheaf of prisoner-interrogation reports, and while they gave a mixed picture of what the prisoners thought about life in North Vietnam and about the war in the South, the general feeling that emerged was that although privation and hardship—including, above all, the effects of the American bombing and artillery attacks and the lack of food and medicines—had caused a drop in morale, the Communists were determined to fight on, believing in their cause and feeling certain of ultimate victory. The most important defector to date, Lieutenant Colonel Le Xuan Chuyen, who was operations chief for an N.V.A. division and had been a Communist Party member for twenty years, left for a combination of personal reasons and because he was convinced that life in the South, with all its shortcomings, was freer and better than life in the North. After long interrogations, the South Vietnamese were so impressed with Colonel Chuyen that they appointed him director of the Chieu Hoi (Open Arms) Center, which handles all the defectors, or returnees. The number of returnees has roughly doubled in the last year—more than fifteen thousand have come back so far in 1967—but very few are old-time Vietcong fighters or cadremen. The great majority came under the sway of the Communists between 1964 and the end of 1965, when the Vietcong were riding high. Consequently, these returnees are, for the most part, people who were simply impressed into service by the Vietcong or found themselves living in Vietcong-controlled areas; as the Communists have been pushed back during the last two years, they have chosen to return to the government fold, very often because they were hungry and knew they would be fed in the Chieu Hoi camps. The reasons most of them cite for coming over are dissatisfaction with treatment by the Vietcong, hard and abnormal living conditions, and the hazards of American bombing and general military pressure.

As a result of a number of major American operations in recent months, notably Cedar Falls, in the so-called Iron Triangle area north of Saigon, and Junction City, in Zone C, in the III Corps area, both heretofore inviolate Communist-base regions, tons of enemy documents have been captured. It will take months, if not years, to translate them all, but many of the more important ones have been translated already, and they reveal a number of significant things about the strategy and hierarchy of the Communists. Perhaps most significant is fresh corroboration of the completeness with which the Lao Dong, or Workers', Party of North Vietnam and the North Vietnamese Politburo control the People's Revolutionary Party and the National Liberation Front in the South, and, in fact, determine the whole policy and course of the war. Since the early part of 1965, the commander of all war operations in the South, and the head of the Central Office for South Vietnam, which directs the total war effort here, has been General Nguyen Chi Thanh. Thanh, who is fifty-two years old, is one of only two four-star generals in the N.V.A., the other being the Defense Chief and top commander, General Vo Nguyen Giap. The extent of North Vietnamese control has been revealed in a number of lengthy confidential speeches and declarations over the last half year by General Thanh, by Major General Tran Do, one of five senior North Vietnamese commanders operating in the South, and by such other high officials as Lieutenant General Nguyen Van Vinh, who is head of the Lao Dong's Department of Reunification and the North Vietnamese government's Reunification Committee, as well as Deputy Chief of Staff of the N.V.A. These men have made it patently clear, sometimes in almost humiliating fashion, that they are running the show in the South and that members of the National Liberation Front are simply puppets who will be told at what moment Hanoi chooses to take steps about anything, including negotiations.

The documents containing these pronouncements, concerning the authenticity of which there is no doubt—they were mostly taken from deep underground fortified bunkers and war rooms—thus make it clearer than it has been before that despite the efforts of the Communists to portray the Front as an independent organization, with its own shadow government and its own missions abroad, the N.L.F. in fact has little remaining identity of its own and very little leverage. This does not mean that the Front will not play a role in negotiations when they begin; it does quite definitely indicate that the North's use of the Front is simply part of a larger game aimed at taking over all of Vietnam.

For example, in a recent speech, General Tran Do frequently referred to "a force of thirty-one million" (the population of North and South Vietnam combined), which he maintained was "morally and physically supported by the whole [Communist] bloc," and, in mentioning the large American buildup, he said, "Objectively speaking, the Americans are no stronger than we. They are very rich but not stronger. We do have the capability to defeat them, because the *whole* nation has concentrated her forces here. . . . We can say openly that we certainly have the right and duty, on a national scale, to help South Vietnam defeat the enemy, to help morally and physically. We can say this bluntly and overtly. [The North Vietnamese had previously denied they were sending men south.] . . . Can we not be expected to bring in our men while the enemy brings in his? Especially when we still have four hundred thousand men available there [in North Vietnam]?" The whole tenor of General Do's speech was that the war would be long and painful. "The Americans are really stubborn, they are really cunning," he said. "They see that they are not able to win by military means, that they can be defeated militarily, so they turn to diplomatic maneuvers to obtain what they cannot seize with their forces. ... Many people in the world are advising us to accept the conditions offered by the Americans. . . . We must not be hypnotized by the peace mirage. . . ."

General Vinh, who in his Reunification jobs works under the direction of Le Duan, the Lao Dong Party's First Secretary and one of the leading candidates for successor to Ho Chi Minh, has made occasional visits to South Vietnam. He, too, has repeatedly talked of the need to win "a final and decisive victory," but he has also set the stage for the expected period of "fighting and negotiating at the same time." The time is not yet ripe for negotiations, he has said, but he has pointed out that "fighting while negotiating is aimed at opening another front, with a view to making the puppet army more disintegrated." Once the fighting in the war has become "indecisive," Vinh has said, the simultaneous fighting and negotiating period begins, and "in fighting while negotiating, the side which fights more strongly will compel the adversary to accept its conditions." In a point-blank declaration of who will call the tune on negotiations, Vinh adds, "The Party Central Committee entrusts the Politburo with the task of deciding on the time for negotiations," and, once that is done, he has said, "We will take advantage of the opportunity offered by negotiations to step up our military attacks, political struggle, and military proselytizing." As one of the "conditions" the Communists will impose, according to Vinh, "the puppet forces must be concentrated in barracks [and] the American troops must be stationed on the wharves."

General Thanh, the field commander, has spent less time theorizing and more time analyzing the war in his speeches, and he is skilled both at exhortation and at making bold and rash statements. In a recent analysis of the campaigns of 1966, he called on his combined N.V.A. and Vietcong forces, plus the admittedly undermanned guerrillas, to defeat as many as "a million or a million and a half American troops." Thanh's figures of the number of Americans so far killed and wounded in the war are multiplied four or five times above the true totals, but he apparently has regarded such exaggeration as a necessary part of indoctrinating and encouraging his own troops. He has said, "The United States has ordered four hundred thousand coffins . . . [but] it makes no difference to us whether we stand against the enemy for two or three years, or even for eight years, of protracted war."

Much has been made by Vietnamese officials and by the Americans of the elections held in April for village councils, and, during May and early June, for hamlet officials. These elections took place in about a third of the total number of twenty-five hundred villages and twelve thousand hamlets in South Vietnam—those considered to be secure, or relatively secure—and roughly eighty per cent of all of those eligible to vote did so, though the figures ranged in different areas from a little over fifty per cent to ninety-five per cent. Despite this turnout, many Vietnamese, and some Americans, too, feel that there was more form than substance to them, and that they were conducted more to impress foreigners—and Americans in particular—than the Vietnamese themselves. It was true that the rural voters did not show much enthusiasm, but, on the other hand, there was no reason to suppose that they would, since their faith in previous governments, as well as in the present one, has never been great.

In both sets of elections, the government had difficulty getting enough candidates to run—a state of affairs reflecting both lethargy and fear of Vietcong reprisals. In each village, six to twelve councilmen were elected, depending on the population; these councilmen then chose a village chief, an administrative committee, and a chief administrative officer, who in effect serves as the local representative of Saigon, while the village chief is the local boss. In many cases, provincial and district officials were barely able to fill the slates, though there were some cases in which semblances of contests took place. "The problem in the villages is still the same," one Vietnamese who is intimately associated with what goes on in the countryside told me. "No one other than old leaders or their friends dared to run. They have no foundation of support among the masses, because the masses know the winners will still all be beholden to the old guard, to the district and province officials they have dealt with for years." The government expects the councils to generate their own self-help projects, and has arranged for them to keep for this purpose forty per cent of all local taxes collected; all such taxes have always in the past been turned over to district and province chiefs, and very little money has ever trickled back down.

This may work, up to a point, but many villages never collected very much anyway, and the central government may have to contribute directly to them if it wants to create any real financial freedom. With the help of the Americans, the Vietnamese also hope to furnish the villages with direct economic assistance, bypassing the provincial and district authorities.

In the last six months, with increasingly frequent attacks on Revolutionary Development workers and police, as well as on candidates, local officials, and civilians in general, it is estimated that Vietcong terrorism has increased by fifty per cent. A recent American study pointed out, "The assassination pattern appears to be directed toward the very best and the very worst officials, against the highly popular and effective government civil servant and against the most corrupt and oppressive local official. Such a policy obviously stimulates mediocrity among civil servants. . . . Potential opposition leadership is the Vietcong's most deadly enemy. Steadily, quietly, and with a systematic ruthlessness, the Vietcong in six years have wiped out virtually a whole class of Vietnamese villagers. Many villages today are virtually depopulated of their natural leaders. . . . This loss to Vietnam is inestimable and it will take a generation or more to replace. By any definition, this is genocide." Unfortunately, if it is genocide, it is also guerrilla warfare in its most refined stage. There are, of course, many Vietnamese, not to mention millions of people abroad, who regard the American bombing of North Vietnam as an example of genocide at its worst.

As Vietnam has economically become more and more dependent on American support, corruption has increased in proportion to the economic disparities caused by the American buildup and the amount of largesse dispensed. With rice production way down, and rubber and fruit production also way off—the latter to some extent because of defoliation of fruit trees in combat areas—the Vietnamese today are almost totally dependent on American aid to survive. The only widespread industry, textile production, is at a virtual standstill because foreign textile imports are ten times what they were only two years ago. Total Vietnamese imports, amounting to almost four hundred million dollars last year, are ten times the total of exports, and more and more of the imports include such luxury items as automobiles and motorcycles, refrigerators, air-conditioners, and television sets. Most of the imported items come in through a commercial import program under which the government furnishes individual importers licenses and funds that are backed up by American dollars. Even though this may be the only way the government can obtain funds to pay its combined total of nearly a million troops and civil servants, the inevitable effect is ever-mounting inflation. Taking advantage of the situation, many Vietnamese, including private businessmen and government and military officials, are reaping profits while they can and paying bribes to do it. The areas of opportunity are varied and wide, ranging from the luxury imports to real estate; a number of generals' wives have made fortunes selling or renting properties to Americans at high prices. In the last few months, new fields for corruption have been developed. Two huge shipments of opium have been seized—one of twelve hundred kilos and the other of two hundred. The drug is said to have come from either France or Thailand, and it is unlikely that it could have found its way here without the help of Army, Navy, or Air Force officers. In an atmosphere like this, of cynicism and opportunism, it is no wonder that the Vietcong, themselves never loath to make or demand payoffs, for goods wanted or transport privileges granted, have further extended their influence. The degree of Vietcong penetration among disillusioned nationalists is much greater today than it was a year or two ago, and Vietcong agents are known to be moving in on the press, on the labor movement, and on the Civil Service.

Despite the apathy toward the local elections, there is already considerable interest in the vote for President and Vice-President on September 3rd, and in the establishment of a new national government following the appointment, by the new Chief Executive, of a Prime Minister. Part of this interest has to do with the basic question of whether there will be another military government or a civilian one, and part of it stems from the larger questions of war and peace—of what steps the new President and his aides may take either to prosecute the war or to move toward negotiations. These are matters that mean more to the average Vietnamese than the personalities of the individual candidates. Almost every Vietnamese I have asked cites, as the things he is principally concerned about, the end of corruption and high prices and a satisfactory end to the war. There undoubtedly will be many people who will vote as individuals on these issues, but pressure groups and blocs will continue to play important and probably decisive roles. The most significant of these groups is still undeniably the military, but the military is by no means a unified bloc, and currently brewing is a bitter fight not only between the military and the civilian candidates but between at least two military factions.

These two factions are represented by Prime Minister Nguyen Cao Ky, who as an Air Vice-Marshal is still head of the Air Force, and Chief of State Nguyen Van Thieu, who is a three-star Army general. Both men, members of the ruling military Directory that has run South Vietnam for the last two years, have announced their candidacies, despite efforts of other military men, and of some Americans as well, to avert a fight between them. Ky and Thieu have never been close, although they have managed to get along for two years, because they couldn't do without each other. Both men over recent months have played a rather childish Alphonse-Gaston game regarding the declarations of their respective candidacies. Ky has on several occasions maintained that if Thieu wanted to run he would not, and Thieu has indicated that he would support Ky if he decided to run. Thieu's policy was to let the more flamboyant, often immature Ky defeat himself by his rash statements, invariably made to the press while travelling around the country. Late in March, just before Thieu went into the hospital for an operation, Ky in effect threw down the gauntlet to Thieu at a meeting of the ten generals who belong to the Directory, formally offering to step aside if Thieu wished to run. At this point, Thieu realized he was being boxed in, that the sentiment in the country was running against a military choice by the military, and that he no longer could count on the strength he had assumed earlier, either among the generals in the Directory or among the members of the Armed Forces Council. It was now apparent that each man was trying to force the other into making a final public declaration of his non-availability. On May 12th Ky announced that he would run, and when asked to comment on a statement by Thieu a few days earlier to the effect he might still run, Ky replied, "Chairman Thieu has the right to run, like any other citizen."

On May 19th, I had an interview with Thieu, and for the first time he said point-blank that he, too, would run. He said he had made the decision as a patriot, after considering all aspects of the matter and consulting friends about whether he would be able to rally a broad front of popular opinion in the fight against Communism. He did not feel that, with both Ky and himself running, the military vote would be split and factionalism encouraged. In fact, he said, it would be worse if there were only one military candidate, because the people would think that candidate was being shoved down their throats. If an Army man declared his unwillingness to coöperate with a civilian President, that was wrong, he went on—in what amounted to a swipe at Ky, who, in an off-the-record speech to his cadet classmates a few days before, had reportedly inveighed against the acceptance of a civilian government, especially one that might be willing to dicker with the Communists.

At this time, there were already eight declared civilian candidates. The first to declare was the venerable Phan Khac Suu, the head of the Constituent Assembly and a former Chief of State during two of the short-lived post-1963 regimes. Suu, a southerner and a former member of the Cao Dai religious sect as well as a veteran nationalist, is a generally respected but not overly admired man—he has never been known for his firm opinions about anything. The civilian with the best chance of winning was one of the last to make his availability known. This is Tran Van Huong, former Prime Minister under Suu, and twice Mayor of Saigon. Huong, who is respected by everyone for his honesty and integrity, was wooed by both Thieu and Ky, particularly by the latter, either to run as Vice-President, a proposal that he peremptorily rejected as an insult because he is a much older man, or to accept the Prime Ministership, which he still might do. The Tri Quang wing of the Buddhist movement, with headquarters now in Cholon, is reasserting itself politically for the first time in many months, and is in a more commanding position than its right-wing opposition, headed by Thich Tam Chau, in Saigon, which supports Ky. Since he is still violently anti-Ky as well as anti-Tam Chau, Tri Quang will support anyone he thinks has a chance to beat Ky.

The Americans are being urged by a number of Vietnamese to resolve the conflict between Thieu and Ky and to persuade either one or the other, or preferably both, to retire from the race for President. If both men quit, Huong would almost surely win. If, in a fair election, Huong ran against one of the military men and perhaps one other civilian candidate, his chances would still be good. The possibilities of deals between now and August 3rd, when the month-long campaign officially begins, are manifold, and deals there are bound to be. At the moment, Ky and Thieu must be rated nearly even, with Ky having perhaps a slight edge, although he has shown an alarming tendency to revert to his wild-blue-yonder style by publicly saying such things as "The people know me very well, and therefore I don't have to campaign for anything." Thieu, who is living up to his reputation as the sly fox of the military politicians, is playing it cool, hoping Ky will outmaneuver and outtalk himself. Huong is playing it even cooler, expecting Thieu and Ky to destroy each other and leave the field open to him.

One has the feeling, over all, of a country in a dangerous state of suspension, with military and political events treated as totally separate phenomena. The gap between the two, despite platitudes about creating a political foundation to prosecute or settle the war, is widened by some of the remarks that have been made publicly. General Thieu, for example, has spoken of the need for fifty thousand or more Americans to remain here for twenty years after a peace settlement has been reached, while Tran Van Do, the Foreign Minister, pledges the removal of all foreign troops from Vietnamese soil within six months of a settlement, or less. Military men still speak of invading the North, while civilians favor the suspension of bombing in the North. Military leaders say they will never deal with the National Liberation Front directly, while civilians say they will confer with anyone on the other side if it helps the cause of peace. Meanwhile, the war goes on bloodily, and this summer of monsoon fighting threatens to be bloodier than ever. Many of the more experienced observers here are convinced that Hanoi will not move toward a settlement until after the American elections in November, 1968, and that the war in the interim will escalate further, with more North Vietnamese troops responding to more American troops.

Escalation has many forms. One senses it not only in the ever-growing numbers of men and machines all over Vietnam but in sadder, more personal ways, too. On the sidewalks of the city today, roaming all day and often until the midnight curfew, one can see small girls and boys of eight or nine carrying their infant brothers or sisters on their backs because their mothers have to work in order to make ends meet for families that hardly ever meet any more themselves.

Saigon

~~~~~~

October 7, 1967

The assumption—primarily an American one—that the Viet-namese elections a month ago have had, or are likely to have, any salutary effect on the war or on the internal political situation here is regarded by most Vietnamese as unwarranted and unrealistic. This reaction can be attributed partly to national cynicism but much more to an enduring conviction that the whole elective pro-cess is simply an American-directed performance with a Viet-namese cast. To a certain extent, this is true; it is very doubtful whether the elections for President and Vice-President and for a sixty-man Senate, which were held on September 3rd, and the forth-coming vote for a hundred-and-thirty-seven-man House of Repre-sentatives, to be held on October 22nd, would have been taking place at this time without American prodding. American officials argue in its favor that we have now replaced a military junta with a constitutionally chosen government, whose election was reason-ably free and fair despite inevitable limitations, and which will be backed up by a duly constituted civilian-military Cabinet and by a civilian National Assembly. This new government, it is argued fur-ther, is superior to the junta in that it can negotiate on a more nearly equal and a more honest footing with the Communists when the time for negotiations comes—though the Americans will, of course, participate in the proceedings and in the making of final decisions.

The case against the holding of elections at this time is more subtle but, in the opinion of most veteran observers here, more substantial. Despite the advisability of establishing some framework of legitimacy, this argument goes, more harm than good is likely to result from force-feeding Western-style democracy to the Vietnamese at such a chaotic moment in their national life. This is so because of the war, because of the fact that, notwithstanding the turnout of voters—which, although subsequently exaggerated by the government, was large—the third of the country that is under Vietcong control remains unavoidably unrepresented, and, finally, because an adequate groundwork for representative government here has simply not been laid. This is true both of the countryside —where the recently revamped Revolutionary Development Program has so far had only scattered impact—and of the cities, where the intellectuals, the professional people, and the various religious elements, if they had been given more time and more encouragement, might conceivably have been able to get together and formulate some sort of logical party system before the voting took place. More time, the critics say, would have been especially valuable in preparing for the Senate election, which turned out to be fairly much of a lottery, with people voting for six out of forty-eight slates of ten candidates each on the basis of party symbols, since they knew little or nothing about the candidates.

This election, particularly the Senate contests, in the opinion of many Vietnamese—in contrast to that of American and foreign observers who briefly watched and hastily praised it—was less free and fair than the election last year for the Constituent Assembly, which, in fact, represented a far greater variety of Vietnamese political, social, and religious elements than the new Senate does. But then, words like "free" and "fair" are relative, and nothing much is achieved by making historical comparisons with the limitations of early American—or early Roman—elections. What is important now that the elections have been held is their impact on other events. There is some danger that the defeated Presidential and senatorial candidates, by pressing charges of rigging, will set off a fresh wave of violence, particularly among the perennially discontented students and Buddhists—two groups whose candidates lost out badly in the Senate vote or else were disqualified before it took place on the ground of being "pro-Communist" or "pro-neutralist." This week the militant Buddhists have been demonstrating in Saigon, and some student demonstrations against the elections have already taken place here, up north in Hué and Danang, and in Can Tho, in the Mekong Delta, but the discontented elements are likely to think twice about stepping up their protests, in view of the setbacks they suffered when they rebelled a year and a half ago. It seems probable that they will choose to bide their time and see what happens.

Although Americans here are expressing hope that the new democratic experiment will succeed as it moves along—that the Vietnamese will learn by doing—there are already various signs that almost everything will in fact remain essentially unchanged. General Thieu, who has expressed his intention of being a strong President, will, following his inauguration early in November, direct the affairs of government on a day-by-day basis through his own inner council as well as through his Premier and Cabinet. He has already outlined some bold plans for revamping and strengthening both the creaky civil administration and the military organization, but even if he does seriously seek to carry out any such plans, it will take some time for his reforms to have any effect. A further hindrance is that there is now a sad paucity of talent available to overhaul the tired government machine. Many able men are doing too well in private business to be interested in government salaries, others are abroad, and still others are not of a mind to coöperate with the military regime. Furthermore, the relationship between the new legislative and judicial organisms and the executive remains unclear. Part of the confusion stems from certain ambiguities in the new constitution and part is simply the product of history—especially the political fragmentation of the last twenty years, since it is extremely difficult for individuals and factions that have worked against each other for so long to coöperate now in a tidy parliamentary way. Once again, those Vietnamese who have been most eager to work closely with the Americans are asking plaintively, "What do the Americans really *want?*"

In talking with old Vietnamese friends, both in and out of the government, I have got the feeling that they are becoming more and more impatient with the Americans' continuing lack of comprehension of Vietnamese attitudes and Vietnamese affairs. Much of this is due to the constant turnover of American personnel here and some of it to a seemingly deliberate ingenuousness on the part of American officials, who seldom develop sustained relationships with the Vietnamese that can lead to new ideas and useful political exchanges. At the same time, the Vietnamese resent their growing dependence on the Americans, militarily and economically; they recognize that although the Americans are not colonialists, there has evolved here a colonial ambiance that can sometimes be worse than colonialism itself. In spite of improved coördination between the American and Vietnamese armed forces, the Americans are more and more fighting their own war and the Vietnamese theirs, which is less effective, though their methods are slowly improving. If a true joint command was ever advisable, it no longer seems even possible—unless, of course, the war broadens to include China, which remains unlikely. Economically, the United States has managed to shore up the country artificially, saving it from a total financial and inflationary breakdown, by pumping in a variety of miscellaneous exports to soak up excess piastres; by building up the so-called infrastructure of bases and harbors, which has furnished well-paid employment to the Vietnamese; and by bringing in some much needed "crisis commodities," most notably rice. Until now, the Vietnamese have had little say in all this, and their main reaction has been just to hope that it would ultimately do more good than harm. Now, having been prodded by the United States into making an experiment with democracy, they want to carry out the experiment in their own way—which doesn't mean they won't listen to American advice if it is realistic and consistent. At the moment, though, American inconsistency is a particular grievance. For instance, in the matter of facilitating peace negotiations—the hope of which was part of the rationale for holding the elections in the first place—the Vietnamese find it hard to understand why the United States, having encouraged a new Vietnamese government to make its own approaches to Hanoi or to members of the National Liberation Front, should itself, a week after the elections, have begun a whole fresh set of maneuvers designed to bring Hanoi to the bargaining table. "Either Washington wants us to make our own accommodations or it doesn't," one of my Vietnamese friends said the other day. "If it does, then it should at least give us an opportunity to do so. To be blunt about it, the Americans should stop talking so much, both about peace and about our great democratic prospects."

The fact is that despite General Thieu's preëlection offer of a bombing pause in the event of evidences of reciprocal "good will," very few people here believe there is any chance of Hanoi's accepting such a bid in the near future. The conviction is growing that the harder North Vietnam is bombed, the more determined the North Vietnamese will be to go on fighting indefinitely. Recent declarations by Premier Pham Van Dong and Defense Chief Vo Nguyen Giap have sounded more bellicose and more confident than ever. Also, even though in the Presidential election the peace candidate, Truong Dinh Dzu, was the runner-up, getting approximately half the number of votes received by Thieu and Ky, most Vietnamese who have given serious thought to possible negotiations believe that it would be a grave mistake to begin negotiating now, except, perhaps, in the way of making preliminary soundings among Vietcong representatives. The reason for this belief is a familiar one: If the new government is going to get anywhere at all in introducing reforms and building more efficient administrative machinery and simultaneously pushing ahead with the still lagging Revolutionary Development Program, it must have time. To start talks now, either under cease-fire terms or under the conditions that the Communists call "fighting and negotiating at the same time," would be to invite ultimate defeat, according to this viewpoint, which does not seem an illogical one in the light of the problems that the new government faces.

The most difficult of these problems, as might be suspected, is that of conflicting personalities, and it begins right at the top, with Thieu and Ky. The two men are almost completely different in character and behavior: Thieu is withdrawn, suspicious, and highly cautious—qualities he has demonstrated throughout his career, although he is now becoming more interested in projecting an outgoing Presidential personality. Ky has always been gregarious, impulsive, incautious, and flamboyant, with a political style entirely in keeping with his career as a pilot. During the Ambassadorship of Henry Cabot Lodge, Ky became the American favorite, and when, at the Guam conference, Ky and Thieu pledged that they would not run against each other for the Presidency, the Americans not only naïvely believed them both but assumed that Ky would be elected, thus maintaining the vaunted "stability" the United States had been proclaiming. When Thieu announced in May that he would run, too, the Americans were shocked and disturbed. Apparently, Ky did not at first believe Thieu but thought he was only bluffing. Then, when it became evident that Thieu meant it, the two men, who had never really liked each other, though they had hung together for two years, set out on a collision course. At the end of June, General Cao Van Vien—who, as Defense Minister and Chief of the Joint General Staff, was the highest-ranking officer in the country—called a meeting of forty-eight general officers in Saigon to settle the issue, which by this time had seriously divided the military.

The meeting, which one of my Vietnamese friends described as a *coup de théâtre,* lasted three days. It was highly reminiscent of a number of such events since the overthrow of Diem, in 1963, in that it was accompanied by such histrionics as tears and patriotic outpourings, which never interfered with the fundamental jockeying for power. The meeting began with the forty-eight generals berating each other for corruption. Some of them suggested that Thieu and Ky both withdraw and let a civilian be elected President. Others said that the civilians would ruin the country and that the junta should just tear up the new constitution and go on ruling without one. General Thieu then spoke, in a humble vein. He said that he realized that some of those in the room resented him and were embarrassed by his actions, and as he said this, according to reports by those present, tears rolled down his cheeks. At that point, Ky offered to withdraw, whereupon, just as he had surmised, a sufficient number of generals rallied behind him to persuade him that he couldn't.

During the second day's sessions, while the customary rumors of a coup by the forces of one man or the other swept the city, Thieu had apparently reached a private decision to quit the race, but overnight, at the urging of his advisers, and especially of his wife (wives have always played prominent behind-the-scenes political roles in Vietnam), he changed his mind, and in the morning he returned to the meeting loaded for bear. He attacked Ky at Ky's most vulnerable point—the Premier's failure to fulfill his promise to eradicate corruption—and listed, one by one, various corrupt activities in the ranks of the police in Saigon and among officials at the district and province level throughout the country. By implication, Thieu was thus attacking Ky's closest ally, General Nguyen Ngoc Loan, a swashbuckling, pistol-packing, erratic officer who was the head of both the police and the Military Security Service. At this moment, histrionics took over completely. Three of the country's four corps commanders are said to have torn off their stars and refused to go back to their commands until the Thieu-Ky deadlock was broken. Thieu is said to have wept again and thanked his fellow-officers for their loyalty. Ky is said to have wept, too, and to have offered once more to quit, and it is said that this time, worn out by the whole performance, the other generals accepted his withdrawal. But they subsequently prevailed upon him to accept the Vice-Presidential nomination, and the American Embassy had no choice but to indicate that it thought this a fine idea. Thieu, the sly fox matched against the leader of the hounds, had clearly won the day.

Before the official election campaign began, on August 3rd, Thieu and Ky appeared together twice, and during the campaign they made only one joint appearance. In fact, neither man really campaigned at all but left the field to the ten civilian candidates, who nevertheless did considerable complaining about the government's treatment of them, in failing to furnish them with transportation and other facilities. The confidence displayed by Thieu and Ky was undoubtedly based on their belief that the superabundance of civilian candidates eliminated any threat of a civilian victory. Their confidence was justified, though the election held some surprises— notably the 817,120 votes won by Dzu and his running mate, as against 1,649,561 for the Thieu-Ky slate, with the preëlection civilian favorites, Phan Khac Suu and former Premier Tran Van Huong, lagging far behind, in third and fourth places, respectively.

Soon after the election, it became apparent that its impressive trappings had covered more irregularities than the official observers realized—although no more than might have been expected in the light of Vietnamese political history and of the fact that military leaders controlled the provincial and district officials who supervised the casting and counting of the ballots. Some cynics have asserted that the whole election was rigged in advance, but the evidence indicates that only some last-minute manipulation took place to bolster the slow-running military ticket. However, within a few days after the election, eight of the defeated civilian candidates—including Dzu and Suu but not Huong—declared it to have been fraudulent and demanded that it be invalidated by the Assembly. The eight have since been joined by twenty-seven defeated senatorial candidates in the formation of a front called the People's Movement for the Struggle for Democracy, which, among other things, has excoriated the United States for approving the conduct of the September 3rd elections. American "interference in Vietnamese domestic affairs will destroy United States prestige," the group declared in a recent statement, adding, in language strikingly similar to that of the N.L.F., that such interference "will force the Vietnamese people to consider the United States as an imperialist power, plotting colonialism in Vietnam and in underdeveloped countries."

The leader of the rebellious octet has been Dzu, a controversial fireball of an attorney, who since the election has been brought into court for a retrial on earlier charges of financial peculations, found guilty, and sentenced to nine months in jail. Dzu's large vote apparently derived from a number of factors, chief among them being a genuine desire for peace among the people, for whom his platform —or at least his white-dove peace emblem—held a strong appeal. Because he obtained heavy support in several provinces where there is considerable Vietcong strength, it seems probable that the Communists ordered some of their sympathizers who held government identity cards and were able to slip back and forth between Communist and government territory to vote for him, more as a gesture of contempt for the government than anything else. Dzu's violently anti-government campaign certainly drew some votes from people who were ready to rally around anyone espousing an anti-government line, and Ky's falling into the trap by counterattacking Dzu as "a dog that should be put in a cage" undoubtedly won Dzu more votes. Finally, it has been said on good authority that Dzu received funds from the French—his six-point peace plan closely resembled French Foreign Minister Couve de Murville's program.

Although there are touches of the charlatan and the opportunist in Dzu, he is not pro-Communist, and some observers here think it would be a good idea for the government to seek his coöperation for the future instead of persecuting him further. However, the government seems unlikely to risk such a course of action. In fact, to the dismay of the Americans, the government has so far done little except to move against Dzu and against Au Truong Thanh, a former Finance Minister who was disqualified as a Presidential candidate on the ground that he was "pro-Communist." If Dzu, as reported, has contacts with the N.L.F.—during the French days, he defended Nguyen Huu Tho, now the leader of the Front, against charges of revolutionary activity—such associations might prove useful at some point. At any rate, the moves against Dzu and Thanh so soon after the elections were a poor idea.

The moment Thieu and Ky were elected, they began a duel for executive control. Formerly, Ky, as Premier, had more actual power than Thieu did as Chief of State. After Thieu's inauguration, in a few weeks, the tables will be turned, for, under the constitution, the President is far and away the principal executive figure, the Vice-President's principal tasks being to act as chairman of three advisory councils—on culture and education, on economic and social affairs, and on ethnic-minority matters. As part of their agreement to run together, Ky, it is said, was promised the right to select the Premier and several of the key Cabinet Ministers, including those in charge of defense and of Revolutionary Development. In any event, Thieu and Ky, and their respective followers, are engaged in a typically Vietnamese war of nerves, and though there have been attempts to call a truce, this contest seems bound to continue. Once again, the other important generals, including the four corps commanders, are involved in the fight, and their support is being sought by both Thieu and Ky. General Loan, Ky's police chief, is known to be egging protesting students on, giving them permission to continue their demonstrations for the time being and also allowing the Buddhists to stir the pot. Even more significantly, Loan has secretly urged the twenty-odd Saigon papers—three have been banned since the election—to attack both the results of the election and the American role in it. Loan and Ky, it would appear, hope to keep the furore over the election going as long as possible and even to discredit the vote if they can. All this appears to prove that democratic forms mean little or nothing where there is no democratic substance.

Meanwhile, no important action has been taken to form a new Cabinet. Various men have been suggested for Premier, including

Huong, who was, in fact, tentatively offered the job a day or two after the elections but rejected it, both because he felt that the elections had not been fair and because he believed that he might be the first victim of the Thieu-Ky struggle. Huong was a logical candidate for the Premiership, because he is a southerner; Ky is a northerner and Thieu comes from central Vietnam, so someone from the South will have to be named Premier in the interests of regional and national unity. Another man who is being mentioned is Nguyen Van Loc, a mild-mannered southern lawyer who was originally Ky's campaign manager and then helped run the joint Thieu-Ky campaign. Loc is not considered a dynamic figure or a particularly able administrator.

A fight for influence between Thieu and Ky in the Senate and, later on, in the House of Representatives also seems inevitable; in fact, there have been reports that Ky and his henchmen have been helping to stir up rebellious anti-election sentiment in the Assembly. Because it was very difficult to determine which Senate slate had won the sixth-ranking position, the final returns were not announced for sixteen days, and this lag was what mainly gave rise to the charges of rigging. Of the six winning slates, only the leading one, headed by former General Tran Van Don, the man who organized the coup against Diem, can claim to be truly independent. Another—the one headed by Tran Van Lam, a pharmacist and a former government official and Ambassador—will probably form the nucleus of a loyal opposition. A third is likely to make some pretense of independence but will probably lean toward the government side, while the three others are considered more or less pro-government. Of the total of sixty senators, twenty-seven are Catholics—a number far out of proportion to the percentage of Catholics in the country's population of close to seventeen million, which is a mere ten per cent. A number of these Catholic senators, though they do not form a solid bloc, are former members of the Can Lao, the quasi-secret society that was the private instrument of Ngo Dinh Nhu, Diem's scheming brother. What is interesting about this circumstance is not so much that it might presage a revival of Diemism as that it appears to reveal an inclination on the part of many voters to forget the past and choose some old familiar faces. It is no longer true, as it was in 1963 and 1964, when the Buddhists were riding high, that everyone who was associated with

Diem is regarded as a pariah. The pendulum has swung the other way, and the Senate vote can be seen as an indication that a good many Vietnamese are gettng tired of the men who since 1963 have unsuccessfully led the country from one crisis to another. Thieu himself is one of the few survivors from the days of Diem—though he also played a part in the anti-Diem coup—and is also a Catholic convert, so his influence in the Senate may be considerable. There is no guarantee, though, that he will be able to retain it indefinitely. Most analysts feel that, in the interests of building a two- or a three-party system, the voters should have been asked to choose two or three men from each slate instead of entire slates of ten. Of the sixty senators elected, no more than twenty can be regarded as even semi-serious politicians or legislators; the rest range from opportu-nists to naïve and inexperienced individuals selected by slate lead-ers in vague deference to that old politician's shibboleth, "balance."

The only slate that shows any promise of developing into a seri-ous party is General Don's, which is called Nong Cong Binh—mean-ing "Farmers, Workers, Soldiers." Though Don, who is widely known and liked, headed the slate, its guiding genius is Dr. Dang Van Sung, a veteran nationalist and onetime Dai Viet leader who publishes *Chinh Luan,* perhaps the best Vietnamese-language daily paper in Saigon. Sung is one of the few men in Vietnam who have sought, since Diem's overthrow, to create some kind of new and workable political alignment here. One of Sung's closest allies is Tran Quoc Buu, the head of the Vietnamese Confederation of Vietnamese Laborers. Buu initially had a slate of his own running for the Senate, but it was disqualified on a technicality. The Nong Cong Binh ticket finally included one of Buu's labor representa-tives, and was elected partly through the support of Buu's federa-tion. Thai Lang Nghiem, another member of the winning slate, recently made the point that only by building a broad worker-peas-ant movement, possessing an identity of its own, can the govern-ment ultimately deal on equal terms with the N.L.F. Nghiem said, "Simply to speak of building 'a broader-based government,' without first creating a real political program, is meaningless, and will lead only to more intrigue."

Whether there will be enough time to do what Nghiem says before a period of negotiating or of "fighting and negotiating at the same time" begins is a vital question. If the effort to achieve political unity is to meet with any success, it must be pushed by the new government, which should try especially hard to consolidate the divergent elements among the Hoa Hao, the Cao Dai, and the other religious groups. The greatest difficulty will be to obtain the allegiance of the Buddhists, who are now more than ever split among themselves and hostile toward the government. The large number of Catholics elected to the Senate has exacerbated this hostility, and the Buddhists, who from the start were violently opposed both to the Thieu-Ky regime and to its American sponsors, are at least united in maintaining, along with the defeated candidates, that the election was crooked, calling it nothing but an American and Catholic plot to keep the generals in power, and vowing to carry on "a fight to the finish against General Thieu." Ever since the defeat of their Struggle Force last year in Danang and Hué, when Ky cracked down on them, the Buddhists have been going through a period of self-examination about their political role. A few weeks ago, Thieu issued a new charter giving official status to the moderate Tam Chau wing—a move that many observers regarded as a mistake, since it gave the radical group, headed by Thich Tri Quang and Thich Thien Minh, new vitality by presenting it with a valid complaint. The militants formed a Committee to Defend the Old Charter, which gave more power to the priests than to the Buddhist lay leaders. Tri Quang is well aware that, after the priests' failure to lead the Buddhists to victory last year, there must be a compromise with the lay leaders, but at the moment his attention is centered on prosecuting his case against Thieu and Ky. This week he led a thousand of his followers on a protest march through Saigon, and then he and four fellow-monks encamped on the lawn of the Presidential Palace. To the surprise of onlookers, Thieu himself emerged from the Palace to engage in a colloquy with Tri Quang. A while later, it was announced that the monk's demand for a change in the charter had been rejected. Tri Quang has said, "We face a dilemma. We cannot be Communists, but if we go with the Americans we will lose the masses. I am anti-Communist; therefore I must be anti-American. If I am not anti-American, I will lose the good cause, the right cause. To fight the Communists, one must have a good cause."

The few voices that really counsel a reconciliation with the Buddhists are listened to politely but essentially go unheeded. Buu, the labor leader, says, for example, "In making our current appraisals, we must ask ourselves, What forces can we rely on? What is our current political capital? Then we must work actively to weld these elements together. The government should create a Ministry of National Unity to evaluate the different groups and help integrate them into the society." Another Vietnamese I know, who is close to the political leadership and is dismayed over the new struggle between Thieu and Ky, says, "If only Thieu could mollify Ky with praise, accept Ky's people in some jobs, and thereby neutralize Ky, and then, having stopped the political maneuvering for a while, get around the country and talk with Buddhists, Catholics, Hoa Hao, Cao Dai, and just plain ordinary people, he could do wonders for himself and for Vietnam, too. Right now, he should be visiting the troops and the villages in each of the four corps areas, letting them know who their new President is, and also letting them know that he means to help them. Just issuing proclamations from Saigon about unity doesn't mean a thing." Another high official, who has worked for both Thieu and Ky, told me gloomily, "Christmas is not far off, then comes Tet—the New Year period—then the American primary elections, and all these will act as delaying factors in the creation of an efficient government."

Efficiency, however, has long been subordinated to two ancient forces: family influence and political corruption, both of which have much more to do with the exercise of power here. Only when this situation is changed will any real progress become possible in the two important areas of Revolutionary Development and Army reorganization. The top Vietnamese and American officials all know this, but the power of decision nevertheless lies with a handful of Vietnamese leaders who arose under the old system and still derive their strength from it. This includes not only the four corps commanders but some other old-line Army men, such as General Vien, the head of the Joint General Staff, not to mention Thieu himself, who used to be a corps commander. These leaders are naturally far from eager to preside over the dissolution of their empire.

Before the election, Ky, as Premier, made the mistake of announcing that General Nguyen Duc Thang would be Deputy Chief of Staff, with far-ranging powers over Revolutionary Development and Army reorganization. Thang, an able man but a loner who suffers from being a favorite of the Americans, made the further

but essentiall a Ky man

mistake of announcing some sweeping reforms, which naturally alienated the Thieu camp, and as a result Thang's future is now in doubt. If he should quit—he has several times threatened to do so, for personal reasons—there is no one around who could take his place, and the Revolutionary Development Program would undoubtedly suffer a serious blow. At present, there are four hundred and sixty-two Revolutionary Development Teams carrying on their work in nearly twelve hundred hamlets. Most of the teams, which are supposed to consist of fifty-nine men each, still average closer to forty men, chiefly as a result of assassinations by the Vietcong. Many of these losses, and the teams' other problems as well, have stemmed from a continuing basic lack of protection. Not only has the regular South Vietnamese Army failed to provide sufficient protection, and thus compelled the teams to provide their own, to the detriment of their assigned development tasks, but the teams have been overextended as a result of unrealistic orders issued to them by Vietnamese division and corps commanders.

Usually, each team works in three or four hamlets, moving from one to another, and remains in one area for six months or more, depending on local needs and on the rate of progress made. Progress is judged by a hundred specific criteria, embracing eleven basic fields of activity, among them the suppression of Vietcong infiltration, the suppression of corruption and exploitation of the people, the development of a democratic spirit of coöperation, the encouragement of anti-Communist activity among the local groups, programs to speed land reform and increase agricultural production, programs to improve sanitation and health, and programs to eradicate illiteracy. The Americans have this all nicely computerized, but one trouble is that not all the criteria are applicable to all hamlets. The problem is made worse by the Vietnamese military commanders. Division and corps commanders use the Revolutionary Development Teams as military or paramilitary instruments for their own ends, assigning them, for instance, to build new hamlets along a main highway solely for military reasons. Used in this fashion, the Revolutionary Development Teams become disillusioned; desertions take place, and the teams fall prey to Vietcong attacks. Though it is true that there are some areas where the teams have functioned well, opening roads and stimulating production, there are still too many places throughout the country where, in the words of one leader, "We go on making the same mistake that Ngo Dinh Nhu made years ago, when he had us build strategic hamlets for show."

This situation will not be improved unless the Revolutionary Development Program can operate on its own, with a minimum of military interference, and this is the fight that General Thang has been waging for some time, against high odds. Even the concomitant secret elements of the program—the so-called Provincial Reconnaissance Units, of ten men each, which are supposed to be counter-terrorist squads—are now frequently consolidated by the Army commanders into company-size units for routine military tasks. Thus, both covert activity of the sort required to root out the Vietcong and the overt social revolutionary influence that the program is supposed to produce become subject to military pressure, and are vitiated by it. There are a great number of farseeing Americans and Vietnamese who are fully aware of the problem, and who are doing their best to solve it in some places, but, in general, their efforts are still being hamstrung. Only the Vietnamese can settle these deeper questions of military-political control, though the Americans, even with the reduction in leverage brought about by their ever-increasing military involvement, could still exert more pressure than they are now. The willingness to do this appears to depend on how bold and how firm Washington, acting through Ambassador Bunker, wants to be in demanding a thorough military-political reorganization, and on whether the United States is now prepared to back up its demands with real threats of deëscalation, and even of withdrawal. The mood—out here, at least—seems too cautious. There seems to be increasing sentiment in favor of just pushing ahead as best we can with Revolutionary Development and pacification, meanwhile depending on American military and economic might to eventually "smother the Communists," as several top-level officials keep saying.

The mere fact that at this point in the history of the American involvement in South Vietnam those in charge of prosecuting policy here can speak of smothering the Vietcong and the North Vietnamese amounts to an admission that politics and ideology have failed. Obviously, in what has always been a political war, there can never be a purely military solution, even if General William C. Westmoreland is given a million troops and North Vietnam is obliterated by bombing. The fact that a growing number of ultra-hawks, here and in the United States (actually, I have always considered them pro-tem hawks), are now saying that if we can't "bomb the hell" out of North Vietnam and "force it to buckle under" we ought to get out indicates the current mood and emphasizes our political bankruptcy. The facts and figures cited to show the increasing effects of the northern bombings and the difficulties the Communists are having in the South are irrelevant to this. It may be that Vietcong recruitment in the South is down from seven thousand a month to thirty-five hundred, that the monthly average of infiltration from the North is down from six or seven thousand to four thousand, and that the total enemy armed strength is not three hundred thousand but closer to two hundred and thirty thousand. It may also be that General Westmoreland's campaign to strike the enemy main-force units and root out the guerrillas at the same time is making slow but sure progress. Even so, there is no sign either that the American people will be patient enough for such a long struggle or that any sort of permanent victory can result, given the political endurance of the Vietcong and their ability to lie low and rise again, as they did in 1946 and again in 1958.

The N.L.F. and its parent, the Central Office for South Vietnam, which directs the war in the South under Hanoi's supervision, do not hesitate to admit their own shortcomings. Their self-criticism is especially harsh in dealing with the work of local Party chapters, saying that these are lacking in zeal, forcefulness, and organizing ability. Such self-criticism is a traditional part of the Communists' agitation-and-propaganda kit. The fact remains that the Vietcong and the North Vietnamese, although they have suffered heavy losses in battle and are unable to sustain an offensive without pausing to renew their strength and replenish their food and ammunition, have amply demonstrated in recent weeks that they can still strike sharply and quickly almost anywhere they want, employing both terror and power. In the I Corps area, in and below the Demilitarized Zone, they are engaged in their only full-scale campaign at present, designed to keep a large force of American Marines pinned down in what amounts to a conventional war posture, and thus prevent them from engaging in the process—more destructive for the Vietcong—of rooting the guerrillas out of the countryside. Elsewhere, there have been few major engagements, and the Americans, the Koreans, and the Vietnamese have been doing what they can, which is considerable, to chase and kill guerrillas and occasional main-force elements in lieu of finding and challenging larger Communist units. All this, however, adds up to a state of irresolution, and is possibly a prelude to the period of "fighting and negotiating at the same time," which could begin within a few months, but, in the opinion of most observers, won't start until after November, 1968.

The confidence of the Communists was well demonstrated in a new political program that the N.L.F. announced in mid-August— the first such major plan issued since 1960. The program was published on the eve of the elections here, and obviously was a calculated attempt to confuse the Vietnamese people about how to vote, and to let them know that they had a positive alternative in the form of a generous offer of coöperation from the Front on a broad basis of harmony and coalition. "The tasks and objectives of the South Vietnamese people in the struggle for national salvation are now as follows," the program, which was broadcast repeatedly all over the country and is now being widely distributed abroad, began. "To unite the entire people, resolutely to defend [against] the United States imperialists' war of aggression, overthrow their lackey puppet administration, establish a broad national, democratic, peaceful, neutral, and prosperous South Vietnam, and proceed toward peaceful reunification of the fatherland." It went on, "The National Liberation Front of South Vietnam constantly stands for uniting all social strata and classes, all nationalities, all political parties, all organizations, all religious communities, all patriotic personalities, all individuals, and all patriotic and progressive forces, irrespective of political tendencies, in order to struggle together against the United States imperialists and their lackeys, wrest back our sacred national rights, and build up the country." Echoing the Chinese Communist line as it has been laid down by Mao Tse-tung's designated heir, Lin Piao, the Front pledged itself to "take an active part in the common struggle of the world's peoples against the bellicose and aggressive imperialists, headed by the United States, for peace, national independence, democracy, and social progress."

The fourteen-point program that followed, which included the first open reference to a "national coalition government," was a compendium of propaganda and promises designed to win the largest possible mass support. Among the points were these: The South Vietnamese constitution and elections must be abrogated and there must be new "free general elections" for a truly representative Assembly, followed by the establishment of a government embracing all "social strata." American "economic slavery and monopoly" must be abolished in favor of a combination of capitalist and Socialist enterprise to improve agricultural production and stimulate industry. Land reform must be prosecuted, through both a redistribution of acreage and rent reductions. The Liberation Armed Forces must be built up "with a view of liberating the people and defending the fatherland." Guarantees must be provided to assure "the rights and livelihood of workers and civil servants," the rights to include an eight-hour day and an incentive system. Women must "be equal to men, politically and economically." National minorities must be protected, and "puppet officers and men and puppet officials" must be "shown leniency" and welcomed back to "the just cause," after which they will be "rewarded and entrusted with responsible jobs." As for unification with the North, the platform said that this would be "realized step by step and through peaceful means on the principle of negotiation between the two zones, without pressure by either side against the other and without foreign interference." In the interim, there would be free movement back and forth and free communication and trade.

There is obviously something here for everybody, and as a declaration of both policy and ideology the platform has considerably more appeal than anything the Thieu-Ky government or any of its post-Diem predecessors have propounded. It also seems obvious that Hanoi, looking ahead to an ultimate period of negotiations, during which some fighting may continue, is giving its southern branch office fresh leeway to make appeals of its own and to justify its representation at a peace conference as an independent entity. This is a factor that cannot be ignored, no matter how close the ties may actually be between parent Hanoi and dependent Front. The only way in which the South Vietnamese government can counter the effect of this propaganda is to establish itself as a going concern and then make its own accommodation with both the Front and Hanoi. Saigon, with the help of the Americans, still has an opportunity to rediscover its own bona-fide southern revolutionary tradition, but at this writing it seems doubtful whether it will be able to meet the challenge unless it stops engaging in the same sort of intrigue and self-serving politics that have impeded its progress for the last five years.

13. Saigon

~·~

January 20, 1968

The Vietnamese have recently been reminding themselves of the last days of the Indo-China War, in late 1953 and early 1954, when political pressure was mounting in France to put a finish to *la guerre sale,* and when a minority of South Vietnamese nationalists were vainly trying to persuade the French colonial hierarchy to grant South Vietnam the sort of independence that would sustain it against Ho Chi Minh's dynamic government in the North. As the current war in South Vietnam enters the third year of its intensive military phase and the second decade of guerrilla combat, there are some striking similarities—and also some significant differences— between the close of the French colonial era and the present period. Despite what President Johnson says about sticking to our commitments, the present American government, like an earlier French one, is being subjected to rising pressures of popular discontent; there is increasing talk, both in Saigon and in Washington, about methods of disengagement—more specifically, about finding formulas for accommodation between the Saigon government and the National Liberation Front. That some sort of agreement between Saigon and the Front, and between Saigon and Hanoi, must ultimately take place is now generally accepted here, while the feeling is growing that negotiations between Washington and Hanoi can deal with the questions of bombing in the North and the pace of ultimate American troop withdrawals but not directly with the question of South Vietnam's political future, which the Vietnamese must settle themselves.

Just how and when this process of accommodation can begin, however, remains uncertain, and, under any circumstances, it will require patience, a spirit of compromise, and a readiness for some calculated face-saving that can only be the product of intricate and typically Asian maneuvering and adjustment. At the moment, in spite of the current peace flurries, the prospects for peace are still regarded here as remote, because, in the words of one Saigon columnist, "no party to the conflict wants or can afford to make concessions." The cynical Vietnamese see little purpose in engaging in semantic contests with the hard-minded men of Hanoi over whether there is special significance to such hints as North Vietnamese Foreign Minister Nguyen Duy Trinh's saying that talks "will" take place on "relevant questions" if we stop bombing the North, whereas he had previously said that such talks "could" take place. There is a conviction that when Hanoi is ready to talk about negotiations, or about a truce or a cease-fire, it will make its desires clear without indulging in word games. This belief, which predominates among thoughtful Vietnamese and among American officials here, is accompanied by the complaint that by continuously emphasizing our desire for peace and expressing our willingness to go anywhere and talk to anybody in pursuit of it we are simply persuading Hanoi to go on fighting.

One highly placed American here recently said to me, in a tone of mixed exasperation and despair, "If you were Ho Chi Minh, and you were told for the fortieth or fiftieth time how eager we are to make peace, wouldn't you figure that, whatever the hardships, this is not the time to quit?" And, as another Vietnamese press commentary has put it, "While the United States may be no less determined to hold out than its allies, the South Vietnamese cannot help having suspicions about actual American intentions, and the North Vietnamese can look forward to further concessions by the United States at the approach of its Presidential elections." All this, naturally, has caused a fresh wave of nervousness in Saigon during a difficult period of post-election political readjustment and has also caused an exacerbation of American-Vietnamese tensions. Even those Vietnamese who dislike us at least as much as they disliked the French are afraid that our withdrawal, whenever it takes place, will be all too sudden, as was that of the French after the fall of Dien Bien Phu in 1954. Partly for this reason and partly out of national pride, the Vietnamese are displaying an increasing resentment at the idea of being prodded into any kind of premature peace move. They want to make it clear that the timing as well as the pattern of eventual negotiations will be determined as much by them as by us.

Any realistic appraisal of the present possibilities for peace must take into consideration the whole sweep of events in Vietnam since the end of the Second World War. Unless this is done, particularly by those who will eventually seek to make the peace, the chances are that the Vietnam tragedy will simply be compounded, and that the war, which has become increasingly cruel and intolerable, will end in a settlement that will prove neither practical nor permanent. Among the basic factors that must be kept in mind are the remarkable consistency of revolutionary thought, strategy, and tactics, and the true genius for organization, that have been displayed all along by Ho Chi Minh, now in his seventy-eighth year. As perhaps the "purest" exponent of Marxism-Leninism in the Communist world, Ho has never veered from his course of seeking Vietnamese independence and unity by the means that have seemed to him most expedient at the time—negotiation, guerrilla warfare, full-scale war, temporary alliance with "progressive" forces (sometimes in the face of opposition from extremists within his own ranks), and an unwavering faith in the justice of his own cause. A number of long-term observers of the Vietnamese scene remain convinced that in 1945 and 1946 the Western world lost an opportunity to deal with Ho as a true national Communist and, by capitalizing on his nationalism, to turn him into a Tito who would create a strong, unified Vietnam as a neutral, or even a "neutralist," state. But most of these same observers believe there is much less chance for a unified Vietnam, under the aegis of Hanoi, to play such a role now. Not only is Ho much older and less active but he has also become embittered after his long years of warfare against the French and the Americans, and meanwhile North Vietnam has become a tougher, more hard-line Communist state. All this is relevant to the making of peace today for several reasons. It explains Ho's reluctance to accept again, as he did at Geneva, a form of compromise that might restrict his freedom of maneuver—his capacity for employing every possible means to achieve his lifelong aim of creating a unified Vietnam. It also places the relationship, in revolutionary terms, between the North and the South in historical perspective.

The possibilities for accommodation must be judged against the background of independent southern revolutionary development, not only since 1945 but in the light of the immemorial divisiveness of Vietnamese society. The long tradition of the people's isolated agrarian life is a vital factor, and today, as in other times of crisis, this sense of isolation, of separate village identity, is behind much of what can be described as the "non-involvement" or "non-commitment" of millions of Vietnamese peasants. In earlier times, whenever the Vietnamese rebelled against their Chinese rulers and, under the inspiration of a series of heroic leaders from the local mandarin class, temporarily fostered a degree of regional or national unity, the natural tendency toward local factionalism sooner or later reasserted itself and allowed new repressive measures to be taken. The French, when they arrived on the scene in the middle of the nineteenth century, encouraged this local factionalism for obvious reasons of their own, and they accepted the autonomous-village system, dominated by a small traditional élite. The incoming colonialists incorporated as much of the system as they could into their colonial structure and then superimposed their own imperial rule, overcoming resistance by means of some of the cruellest measures in the history of conquest. As the people reacted and resistance movements spread, whole villages were razed by the colonial soldiers for harboring opposition leaders or guerrillas. It took the French half a century to "pacify" Indo-China. During this period, despite the rising hatred for the French, there was actually very little local political awareness of consensus. As Joseph Buttinger has written in his classic *Vietnam: A Dragon Embattled,* ". . . the really tragic aspect of the . . . tradition-bound rebel movement was not the number of its victims but its political futility. . . . Not only was nothing achieved; nothing was learned either—neither by the defeated rebels nor by the victorious French." Except for the occasional outbursts of violence, village life generally went on as it had for centuries. Custom and religion continued to blend in a local synthesis of ancestor worship, animism, Confucianism, and mixed forms of Buddhism, which eventually led to the formation of quasi-political sects, the Cao Dai and the Hoa Hao. For the French, the fragmenting of Vietnamese society proved both profitable and convenient.

The Communists, from the outset of their activity in Indo-China, in the late twenties, rejected the élitist outlook of the old mandarin nationalists and directed their appeals to the Vietnamese people as a whole, concentrating on economic and social goals. They also readily adapted themselves to the traditional Vietnamese clandestine and conspiratorial climate. During 1930 and 1931, the Communists succeeded in organizing peasant revolts throughout Indo-China, particularly in Annam, though these were directed more at local landlords and pro-French elements among the Vietnamese than at the French themselves. The French crushed these rebellions, killing an estimated ten thousand Vietnamese and deporting fifty thousand more. Even so, there was, beginning in 1932, a gradual reëstablishment of the Communist movement in Cochin China, the southernmost colony, led by Tran Van Giau, a young revolutionist who had just returned from studying in Moscow. These years of slow rebuilding of the underground Party machine, which included a bitter struggle at one point between the Stalinists and the Trotskyites, contributed much to the development of a separate southern revolutionary ethos, which still exists. Intrigue for the sake of intrigue often was the rule, and the results were destructive, which helps explain why there remains so much mutual distrust and suspicion among the Vietnamese in the South today and why it is so difficult to create effective political parties in the modern sense.

It is against this backdrop that the present war must be seen and that the chances for reaching some sort of accommodation in the South must be gauged. In a sense, all that the Americans have done in Vietnam since 1946, when they began helping the French, and particularly since 1954, when they assumed their own role, largely at the instigation of John Foster Dulles, is delay the process of revolutionary development. The delay has affected the shape and the substance of the southern revolt, and this is apt to be significant when negotiations begin. At the end of the Second World War, when

Ho Chi Minh established his rule in the North, his Vietminh network in the South was operating semi-independently, under its own regional and local leadership. In the fall of 1945, the Vietminh, having failed in an attempt to seize and hold Saigon, went underground again in the southern countryside. Then Ho's agents travelled south to try to pull the Vietminh elements together. The agents partly succeeded, but the local Vietminh continued, under its own largely southern leadership, to fight its own sort of guerrilla war against the French—a war different from that waged by Vo Nguyen Giap in the North, as he moved from guerrilla tactics, through the stage of mobile warfare, into the counter-offensive stage that culminated in Dien Bien Phu. Clandestine activity continued to be the rule in the South, even after the Geneva settlement, when many Vietminh cadremen were left behind while some eighty thousand of their fellow-Communists went north—to return after 1958, when guerrilla activity was resumed. And in 1960, when the National Liberation Front was established, it was not surprising, as Douglas Pike, the author of *Viet Cong,* and a thorough student of the Vietcong and the Front, has pointed out, that its various component groups—Buddhists, young people, women, professional associations, and so on—were modelled on the clandestine protective bodies in the tradition of the Vietnamese *ho,* the patrilineal social group, deriving from an individual's great-great-grandfather. From the outset, the Front, using its secret network in the villages and portraying itself as "the sole genuine representative of the South Vietnamese people," had political power as its objective. Such power was to be achieved through the so-called *khoi nghia,* or general uprising, and through a combination of political and armed *dau tranh,* or struggle movement.

In any analysis of the Front as a southern phenomenon, dominated and manipulated by Communist cadremen but by no means consisting only of Communists, even at the leadership level, and in any appraisal of means by which accommodation with the Front can perhaps eventually be negotiated, the Front's weaknesses and strengths must also be considered. The weaknesses, carefully analyzed by the Front itself, are revealed in transcripts of its self-criticism sessions. Self-criticism as a Communist weapon of flagellation can easily be misunderstood. Its impact derives not only from exhortation, and from constant study of the theoretical and practical mistakes that have been made, but from purposeful exaggeration, which seeks to produce something close to acts of penitence as a means of restimulating the urge to rebel. In this sense, self-criticism is a steady process of therapy through catharsis. The longer the war has gone on, and the more difficult it has become for Vietcong troops to maintain their morale in the face of disease, shortages of food, and, above all, the tremendous firepower the Americans have thrown at them, the more important this process of reinvigoration has become. After years of privation and struggle and of being kept on the run, even the most ardent believer is bound to develop doubts. Dedication gives way to disillusion, and when a man is ill and weak, persuasion and a pep talk are less effective remedies than penicillin.

Probably the most important date for the analyst, and the potential negotiator, to keep in mind in appraising the possibilities of peace through accommodation is January 1, 1962. It was on that day that the People's Revolutionary Party was founded. The P.R.P. was described as "the Marxist-Leninist element of the National Liberation Front," and, privately, members of the Lao Dong Party in the South were told that the P.R.P. would thenceforward represent the Party there. According to what Pike and others have since concluded, Hanoi decided to set up the P.R.P. as a hard "inner pyramid core," reinforcing the loose Front pyramid, with its village base, because the North Vietnamese felt that a sense of "ideological isolation" was growing in the South and that this could lead to separatism. (The Russians, incidentally, had warned them of this.) The P.R.P. has now assumed direct control in all Front villages, with P.R.P. members handing down orders to all sub-groups and local bodies, and establishing all the guidelines.

The present N.L.F.-P.R.P. policy on negotiations is to resist them, on the ground that the American position is constantly growing weaker both militarily and morally; the first of these qualifiers is surely wrong, but the second is probably right. Victory, the Communists maintain, can and eventually will be achieved without negotiations of the sort that proved so ineffective at Geneva. Instead of risking possible internal division by altering their course, they are determined to fight on, one way or another; their announced alternative strategy of "fighting and negotiating at the same time" comes into prospect here, as does the stress on "national salvation." In its 1967 program statement, the first major one it has issued since 1960, the Front repeatedly emphasizes this theme of national salvation, which will eventually lead to reunification but not until "a democratic, peaceful, neutral, and prosperous South Vietnam is built." Although the word "coalition" does not appear in the statement, Front leaders have acknowledged that the coalition idea is implicit in the program, while making it perfectly clear that any coalition in which the Front participates must be completely dominated by the Front, using the technique of the well-organized minority that gains and holds power over an amorphous, less deeply dedicated, and poorly indoctrinated majority.

Given the Communists' dedication, conviction, and patience, and their ability to adjust themselves to either a "front-door" or a "back-door" approach to seizing power, the chances of achieving a balance of forces in the South—of building independent political parties and creating a true new consensus—may seem slight. Nevertheless, this appears to be the only sensible way out of the Vietnam predicament, and the chance must be taken, even if it involves the risk of Communist domination. To the degree that the government enters into this attempt in a true revolutionary spirit, making good, even belatedly, on its own revolutionary promises, the risk will be reduced. What, in effect, we are now confronted with in Vietnam, after so many missed opportunities for creating a valid political entity—and we Americans are as much to blame for these missed opportunities as the French were before us, and almost as much as are the floundering Vietnamese themselves—is a last race against time.

First, one must ask the question: Can the non-Communist Vietnamese, despite fatigue, and despite the tremendous problems of reorganizing the military and civil administration, of dealing boldly with corruption, and of facing up to the absolute necessity of creating a fresh political climate, still manage not only to win popular support but to attract some of those in and around the National Liberation Front who believe in the southern revolutionary ethos and are disillusioned by the harsh and often contradictory dictates of the P.R.P.?

Second, having come this far, will and can the Americans demonstrate the added patience, in a turbulent election year back home, that would enable the Vietnamese process of accommodation to begin judiciously, whatever Hanoi does or does not do about negotiations? It is not just a question of how intolerable the war has become. What is involved is a tough calculated risk, the careful weighing of both moral guilt and responsibility against the future of American foreign policy in Asia, which is concerned with far more than the containment of Communism. The widely held fear that if we stay in Vietnam much longer we will lose whatever worthwhile influence we might continue to have in Southeast Asia in the future does not accord with the views of most of the states-men and political observers I have talked with in all parts of the region during the past year. They include such Socialist leaders as Prime Minister Lee Kuan Yew of Singapore and Foreign Minister Adam Malik of Indonesia, who, eager though they, too, are to see the war ended, firmly believe that the manner and method of our disen-gagement is perhaps the most important single question that Asia has been confronted with since 1945. Even Prince Sihanouk of Cam-bodia, who is strongly opposed to the war and to our role in it, has expressed the opinion that a precipitate American withdrawal from Vietnam, followed by a reduction of our commitments else-where in Southeast Asia, would be disastrous at this juncture.

A third factor in the equation, as the South Vietnamese and many Americans here see it, is that Hanoi and its southern P.R.P. adjunct will decide on their own, despite what they say about continuing the present fighting indefinitely, how and when to enter a fighting-and-negotiating-at-the-same-time phase. Many observers here have wondered why Hanoi has not already entered this phase, since the social and economic deterioration that has accompanied the incon-clusive political struggles since the fall of Ngo Dinh Diem in 1963 seems to have offered the Vietcong countless opportunities for an open political contest under conditions of continuing guerrilla war-fare. It would appear to be more prudent for the N.L.F. to protect and sustain its guerrilla organization in the villages, which is now being weakened by attrition, than for it to continue fighting and losing as many men as it is and thereby making itself increasingly dependent on northern replacements. It may be, of course, that Hanoi is fearful of losing control over the Front, which presumably could happen if it allowed the Front to revert to the old style of independent guerrilla warfare while negotiations dragged on. An-other factor in the situation is, of course, China; for Hanoi to call a halt to the war now would almost surely jeopardize its relationship with Peking.

There are signs that the phase of fighting and negotiating at the same time may be coming much closer—that Hanoi, both because of the heavy bombing of North Vietnam and because of its own manpower problems, may be ready to take the risk of altering the nature and course of the war. The war would simply shift gears, but the shift could encourage the accommodation process, if the government in Saigon should become strong enough, and prove imaginative enough, to react to it. Instead of employing the tactics of all three classic stages of insurrectionary warfare, from simple guerrilla action to offensive-attritional campaigns to full-scale counter-offensives, the war may tend to be waged solely, or primarily, at the second level. The manner in which the Communists have conducted the war in recent months indicates that they have adopted this approach, with partial success. They have sought, sometimes at a heavy cost in lives, to keep us engaged on their terms instead of allowing us to decide the time and place of battle. In the I Corps area, just south of the Demilitarized Zone, they have continued to pin down the American Marines and to prevent the Americans from maneuvering freely, especially south of Danang, where the Vietcong have been solidly entrenched for many years and the Marines have never had more than sporadic success in pacifying the villages. In the II Corps area, notably two months ago at Dak To, near the Laotian border, in the second most violent battle of the war, the Communists suffered estimated losses of sixteen hundred men while themselves killing almost three hundred Americans and a hundred South Vietnamese in a bloody three-week-long struggle for a series of hills that were of no particular value to either side, except that if the Communists had not been halted there they would have moved on to the strategic provincial capital of Kontum. In American terms, Dak To was obviously a victory, yet for the Communists, who do not think as much about losses as we do, it could not be called a complete defeat, as was the prior battle at Loc Ninh, farther south, near the Cambodian border, where their losses were at least eight times ours. A primary Communist aim at Dak To was to draw American forces away from the coastal areas of Phu Yen and Binh Dinh Provinces, and they succeeded in doing this. Significantly, however, the Vietcong were unable to take advantage of these American withdrawals either to regain lost ground in the east or to gather and stock rice, as they seek to do each harvest season. Now the Communists are instead likely to concentrate on the III Corps area north of Saigon.

In stressing the theme that the war in Vietnam is bound to be a protracted one no matter how it is pursued, the challenge the Vietcong face is no longer so much one of convincing the villagers that there will be social and economic panaceas in a future Communist society as one of simply convincing them that, come hell or high water, the Vietcong are going to win this war and the peasants had better stick with the winner. If coercion is necessary to persuade the peasants that victory will be achieved, then coercion will be employed. This approach holds obvious risks for the Communists, the greatest being that of alienating the very people they want to recruit—even though it is probably true that the average Vietnamese peasant is sufficiently tough-minded to be persuaded less by doctrine, or by coercion, than by his own hard estimate of which side is going to win. In the last year or so, the Communists acknowledge that they have lost dominion over a million people, many of whom have become refugees seeking sanctuary from American bombing. The Vietcong's claim of still controlling five million of an estimated total of seventeen million South Vietnamese is denied by the Americans, who set the figure at seventeen per cent of the population—less than three million people—and list roughly the same percentage as "contested." In most places, however, the organization built up by the Vietcong over a period of many years has remained relatively intact, and it would be a grave mistake to assume otherwise.

The government, for its part, has made many attempts over the last six years, with the help of the Americans, to create an alternative rural organization, and so far not one of these attempts has succeeded. The present effort, under the Revolutionary Development Program, is the most elaborate and scientific one to date, but it is still only getting up steam. Of the thirty-five thousand R.D. men, in fifty-nine-man teams, at present working in about a thousand hamlets, only half are effective. Under a new evaluation system, which makes use of computers, 8,650 hamlets, out of a newly listed total of 12,650 in South Vietnam, are being rated on a scale of "A" through "E" according to eighteen indicators, half having to do with security and the other half with development. The remaining four thousand hamlets, mostly small ones, are controlled by the Vietcong. The standards employed, says Deputy Ambassador Robert Komer, who is in charge of the American side of the pacification program, are quite high; he cites the fact that only a few more than two hundred hamlets are rated "A" today—though almost all of these are big ones, with a total population of nearly seven hundred thousand. Recently, in explaining the hamlet-evaluation system, Komer said, "A 'D' hamlet is one where Vietcong military activities have been reduced . . . [although] there is still Vietcong activity in the hamlet at night. Some Vietcong cadremen have been eliminated and leaders neutralized, but there may be terrorism and taxation at any time during the month. On the other hand, there is more local protection than there is in an 'E' hamlet. Local participation in hamlet management has begun. A Census Grievance Program has started. Census Grievance Teams provide a blueprint of a village, tabulating each household and noting the sympathies of each family, and also the desires of the hamlet population for schools, bridges, wells, and the like. Some medical teams are visiting the hamlets periodically. There is a beginning of hamlet education and welfare activity, and a certain amount of economic development is going on." There are about two thousand "D" hamlets at present, with a total population of two million. "B" hamlets account for three and a half million people, "C" hamlets for something over four million, and "E" hamlets for about three hundred and fifty thousand. The slowness of the economic-development programs has hampered the project as a whole, and the increase in the relatively secure population during 1967 has been estimated at about five per cent.

One may wonder whether socio-economic progress can ever be adequately measured by computers, but the hamlet-evaluation system does seem to be more effective than any other system so far devised in avoiding rash estimates and predictions of the sort that have consistently been made in the past in Vietnam. What it inevitably leaves out is the human factor, and it is on this that everything ultimately must depend. Besides, it cannot judge the true impact on a hamlet of clandestine activity, and this is the vital weapon of the Vietcong. Critics of the pacification program, the American side of which was taken over by the military last year, have charged that it is too big and sprawling, and that the loss of its civilian character is to be regretted. The bigness of the new nationwide system has proved to be a handicap in that it has reduced the sort of local activity that is best able to deal with the Vietcong in truly "counter-revolutionary"—that is, ultimately revolutionary—ways.

There have recently been some indications that this problem is at last being realistically confronted. Plans have been completed for a thorough training this year of the hundred and forty thousand members of the local Popular Forces, who operate at the village level under the control of district chiefs, and who will take over most of the security functions of the pacification program in the hamlets and villages from the regular armed forces (A.R.V.N.), which have never adapted themselves effectively to pacification duty. On the covert side, the most important innovation is a revised counter-intelligence plan, called the Phoenix Program, which is certainly long overdue. For the first time in all the years of American involvement in Vietnam, an attempt is being made to bring together and coördinate at the vital district level all the intelligence resources of both the Americans and the Vietnamese. That is, the data collected by United States military intelligence sources, including outlying Special Forces units and their Vietnamese informants; by the ten-man Vietnamese teams called Provincial Reconnaissance Units, which are trained by the Central Intelligence Agency, and are mostly counter-terror and counter-assassination squads; by the Vietnamese Army intelligence services; by the Census Grievance Teams; and by the eleven thousand members of the Police Field Force, a special unit of the Vietnamese police that works locally and usually covertly—all will be collated and analyzed by a joint American-Vietnamese team at each district headquarters in the country. When prisoners are brought in, or defectors surrender, for example, everything they have to say will be carefully studied and appraised under one intelligence directorate. Whatever the dangers of creating a new bureaucracy, the establishment of a unified intelligence-gathering organization and an improved national police system, employing more local policemen, is a step in the right direction, and one can only wonder why it wasn't tried sooner.

Rooting out the Vietcong infrastructure is only the beginning of the challenge faced by the government. This challenge involves the long process of coming to terms with a whole set of local and regional societies that have their own historical importance. Included among them are not only the religious groups—the Catholics, the various kinds of Buddhists, the Cao Dai, and the Hoa Hao—but also the two dozen or so tribal groups inhabiting the highlands, parts of the northern mountainous regions, and some of the areas bordering Laos and Cambodia. Among these various bodies, the Vietcong, and the Vietminh before them, far more than the central Saigon government, have, as Gerald Hickey, the author of *Village in Vietnam,* has put it, "penetrated the attitude-value system" of hundreds of thousands of people, most notably in those areas where the Communists have held sway for decades. In the areas where the Communists are not so strong, however, or where they have lately suffered military setbacks, the opportunities for accommodation between the government and these societies are manifold, and an imaginative pacification process, backed by a good counter-intelligence net, could help to achieve it. Considerable progress has already been made—in the tribal highlands, for instance, where, after years of failure resulting largely from a traditional antipathy between the Vietnamese and the Montagnards, the Vietcong influence has been lessened in a number of the provinces by an organization named FULRO—an acronym for Front Unifié de Lutte des Races Opprimées. The government has also managed a degree of accommodation with many of the million and a half or two million members of the Hoa Hao sect, which operates mostly as an independent element in the southwest part of the country—something of a feat, since both the Hoa Hao and the Cao Dai, which has about a million members, have themselves remained split into various factions. If these separate and collective voices are allowed to speak out, they can assist in the incorporation of some Vietcong elements into the larger political framework of accommodation. The areas of "pure," or total, Communist influence, which would also be incorporated into the framework eventually, and would be represented by the Vietcong as such, would thereby be reduced. "Coalition" thus appears at least possible on terms other than Communist domination.

If one calculates that the Hoa Hao, the Cao Dai, the highlanders, the Chinese (most of whom live in Cholon, the Chinese part of Saigon), and the Khmer and Cham elements (both remnants of former powerful empires in Southeast Asia) total around six million—roughly a third of the population—then it becomes obvious that national *consolidation* is fundamental for national salvation. In the years since 1954, despite the efforts of a number of individual Vietnamese who have been deeply concerned with this crucial question of consolidation, or assimilation, very little has been done to create the sort of cohesion that would effect it. The opportunity still exists, but if the historic disunity of Vietnam is to be ended, and what the government now calls "national reconciliation" is to amount to more than trying to lure random Vietcong elements over to its side, the process must take in the entire social spectrum.

Unless the new government of President Nguyen Van Thieu moves far more quickly than it has moved so far to consolidate its own position and reconcile its internal differences, its chances of engaging successfully in the process of accommodation will surely look dim. More than four months have elapsed since Thieu and Vice-President Nguyen Cao Ky were elected, and it has been more than two months since they formally assumed office, and very little has been accomplished, despite all sorts of plans and promises. The fact is that in Saigon today there is not one government but a whole series of governments and would-be governments. At the top is Thieu. Sitting alongside him, as Secretary-General of the newly established Office of the Presidency, is Nguyen Van Huong, who is a former leader of the Dai Viet, the old nationalist party, and a close friend of Thieu's. He is more or less an Assistant President, charged primarily with seeing to it that the Cabinet of Premier Nguyen Van Loc performs its proper function of carrying out the President's policies and the country's laws and regulations. As for Loc, a mild-mannered lawyer-poet, he is hemmed in between Thieu and Vice-President Ky. Ky has his own Office of the Vice-Presidency, and, having emerged from a period of obscurity following the election, seems about to play an active political role again. The relationship between Thieu and Ky, though it is calmer on the surface than it was at first, remains shaky at best, and both men, as well as Huong and Loc, are engaged in building their own power bases. The executive is thus at least quadripartite, and Thieu's reluctance to take the firm steps he keeps promising Ambassador Ellsworth Bunker and others he will take has made the situation more complicated and confusing.

There are also a number of other executive or quasi-executive arms or branches. The National Police Chief and head of the Military Security Service, General Nguyen Ngoc Loan, who is more intent than anyone else on defending Vietnamese sovereignty against American encroachment, is a continuing power in his own right, and so is his assistant, Nguyen Thanh Tung, known as Mai Den, or "Black Mai." Loan, who has done what is generally regarded as a good job of tracking down Communist terrorists in Saigon, will control the police functions under the new coördinated intelligence scheme, and this will increase his authority further. Finally, there remains the executive influence of the military. Although the four powerful corps commanders were supposedly to have been shorn of political power, their military-political influence remains strong. So does the vestigial influence of the former National Leadership Committee, made up of generals and of a smaller "inner" military committee headed by Thieu. Thus, there can be said to be eight overlapping areas of executive influence, or eleven, if one wants to count each corps commander separately, a form of reckoning that is still warranted.

The Senate and the House of Representatives must also be counted as would-be governments in their own right. The hundred-and-thirty-seven-man House includes some sixty-five Buddhists, thirty-five Catholics, and thirty-seven members affiliated with other religious groups or serving as independents. A so-called Democratic bloc of about fifty is generally considered pro-Ky and pro-Loan, rather than pro-government as such. The rest of the House is composed of smaller groups associated with Catholic and Buddhist factions, or with Dai Viet or chauvinist southern factions. Basically, the House has not yet really taken shape. The Senate, in many respects, represents the best hope there is today for the creation of both a political conscience and a power base for the divided and uncertain executive. It, too, is still in the process of organizing itself into blocs, but since it is composed of only sixty members, the process is potentially easier. The Catholic membership of the Senate totals twenty-seven, or almost half—though the Catholics in South Vietnam amount to around ten per cent of the population—and the Catholic senators have taken over the chairmanship of most of the important committees. Thieu is a Catholic, and just how important the Catholic ascendancy in the country will become is as yet hard to tell. This week, the country's seventeen Catholic bishops asserted both their independence and their importance by issuing a call for a cessation of the bombing in the North and for peace talks "right now," and they also implicitly criticized the Thieu government by deploring "laziness, hypocrisy, and corruption." The encouraging thing about the Senate, in any event, is the presence there of twenty or twenty-five members who either are bona-fide intellectuals or legitimately represent the various mass movements or religious groupings, such as the Hoa Hao. These senators, several of whom have had long experience in the nationalist movement, both underground and in the open, are concerned about the national process of consolidation, reconciliation, and accommodation, and they are now in a position to prod the government into taking the steps that everyone is waiting for. These include a drive against corruption, which has so far existed only in token form, and the reorganization of the Army and the civil administration, which Thieu has been referring to constantly but which has not yet got off the ground.

Ambassador Ellsworth Bunker is fully aware that American leverage has been reduced by time, by the impact of our vast commitment of troops and money, and by the inevitable ultranationalist reaction of the Vietnamese—much of which, it can be said, is justified. Bunker may be somewhat too sanguine about Thieu's promises, but he sees Thieu often and is aware of the President's peculiarly cautious and suspicious temperament—the antithesis of Ky's impulsive one. If anyone can persuade Thieu that time is running out for everyone, and that at least some of the promised basic reforms must be instituted in the next month or two, it is Bunker, the quiet septuagenarian New England diplomat-businessman, praised for facilitating accommodation in Indonesia and the Dominican Republic, who has been introduced into the complicated Vietnamese situation as a counterfoil, in an odd kind of way, to that other cagey septuagenarian, Ho Chi Minh.

Accommodation is undoubtedly the only way out. The Vietnamese are touchy these days about being pushed into it by us. Nevertheless, the idea has taken hold, and it seems bound to gain momentum. To the degree that we can encourage it, through suggestion and persuasion, we may be able, at this very late hour, to reconcile our own confusion of policy and purpose in Vietnam, extending over two decades, while at the same time truly helping the Vietnamese. When, or if, reconciliation and accommodation begin to occur, they will do so, it seems likely, at the lowest levels —in the hamlets and villages of this stricken country, where the tradition of local autonomy still obtains, and must be reaffirmed. Any negotiations to come, involving smaller and greater cease-fires, cessations of bombing, and even international conferences, will succeed or fail, ultimately, on the basis of how well the Vietnamese who care about the future of their country have been able to work out their own solutions despite their own long history of divisiveness.

14.   Saigon

March 2, 1968

By their unique and audacious attacks of late January and the first weeks of February on Saigon and Hué and some thirty other provincial capitals, along with seventy district towns throughout South Vietnam, the Communists have suddenly altered the nature and course of the whole long and painful conflict here and, at least momentarily, are in a stronger position than ever before to set their own terms for negotiation. Nevertheless, it remains questionable whether the North Vietnamese and Vietcong strategists will succeed in their daring gamble to touch off and sustain a widespread urban insurrection while simultaneously continuing major attacks against Allied forces elsewhere in the nation and maintaining pressure on the rural hamlets and villages. No firm answer to the question is likely to be forthcoming until the present winter-spring Communist campaign reaches its expected climax, sometime between now and the end of May. Equally questionable is the nature of the Saigon government's response to what has been at once a deep national shock and an opportunity for the country to rally its strength and try to find the kind of unity and purpose that it has so evidently lacked at least since the fall of the Diem regime in 1963.

The war in Vietnam has always been full of contradictions and imponderables, but in attempting to comprehend and evaluate the stunning events of the past few weeks three tentative conclusions may be offered. First, the attacks on the cities—whatever degree of success or failure they may be judged to have had—cost the Vietcong heavily. Second, the reaction of the Saigon government to date has been good in some respects. It has dealt swiftly and fairly effectively with the emergency social and economic problems created by the tremendous damage and dislocation, which, as the Communists correctly anticipated, were caused in large part by American and South Vietnamese counterattacks. And although in other respects, notably the more important political and psychological ones, developments have been slower, a belated beginning has been made, in the third week of February, to create a broad front that represents all elements of Vietnamese society, by getting prominent leaders in the political, religious, social, labor, and other spheres, who have never worked together before, to coöperate in dealing with the crisis. Third, the winter-spring offensive will almost surely be marked by a significant number of coördinated sequels to the attacks that were launched on the cities in late January, at the time of Tet, the Vietnamese New Year holiday. The strongest possibility is for a continued offensive below the Demilitarized Zone that divides North and South Vietnam—an assault on the mountain base of Khe Sanh, in the west, or renewed attacks on the eastern bases of Con Thien and Gio Linh and the cities of Hué and Quang Tri—accompanied by another major effort in the highlands area around Dak To, near the Laotian border, and by fresh attacks on half a dozen other cities in the highlands and farther south.

There is considerable expectation here among military and diplomatic officials that if the Communists achieve any degree of success in this phase of their 1968 campaign, they will offer to negotiate on the basis of their controlling much of the western half of South Vietnam, just as they control the eastern and central parts of Laos. The alternative, the Communists will suggest, would be more of the same protracted war, which they are willing to wage indefinitely. If the United States unconditionally stops bombing the North, negotiations on "all relevant problems . . . will begin . . . on the basis of the 1954 Geneva agreements," according to the latest statements from Hanoi, but at least one high-ranking diplomat, who has just returned from the North Vietnamese capital—Ormond W. Dier, the head of the Canadian section of the International

Control Commission—says that the mood there is more intransigent than ever, and that there is no sign of any desire to negotiate now. As their euphoric broadcasts of exaggerated claims of success during the Tet attacks indicate, the Communists are relishing their present position and feel that they will soon be able to force new concessions from Washington, if not from Saigon. Their apparent purpose was, and is, to strengthen their underground bases in urban areas in order to be in a better position ultimately to force the kind of coalition solution they want and hope to control from the outset. An urban coalition would then be extended to the countryside—in effect reversing the classic Chinese Communist formula of forcing a decision in the rural areas while encircling the cities and letting them "die on the vine." And then the Vietnamese Communists' control of the border regions around Cambodia and Laos, part of the highlands, and some key cities and towns would become the basis for continuing to "fight and negotiate at the same time" in an effort to obtain the all-embracing, "final" coalition, dominated by the National Liberation Front.

Nothing like the coördinated and synchronized Tet offensive against the cities occurred earlier in this war or in the war with the French. As for what happened here in Saigon, the only comparison that can be made is with the situation in August and September of 1945, when the so-called Committee of the South, a group dominated by the Vietminh, peacefully established itself as the city's ruling government; after a month it was thrown out by a combined force consisting of British occupation forces, returning French commandos, and Japanese troops that were pressed into service before being shipped home. Ten years later, in March, 1955, a non-Communist attempt to seize the city from the Diem regime was led by the Binh Xuyen, a religious sect dominated by racketeering elements, but that, too, failed; the Binh Xuyen were defeated in sporadic fighting that lasted about a month. In both these instances, however, Saigon, though somewhat damaged, was not badly disrupted and did not suffer anything like as much physical destruction as it did in the period that began on the early morning of January 31st, when the Communist attack on the capital was launched, and ended on February 7th or 8th, when, except for some isolated sniping and other acts of harassment, the situation had—for the moment—become comparatively calm.

During the second week of February, I rode through the city, including the Chinese section of Cholon, which bore the brunt of the attack, and I flew over it in a helicopter. A dozen separate areas, comprising perhaps sixty or seventy blocks, had been totally burned out. These were almost all residential areas. From the air, I saw a number of fires still burning or smoldering. Most of the damage was the result of rocket attacks by American armed helicopters or other planes, though some of it had been caused by artillery or ground fighting. The civilian death toll in the city, as of now, is said to be six hundred, with more than four thousand civilians wounded. Fortunately, most of the population of the totally destroyed areas, which were the areas most heavily infiltrated by the Vietcong, had either been evacuated or had fled in advance of the Allied bombardments. Approximately two hundred thousand people are now homeless, and are living in municipal refugee centers or with relatives. The damage to private homes in Saigon has been estimated to run to twenty-five million dollars, but this is only a preliminary figure; the over-all damage to property is certainly much higher.

Two weeks after the attacks began, four of Saigon's nine districts were still considered "red"—that is, insecure and unsafe—and the whole city was still under a partial curfew. Government offices and some restaurants and stores in certain parts of the city were open four or five hours a day, but Saigon could not be said to be functioning at more than a half or a third of its normal pace, and complete recovery will unquestionably take a long time. The public utilities are operating, and there is enough food; ample amounts of rice and adequate amounts of pork are being distributed at emergency relief centers set up all over town. As for the Americans here, who have also been subject to the curfew, they have been getting by. The Army post exchanges reopened a week after the attack, and the Western-style food in the billets and hotels began to improve then, too. However, I did ride in a jeep up a narrow driveway in Cholon at dusk one day with a worldly sergeant who was stopping at his girl friend's house to pick up a full Vietnamese dinner pail. "A little reverse relief," he said. "It's better than the Spam I've been eating."

It has been harder to assess the damage elsewhere in the country, partly because the Communist attackers knocked out communication facilities wherever they could. It is known, though, that conditions are much worse up north in Hué, where in mid-February about a thousand Communists were still fighting bitterly in some parts of the town. American Marines and South Vietnamese troops were battling block by block and, in the old Citadel section, house by house. At least half of Hué seems to have been destroyed or damaged—the first time that this lovely and gentle northern city, sitting right in the eye of the hurricane, has felt the direct physical impact of the war. In most of the other major cities that were attacked, the amount of destruction apparently runs between twenty and thirty per cent. Among the worst hit were My Tho, Ben Tre, and Vinh Long, in the Delta (I visited Vinh Long and found a quarter of the city's homes burned out or in rubble), and Ban Me Thuot, the so-called capital of the Montagnards, or tribal people, in the highlands. Although the Communists may have failed to rally the Montagnards to their side, they came very close—far closer than elsewhere—to creating the sort of mass uprising that they had hoped to achieve throughout the country. Some six thousand tribal people, mostly members of the Rhade and Mnong tribes, were assembled by the invading forces and were marched toward Ban Me Thuot during the attack on the city, which occurred on January 29th, two days before the assault on Saigon. Columns of tribesmen, waving banners, were dispersed by heavy ground and artillery fire on their flanks, but the attackers first did a lot of damage and, it is estimated, set back by at least half a year the government's recent, and belated, program of helping the mountain people and giving them some degree of self-expression.

On a nationwide basis, the Communists have seriously disrupted the Revolutionary Development Program, through which the government has been attempting to provide economic and social assistance—as well as a measure of security—in village areas. In moving up to infiltrate the cities, they did not stop to attack the widely dispersed Revolutionary Development Teams, but the disruption of communications caused by the city assaults, to say nothing of their psychological impact, has had a drastic effect throughout the countryside. In some places, the fifty-nine-man Revolutionary Development Teams have been reassembled and are trying to get started again, but in many others the teams, along with their protective screens of Regional and Popular Forces, have not yet been heard from, and American officials estimate that the whole program, which was just beginning to make some small headway, has lost three or four months, and maybe more.

As for the total nationwide casualty figures, it may be some time before the true picture emerges. The Allied figures of about four thousand American and South Vietnamese military dead and twelve thousand wounded are relatively accurate, but the figure of five thousand two hundred Vietnamese civilians dead by the third week of February is unquestionably low—the heavy totals in Hué, for example, were not included—and the figure of twenty thousand civilians wounded is low, too. In addition, there is some doubt about the accuracy of the Allied claim of thirty-six thousand Communists killed between January 29th and February 18th. This supposedly includes only those Vietcong commandos and main-force units and North Vietnamese troops that attacked the cities, but it is conceded that it may also include several thousand civilians. Since the Communists committed between fifty and sixty thousand troops to the city attacks, and since the minimum ratio of wounded to dead is calculated to be one and a half to one, the Allied claim would indicate that virtually the total attack force of the Communists had been put out of action.

What remains hardest to gauge, and is therefore most tantalizing, is the calculation that made the Communists willing to pay such a heavy price for the limited rewards of their Tet offensive. As is always true of the Communists, the military objectives were undoubtedly reckoned carefully in terms of political purposes. These objectives and the campaign to achieve them must be considered not only in relation to the general situation in South Vietnam and to Hanoi's judgment of it—and, for that matter, to its judgment of world reactions and particularly of American public opinion and policy—but also in relation to the internal political situation of North Vietnam. Although North Vietnam is a young country in demographic terms—seventy-five per cent of the population is under thirty-five—and although only about eleven per cent of the total available manpower is engaged in military duty of any kind, there has been considerable economic deterioration and dislocation as a result of the pressures of the long war, and especially the American bombing. The country's transportation and communication systems are constantly being destroyed, repaired, and destroyed again, and although there is enough food to get by on, it is known that for almost all major commodities, including rice, there is now a black market, in which prices are as much as ten times the controlled prices—ample evidence that serious strains exist.

According to some reports, an increasing sense of impatience has been reflected in the North Vietnamese Politburo, where more or less open dissatisfaction has been expressed over the way General Vo Nguyen Giap, the Defense Minister and Commander-in-Chief, has been conducting the war. He has been criticized for not adapting sufficiently to the present difficult circumstances resulting from the tremendous weight of American technology. The military realities, especially air mobility and gigantic firepower, have made the current war altogether different from the one the Vietminh waged against the French, and though no one denies Giap's military genius, there is some feeling that he has been thinking too much in terms of that war; that is, he has been pursuing the classic three-phase strategy originally developed by the Chinese Communists, and refined by Giap himself, of advancing from a period of guerrilla resistance to one of mobile warfare, involving both defensive and offensive action, and then to a period of full-scale counter-offensive and general uprising. In the six years before mid-1965, when the Americans came to Vietnam in force, this classic approach had worked so well that the Vietcong were on the verge of launching their general offensive in the highlands and following it up with a decisive attack in the cities. But once the highlands offensive had been prevented and American pressure on the ground and in the air had begun to build up, the Communists were forced to improvise and experiment. Their traditional care and caution—mainly Giap's —in "preparing the battlefield" before beginning a major attack gave the Americans repeated opportunities to throw them off balance with mobile search-and-destroy operations, heavily supported by planes and artillery. The Communists also lost some of their long-held secret base areas in the jungle as a result of major American attacks on these sanctuaries, and by the end of 1967 their guerrilla ranks were reduced from about a hundred and twenty thousand to seventy thousand. None of this meant that the Vietcong and the North Vietnamese were on the verge of defeat, but it did prompt Giap to revise his strategy and, in effect, adopt a bolder plan than he has followed customarily. And regardless of whether or not the impetus came from Hanoi, the situation in the South made a change essential: with the increasing delay of a general offensive in the countryside, the population in the cities was in danger of forgetting about the Communists' revolutionary aims. The urban people felt comparatively secure, and if they were not pro-government, they were not pro-Communist, either; for the most part, they were cynically neutral. In fact, instead of "dying on the vine" many city people were thriving on the American cultivation of it, and the rest were at least managing to survive better than their rural compatriots, who were constantly subjected to the brutalities of the war.

It seems likely that Giap reformulated his stragegy in mid-1967, when he began to plan the present winter-spring campaign. He had been successfully, although with a heavy loss of life, pinning down large numbers of American Marines and some South Vietnamese troops below the D.M.Z. Last fall, he started large-scale attacks at Loc Ninh and Dak To. His losses continued heavy, but there were psychological benefits: he succeeded in arousing further dissatisfaction in the United States over the seeming endlessness and futility of the war. Giap also stepped up his attacks against Allied air bases, communication and transportation facilities, and logistic centers like ammunition dumps and warehouses. Giap apparently now believes that by stepping up the general offensive he may make the Americans so tired of the war, both militarily and psychologically, and the South Vietnamese so disillusioned and disorganized that a peace settlement favorable to the Communists can be reached.

Some analysts believe that Giap's new strategy indicates desperation on the part of the Communists now that they are under severe pressure in both the South and the North, and, further, that the daring decision to reverse all previous revolutionary-warfare doctrine and attack in the cities without having first fully prepared the countryside offers a classic example of the Communists' mistakenly believing their own propaganda, and thus assuming that the people of the cities would welcome them without reservation. Other experienced students of Communism and of the Vietnamese situation disagree. Despite what appeared to be an all-out offensive, in which Giap employed throughout the country about half of his total Vietcong main force of a hundred and eighteen thousand and also between five and ten thousand North Vietnamese soldiers, these analysts doubt that he and the other Communist leaders expected to achieve their maximum military and political objectives in a first assault. The actual objective, these experts say, was a limited one, involving certain definite short-term risks, and it was based on the assumption that losses would be heavy but were justifiable in preparing the final battleground in the cities and in the countryside simultaneously.

If the Communists did indeed make the decision, for tough-minded political reasons, to set up the "objective conditions" for the third, and final, stage of their general offensive, they must have had several purposes in mind. Tactically, they wanted to create a big sensation in the United States and elsewhere in the world. Strategically, the drive on the cities was meant to draw attention away from the slow tempo of their military and political offensive in the rural areas and to prove to the urban people that the Saigon government and the Americans could no longer protect them, since the Vietcong were capable of striking anywhere at any time. A second strategic purpose was to strengthen the Communists' underground bases in the cities, and to use these urban organizations for collecting taxes, food, and medicines, for distributing propaganda, and—most important—for hiding weapons and making other preparations for the next assault. In all this, the Communists achieved at least a qualified success in their Tet offensive.

Certainly there was no reason for the Americans or the Vietnamese government to doubt that some big offensive would take place at the time of Tet, and that its primary objective would be the cities. As it turned out, the assaults were astonishingly well coördinated, although there are some indications that the synchronization was not perfect. For instance, there is evidence that the attack on Saigon was originally scheduled to take place on the morning of January 30th instead of on the morning of January 31st, and thus follow the attacks on Ban Me Thuot and some other places in the highlands by one day instead of two. An attack of some sort on Saigon was expected by the police, but it was believed that this would come at the end of Tet, and not at the beginning, although on the evening of the 29th of January the Americans warned that something big was brewing and would probably take place within twenty-four hours. About a week before the attack, a cache of forty AK-47s—the guns in widest use among the Vietcong—was discovered in the city. This prompted General Nguyen Ngoc Loan, the

Chief of the National Police, to order a state of alert, and all but fifteen per cent of his police were assigned to duty during the Tet period.

Even so, there was no hard intelligence that the Vietcong would mount a multiple attack early in the morning on the thirty-first, aiming at such targets as the American Embassy, the Presidential Palace, the Joint General Staff Headquarters, the Tan Son Nhut Airport, the radio station, and South Vietnamese Naval Headquarters, or that the Saigon assault would be only one of many coördinated attacks throughout the country. The fact that the Communists were able to infiltrate so many men and weapons into the city without being detected indicated an astonishing amount of successful covert planning and organization, and it also showed that an effective underground was in existence in and around the city despite General Loan's earlier success in breaking up some elements of it. Many weapons were systematically smuggled into town weeks in advance, and were hidden in homes and in cemeteries, among other places. The agents who were to direct the attacks arrived several days in advance, and went to assigned houses, where they waited to give orders to the incoming commando units, consisting of from three to fifteen men each, that constituted the initial assault wave. On the eve of the attack, a general order of the day was issued to all participants by the headquarters of the National Liberation Front. It began with a special Tet poem written by Ho Chi Minh. Then came a statement that the assault on South Vietnamese and American installations was designed "to restore power to the people, liberate the people of the South, and fulfill our revolutionary task of establishing democracy throughout the country." The order continued, "This will be the greatest battle ever fought in the history of our country. It will bring forth worldwide changes, but will also require many sacrifices." An additional order, which referred to "the confused Americans, who are bogged down and hurting badly" and to "the expected disintegration of the Puppet Army," called on the troops to punish drastically all high-level traitors and all tyrants and to "establish a people's revolutionary government at all levels." All the attacking commando units were told that there would be a popular uprising, and that large elements of the South Vietnamese forces would desert and join them.

A distinction must be made between these commando units and

the four thousand Vietcong soldiers, in two separate battalions, who attacked the city from the south and the north. (Eventually, parts of five Vietcong battalions were in the city.) The commandos, who wore civilian clothes, were simply given orders to infiltrate into town by motor scooter, by boat, by truck, on bicycles, and on foot, and then go to designated houses, where they would get their specific instructions and, if they did not already have them, their weapons; in some cases, they were also given uniforms, including red armbands. Most of this infiltration took place on January 29th and 30th. Once the commandos had received instructions to attack specific targets—and some of the units were not assigned their objectives until almost the last moment—they became, in effect, suicide squads, since most of them had no contingency or withdrawal plans and were carrying out their orders in the expectation that they would be supported by the incoming main-force units and by the promised popular uprisings. Subsequent accounts by commandos who surrendered or were captured indicate that although ninety per cent of them detected no signs of popular support, almost all of them kept fighting until they ran out of ammunition and food, a day or two later.

Apparently, it was not expected that all the initial targets would be held—for instance, the American Embassy, which was attacked at 2:54 A.M. on the thirty-first by a score of commandos, all but two or three of whom were killed by the time the Embassy compound was resecured, six hours later. The Embassy attack was undoubtedly for show purposes, to prove to both the Vietnamese and the American people that the very symbol of "imperialist power" was vulnerable. In the case of other objectives, such as the radio station, which was captured and then blown up during a government counterattack, and the Joint General Staff Headquarters, near the airport, it was apparent that the Communists hoped to hang on with combined groups of commandos and regular soldiers until main-force troops arrived, later in the morning.

An interrogation report on a twelve-man commando squad that attacked the Naval Headquarters, along the Saigon River, throws considerable light on the detailed plans the Communists drew up. The attack, one of the boldest that had been conceived, was designed to capture the headquarters building, to employ three machine guns on its roof to neutralize the guns aboard several small

Navy vessels in the river, and then to capture these ships and use them as ferries to bring two Vietcong battalions into the city from the far shore. If the plan had succeeded, it could have affected the entire situation in Saigon quite significantly. When the attack began, early in the morning, the commandos quickly killed three Navy guards and managed to blow a hole in the side of the headquarters building, but, thanks to a general alert that had gone out six hours earlier, all twelve commandos were killed or captured. One of the survivors said that he and two other members of the team had come to Saigon together from Ben Tre, in the Delta, a day and a half in advance, carrying false identification papers; they had been told to go to a downtown movie theatre and, when they came out, to look for a man with a distinctive mark on his shirt. They did so and met the man, who took them to a house on Le Van Duyet Street, where they were told what their mission was. None of the four groups of three who met in the house had known each other until late on the evening of the twenty-ninth; in fact, they all came from different parts of the country.

The death of one or two Communist leaders of high rank, and also of some battalion company commanders in Saigon, may account for what appeared to be a degree of confusion, and even aimlessness, on the part of some of the commandos and main-force soldiers after the attack. Significantly, the Communists did not reach one of their principal Saigon objectives—the city prison, where they had hoped to liberate some five thousand persons, many of them Vietcong members or sympathizers, although elsewhere in the country, most notably in Hué and Quang Tri, they did free about five thousand prisoners. After the first two days, a good many of the Saigon invaders seemed to be confused about what part of the city they were in; quite a few were captured when they asked directions. Initially, the infiltrating commandos carried out their tasks of sniping, attacking key government positions, and assassinating officials with precision. As the days passed, however, the pattern of terror became less discriminate. Men and women who were simply suspected of helping the government had their hands cut off or were otherwise maimed. Generally speaking, though, the Vietcong behaved well toward the population. Some of them even went about helping people whose homes had been destroyed by American or government planes.

At the time the Saigon attack took place, mixed elements of some ten South Vietnamese battalions were in the city, in addition to the police. There was little cohesion among them, and the danger was at its greatest when the attacking elements from the direction of the airfield moved into the city. The Communists were trying to cut the city in half, using two main-attack elements, from the north and the south, and not until the second or third day were government reinforcements in a sufficiently strong position to keep the Communists from overrunning the city from Cholon toward the center. Even then, if it had not been for American and South Vietnamese air and artillery support, the attack might have succeeded. The Communists took full advantage of the fact that most of the damage was the result of Allied bombing and shelling, and they began stressing this in their first broadcasts to the world. Although there were occasions when government troops behaved toward the people with their traditional contempt and cruelty, by and large they conducted themselves a lot better than they might have been expected to in such a crisis. They fought especially well considering that many of their units were at half strength or less because of the Tet holiday period. General Loan's police force, which was near its full strength of seventeen thousand in the city, also fought well. The police and intelligence agencies of the government worked around the clock to keep up with the flow of information that might give them further clues to the Communists' plans. In addition to questioning prisoners intensively, they employed a number of modern devices to check persons brought in for interrogation. For example, they used an ultraviolet machine on the hands of suspects to determine whether they had fired a gun within three days.

The Americans' role during the attack was principally to throw a ring of troops around the city in order to keep reinforcements from coming in and the Communists already in the city from escaping. Nevertheless, there apparently was some movement in both directions. American tanks with infrared scopes that can pierce the darkness have roamed the outskirts of town from dusk to dawn, and flares have been filling the sky for many nights. By the fifth or sixth day, however, it was apparent that the back of the attack had been broken. About a thousand Vietcong, mostly operating in small groups, were then left in the city, and by the eighteenth the number officially given out was five hundred, but no one could estimate how many were in hiding, possibly awaiting a signal that a second major attack was beginning.

Together, Hanoi and the high command of the National Liberation Front prepared a number of special political programs for the Saigon attack. These programs were designed to have a spontaneous appeal of their own, and were therefore to be kept separate, at least at the beginning, from the program of the Front itself. Part of the idea, apparently, was to create a coalition of a new sort, with which the Americans could negotiate if they wished—the expectation, or hope, being that the Saigon government would collapse and disappear from the picture. The first troops sent into Saigon were called "revolutionary troops," or "troops with a cause," as distinct from the usual Vietcong "liberation forces," which were to follow. Defecting government elements were to be described as "troops to fight for a cause," and were to become probationary forces of the new revolutionary high command, which would afterward be embraced by the National Liberation Front. This was obviously all part of the special mystique surrounding the anticipated "general uprising," with which all the combatants had been thoroughly indoctrinated. For every combatant with a weapon, it is thought, one political officer was infiltrated into town.

The most important element of the independent coalition government that was supposed to take shape in Saigon was to be the Alliance of National and Peace Forces, or the National Alliance for Peace and Democracy, as it has also been called. This was formed January 31st, according to a barrage of broadcasts that began immediately on Radio Hanoi and on a clandestine radio of the Front somewhere near Saigon. Leaflets announcing the formation of the Alliance were also distributed throughout the city. The Alliance was ostensibly composed of "intellectuals, industrialists, representatives of political parties, and representatives of religious organizations," and its appeal was directed at the urban middle class. It had a four-point platform, calling for the overthrow of the government of President Nguyen Van Thieu and the substitution of a "power representing all strata of the South Vietnamese people"; for the withdrawal of all American forces and the establishment of an "independent, democratic, peaceful, and neutral South Vietnam"; for the restoration of "national sovereignty"; and for subsequent negotiations with the National Liberation Front, "in order to enforce the above aspirations." Much of this was obviously designed to detach the Americans from the South Vietnamese and give Washington a way of reaching an accommodation with "independent forces" that were not formally a part of the National Liberation Front.

In Hué, a similar group was established, calling itself the National Democratic Peace Alliance Front of the Central Part of Central Vietnam, and its purposes, which were much like those of the Saigon Alliance, were broadcast from the Hué radio station as soon as that was captured. Later, as the fighting in Hué intensified, the Communists announced the establishment of a Committee to Form the People's Government, and Radio Hanoi quoted a "liberation-army commentator" as saying that the entire countryside of Quang Tri and Thua Thien, the two northernmost provinces, had been liberated. Whereas the approach in Saigon has been to suggest that the Communists want to create "a movement open to Western-style democracy," in the words of one captured cadreman, the emphasis up north has been on separating that part of the country entirely from the areas to the south—perhaps in preparation for talks on unification. An attack on Khe Sanh or other northern bases would clearly support this strategy. In addition to the purely political organizations, a variety of groups were formed in Saigon, Hué, and elsewhere in an effort to draw government soldiers and "Buddhist Army men," among others, into what were collectively described as the Patriotic Armed Forces. These were the hoped-for defectors who would ultimately qualify to become part of a new revolutionary mass organization.

After the first few days, Radio Hanoi and the National Liberation Front radio began to play down the various new organizations and fall back on the Front itself as the only true revolutionary body in South Vietnam. However, the new organizations have by no means been given up, and as late as February 9th Wilfred Burchett, a correspondent with close Communist connections in Hanoi and elsewhere, quoted Nguyen Van Hieu, who is the Front's chief representative in Phnom Penh, Cambodia, as saying that the Saigon "Puppet Government" no longer existed, having been replaced by "autonomous People's Committees." On the question of negotiations, Hieu said that the problem of setting up "a provisional government" was an "agenda item" that would be "decided through consultations with other revolutionary forces and in the light of future developments." If there had been any question about these new organizations' having been created as ploys in a ritual leading in the direction of negotiations, Hieu's interview should have removed all doubts.

When the attacks began, President Nguyen Van Thieu set up a National Recovery Committee and appointed Vice-President Nguyen Cao Ky to be its chairman. Though the Committee has been successfully performing its function of distributing emergency relief, it has had no success at all in creating the sort of united political front that has been lacking for so long. The trouble, as usual, has been personal and political rivalries, and a lack of central leadership. If ever there was a need for a single national leader, it is now, but President Thieu, who is by nature a cautious man, given to withdrawing in a crisis and then trying to pick up the pieces, has been reluctant to take charge. His appointment of Ky, who has been his political rival, to head the Committee was a mistake, most observers feel, despite Ky's capabilities and the fact that he had very little to do as Vice-President. It was not that Ky would misuse his new post but that the appointment would inevitably serve to dramatize his differences with Thieu and give fresh encouragement to the ambitious underlings surrounding each of them. As things turned out, Ky soon resigned as chairman of the Recovery Committee, but the differences between his supporters and Thieu's have remained aggravated by the Tet crisis. Ky has more support in the National Assembly, and Thieu's appearance before a joint session of the Senate and the House of Representatives early in February to ask for emergency powers to deal with all economic and financial matters for one year did not go over well. The feeling of the legislators is that his request was unnecessary under the constitution, which already allows him to declare an emergency and take required steps to deal with it without seeking added executive authority. In political terms, it is felt, Thieu would have been wiser to "act like a President" from the outset of the crisis, perhaps setting himself up as the head of an emergency task force, aided by Ky and Premier Nguyen Van Loc and the Americans. In this way, he could have taken full advantage of the critical situation to forge the needed political unity. Instead, there has been an increase in factionalism and bureaucratic confusion during the recent weeks of crisis.

A new group called the Committee to Organize the People for the Safety of the Nation has now been formed, which represents a belated effort to rise above divisiveness and form a united front representing all anti-Communist forces in the country. "This is the answer to those who have long thought the nationalists are incapable of getting together," one member of the new group told me somewhat defensively. At least it does include an appreciable cross-section of Vietnamese society, and it is the first political group to do so. Thus, it could serve as an effective anti-Communist front if it manages to hold together. Though Ky has avoided any formal connection with it, most of its leaders are either pro-Ky or more inclined to support him than Thieu, and, in spite of Thieu's blessing, it risks being regarded as a pro-Ky body. The Committee's plan envisions arming some carefully chosen civilians in each block area, and instilling a will for self-help and self-defense in the population as a whole. There are those who regard the arms project as dangerous, particularly in view of the Communists' head start and of the danger that the guns, no matter how carefully they are distributed, will fall into the wrong hands. Meanwhile, as the debate goes on, time is being lost, and simply dispensing rice and medicine —and even rebuilding houses—is not enough. What is desperately needed is political leadership at the top to create unity, both within and apart from the government, and so far no such leadership is in sight. The Americans, as usual, are sitting on the sidelines and keeping their fingers crossed, making their recommendations and hoping for the best.

Everyone is waiting for the Communists to drop the other shoe. Sooner or later, it is generally agreed, the shoe will be dropped somewhere, whether at Khe Sanh or some other place in the north, in the highlands, in Saigon, in the Delta, or in several of these simultaneously. If the Communists do launch a followup to the Tet offensive soon, they will almost certainly have to use many more North Vietnamese troops than they did before. Approximately sixty thousand North Vietnamese troops are in the country, and only about ten per cent of them took part in the Tet attack. Despite what the Americans said initially, Giap also has sixty thousand main-force Vietcong troops he did not commit during Tet, but he cannot afford to spread himself too thin by using all these in another attack on the cities, and he will need time to recover from the casualties he has already suffered. Most experts are convinced that the Communists will be more selective in the next phase of their winter-spring campaign, and that belief seems to have been corroborated by the harassment actions that have taken place in the last few days, mostly on airfields around the country. Even as the Hué battle continues, Giap has begun probing other American and South Vietnamese bases below the D.M.Z.—Con Thien, Gio Linh, and Camp Carroll in the last few days. He is apparently trying to get the Americans to disperse their forces. Some American military planners, pointing out that we have far more ability to maneuver around Khe Sanh than the French had at Dien Bien Phu, advocate that we take the bull by the horns and, instead of waiting for the Communists to attack the place, go out and chase the four North Vietnamese divisions in the area with a combination of air power, artillery, and ground strikes. Khe Sanh itself, they maintain, is important only as part of the larger complex in Quang Tri Province, and we cannot afford to remain pinned down in that one part.

To anyone speculating on what might happen in the next three or four months, there seems little doubt that a conclusive phase of the war has begun. The Saigon government, despite the great military strength it has acquired from its American Allies, still lacks political motivation. If the Communists choose to enter a period of "fighting and negotiating at the same time" after another offensive, and if the conditions are established for political accommodation to begin, then Saigon will be tested by both risks and opportunities as never before. What the Communists have accomplished in the last three weeks is to throw an immense political burden on the Saigon government while placing the Americans in a kind of diplomatic limbo and keeping the possibility of negotiations in their own hands more firmly than ever.

15. Saigon

~~~~~~

March 23, 1968

In the month and a half that has passed since the Communists launched their Tet offensive, there has been a great deal of bracing talk here, and some bracing action, but for the most part the response has been the conventional one of trying to repair the damage that was done and get going again with old formulas and programs, instead of facing the realities of what is undeniably an entirely new situation. Under these circumstances, it is increasingly difficult to accept the argument of those who claim that the Tet offensive was primarily an act of desperation on the part of the Communists because of the heavy military pressure to which they were being subjected in the countryside. Hanoi's assessment of the vulnerability of the cities seems to have been thoroughly vindicated, and the assault on the cities and towns—the final total was a hundred and two—must be regarded as a carefully calculated action that is part of a synchronized political and military effort to end the war as soon as possible on Hanoi's terms. Despite the heavy losses the Communists suffered, many of which they have already recovered through recruitment in the countryside, the North Vietnamese and the Vietcong attained two major objectives. First, they greatly disrupted the operations of the government, whose second- and third-echelon officials in many of the provinces and in some of the cities were killed or captured, or have for one reason or another been absent from their posts ever since, or are able to work only ineffectually under conditions of civil chaos and bureaucratic confusion, made worse by a breakdown in communications. Second, the Communists succeeded in producing or increasing disunity between the Vietnamese and the Americans—and the Americans have also become more divided among themselves and more disheartened than they have been at any time since the independent United States commitment here began, in 1954 and 1955.

The growing breach between the Allies is demonstrated by continuing South Vietnamese comments, most of them unjustified, that the American response to the Tet attack was unduly slow, and by South Vietnamese expressions of pride in the relatively good performance of the government troops. A few days ago, Van Minh, a pseudonymous local columnist, derided the vaunted American military mobility as purely technological and geared primarily to the selfish protection of American bases. "While the Americans may be utterly unable to adjust themselves to the terms of this strange war, it is by no means too late for the South Vietnamese armed forces to de-Americanize themselves and start fighting the simple way and beating the Communists at their own game with as little American tactical support as possible," Van Minh wrote. "This may be extremely difficult at first, but it is worth the trouble for many strategic, tactical, and especially political reasons. . . . To stop smoking is painful during the first few days, but people feel better and better every day after they have done away with their undesirable and costly habit."

There are few Americans here who haven't wished that the South Vietnamese were capable of doing just what Van Minh suggests. Unfortunately, they are not capable of it. If the whole American effort seems on the verge of failure, this is surely due in large measure to South Vietnamese intransigence, to absence of South Vietnamese leadership, and to a deep-seated lack among the South Vietnamese of social and political motivation. It is almost certainly too late now to hope that the Tet events have shocked the Vietnamese into taking steps that might finally deal in a revolutionary way with what has always been a highly revolutionary situation. The most dramatic step the South Vietnamese government has taken so far is to replace eight province chiefs and to fire two incompetent corps commanders. One of the new corps commanders is a mediocrity, but the other, Major General Nguyen Duc Thang, who argued in vain for abolishing the whole corps setup, has at least moved swiftly to get his troops to fight at night, and he has also chosen to live in a trailer rather than in his predecessor's fancy house. By and large, however, the gears grind as slowly as ever, and the most serious lack of all is a feeling that the country can and must be saved from internal collapse as a result of immobility and corruption.

The Communists, who could have struck sooner but waited until now, may have achieved nearly perfect timing, even though they did overestimate the popular response they would get and underestimate the government's ability to survive. In a purely military sense, the North Vietnamese and the Vietcong probably cannot count again on the element of surprise to the extent they did during Tet, although they continue to hold the military initiative in most parts of the country, but politically and psychologically they are still capable of springing a number of surprises. They are favored not only by their own proved ability to wage both guerrilla and semi-conventional warfare but also by the government's utter inability, after all these years, and despite the kind of whining bravado represented by Van Minh, to cope with it. The result is a continuing erosion of morale and a growing sense of foreboding. Vietnamese I have known for many years are as frank as they are sad these days in their prognoses; they sound more and more like men who know they are suffering from an incurable malady.

The sense of doom may not be warranted on military grounds, but in all other respects there seems little reason for optimism. There have been fresh rumors of coups and assassinations, and though the Americans have let it be known that they would not countenance any such actions, there seems to be little they could do about it if the Vietnamese were foolish enough to attempt them—except, perhaps, get up and leave. The South Vietnamese Senate and House of Representatives have rebuked President Nguyen Van Thieu by overwhelmingly turning down his request for one year's emergency powers. Despite the evident need, there has been no real effort made to create a sense of unity at the top. Thieu's inner circle now contains two separate political groups—one headed by his brother,

Nguyen Van Kieu, and the other by his Secretary-General at the Presidency, Nguyen Van Huong—and these groups, in typical Vietnamese fashion, are squabbling with each other. About all they agree on is not joining a new and still quite amorphous political group called the National Salvation Front, the original name of which, when it was set up after Tet, was the Committee to Organize the People for the Safety of the Nation. The Front, which is headed by Senator Tran Van Don, held a meeting in Saigon on March 10th that managed to bring together almost two thousand political, religious, and tribal representatives from all over the country, and also representatives of labor, youth, social, and professional organizations. Like all other such groups through the years, the National Salvation Front has from the start been divided by internal suspicions and jealousies. It could, however, turn into an anti-government party, and this is one reason that Thieu has been reluctant to let his people join it. Another reason is Thieu's conviction—at least partly justified—that the Front prefers Vice-President Nguyen Cao Ky to him.

The Americans have worked behind the scenes to foster political unity, but, as usual, they have received little more than bland promises. One of the main causes of discontent has been the government's action in taking Thich Tri Quang, the militant Buddhist leader, into custody; this kept the Buddhists he represents as anti-government as ever, and thus restrained them from joining the National Salvation Front. Militant Catholics have also stayed out of it, and so have the representatives of the Cao Dai sect. "We have been engaged in salvation for twenty-five years and have been treated by the same doctors with the same medicines. What we need is some new ones," one critic of the Front has said. Many of the Front's organizers are northerners, who have traditionally been mistrusted by—and, in turn, have mistrusted—southern groups such as the Cao Dai and the Hoa Hao. All in all, it seems impossible, even under conditions of the gravest urgency, for the Vietnamese to get together.

One aspect of the continuing Communist political offensive that will almost certainly acquire increasing importance is a tie-in that Hanoi and the National Liberation Front have established with some of the neutralist Vietnamese leaders in Paris and in Phnom Penh, Cambodia, and also with a number of Vietnamese in Saigon,

including some in and around the government, who may be thinking in terms of a possible accommodation with the N.L.F. and
Hanoi. This development is clearly related to the attempts that the
Communists made during the Tet offensive to establish new Front
"alliances" and "committees" in Saigon and Hué as the nuclei of
new local governments. Like everything else about the offensive,
the links with Paris and Phnom Penh were prepared with great
subtlety and care over a period of many months, and they apparently have at least an indirect connection with the French policy of
wanting to see the war here ended, the Americans sent scuttling,
and the French given a chance to reëstablish economic and political
ties with their former Indo-China empire. The over-all plan is said
to have called for neutralists here and abroad to come together
after the Tet offensive had paralyzed the country and establish a
kind of "middleman" neutralist government, which would receive
the blessings of both Hanoi and the N.L.F. and would negotiate for
peace. After that, there would be a complete takeover of the new
coalition by the N.L.F. and the Lao Dong Party of North Vietnam.

Several Vietnamese known for their neutralist leanings converged on Phnom Penh from Paris at the end of January, and arrived in Saigon just before the Tet attacks. At least two of these men
held high positions under Diem, but another, interestingly enough,
was Pham Van Binh, the former governor of what is now North
Vietnam during the pre-Diem regime of Emperor Bao Dai. Two
years ago, I have been told, Hanoi urged Bao Dai to return to South
Vietnam from his exile on the Riviera, possibly as a member of a
neutralist interregnum. Bao Dai refused, but those who look for
fresh omens have been especially struck by the sudden arrival in
Saigon of a dozen or more French correspondents. I have been told
that the French business community here had definite knowledge
that some important Communist action would take place at Tet,
and that many of them left the country temporarily or sent their
families out.

Since the Tet attack, the Communists have maintained their
countrywide harassment of cities, airfields, and various Allied installations, primarily with rocket and mortar fire. They have made
occasional fresh ground assaults against about a dozen cities,
mostly in the Delta, and particularly on March 3rd and 4th, when
it seemed that a second wave of the offensive might be beginning.

They have recruited as many as thirty thousand new troops, rang- ing in age from fifteen to forty. Most of the recruiting has been done in the Delta, where the Communists moved in to fill the vacuum in the countryside following the withdrawal of American and govern- ment troops to positions of defense around the cities and the towns. Hanoi has continued to infiltrate troops both to reinforce the North Vietnamese forces now totalling a hundred and twelve thousand men in South Vietnam (five more North Vietnamese divisions are said to be alerted to move south) and to build up the main-force Vietcong units that suffered the heaviest losses during Tet. As these reinforcements have arrived, by way of the Ho Chi Minh Trail, some have gone down to the central highlands, where at least seven North Vietnamese and five Vietcong battalions are concentrated around Dak To, Kontum, and Pleiku, and the rest have been shuttled eastward through the A Shau Valley, in the north, and into Commu- nist-held areas south of Hué and Danang. Supplies—primarily am- munition—have come in along with the troops and also through Cambodia, as even Prince Sihanouk now admits. Across the whole area below the Demilitarized Zone, the Communists have demon- strated a remarkable flexibility and capacity for maneuver in the region extending from Khe Sanh to the coast and then slightly south to Quang Tri and Hué. The next major Communist attack, which is expected soon, could start below the D.M.Z., but threats have also been made against Saigon, and even the Delta.

In and around Saigon, where a strict curfew has been only slightly relaxed and commercial life is still functioning at no more than half speed, the situation continues to be critical. There are three Communist divisions to the north and northeast of the city, and other units, of up to regimental size, to the west and to the east. There have been probes only a few miles from the city, but so far the Communists have not carried out their repeated threat, dis- seminated by word of mouth and by leaflets to the already jittery population, to make another attack on the city itself. My room boys at the Hotel Continental daily bring me new reports and show me leaflets advising them and their families to get out of town. Vast quantities of 107-millimetre and 122-millimetre rockets are being brought into areas close to the city along the myriad canals, which at this time of year are fully navigable by boats a good deal larger than sampans. These weapons are being secreted along the banks in clusters of four or five. There is little doubt that the city is being heavily infiltrated. The Communist underground in Saigon, and especially in Cholon, the Chinese section, has remained essentially intact since the Tet attack. Literally thousands of people, including prostitutes and "cowboy" hoodlums, are part of this intricate organization. Secret caches of weapons are still being established everywhere in the Saigon area, and different parts of Cholon are said to be connected by tunnels running from street to street and from house to house.

The situation in the north, where I spent the first week of March, is, if anything, more critical than the situation in Saigon. The Communists held Hué for most of February, and they have now massed nearly twelve thousand troops around the city, which, being still in a state of shock, is both militarily and politically vulnerable. Nothing I saw during the Second World War in the Pacific, during the Korean war, or in the Vietnam war so far has been as terrible, in terms of destruction and despair, as what I saw in Hué. Before the Tet offensive, the city's charm and beauty were often compared to those of Peking. Now much of the city—particularly the old, walled part of it on the northern side of the Perfume River, which is known as the Citadel, and which includes the Imperial Palace—is in complete ruins. There are ninety thousand refugees or people receiving aid in Hué. Women and children wander crying through the rubble, picking up the broken bits of their possessions, gathering watercress from the ponds to eat or sell, collecting bricks, begging from strangers. I walked down Le Loi Street, on the south side of town, and found a once lovely waterfront park littered with garbage and broken telephone wires. The large hospital area was packed with refugees. Nearly four thousand civilians were killed in Hué, most of them by the American air and artillery attacks that were called upon to dislodge the North Vietnamese and Vietcong forces, which held the city stubbornly as long as they could.

In Hué as elsewhere, both the American and the government forces, caught off guard, reacted belatedly to the Communist attack, which began early on the morning of January 31st, when the city was teeming with Tet celebrants. The bitter fighting dragged on, costing some of the Vietnamese and American Marine battalions half their strength in killed and wounded, and the Americans cursed the bad weather, which favored the Communists. At last, when the clouds lifted, the Americans called in their helicopter gunships and their heavy artillery. There was a great deal of house-to-house fighting, but the American Marines, unaccustomed to fighting in cities, operated as if they were taking hills instead of houses: they probed and then withdrew, and relied on heavy weapons. If this tactic saved some American lives, it also added greatly to the number of Vietnamese corpses. Throughout the city, along the sidewalks, in the gardens of houses that are still standing and amid the rubble of houses that aren't, crude graves—simple oblong mounds of earth marked by a stick with a name on it, and perhaps a twig or a small plastic flower—tell the story of the death of Hué.

Nothing that the Americans did, including some looting by young, inexperienced Marines, excuses what the North Vietnamese and the Vietcong did to the city. In the words of Robert Kelly, the previous senior American adviser in the area, who was sent back to Hué when his successor was one of thirty American civilians killed, captured, or missing during the battle, "Hué was like a naked woman. The people of the city just didn't believe the Communists would ever do this here." Kelly, who has six years of experience in Vietnam and is about to leave, is deeply committed to the Vietnamese people and believes strongly in the necessity of our involvement in Vietnam, but he has also been highly critical of the American failures here. His difficulties are typical of Americans who have genuinely tried to improve the people's welfare in the face of apathy, corruption, official Vietnamese obstruction, and American policies that are frequently confused and contradictory. Surveying the ruins of Hué, Kelly spoke bitterly of the lack of interest some people had shown in anything but saving their own skins and either getting out or, as in the case of officials in power, making money out of the relief programs.

Even before the Tet offensive, Hué's officials were widely known for inefficiency and corruption. The Mayor, Lieutenant Colonel Phan Van Khoa, who was also chief of Thua Thien Province, is said to have had two days' warning from the Vietcong that the attack was coming and hid for six days in the rafters of a hospital. He later explained that he had let the Communists enter the city so that they could be trapped there. When he came out of hiding, Khoa lost no time in making money out of the emergency shipments of rice sent into the stricken city. Finally, this past week, President Thieu

visited Hué and fired Khoa, but what the city's government desperately needs is not just a reshuffling of officials but a complete overhaul. Certainly nothing will be accomplished by simply resuming
where things left off when the Tet attack began. Not only is Hué's
spirit broken, but it is a bureaucratic mess. The Communists raided
the city treasury, stole all the records, and destroyed the water, gas,
and electric systems. Some progress could be made toward establishing a degree of administrative and political stability by giving
more authority to six Revolutionary Development Teams that are
in Hué because they had to flee from nearby hamlets during the Tet
offensive. These teams, made up of some fifty men each, have already been assigned to help with relief work in the city, and they
will probably not be able to get back to their hamlets for some time
anyway, especially if military action starts again.

After leaving Hué, I flew in a small observation plane over Khe
Sanh. In the past two weeks, according to intelligence reports, the
North Vietnamese have moved part of one of their divisions around
Khe Sanh to the east, into the vicinity of Camp Carroll, the artillery
base fourteen miles away, and have moved another part farther
east, into the vicinity of other Allied bases. But they still have major
elements of two divisions, totalling fifteen thousand men, in the
hills around Khe Sanh, where the Americans and the South Vietnamese have some six thousand troops. The Communists have assembled a tremendous arsenal in the surrounding hills and
constantly throw rocket and mortar shells into the base, which
consists of little more than an airstrip and some fortified bunkers.
The enemy's heavy artillery is hidden away in the mountains, as it
was when the French made their disastrous stand at Dien Bien Phu.
The Communists are also believed to have "red-eye" missiles,
which are attracted to a target by heat, and to have not only Rus-
sian-built tanks but Russian fighters and bombers that can come
down from North Vietnamese bases, do their bombing and strafing,
and then land at some newly built emergency airstrips just north
of the D.M.Z. An attack on Khe Sanh has been expected ever since
Tet, and the general assumption has been that it would come soon
—certainly before the end of the month, when the monsoon
weather will more or less clear, enabling the Americans to count on
increased support from the air.

There has been considerable debate about the wisdom of the

Americans' getting themselves into a static defensive position at Khe Sanh, but the justification—which clearly impresses a majority of our officers, at any rate—is that the base must be protected because it stands at the focal point of the entire southward invasion route. Unfortunately, the Americans allowed the North Vietnamese to invest the base heavily before they began their own buildup, so they have not been able to take the offensive and maneuver around it. The Dien Bien Phu analogy can easily be carried too far, but it makes an interesting study nevertheless. For example, a new "provisional corps" area was created this week in the two northernmost provinces, to be headed by Army Lieutenant General William B. Rosson, who in respect to all operational matters is supposed to be responsible to the American commander in I Corps, Marine Lieutenant General Robert E. Cushman, Jr., in Danang, but will actually be taking orders from General Westmoreland, in Saigon. There has always been jealousy between the Marines and the Army, and the Marines don't like the idea of having a new headquarters superimposed on them, any more than they liked losing operational control over their Marine air wing to the Air Force. The Vietnamese are recalling a parallel situation in the Indo-China War, when two French generals had different ideas about defending Dien Bien Phu and attacking in the Red River Delta. "The French had Navarre and Cogny," it is pointed out. "You have Rosson and Cushman."

While flying over the base, at altitudes ranging from several hundred to several thousand feet, I got a clear picture of the countless trenches that the North Vietnamese are building, some of which run almost to the edge of the airstrip. During the whole time our plane was over Khe Sanh, the pilot kept switching back and forth among four or five radio channels with which he had to keep in touch in order to guide in the large C-130 transport dropping supplies by parachute. In the background, over another channel, the Armed Forces Network Vietnam station in Saigon played soft jazz, and at one point, just as a big transport was dropping some supplies by parachute at the western end of Khe Sanh, we heard a news bulletin that President Johnson was still considering whether to dispatch two hundred thousand more troops to Vietnam.

16. # Saigon

~~~~~~

June 29, 1968

While the pattern of the negotiations in Paris is not yet clear, the consensus here is that there will be no final settlement for years and that we are now getting, in Vietnam, a significant preview of the slow-moving drama for which the Paris talks have so far provided only a tiresome prologue. While considerable fighting has been going on since the beginning of May, and it is likely to spread during the coming months, the essential struggle remains political. Although the Communists retain the military initiative in many places, and in some cases can still count on the element of surprise, they have basically been denied one of their most important assets —the opportunity for careful preparation of the battlefield. In the past, their detailed planning of every aspect of impending battles has involved steps ranging from the caching of food and weapons and the building of emergency underground hospitals to the preparation of models of the terrain. Mobile American and South Vietnamese spoiling operations, conducted with the aid of troop-carrying helicopters and supported by heavy air and artillery assaults, have now effectively deprived the Communists of this advantage. Their ability to carry out harassing actions, as they have against Saigon for the past several weeks, is certainly undiminished, and as rockets and mortar shells have continued to drop into the capital the population's nerves have begun to wear thin. But nowhere, with the possible exception of the central highlands—where there are estimated to be elements of two North Vietnamese divisions secreted in jungle bases near the Cambodian border—are the Communists being given a chance to mount and sustain a new major assault. Thus, militarily, they may again be faced with the need to develop a new strategy, and it is quite possible that in due time they will be forced to switch from overt military action back to their own highly developed forms of guerrilla warfare.

Since Tet, new political tactics have been designed to meet the strategic requirements of what Hanoi calls "fighting and negotiating at the same time." These may be described as the careful preparation of the political battlefield to deal with various contingencies that may result from the Paris talks, and in this realm, where the Americans can offer the South Vietnamese only advice and some assistance, the Communists must still be granted a considerable edge. This does not mean that Hanoi and its southern representatives are not having trouble politically as well as militarily. Perhaps most important are their problems in that area where these two principal prongs of insurrectionary warfare come together, at the critical village and hamlet level. The Communists are finding it harder to recruit new guerrillas, to fight either in local areas or in the regional and main forces, and this is the chief reason the main-force military units, totalling about a hundred and twenty-five thousand, are now dominated by some eighty-five thousand North Vietnamese troops—who are currently being infiltrated at a higher monthly rate than ever. There has been increasing resentment over harsher methods adopted by the Communists, who, since Tet, have been prompted more and more to substitute terror for quiet indoctrination and persuasion. The causes of the villagers' resentment include the kidnapping of boys and men from fourteen to forty-five to serve as soldiers or laborers, the increased forcible recruitment of women, and the shooting of those suspected of being government spies. During the attacks on Saigon and other cities in the last few months, the open resort to terror has represented a calculated risk on the part of the Communists; they have gambled, not without justification, on the assumption that the popular resentment against their rocket and mortar attacks on civilian areas and their infiltration of bands of troops will be less than that aroused by the destruction of homes by retaliating American gunships and by the often indiscriminate and wanton counterattacks of government forces. In the countryside, the villagers' response to the increase of terror and the continued intrusion of the war on their lives has been new resignation and despair. As they flee toward the still relatively safer urban areas, they may not love the government more but they seem to be loving the Communists less.

Despite all this, the Communists appear to be preparing the political battlefield for the forthcoming months much better than the Saigon government, because they know what they want and they know how to use their still intact rural and urban apparatus to go about getting it. Furthermore, their appeals, in patriotic as well as in revolutionary terms, still carry considerable weight, particularly when they are directed against the "white American invader" whose "lackey" is "the corrupt Thieu-Ky clique." Whatever degree of distortion and untruth there may be in the Communists' appeals, the historic struggle for the independence of Vietnam, which they have long dominated (and which to a large extent they have subverted), remains a real one, and the government has not succeeded in capturing the revolution for itself. Since Tet, as new social and political problems have emerged, and as the people have become more conscious of the Communist threat and of the extreme means the Communists are now willing to adopt to achieve their ends, neither the Vietnamese government nor the Americans have yet been able to deal with the challenge in a positive and comprehensive manner. As a Vietnamese whom I have known well for a long time put it the other day, "There has been no real effort to study the meaning of the Tet offensive and what has taken place since in the total context of the war. You Americans still don't have a policy— you just have measures. It's the same with us. We improvise, take single steps to improve the situation, and even then—as in the case of our recent new plans for national mobilization—we flounder around for weeks as our President fights with our Senate and House. There is no constitutional machinery for compromise. Nothing is done in political terms to bring together the constructive social forces that still exist in this country. There is fluidity and plenty of rivalry, but no tactical mobility and no attempt at achieving a consensus.

"There is much we must blame ourselves for, but much of what has happened is your fault. At the end of the Second World War, you decided who should go where in Asia and occupy what. The French returned here—and you helped keep them here, with your guns and your money—for nine more long years. It was natural enough that the French should try to manufacture a fake nationalism with mandarin officials, but why did you have to do the same when you moved in, in 1954? You came to Vietnam without any preparation and therefore without understanding, yet you forced us to adjust to your anti-Communist objectives without helping us develop our own democratic ones. You were afraid of Diem, until it was too late to get him to change his ways and to get rid of his brother Nhu. You ended by creating a vacuum the Communists were best prepared to fill. The strongest non-Communist political party in the country became USAID [the American economic-aid program], and now you wonder why so many Vietnamese are corrupt. You brought an American army here, and you made a Western army out of ours, but it has never been a national army and it still doesn't know how to fight a war of insurgency or how to deal with the people. We are no longer the makers of our own destiny. We are the victims of your global policy."

These are very strong words, but after many years of experience in Vietnam I cannot contradict them. My friend said, in conclusion, without any implied cynicism, that, despite all our mistakes of omission and commission, "if the Americans had not come to South Vietnam, we would have gone Communist long ago, so we do not regret your being here—and we will do everything we can to keep you here, because we need you even more, economically, without a war."

It would be nice to be able to say that, given the gambles the Communists have taken and the heavy losses they have suffered—the Allies claim this year to have killed ninety-two thousand of the enemy by mid-May, which equals the total claimed for all of 1967—the government is now in a stronger position to regain some of the political and military ground it has lost and to win over elements of the population that it has previously neglected or antagonized. Unfortunately, I do not think this is the case. There is reason to be pleased, certainly, over the selection as Prime Minister of Tran Van Huong, a respected, independent-minded, and honest nationalist, in place of the colorless Nguyen Van Loc, but almost everyone agrees that it would have been better if Huong had been appointed initially, which might have been possible if the Americans had made absolutely clear their determination to protect him from encroachments by the military. The Americans chose instead to concentrate on building up Thieu at the expense of Ky, their earlier favorite— a process that has now culminated in the almost complete eclipse of Ky and his aides, including the just deposed National Police Chief, Major General Nguyen Ngoc Loan. Thieu, who plots and moves carefully and cautiously, has played his cards well. First, he mollified Ky by giving him a man of his choice, Loc, as Prime Minister. Then, when he felt himself in a strong enough position, he got rid of Loc and belatedly called on Huong, who agreed to take the job despite the fact that, in addition to being in a weak position constitutionally vis-à-vis the President, he now has little political leverage at present against Thieu and his fellow-generals. Even Huong's closest friends and well-wishers don't give him more than a twenty-five-per-cent chance of making something of the job, and they feel that Thieu will simply use him as a convenient instrument to eliminate any remaining opposition from Ky or anyone else. As one of Huong's friends has said, "The P.M. is like a baby born in prison."

Huong, who favors peace with "honor and real guarantees" and is against any kind of sellout to the Communists, made an excellent initial televised address to the nation, bluntly telling the people, "We are invaded, we are dependent, our ranks are divided." The divisiveness was underlined by the difficulty he had in choosing a Cabinet. He wanted a group representing various religious and political elements, but he ran into trouble getting a number of those he approached to agree to work with one another or to take one specific job instead of another. The end result was scarcely a Cabinet calculated to have a strong popular following or a strong civilian image of its own, and it will be up to Huong alone to provide that. His modesty has won him new friends—probably more than when he previously held the Prime Ministership for a frantic and futile three months in 1964-65—and so have his wry comments on his problems. About his predicament in forming a government, he said, "I went to the market to buy good fish, good shrimps, and good chickens to cook delicious dishes for my guests. Unfortunately, I did not find what I wanted, so I had to improvise."

The main problem Huong faces, that of rallying the many disparate elements among the South Vietnamese, will not be made easier
by the prevailing popular mood, which is perhaps more difficult to
define at present than at any time since the "big war" mounted by
the Americans began in 1965. It might best be generally described
as one of watchful waiting—*"attentisme"* is the French word—but
there are various new shadings, ranging from quiet withdrawal to
nervous anticipation over the possible departure of the Americans
and a growing predilection for neutralism. These reactions are
most prevalent among urban intellectuals and professional people,
whose views scarcely reflect those of the bulk of the population in
the countryside but do represent the opinions of some important
groups, including religious ones—elements among the Buddhists;
the Hoa Hao and Cao Dai sects, for example—which are either
willingly or willfully disaffected toward the government and look
forward to its disintegration, so that they can pick up the pieces.
Such groups talk vaguely of *their* programs, even of *their* revolu-
tions, but their approach is essentially negative or opportunistic.
Among their ranks, however, are some genuine nationalists who
believe in a real unity of forces, and they may yet create a new
resistance in the South in the event of a widely unpopular peace or
a permanent stalemate. Other organizations, such as the Confederation of Vietnamese Laborers, which represents the largest group
of unions and which is moving for the first time into the political
arena, have begun to come forth with specific programs for building
meaningful political parties and even for creating a "people's
army," in the expectation that the war will go on indefinitely.

Decentralization, including local self-defense in the cities, villages, and hamlets, has become a rallying cry for a variety of groups
and individuals, including Vice-President Ky, who has mixed his
recent xenophobic line with a fresh nationalist fervor; he has
spoken out against "colonial slavery," obviously referring to the
Americans, and has even had favorable things to say about Ho Chi
Minh. Both Thieu and Ky, while politely vying for power, have
quietly thrown out their own political fishing lines. They have kept
in touch, through their separate agents, with neutralist Vietnamese
groups in Phnom Penh and in Paris. In Thieu's behalf, according to
a reliable source, a member of his private planning staff, named Le
Trung Kim, who is an agricultural engineer by profession and who

has had close neutralist associations in the past, has been circulating among the Vietnamese expatriates in Paris, most of whom are neutralists, and probably among members of the Hanoi delegation as well. A story that has floated out of Eastern Europe and that is being repeated here has it that Thieu might, under certain circumstances, be acceptable as a neutralist front man in a future government that included the Communists. Thieu himself, while he has given no indication of his willingness to play such a game, has said he will talk about the future with *individual* members of the National Liberation Front, but he has remained adamant about not negotiating with the Front as such. As for Ky, he, too, has his man in Paris, who was sent there by his close friend, the just dismissed police chief, General Loan. This man's name is Le Doan Kim, and though he is no relation to the other Kim, he has also been close to the expatriate neutralists in the past, and for the last two years he has been moving back and forth between Europe and Vietnam via Phnom Penh, apparently more in the role of an *agent provocateur* than anything else. Interestingly, Hanoi has privately encouraged these neutralist ploys. Jacques Duclos, a member of the Central Committee of the French Communist Party, said, after a visit to Hanoi last March, that Le Duan, the First Secretary of the Lao Dong Party of North Vietnam, told him that the future government of South Vietnam could include both "pro-French and pro-American neutralist elements."

On the badly fragmented government side, there is only fuzziness and confusion in approaching the question of South Vietnam's postwar status. Once again there has been no preparation of any political battlefield. And this is simply a further reflection of the incontrovertible fact that the Communists, under that redoubtable superorganizer Ho Chi Minh, captured the nationalist movement of the country back in 1945, killed or dispersed the anti- or non-Communist leaders and elements that had originally joined them in the broad Vietminh Front, and ever since have determined the course of the Vietnamese revolution. The dozen or so members of the ruling Politburo in Hanoi, whatever their attitudes toward pro-Chinese or pro-Russian factionalism, have held together more tightly than any other Communist ruling body in the world and have been able to shift their military and political strategy as they have seen fit over the years—advancing, retreating, and modifying.

Countless successive governments in the South, under the French, under Emperor Bao Dai, under Diem, under the seemingly endless procession of military and shadow civilian bodies and leaders— juntas, councils, troikas, directories, Chiefs of State, Presidents, and Prime Ministers—have unavailingly sought to contend with this precisely steered Communist machine. There have been in the South countless economic, social, and political experiments—from the early French-sponsored *agrovilles* and the Diem-sponsored strategic hamlets to today's Revolutionary Development schemes and "new-life" hamlets, and from hand-picked advisory councils and national assemblies under the French and Diem to today's elected legislature and local village and hamlet councils—yet none of these, including the present "legally elected" government the Americans so avidly sought (prematurely, in the opinion of many observers, including this one), has served to rally or inspire the country or to effectively counter the better-organized, more single-minded Communist apparatus.

As a consequence, whatever the reasons that prompted Hanoi to go to Paris—whether the Communists were "hurting" that badly, as the American military likes to say, or whether they are simply seeking to buy time—the blueprint that the leaders in Hanoi have for South Vietnam today is unmatched in clarity and incisiveness and political convictions, and perhaps unmatchable by anything the Americans or the South Vietnamese can offer. This blueprint, over the last few months, has become even clearer. In its most fundamental form, it was revealed, in 1965, in "Four Points," published by Hanoi, and "Five Points," published by the National Liberation Front. These two manifestos stipulated as most important the complete withdrawal of the Americans and South Vietnam's ultimate reunification with the North without "foreign interference" and in accordance with the "popular will," as exemplified by the Front. The accomplishment of these objectives represents the Communists' Program Maximum, and it was their hope that by achieving a knockout victory with the Tet offensive they would be in a position to force the Americans to back down and out. The offensive failed, but its sensational impact undoubtedly helped prompt President Johnson's decision to reduce the level of the bombing of North Vietnam and to offer to negotiate. Hanoi's acceptance of the offer to start preliminary talks, on its own terms, prepared the way for the achievement of the Communists' Program Medium or Program Minimum—which, though Program Maximum has still not been discarded, represent, respectively, a carefully calculated first line of retreat and then, if necessary, a second line of retreat. The medium objective, which could presumably be reached after protracted and probably secret talks in Paris or elsewhere, is a coalition government, which the Communists would hope quickly to control. The minimum objective is a lesser form of accommodation in the South, assuring freedom of activity for all political elements, through which the Communists would seek to gain control through new nationalist political parties.

By continuing and even stepping up the fighting while talks go on, the Communists hope to achieve two things: first, to convince the Americans and South Vietnamese that they are still able to wage a protracted war, and, second, to persuade the South Vietnamese people that they cannot lose. It should already be clear that the area of maneuver for the Communists in Paris is greater than that for the Americans, principally because we expressed only minimum demands at the outset—i.e., we requested some reciprocal action for stopping all the bombing—while, even if the Communists' maximum and minimum demands were not openly stated, the potential range of these demands is apparent. For instance, should there be a discussion about establishing a bigger and better buffer zone between North and South Vietnam, Hanoi would undoubtedly lay claim to Quang Tri and Thua Thien, the two northernmost provinces of South Vietnam; it has all along controlled large parts of both, and administratively and militarily it has for some time considered them to be part of its southernmost military region. By extension, Hanoi would very likely also claim the two northern Laotian provinces of Phong Saly and Houa Phan.

If Hanoi is thinking in terms of protracted negotiations, as is likely, the debate over such demands or issues could drag on for months, to be finally compromised or abandoned, all of which would admirably suit its "fight and talk" strategy. The United States would be almost continuously on the defensive, and, in its anxiety to find something substantive to talk about, would repeatedly find itself forced to devote serious consideration to Hanoi's most extreme demands. What worries the South Vietnamese, even those among them who believe in some sort of ultimate accommodation, is that American impatience might lead to a premature settlement, which would, in effect, amount to political surrender. By and large, virtually all South Vietnamese I have spoken with, in and out of the government, pro- or anti-American, feel that we forced negotiations too soon, before the Saigon government and the country at large were militarily and politically ready for them. They are afraid that, as was the case with Premier Mendès-France in 1954, President Johnson will be racing against the clock, and that, his insistence upon "peace with honor" notwithstanding, he will try his hardest to reach an agreement of some sort before he leaves the White House. While everyone here wants peace, too, there is a feeling that if the military regime starts dealing with the National Liberation Front without first building up more mass support, the outcome will be disastrous.

In contrast to the government's lack of readiness, the Communists' preparation of the present political battlefield dates back at least to 1966. While the Communists were opposed to negotiating too early, they hoped, as a result of their 1966-67 military campaign, to turn the tide sufficiently so that they would be in a position to start talking. Despite American escalation, the North Vietnamese tried to keep to their schedule, and late in 1966, according to a captured top-level cadreman named Le Ngoc Lan, alias Ba Tra, with whom I have just had several long conversations, Hanoi so informed both Moscow and Peking. Ba Tra corroborated a report that Prime Minister Pham Van Dong at that time travelled secretly to Moscow and obtained the Russians' pledge of continued military and economic aid, as well as their approval of Hanoi's peace plans. Le Duan simultaneously headed a delegation to Peking; not unexpectedly, he ran into trouble when the Chinese insisted that the North Vietnamese continue fighting indefinitely—or for "seven more years," if necessary, by which time, said Mao's representatives, China would be strong enough to resolve the situation. However, the North Vietnamese in Peking stuck to their proposed timetable. As Ba Tra told me, he and other ranking cadremen were informed of their government's decision, and of consultations with the two Communist powers, at a secret jungle meeting northwest of Saigon in April, 1967.

A thin, soft-spoken man, now fifty years old, Ba Tra was born in the South and attended school in My Tho, where Prime Minister

Huong was one of his teachers. He joined the resistance of 1945 and became a Party member four years later. He never went to North Vietnam but always operated in the South, and after 1955 he worked steadily among the intellectuals and bourgeoisie in Saigon, first in the open, and, after 1958, underground. Beginning in 1966, Ba Tra told me, he and others of his group convinced the Front that it had to make "a special appeal to people in the urban areas, particularly to bourgeois and intellectual elements who disapproved of the government and who were sympathetic to our cause but believed the Front was 'too Red.'" With the approval of Hanoi, Ba Tra received permission to establish a number of legal fronts that would come out in favor of national sovereignty, freedom, democracy, and peace; the term "neutrality" was not initially used, because it was felt that this would be too much of a Communist giveaway. The first group he helped promote was the Committee for the Protection of the National Culture. Additional organizations and fronts that Ba Tra and his associates secretly helped create included the Committee for a Self-Sufficient Economy, the Association for the Protection of the Personality of Vietnamese Women, the Association for Improved Relations Between Vietnamese Classes, and the Movement for Student Autonomy. By mid-1967, these organizations had spread their wings and were gaining increasing support among university professors and other intellectuals, as well as among members of the bourgeoisie, but when Ba Tra and some other top-level Front cademen were arrested in the spring and summer of last year, the various groups fell apart and most of the unwitting members realized they had been used as Communist dupes.

Although they had suffered a setback, the Communists by no means gave up their tactic of creating new fronts, and in the months before this year's Tet offensive, which they hoped would trigger what they called "the general uprising," they established a whole new series of political "alliances," designed to attract intellectuals and prominent professional people; territorial "administrative organizations" in the provinces and cities; "insurrectionary committees"; and proselyting "armed-forces groups," which, among other things, were supposed to encourage military and civilian defectors from the government side. As the National Liberation Front itself pointed out, there was nothing new about this tactic, which had been applied successfully in North Vietnam in 1945, when the Communists established first the Vietminh Front and later the Lien Viet and Fatherland Fronts. "The more allies we can find, even precarious ones and temporary ones, the better," one document said. "A sound Front policy is one of the decisive factors for a successful revolution. It is only when the Front has real strength that it can secure the participation of in-between forces and recruit in-between classes such as nationalist bourgeoisie who are opposed to imperialism in certain respects but are essentially reformers and compromisers."

According to Ba Tra and others, the long-term strategic goals of Hanoi and the Front were first to create a "Socialist" state in South Vietnam and then to tie it to the Communist North, but the tactic governing the various alliances and committees during the Tet offensive was to stress "peace, neutrality, and coalition government." All the bodies and groups established just before and during Tet had different names—at least seventeen were identified, and the Vietcong and Hanoi claimed that "hundreds" of others had been created throughout the country. The principal urban alliances were not supposed to represent new revolutionary movements in themselves, at least not initially, nor were they to be overt Vietcong organizations. They were to act as independent "united-front" groups, and after demanding the withdrawal of American troops and establishing their *bona fides,* they were to portray themselves as the true representatives of the people in negotiating for a coalition government, *not with Saigon but with the National Liberation Front.* From the outset, both the Front's Liberation Radio and Radio Hanoi acted as channels for disseminating the various communiqués and appeals of the "spontaneous" organizations, all of which—with the exception of two in Hué, the only city held by the Communists until almost the end of February—were short-lived, as the general uprising failed to materialize and the Vietcong were forced to retreat within hours or days from the urban areas they had attacked.

In Hué, the National, Democratic, and Peace Alliance Front and the Thua Thien Province–Hué People's Revolutionary Committee were both headed by Le Van Hao, a former professor of anthropology at the universities of Saigon and Hué. The first appeal of this particular Front, read over the captured Hué radio on February 1st and later rebroadcast by Hanoi, declared, "Dear compatriots: We cannot stand with folded arms and see our country fall into the hands of the U.S. aggressors and the Thieu-Ky clique of traitors. We can no longer endure slavery, exploitation, poverty, and misery. We cannot let the U.S. aggressors and their lackeys prolong a war which only serves their selfish interests. We only want independence, sovereignty, freedom, democracy, peace, neutrality, food, clothes, and land." In the weeks that followed, as the Communists clung to Hué and a fierce battle raged in that old city, Le Van Hao issued several more communiqués, as well as open letters to U Thant at the United Nations and to the heads of various nations, denouncing American policy and acclaiming the deeds of the revolutionary forces. The Thua Thien People's Revolutionary Committee finally announced the establishment of a provincial administration and outlined a new revolutionary-government program. When the Americans and the South Vietnamese at last recaptured Hué, the revolutionary groups, led by Le Van Hao, left the city with the Communist troops and set up new headquarters in the nearby jungle.

The post-Tet political activity of the Communists has to be placed in historical context. In 1964, at the hamlet and village level in the Communist areas there theoretically existed a three-level organization: the local chapter of the People's Revolutionary Party, which is the South Vietnamese wing of the Lao Dong Party in the North; the National Liberation Front and its various member groups, for farmers, women, youth, and so on; and the so-called Autonomous Administrative Committees, or Village Liberation Committees, which were supposed to be modelled on the local People's Councils in North Vietnam. These committees were ostensibly chosen by "elections" but in fact were appointed by the local cadres of the P.R.P., who headed the Party's sections on finance and economy, security and propaganda, and so on; the P.R.P. also increasingly tightened its control over all the branches of the N.L.F. Late in 1966, the establishment of the Liberation Committees was postponed, and the broader "peace, neutrality, and coalition government" tactic referred to by Ba Tra was adopted instead. But a year later, when the Tet offensive was being planned, the Communists ordered the establishment of the Liberation Committees resumed and said this job should be completed by the end of January, 1968. Specifically for coalition purposes, they were to form a Vietcong structure parallel to that of the government. By the time the Tet attacks took place, an unknown number of these committees had been set up.

An important directive from the Central Office for South Vietnam—Hanoi's southern administrative arm—dated March 5th, made it clear that in the wake of the limited achievements of the Tet offensive the new plan was a flexible one, designed to meet the demands of continued fighting while the approach to local accommodation and coalition government continued. The emphasis in this document was on consolidating local strength in order to achieve one of three options: total victory, coalition, or a return, if necessary, to protracted war. There was no longer any specific reference to the general uprising. Village People's Liberation Councils were now to be set up in the Communist areas; there were to be fifteen members in villages with a population of three thousand or less, from twenty to twenty-five members in villages of from three to five thousand population, and from thirty to thirty-five in those with more than five thousand. Below these Councils, Village Liberation Committees of from five to seven members were to carry out the orders of the Councils and supervise military and security matters, food production, finance, information and cultural affairs, and education and health.

What the Communists called the "second phase" of their "winter-spring offensive" took place on February 17th-18th, when scores of cities and towns throughout South Vietnam were attacked—most of them by rocket and mortar barrages and not by ground forces. The "third phase" involved the more serious attacks that began on May 5th and lasted approximately a week. Unlike the Tet offensive, which was conducted by the Vietcong while North Vietnamese troops were held back, the May drive was mounted almost completely by North Vietnamese forces. This time, although there again was evidence of careful planning, the Communists did not have the advantage of complete surprise. Individual attacking units, many of them under strength, lacked the knowledge of the local terrain and of the cities that the Vietcong troops had had at Tet, and a number of them got lost. The bulk of the forces that attacked Saigon were intercepted to the north and never reached their objectives. Those that did reach the fringes of the city, from the south and west, fought hard but suffered heavy casualties, and were driven from the suburbs by mid-May. Nevertheless, the May offensive did show that the Communists still packed a heavy punch and that they were still able to attack in the cities as well as in the countryside; the harassment and infiltration tactics that they have practiced since show further that they have applied the lessons learned during both Tet and early May, and that they are now making the most of small-scale attacks, in up to platoon strength, while capitalizing on their new capability to hurl heavy mortar shells and rockets into Saigon from hidden locations two or three miles away.

Perhaps more important, the Communists, having tested their new political apparatus, have now established a functioning umbrella organization to deal with the future problem of coalition. This is the Alliance of National, Democratic, and Peace Forces of Vietnam, which was formed at a meeting on April 20th and 21st "at a locality near the Saigon-Cholon area," according to Liberation Radio, and was attended by "many notables, intellectuals, scholars, teachers, students, writers, influential businessmen, civil servants, private-enterprise employees, and officers of all sections representing different political and religious organizations in southern cities." A few days later, the Communist radio network and press agencies made public a communiqué and a manifesto issued by the new Alliance and named the members of its ten-man central committee, headed by a well-known Saigon lawyer named Trinh Dinh Thao. Thao and his fellow committee members had apparently left Saigon for secret headquarters, believed to be somewhere in the Delta, during the previous month.

The communiqué declared that the opening conference had been "aimed at working out a unified line and unifying the organizations of various alliances which have emerged and are vigorously developing in the towns." It excoriated the United States for having "sabotaged the Geneva agreements on Vietnam" and "rigged up a series of puppet governments . . . launched a war of aggression against the South Vietnamese people, and turned South Vietnam into a new-type colony of the U.S." The Alliance, according to the communiqué, had "gradually emerged" with the aim of "uniting all patriotic forces and individuals determined to resist foreign aggression, overthrowing the Thieu-Ky puppet regime, establishing a national coalition administration, and achieving independence, democracy, and peace" as a preliminary to "the reunification of the country through consultations and negotiations between the South and the North on an equal footing." Significantly, the communiqué made only one mention of the National Liberation Front, to which the Alliance conveyed "sincere greetings of solidarity," and which it described, almost patronizingly, as "a patriotic force that has made worthy contributions to the cause of national liberation." The Alliance did promise to "coördinate actions" with the N.L.F., saying that the latter "cannot be absent in the settlement of any problem in the South," and giving its own summary of a future program for South Vietnam, which amounted to a synopsis of the Front's program of August, 1967. But the Alliance also specifically said, without mentioning the Front, that it was "prepared to enter into discussions with the United States government" to end the war, obtain the withdrawal of American troops and the dismantling of bases, and secure recognition of South Vietnam's "national independence and sovereignty."

The purpose behind the Alliance of National, Democratic, and Peace Forces, which was almost certainly created by Hanoi, was to give the appearance of an independent group that, for coalition purposes, could seem to operate separately from the National Liberation Front. Hanoi no doubt felt that the Front had become compromised by its obvious dependence, despite denials, on North Vietnam. It was not that the N.L.F. had no southern identity of its own, or that it did not include some non-Communist nationalist elements; it was simply that, for tactical purposes, it was deemed wise to create another organization that could act as a bridge between the urban intellectuals and the Front's rather remote membership. Moreover, by setting up the Alliance, the Communists created a new instrumentality that they could use in various ways; its initial advantage was its ability to bring the other alliances, fronts, and revolutionary committees around the country under one banner, and it was significant that the Hué Alliance and the Thua Thien People's Revolutionary Committee lost no time in joining the new umbrella Alliance and accepting its "leadership." Thich Don Hau, an aged Buddhist monk who had become vice-chairman of the Hué Alliance, also became a vice-chairman of the new Alliance. Similarly, a Saigon-Cholon-Gia Dinh Alliance of National, Democratic, and Peace Forces, formed early in May, expressed its full support for the Alliance.

Late in May, Hanoi sent south, to supervise all military and political matters, one of its top Politburo members, Pham Hung, who was also serving as First Deputy Prime Minister. Hung, born in the South, spent fourteen years in prison on the island of Poulo Condore under the French. After his release, in 1945, he became one of the most important Vietminh figures in the South, in charge of political and security operations. He went north in 1955, and there he subsequently held various top jobs supervising financial and economic affairs. His return to the South, after an absence of thirteen years, seemed an obvious indication of the importance with which Hanoi regarded the whole new coalition gambit while negotiations began in Paris. It was no accident, either, that shortly after the Paris negotiations got under way a North Vietnamese spokesman, when asked who should represent South Vietnam at the peace talks, replied, "The authorized representatives of our fellow-elements in South Vietnam, not the stooges in the South. It is the National Liberation Front and the other authorized representatives—that is to say, the Alliance [of National, Democratic, and Peace Forces]." The Alliance was also welcomed into the international Communist limelight by Moscow, Prague, and other Eastern nations, and by Algeria and Cuba.

So far as is known, none of the ten members of the Alliance's central committee belongs to the Communist Party in Vietnam. One, a well-known woman obstetrician in Saigon, Dr. Duong Quynh Hoa, was, and may still be, a member of the French Communist Party; when arrested by the Saigon police in 1960, she admitted to having joined the Party while studying medicine in France. The other nine on the committee represent a cross-section of leftist intellectuals. Trinh Dinh Thao, the chairman of the group, is a northerner who settled in South Vietnam after studying law in France. He led a pro-Vietminh Peace Movement in 1954, and was thereafter deported to the North, but was allowed later to return south. He was arrested twice again in the last three years for being involved in anti-government peace activities, but was let go both times. Ton That Duong Ky belongs to an old mandarin family from central Vietnam; he was a popular professor of history at Saigon University until he, too, was deported to North Vietnam, in 1965, for anti-government peace activities. He slipped back south sometime in the last year or so. Ky and Thich Don Hau, the monk from Hué, both have a strong following in central Vietnam, and the latter's presence in particular points up the Communists' awareness of the importance of obtaining Buddhist support. Lam Van Tet, an elderly southerner from the Delta, has a long record of joining protest movements, and is regarded as a sort of Vietnamese Bertrand Russell. Two student leaders lend emphasis to the Alliance's desire to proselyte among both college and high-school students.

Whether, on the government side, Prime Minister Huong, starting from scratch, can create any kind of consensus for negotiations in the diffuse and embittered political climate of South Vietnam highly problematical. While the government preaches "national reconciliation," it is still all too apparent that what is required in South Vietnam today is a complete overhaul of institutions. It may be too late to achieve such an overhaul now. But, in the light of the imperatives created by negotiations, it is not too late to hope for certain reforms and improvements, especially in the areas that seem likely to become the decisive ones in the months ahead. These include the gathering and use of intelligence and the creation of an apparatus that can make the South Vietnamese, particularly those in the hamlets and villages, less vulnerable to Communist penetration. An optimistic American general, harking back to Mao Tsetung's famous image of the Communist leaders as fish and the people as the sea in which they swam, said recently, "The sea is getting somewhat less compatible." This may be so, but if ideology rather than organization was at one time more important to the Communists it surely no longer is; their success in creating and sustaining their so-called infrastructure, which amounts to a subterranean government and depends on a whole network of couriers, tax collectors, agitprop workers, spies, and directing cadres, is an organizational accomplishment that dates back over a period of thirty years in South Vietnam.

Some recent improvements have been made in the methods of collecting and using intelligence. In about two-thirds of the approximately two hundred and forty districts in the country, so-called DIOCs—District Intelligence Operations Centers—have been set up under the Phoenix Program for coördinating the gathering of intelligence, and similar centers have been established in thirty-nine out of the country's forty-four provinces. There are an estimated sixty-five thousand to eighty thousand members of the Communist infrastructure in South Vietnam, most of them People's

Revolutionary Party members who operate completely covertly. So far this year, according to Robert Komer, our top man in the pacification program, some five thousand arrests have been made of alleged members of this infrastructure. The hope is that by the end of the year the total will be twelve thousand. Aside from the members of the infrastructure who have been arrested, some have been killed by government assassination squads. Nevertheless, it is still debatable how much the Communists' capability really has declined. So far, they still seem able to replace cadres they have lost.

If, in sum, the government's belated effort to track down and eliminate members of the Communist secret apparatus is accomplishing something, the cumbersome and corrupt police system is not designed to gain the people's confidence, especially since they have been neglected and abused for so many years. The government workers who could rectify this are the Revolutionary Development cadres, but unless they have more support and protection they will be unable to make sufficient headway. The Communists are fully aware of the threat posed by these cadres, which is why they have increasingly made them special targets for assassination. Without a covert "black pajama" apparatus of its own, however, the government is unlikely to succeed. It can perhaps disturb, but it cannot destroy, the Communist apparatus, and it can do little to alter the Communists' basic blueprint, which is to continue fighting in Vietnam and talking in Paris indefinitely if need be. Both sides are seeking to win over as much of the population as possible before either of the two eventualities the Communists envisage: a coalition government or a political-party system that Hanoi would ultimately dominate. Despite the military setbacks the Communists have suffered, they are not losing politically in Vietnam today. How much this is due to their own tactics, and how much to the ineptitude of the South Vietnamese government and the Americans, is a moot question, but there is scant reason to doubt that the options at the moment belong to Hanoi.

17. **Paris**

$\rightsquigarrow\rightsquigarrow\rightsquigarrow\rightsquigarrow\rightsquigarrow\rightsquigarrow\rightsquigarrow\rightsquigarrow$

November 16, 1968

Since President Johnson called off the bombing of North Vietnam on October 31st, pushing the Paris peace talks toward a new phase, it has become increasingly apparent here that what happens in South Vietnam during this period will be at least as important as what happens at the conference table or behind the scenes in Paris. Paris, in one sense, will serve as a screen onto which the events in Vietnam, both political and military, are projected. It will be somewhat as if a stage play and a film of a single story were being presented simultaneously, and the audience—the rest of the world —had to determine which was the more meaningful performance. Something like this has been occurring during the last month, and has perplexed everyone, creating new doubts about the ability, and even the desire, of men to order their affairs and speak with each other in ways that can promote understanding. To say that the confusion has been mainly a matter of semantics is too simple— though the different meanings given specific words and phrases by the parties involved have played a large part in compounding that confusion. More significant has been the political purpose behind the obfuscation, the purpose not only of each of the major parties involved—the Americans, the North Vietnamese, the National Liberation Front, and the Saigon government—but also of each of a number of moderators. Among these are the Russians, who are believed to have been instrumental in persuading Hanoi to modify its earlier insistence on an unreciprocated and permanent bombing halt, and, to a lesser extent, the French, who, as hosts, have acted with aplomb and courtesy in stimulating private dialogues here between the representatives of Washington and of Hanoi. It was these dialogues, in progress for weeks apart from the formal meetings, that led to compromises that have now theoretically elevated the discussions from the level of propaganda duels to the level of substantive negotiation over ways of achieving peace on the ground in South Vietnam and in the hearts and minds of the various groups in conflict there. It is the latter factor, of course, dependent as it is upon what those engaged in the protracted struggle still expect to achieve in terms of political power or mere survival, that has been the vital subjective element all along, here in Paris for the last five months and in Vietnam itself for the last several years and especially during the last year.

On the basis of what I have observed in Paris during the past fortnight, and what has been happening in the United States and elsewhere, the current scenario (a favorite word among Americans at the negotiations) can be described as follows: The North Vietnamese, having decided a month or more ago, for various reasons, to negotiate seriously instead of just asserting that negotiations were desirable, reluctantly made some secret admissions and concessions that defined the lull in fighting during September and October as amounting to a pullback of their forces. These concessions, which were tantamount to a political signal to Washington, included something less than Hanoi's previous demand for a completely unconditional bombing halt. Hanoi has consistently refused to admit, publicly or privately, that it agreed either formally or tacitly to any kind of reciprocity in return for the cessation of the bombing, but it did let the Americans know privately that, in the event of a halt, certain "circumstances" would obtain; i.e., the withdrawal of its troops northward across the Demilitarized Zone dividing North and South Vietnam. According to the Americans, Hanoi and Washington also agreed privately to seat delegates from the National Liberation Front and from the South Vietnamese government, *but not as separate entities*. The North Vietnamese, on the other hand, maintain that the American interpretation of what took place in the secret meetings is, in polite terms, a "subjectivist" one, or, in less polite terms, simply a "fabricated" one. At any rate, it soon became apparent that the terms of the arrangement had been inadequately worked out, and that whatever deal had been made meant different things to the two major parties as well as to their separate Vietnamese associates. The South Vietnamese, having been apprised in advance of the bombing-halt announcement and of the proposed seating plan, and having known for some weeks that such an arrangement was imminent, suddenly balked. For reasons best known to President Nguyen Van Thieu—a highly suspicious man, who was apparently upset by what he deemed President Johnson's highhanded and unilateral tactics, and who was worried over the lack of precise definitions of the status of his government vis-à-vis the National Liberation Front—the South Vietnamese postponed indefinitely any formal appearance at the peace sessions. Relations between the Americans and their Vietnamese partners thereupon reached the lowest point yet in this strange and often miscomprehended alliance, with each side privately and openly blaming the other for their differences.

As a result of Saigon's absence—which President Johnson had at the last moment anticipated, declaring in his speech that the South Vietnamese government was "free to participate" in the talks, thus implying that it was also free not to—the first full "new-phase" Paris meeting, scheduled for November 6th, was called off. Whoever was at fault—and there are several versions of what happened and of whose tactics were more tactless—the spat between Saigon and Washington has played into the hands of the North Vietnamese and their country cousins, the National Liberation Front. Together, they have had a propaganda field day, proclaiming their willingness to proceed on a three-way basis, but placing complete responsibility on the Americans if Saigon maintains its refusal to take part. The circumstances have been particularly embarrassing for Washington, not only because of the emphasis that President Johnson has repeatedly placed on Hanoi's unwillingness to talk "seriously" about deëscalating the war and proceeding with other aspects of peacemaking but also because he warned Hanoi in his October 31st speech that "we have a right to expect . . . prompt, productive . . . and intensive negotiations" and that "our people will just not accept deliberate delay and prolonged procrastination again." As far as Hanoi and the newly arrived representatives of the N.L.F. in Paris are concerned, the Americans have simply reneged on their "assurances" that their South Vietnamese "puppets" would appear on time, and the shoe of procrastination is on the other foot.

Sooner or later—and at present the betting is on sooner—Saigon is bound to send someone to represent it in the discussions, for all observers agree that it cannot afford to stay out of them for very long. Its chief observer here, Pham Dang Lam, is returning to Paris this week from Saigon, and there are reports that additional delegation representatives will arrive "soon." However the seating formula is worked out, there will no doubt be some sort of meeting among all four elements during the next week or two, but Richard Nixon's election, it is generally agreed, may cause new delays as all sides reassess their positions. Underlying the many difficulties of working out new rules of procedure and a new agenda—steps that could in themselves take weeks, if not months—remains the fundamental question of status. The Americans continue to maintain that a brand-new empty table has been set, with places for just two parties, the United States and North Vietnam, though each will be allowed to bring along as many guests as it wants. Hanoi, however, has continued to claim that the Front is to sit at the table as an "independent voice," and that this is no more than "right and realistic," because the Front is the "authentic representative" of the people of South Vietnam. Mrs. Nguyen Thi Binh, the diminutive, comely, and tough-minded pro-tem head of the Front delegation, naturally echoes this view, and there is very little likelihood that it will change when, as is expected, one of three top Front officials, Tran Buu Kiem, Nguyen Van Hieu, or Huynh Tan Phat, arrives here later on. Which one is chosen to come will be significant. Kiem is, in effect, Foreign Minister of the Front, and is regarded as a hardline man with close ties to the People's Revolutionary Party, the southern offshoot of the Lao Dong Party. Hieu, also known as a hard-liner, has been the Front's spokesman and representative in Phnom Penh, and has acted as a sort of roving ambassador for it in Europe from time to time. Phat, who is the Front's Secretary-General, has more solid southern roots than the two other men, though they also are southerners. A rivalry is said to exist between Kiem and Phat. If Phat, who is known as a more outgoing and conciliatory man, should come to Paris, either now or later, there is some feeling that this might help build bridges and promote an accommodation with non-Communist elements in Saigon outside the government, or perhaps even with some members of the government. The Front is now stressing the concept of coalition "with patriots but not with traitors"—meaning, by "traitors," men like President Thieu and Vice-President Nguyen Cao Ky—while Saigon still adamantly refuses to accept coalition under any circumstances with the Front as such. If Kiem or Hieu should come here, it would probably signify a tougher line, in keeping with the policy the Communists are now obviously ready to pursue—that of "reverting to protracted war" and "fighting and negotiating at the same time."

In analyzing the Communists' present position both in Paris and in Vietnam, weight must be given to a speech made to Party workers last summer by Truong Chinh, the third-ranking member of Hanoi's Politburo, in which the policy of "reverting to protracted war" was set forth. The speech, which was made public only late in September, must be considered in the context of this year's remarkable military developments in Vietnam. Prior to the Tet offensive, there was a debate in Hanoi over whether to launch an all-out offensive or, in the face of the Americans' superior firepower, to go on fighting a defensive war in the South. Le Duan, the Secretary of the Lao Dong Party, who is generally regarded as the No. 2 figure after Ho Chi Minh, favored the offensive, and won out, with the result that General Vo Nguyen Giap was ordered to launch the Tet attack. As everyone knows, the assaults on Saigon, Hué, and a hundred other cities failed to achieve their basic military objectives and were very costly to the Communists. However, they did disrupt the entire apparatus of the Saigon government, bringing its pacification program in the countryside to a virtual halt, and thus benefitted the Communists psychologically and politically. Not only did the Tet offensive give impetus to numerous local and regional "revolutionary" bodies but it also created a new and serious vacuum in the rural areas, where the Communists were able to form additional "autonomous" and "people's" committees in scores of villages. These new committees, created by cadres of the People's Revolutionary Party, are likely to be the real instruments of the Communist political power thrust in the future, with the Front and the Alliance of National, Democratic, and Peace Forces, set up after

Tet, serving as broad national spearheads. The Truong Chinh speech came after the failure of the Communist offensive in May, but when one takes into account Hanoi's decision to enter serious negotiations, and the continued heavy losses the Communists have taken since August (in the last three months, they are reliably said to have had more men killed than the twenty-seven thousand the Americans have lost in the entire war), the speech assumes even more significance.

After warning Party workers to "overcome pacifist ideas" and "grasp the motto of long-drawn-out fight," Chinh said, "We must attack the enemy with determination to fight and win. But at times, under certain circumstances, we must shift to the defensive to gain time, dishearten the enemy, and build up our forces for a new offensive. . . . A truly profound and broad revolution of the masses of people to seize power must naturally coördinate political struggle —including general strikes, market strikes, school strikes, office strikes, political meetings and demonstrations, show-of-force demonstrations, and so forth—with armed combat." He said it was theoretically sound to build "a united front with a broad basis," but "to insure the success of the revolution the Front has to base itself on a solid worker-peasant alliance and be led closely by a Marxist-Leninist Party." Such a party, with "a maximum platform," Truong Chinh added, must never share its "right" to exert complete revolutionary leadership "with any party whatever, and must absolutely not allow the national bourgeoisie to lead the national unified front."

Despite, or perhaps because of, Truong Chinh's hard line, which seems to show that the Hanoi government will continue to try to control developments in South as well as North Vietnam, Hanoi has been determined to obtain some recognition of the Front from the United States. There is a historical parallel here. Back in 1951, as the North Vietnamese are fond of recalling, when the Russians unavailingly sought to obtain some recognition for the Vietminh in the United Nations, the French described the Vietminh as "nonexistent phantoms." Three years later, at Geneva, the chief North Vietnamese delegate, Pham Van Dong, took special delight in pointing out that the phantoms, having just defeated the French at Dien Bien Phu, had "acquired flesh and blood." The situation is the same today with regard to the Front, say the North Vietnamese. "Now the

United States can't ignore the reality," they maintain.

The position the Front is to have at the peace talks thus remains a bedrock issue for Hanoi. In the private talks during the tea breaks at the old Majestic Hotel, on the Avenue Kléber, and, more important, at the secret sessions held in various private homes in the city during September, the North Vietnamese gave the "signal" the Americans were waiting for, and its gist was that they were willing to make certain concessions in order to facilitate a bombing halt and obtain a seat for the Front at the meetings. During the lull in the fighting between mid-June and mid-August, the French, and perhaps also the Russians, had counselled the Americans to recognize that the slowdown had political implications. A number of American officials, including some members of the American delegation in Paris, are said to have agreed, but the White House remained dubious and failed to respond. The fighting in the South, including the rocket assaults on the cities, then picked up again, and so did the bombing of the North below the Nineteenth Parallel —the limit set by Washington. In September, however, for a combination of reasons, Hanoi decided to make privately explicit what had been implicit before.

Secret activities proceeded at a fast and furious pace in the next fortnight, both in Washington and in Paris, and presumably in Hanoi, too. By mid-October, these activities had produced the first "package deal," whereby, in return for promising to withdraw its troops across the Demilitarized Zone and assuring the Americans that their troops below the D.M.Z. would not be attacked by artillery or other means, and perhaps also implying that Communist units drawn back into Laos and Cambodia would remain where they were, at least temporarily, Hanoi obtained the Americans' promise to end the bombing and "all other acts of force" in North Vietnam. The phrase used, according to the North Vietnamese, was *"sans conditions,"* which they read to mean "no reciprocity," but the fact is that President Johnson did not mention the word "unconditional," or the phrase "without conditions," in his October 31st speech; on the contrary, he said, "We could be misled—and we are prepared for such a contingency." Johnson was said to be disturbed over the lack of any written agreement. By this time, the North Vietnamese had already dropped the word "permanent" in their demands for a bombing halt, and now they reluctantly accepted the prospect of a continuation of American reconnaissance flights over their country, even though they continued to claim in Paris that these flights were a violation of their sovereignty.

When the package was presented to the Saigon government, on October 8th or 9th, President Thieu expressed concern over allowing the role of the Front to be equated with that of his government. However, he appeared willing to accept the package as a whole. On the morning of October 16th, though, a few hours before the bombing halt was to be announced by President Johnson, Thieu apparently had fresh qualms and repeated his objections more strenuously. Although, like Johnson, he had played his cards close to the vest—throughout this crucial period both men acted more than ever like lone wolves—the South Vietnamese President was obviously worried about the hawks in his National Assembly and in the Army who wanted both the war and the bombing to continue. At any rate, the Americans held off the bombing announcement in the hope that Thieu could drum up more support for the new position in a few days' time.

It may be argued, and perhaps it will be for a long time, that if President Johnson's bombing halt had gone through in mid-October he would have more clearly proved the sincerity of his professed search for peace and Hubert Humphrey would today be the President-elect of the United States. In any event, the result of the South Vietnamese demurrals in mid-October led to another frantic period, during which a second package was completed. This also failed to satisfy President Thieu. In fact, in most respects he had become more recalcitrant. He wanted an unequivocal assurance from Hanoi that it was ready to enter into direct and serious talks with the Saigon government, and that the participation of the Front in the talks would not be just a ruse and the first step toward creating "a spurious coalition government."

Hanoi, as the United States well knew, would never make such concessions, and during the latter part of October Ambassador Ellsworth Bunker in Saigon saw Thieu a dozen times in an effort to make him modify his position. (As one American official afterward commented, "Anyone who still thinks the South Vietnamese are our puppets after this is crazy.") At one point, Bunker thought he had convinced Thieu, and he told Washington so, two days before Johnson's speech. But the Americans had mistaken their man. A few hours before the bombing halt was announced, Bunker and Deputy Ambassador Samuel Berger saw Thieu again. Thieu was particularly upset by a rocket assault on Saigon that evening, in which nineteen worshippers in a Catholic church had been killed and many others wounded. He agreed that any rift with the Americans would be disastrous, and he or Vice-President Ky—it is not clear which—suggested that the bombing halt be announced but that other details of the package, including a definition of the exact role of the Front in Paris, be left for later discussion. The Americans said that was impossible, and, as tempers flared, Thieu muttered in Vietnamese to Deputy Ambassador Berger, who didn't hear him, "Are you representing Hanoi or Washington?"

In any case, the conditional, rather than unconditional, bombing halt the Americans announced on October 31st served Saigon's interests. As for Hanoi's promise to halt rocket and mortar attacks on South Vietnamese cities, that seems to have been much more conditional. At the time of the attack on Saigon that incensed Thieu, the Americans were still bombing the North, avowedly for the last time, but more indicative of what may lie ahead was a rocket attack, three days after the bombing halt went into effect, on the Delta city of My Tho, which killed five people. By November 7th, Saigon claimed, sixteen more rocket assaults on cities and villages had taken place. Hanoi may well argue now that since the new conversations in Paris have not yet begun, and since the Front has not yet been seated, it cannot guarantee control over what the Front does militarily—and the Front's men do most of the rocketing.

However, nothing substantive is likely to start until a Saigon delegation comes to Paris. Feelings in the South Vietnamese capital by the end of the first week of November were still running high. There was no doubt that, beyond their fears and suspicions of the Paris formula, the South Vietnamese were deeply resentful of what they judged to be American attempts to railroad them into accepting it. Their attitude was summed up by Thieu's comment that his government "is not a car that can be hitched to a locomotive and taken anywhere the locomotive wants to go." One prominent neutral diplomat has suggested to the American delegation in Paris, "Saigon is in a fever now. You must let it quiet down." It seems likely that, in view of Nixon's election, Washington will be obliged to follow this advice, despite Johnson's undoubted desire to advance the cause of peace before he leaves office. Although Thieu and his aides had some misgivings as to where Nixon really stood on the Vietnam question, they undoubtedly bet on his victory. Now their desire to weigh the President-elect's avowal that he would not force a coalition government or "sell out to Communism" against his pledge to end the war as soon as he could and get on with other matters will probably provoke them to take their time in committing themselves fully to the Paris discussions, if for no other reason than that the peace talks are bound to move slowly anyway during the American Presidential transition.

Saigon still has to adjust to the facts of life about the Front. Privately, most South Vietnamese officials, including President Thieu himself, have already admitted that the Front cannot be excluded from any settlement. But some sort of face-saving formula for dealing with the Front, beyond the often expressed policy of accepting recanting individual members in the Saigon government, must still be found. One suggestion that is heard here is that the American scheme for seating the Front and Saigon delegations at the peace table as "guest participants" could be more explcitly spelled out. This might be done by accepting the Front and Saigon as *de-facto* representatives of their respective constituencies and postponing *de-jure* status until an election plan for South Vietnam can be made. Hanoi's initial reaction to this, however, is negative, and it continues to insist that the Front be accorded full independent status at the Paris talks, without any qualifications. The Front, of course, says the same thing. Thieu still maintains that his government must deal directly with Hanoi on a *de-jure* as well as a *de-facto* basis. As for Thieu's newest proposal, advanced on November 8th, to have the Americans sit as *his* "guests," instead of vice versa, Hanoi's reaction has been predictable. "It makes no difference to us if the master leads the horse or the horse the master," I was told by a North Vietnamese. "The Democratic Republic of Vietnam [Hanoi] will speak for itself, as will the Front."

No delegation sent to Paris by Saigon will carry much weight unless it represents at least a broad cross-section of South Vietnamese political life and contains some spokesmen for the most important elements in South Vietnam, which include the majority Buddhists—militants as well as moderates—and the religious sects, the Hoa Hao and Cao Dai, along with the minority Catholics, who dominate the Thieu government. South Vietnam's history of fragmentation since 1946 does not augur well for this kind of representation, but the country's very survival now seems to depend upon it. Divisiveness is still endemic, and rivalries still exist across the board in politics, in the Army, among the religious groups, and so on. Over the last few months, several organizations, such as the National Congress for the People's Salvation, headed by General Tran Van Don, have been formed, but they have proved unable to work together, and there is nothing on the Saigon side to compare with the Communists' Alliance of National, Democratic, and Peace Forces. Premier Tran Van Huong has succeeded in stressing civilian leadership as a counterbalance to that of the military, but he is still subject to Thieu's orders. In the last week, the Communists in Paris have begun to refer to the "Thieu-Ky-Huong clique."

None of this diminishes the problems that the Communists also face. Though they accept the fact that they can at this point no longer win a quick military victory themselves, they are obviously more willing to risk a political fight than Saigon is, both in Paris and in South Vietnam. They, too, are fully aware of the possible implications of the American elections and Nixon's victory. "The defeat of Johnson and Humphrey was the result of the policy of intensifying the war," I was told by one of them. They also face a problem of southern leadership—there is no one like Ho Chi Minh among their supporters in the South, and they now admit that the reunification of the North and the South is a long way off. The great advantage they have is that they can face the problems of peace and address themselves to the people of Vietnam, and to the rest of the world, as Vietnamese nationalists as well as Communists. The fact that they are Communists does not detract from their arguments in behalf of independence, for which they have been struggling for twenty-five years. In this sense, it may be said that Thieu's contest with the Americans in the last month may have done us some good, for it has redressed the puppet image. If the South Vietnamese can now stand on their own feet and, as non-Communist nationalists, finally establish some sort of consensus, there will be a chance for them to win the peace, or at least not to lose it.

What has become more apparent in the last month here in Paris is that, whatever happens, the Vietnamese themselves will determine their own future. No one is talking at this point of another

Geneva conference, and it seems doubtful that anyone wants one, including the Russians and the Chinese—although they, as well as the Americans, the British, the French, and some of the smaller nations involved in the Vietnam war, will all seek to influence the eventual peace talks. The Russians have their own reasons for wanting the Vietnamese war to end, including their problems in Eastern Europe and their long-term plans to regain an influence in Southeast Asia, not to mention their ideological struggle with China and their desire to achieve a détente with the United States. The Chinese, despite their reported initial opposition to the peace talks and their belief in continued and continuing wars of liberation, are in a somewhat different position. They have seen the North Vietnamese slip slowly away from their political orbit and toward Moscow's in the last year, even though Hanoi must remain dependent on the Chinese for guns and ammunition if the fighting continues. But Peking is also aware of another factor, often overlooked. Surrounded by American bases and influences in Japan, South Korea, Okinawa, the Philippines, Taiwan, and Thailand, the Chinese might best serve their own interests by getting the Americans out of Vietnam, and perhaps pave the way thereby for the reëstablishment of some sort of diplomatic relations with the United States. This may partly account for the fact that Hanoi has been able to persuade Peking of the logic, as well as the necessity, of moving ahead with the negotiations now.

As for the Americans, the members of our delegation in Paris are, for the most part, biding their time. Obviously, their future actions will depend on what Nixon wants to do about Vietnam. The possibility of Averell Harriman's remaining in Paris as the delegation chief is remote; he is a loyal Democrat and no admirer of Nixon. Cyrus Vance, his able deputy, may remain for a time, as a bridgebuilder between this administration and the next, but he, too, is not eager to stay. For the next few weeks, at least, the jockeying and the propaganda will continue, but no one expects much to be accomplished, except perhaps some tentative redefining of the difficult question of the status of the Front and of Saigon. Sooner or later, everyone says, a new phase of the conference will begin, but now there has been a distinct letdown. Among most of the delegates, there is only an air of quiet, watchful waiting.

18.   **Saigon**

January 13, 1969

Not since November, 1963, the date of the *coup d'état* that ended the regime of President Ngo Dinh Diem, has there been such a mood of impending change in Saigon. But whereas five years ago this was accompanied by exhilaration and hope, the atmosphere today is heavy with apprehension about the possible course of events both here and in Paris. To go further back, to the end of the Indo-China War, in 1954, when Diem came to power, there was then a similar mood of fear and doubt, until Diem took firm charge. Unlike Diem's First Republic, which never could claim to be a democracy, the present, year-old Second Republic, directed by President Nguyen Van Thieu, does claim to be one. Many Vietnamese, however, maintain that Thieu is as powerful under the 1967 constitution as Diem was under that of 1955, which he interpreted exactly as he saw fit. To be sure, the current legislature, unlike Diem's rubber-stamp Assembly, has expressed independent opinions on a variety of matters, including the conduct of the war and of the peace negotiations, and, as a result, Thieu, who at first all but ignored it, has had to learn to live with it, like a man with a nagging wife. But the power to make all major decisions has remained firmly with the President, subject only to irregular consultation with a handful of advisers. In contrast to Diem, who came to be guided more and more by the mystical insights of his brother Ngo Dinh Nhu, Thieu trusts no one. In the words of one American here, "He is his own Nhu." Although his habit of deciding things alone, often after prolonged inner debate, and without giving anyone else a clue to his thoughts, has surrounded him with a sort of mystical aura of his own, he has also won considerable respect for his astuteness. "Thieu will never be a statesman, but he *is* becoming a politician," a Vietnamese who is not one of his ardent admirers grudgingly admits.

Whatever Thieu's compatriots think of him, and he is by no means first in the hearts of his countrymen, a considerable number of Americans here hold the opinion that only a government such as his—centralized in its direction and at least avowedly benevolent in its aims—can keep the Communists from eventually taking over the country, irrespective of the kind of formula evolved in Paris. These Americans say that in the earlier Diem and post-Diem days opportunities to build Western-style democracy in South Vietnam were lost, and it cannot be effectively imposed in a short time at the climax of a brutal and destructive war. Vietnamese society has traditionally been authoritarian, even when there has been a certain amount of local autonomy. The French colonists simply took over the old mandarin system and adapted it to their own needs. During the eight years of the Indo-China War, the old colonial structure, though it was being modified by slow and restricted grants of independence, disintegrated and then collapsed. When Diem imposed his own system of authority, his first failure was his rejection of a chance to broaden his base of support by holding village elections, and his more serious failure was his inability to rationalize and organize his administration; a lack of efficient organization has plagued all South Vietnamese regimes since.

In sharp contrast, good organization, combined with effective leadership, has all along been the Communists' chief asset. The Saigon government's need to emulate its enemy in this regard has never been more apparent than it is at the moment, for the military advantage has now swung firmly in its direction while the political indicator remains on dead center—or, if anything, still pointing toward the Vietcong in the rural areas. Even if the government's claim that it now controls some seventy per cent of South Vietnam's population—forty per cent of which, including refugees and other displaced persons, currently lives in the cities—is statistically accurate, the statistics do not provide a true picture of the situation. The remaining thirty per cent is about equally divided between people living in "contested" areas and people living in areas that are admittedly controlled by the Communists, and the government's response in these areas so far either has been nil or has been limited to the presence of isolated platoons in contested hamlets. And in the cities—particularly in Saigon and Cholon, its huge Chinese section —the underground Communist apparatus remains strong, as can be seen from the arrest here in the last several weeks of more than four hundred Vietcong agents, about a quarter of whom are said to have been members of "sapper" units or of what are known as "special-action squads," both of which are devoted to carrying out acts of violence and terror. At least that many agents are still roaming the city or hiding out nearby.

Probably the phrase one hears most in Saigon these days is "gaining time." The fear is widespread that there will not be enough time for the country to organize itself before some sort of settlement is reached in Paris—if only a preliminary one involving a cease-fire and planned troop withdrawals. This fear, combined with suspicions that have been nurtured by statements from high-ranking American officials like the outgoing Secretary of Defense, Clark Clifford, has made the Vietnamese attitude toward the Americans even more ambivalent than usual, the general belief being that we railroaded the Thieu government into the Paris meetings without giving it enough time to get ready. Many Americans here, for their part, are even more doubtful than usual about the desire and the ability of the Vietnamese to prosecute the war by themselves, and these Americans, who include ordinary soldiers, are commenting more freely than ever before on what the war has cost them, personally and collectively, and on what it has and has not accomplished. Among the military, there are complaints both about the outgoing Johnson administration's lack of candor and about the wisdom of fighting a limited war with limited objectives and then negotiating something tantamount to defeat just when, as they see it, victory is imminent. The critics also have pointed out that in this difficult period not one but three different American policies seem to have been followed—one in Washington, one in Paris, and one in

Saigon—and that, under the circumstances, it is no wonder the Vietnamese are both confused and annoyed. The principal question now being asked is whether President-elect Nixon will move still more rapidly to deëscalate the war and withdraw American troops or whether he will proceed slowly enough to permit the careful "re-Vietnamization" of the conflict that should accompany its "de-Americanization."

The most important problem remains that of giving significant numbers of the Vietnamese armed forces enough time and experience to operate effectively on their own. American military men today rate as excellent one Vietnamese division (out of eleven), two or three independent regiments, and some special élite units; two divisions are considered outright poor, and the rest are said to be improving, at varying rates. Even if they continue to improve, they will still need American helicopters and other logistical aid, and even if it is assumed that this aid will be continued when American troops begin to pull out, the Vietnamese will need considerable time in which to learn how to manage the complicated techniques associated with it. Half a dozen or more studies, both military and civilian, are under way, with the help of the inevitable computers, to determine just how soon and under what conditions the Vietnamese can master these techniques, and to estimate the amount of continued American support that will be required in the interim period. One formula suggests an annual eight-billion-dollar, two-hundred-thousand-man American commitment over the next two or three years, instead of the present thirty-billion-dollar-a-year effort involving five hundred and forty-five thousand men, but it seems doubtful that Congress, in its present mood, or the American people it is supposed to represent will accept even those figures.

It would be a mistake to suppose that the Communists, in Paris, in Hanoi, and at the jungle headquarters of the National Liberation Front (now thought to be in Cambodia), are unaware of the dimensions of Saigon's and Washington's predicaments. Up to now, it has been customary to say that time is on Hanoi's side—that the North Vietnamese have always meant what they said about being willing to fight for twenty more years if necessary. But they and the Vietcong have been taking a beating—between a hundred and a hundred and fifty thousand men were killed during 1968; the North Vietnamese have been enduring increasing hardships and experiencing increasing administrative difficulties at home, and they run the risk that the bombing will be resumed if they keep up their offensive in the South, though American and world opinion make any resumption unlikely. The policy of protracted warfare recently pronounced by Truong Chinh, a top-ranking member of the North Vietnamese Politburo, certainly represents a long-term gamble, just as the strategy of his chief rival in Hanoi, Le Duan, First Secretary of the Lao Dong Party, who planned the quick, concentrated attacks on the cities last winter and again in May, represented a short-term gamble—one that, although it failed to achieve its military objectives, shook the Saigon regime badly and set back many of its programs. The political and military campaigns that the Communists are now mounting seem to have somewhat less ambitious objectives than those of the Tet and May attacks. They are primarily aimed at eroding as much of the South Vietnamese strength as possible. But they are bold enough to suit either alternative at the conference table—a cease-fire followed by some troop withdrawals, which would leave the political situation wide open during further negotiations, or the first step in the Truong Chinh strategy of gradual attrition, aimed at wearing American resistance down even further and stimulating our withdrawal, which conceivably would enable the Communists to win wider concessions.

The current political offensive is being directed by hard-core Vietcong units, who have launched new peace groups in Saigon and elsewhere. The aim of these units is to support the propaganda line of the National Liberation Front in Paris and, by keeping the Saigon government off balance and by inhibiting its efforts to operate cohesively, to put the onus of obstructing peace on Saigon. The new groups, and especially one called the Movement to Struggle for Peace, have demanded the creation of a "peace Cabinet"—an apparent effort to drive a wedge between the Thieu government and those more eager to negotiate. The groups were started early in November, to supplement the activities of the Alliance of National, Democratic, and Peace Forces of Vietnam, which was set up last spring. In recent months, the Alliance has drawn perceptibly closer to the Front, and now the two groups are issuing joint communiqués, the Alliance having dropped its pseudo-separatist line to declare that the Front must play the "decisive" role in negotiations.

However, the fact that both Vice-President Nguyen Cao Ky and Premier Tran Van Huong have obliquely suggested the possibility of purely political discussions in South Vietnam with the "insurgents" while Hanoi and Washington are simultaneously discussing in Paris a cease-fire, troop withdrawals, and policing formulas still presages a future role for the Alliance as a middleman group.

The peace Cabinet theme has been repeated almost daily, in one Communist broadcast or another, since early November. The militant Buddhists who helped to overthrow Diem have also adopted this line. At the end of November, Thich Don Hau, the aged vice-chairman of the Alliance, who is hiding somewhere near Hué, called on all "peace-loving organizations" to "isolate the Thieu-Ky-Huong clique" and replace the "Cabinet of War" with a "Cabinet of Peace, qualified to attend the Paris talks." In Saigon, the Buddhists of the An Quang Pagoda group, led by Thich Tri Quang and Thich Thien Minh, later issued a similar call for a peace Cabinet, and Buddhist chaplains in the field began privately urging soldiers, mostly recent draftees, not to sacrifice themselves to the cause of war but, rather, to lay down their arms—with the result that about fifty deserted and returned to Saigon, where they are said to be hiding out in pagodas. During the second week of December, a Buddhist motorcade of fifty cars, bearing representatives of left-wing student and labor groups, toured the Mekong Delta. In several provincial and district capitals, religious speeches were interspersed with calls for a new Saigon government.

All this was well synchronized by the Communists with the birth of the Movement to Struggle for Peace, which held an organizational meeting at the An Quang Pagoda late in October and a large rally in Saigon on November 10th. The rally was attended by a number of young liberal Catholic priests and a wide variety of clerical and lay religious leaders, by members of a dozen or more left-wing labor unions, and by lawyers, doctors, teachers, and journalists. The Vietcong cadremen who organized the meeting stayed in the background. Another meeting resulted in the arrest of three students, who were given jail sentences, and this in turn resulted in the issuance of a student manifesto. Since the Paris talks had technically started, the government was in a dilemma; it refrained at first from cracking down on the peace movements, but now it seems determined not to let the situation get out of hand.

The main Communist military effort at present appears to be concentrated in the III Corps area to the west and north of Saigon. By early December, there was evidence that four divisions temporarily withdrawn to Cambodia had begun to move back into South Vietnam along the infiltration routes leading to Saigon. It seemed unlikely that the Communists intended to launch another full attack on Saigon, in view of the heavy losses they had suffered previously, but they apparently did want to infiltrate sapper and special-action squads and other small elements into the city—and even, if they could get away with it, a military battalion or two. Another of their apparent objectives was to attack as many district capitals in the III Corps region as possible. American intelligence officers continue to expect these attacks momentarily. In the I Corps area, immediately below the D.M.Z., there was some activity as the year drew to its end, with the Communists bringing supplies down from North Vietnam to storage points just above the demarcation line, but there have as yet been no signs of movement across either of the two main infiltration routes from Laos into South Vietnam—Highway 9 and the A Shau Valley—though troops were seen storing supplies in the western end of the valley. It is in the IV Corps area—the Delta, which is still the stronghold of the Vietcong rather than of the North Vietnamese, who now predominate everywhere else—that the Americans and the South Vietnamese have made the greatest progress in recent months. Some long-established infiltration routes from the sea and from Cambodia have been cut, and the Communists are suffering more losses than they can replace, while the number of those rallying to the government's side has risen sharply. The improvement in the Delta also reflects increased zeal on the part of the Regional Forces, which is partly attributable to their recently having received new M-16 rifles from the Americans. Their numbers have now risen to two hundred and seventeen thousand, which, added to the hundred and seventy-three thousand Popular Forces and the four hundred and twenty thousand regular South Vietnamese Army, Navy, Marine, police, and auxiliary elements, will soon bring the total of government men in uniform to almost a million. In contrast, there are between eighty and ninety thousand North Vietnamese troops in South Vietnam or just beyond its borders, and the strength of the Vietcong main-force elements is less than fifty thousand; their regional and local forces have also suffered heavily, and may have dropped below a hundred thousand.

Allied intelligence has slowly continued to improve under the coördinated Vietnamese-American Phoenix Program. About two thousand members of the Vietcong infrastructure (V.C.I.) are being arrested each month, but the great majority of these belong to the less important categories. However, some big fish—district heads and propagandists—have been caught. One important arrest frequently leads to a flock of others, as happened in Saigon late in November, when a Vietcong captain who was deputy head of a sapper unit assigned to one of the Vietcong sub-regions that now ring the capital was apprehended trying to renew a government identity card that was phony. Within a fortnight, on the basis of information the captain gave, more than a hundred V.C.I., mostly lower-rung workers but including several military and political proselytizers and some squad and cell leaders, were rounded up in the city. However, the Phoenix Program is still not functioning as smoothly as it should, because it is still impeded by parallel chains of command and by the reluctance of district chiefs and police officers to be either sufficiently coöperative or sufficiently aggressive.

Another sign that the Communists may be having some difficulty with their political units is the increasing proportion of women on the Village Liberation Committees—or Revolutionary Committees, as they are also called. These groups, which have been set up by the People's Revolutionary Party over the past several months to replace earlier Party committees or administrative bodies in the Communist-controlled hamlets and villages, in effect constitute new governments at the rural level. Previously, the Party committees governed in the name of the National Liberation Front, but now they are supposed to govern in their own right and to constitute the nuclei of district and provincial Party committees and councils. According to radio broadcasts, captured documents, and interrogations of defectors and prisoners, the Communists claimed that by early November they had held elections setting up seven Province Liberation Committees, five committees in major cities, thirty-six District Liberation Committees, and 1,241 Village and Hamlet Liberation Committees, but intelligence analysts doubt the accuracy of these claims. Many such committees are simply appointed "shadow" groups. No one, though, denies that the Communists are making strenuous efforts to build up their Party machines in Vietcong-controlled areas and contested areas—underground committees are said to exist in two of Saigon's nine precincts. In their propaganda, the Communists are forever making references to the "democratic process" by which the new committees have been chosen, but these do not conceal the efforts being made by trusted Party members or candidates to move in and take control of as many hamlet and village administrations as possible before negotiations in Paris lead to precise political formulas, including local elections on a one-man, one-vote basis.

At the moment, the Communists are not thinking about elections so much as about their chances of consolidating their hold in the contested areas militarily, through propaganda and, when necessary, through terror. The incidence of terrorism has increased in recent months. Between January 1st and December 1st of 1968, more than five thousand civilians were killed by terrorist action in South Vietnam, in addition to nearly seventy-five hundred who lost their lives in the wave of attacks during Tet. A good many local officials, including hamlet and village chiefs, police officers, and workers for various government organizations, were assassinated, but most of those killed during the year were ordinary villagers suspected of coöperating with the government. This is the iron hand of the Communist program, but the velvet glove of accommodation is also being more widely felt, and in certain areas, including the region around Saigon and parts of the Delta, an increasing number of families and individuals in out-of-the-way hamlets are being visited clandestinely by Vietcong agents. Some of the agents are local friends or old acquaintances who suddenly reappear after years of absence, and others are newcomers, but in either case these men—or, sometimes, women—discuss the approach of peace, the withdrawal of the Americans, and the corruption and failures of government officials, and in other ways seek to build between themselves and the peasant families bridges that, however tenuous, may prove to be vital in the future.

Some of those who know the Communists best—both among high-level defectors and former members of the Vietminh during the war against the French—have suggested the method by which the Vietcong will continue to infiltrate the hamlets and villages in the months ahead. One of these experts, Lieutenant Colonel Nguyen Be, who was once a Vietminh battalion commander and who now runs the training center for Revolutionary Development workers, at Vung Tau, says that prior to a cease-fire the Communists will try to assert their hegemony in as many rural communities as possible and install administrative machinery composed of local "people's cadres," partly as a screen for the activities of covert agents. Be goes on to say that between the signing of a cease-fire agreement and the date it goes into effect—a period of three or four months, probably—Communist agents in government-controlled areas, including the cities, will pose as hoodlums and petty criminals, and will denounce or pick fights with nationalists who preach patriotism and order. When the cease-fire becomes operative, Be warns, Communist agents will begin a subtle process of accommodation with government officials, seeking to win their confidence by entertaining and flattering them. Meanwhile, the *agents provocateurs* will continue to harass and intimidate the non-Communist nationalists, who will become more and more afraid to speak their minds. Many of them will leave the cities and towns to return in fear and disgust to their rural homes, only to find Communist workers already installed there, who will denounce them for their "crimes against the people." Since many ordinary people suffered during the war at the hands of the government soldiers and police, and met with discrimination from officials, this campaign of denunciation will get a ready popular response. The situation will be further aggravated if, as Be fears, non-Communist members of the N.L.F. who lay down their arms and return to government areas to live are kept under police surveillance and treated as outcasts, despite government promises to reaccept them into society. If the government does not allow such people to take part in an open and legitimate political struggle, which would enable them to gain elective offices and jobs, they will become the nucleus of yet another separatist resistance movement guided by the Communists, and, in Be's words, "thus will the cruel cycle begin anew."

Be's analysis, whether it is unnecessarily dire or not, raises the question of how to deal with the Communists during negotiations and after some sort of settlement is reached. A compromise of one kind or another is inevitable at Paris, most Vietnamese agree. Probably, despite the protestations of Thieu and other government officials, the N.L.F. either will become part of a new coalition or will be allowed to function as a political party. But most Vietnamese fear that even if the Communists should be forced into the open, they would gradually succeed in taking over the country. The first stage in the takeover, it is thought, might be a liberal democracy, like the French Third or Fourth Republic. A period of conflict would ensue, leading to a Communist-dominated coalition. Such a coalition would be neutralist in its foreign policy, and its internal policy would remain anti-Communist on the surface but would in fact be Communist-controlled. American disengagement would create rising anti-American feeling, and only non-Western foreign aid, mostly from the Communist bloc, would be accepted. Finally, as the government lost the support of the West and came to depend more and more on Communist assistance, a military-political coup would solidify Communist rule.

The only way to avoid all this, according to some of the tougher Vietnamese, is to devise a counter-stratagem. "We should not deceive ourselves," one of these Vietnamese, who has had many years of experience in dealing with the Communists, has said. "We remain politically and organizationally weak, and they are strong. They will obviously try to sabotage the peace, and our job will not be made any easier by the fact that after a cease-fire some government troops are likely to go over to the other side, and many of the common people will fall victim to Communist propaganda or otherwise make accommodations with the Communists. Our best course might be to allow the Communists to operate openly for two or three months and then crack down on them. We may have no other choice, for if our population is divided we will not be able to engage them in an open political fight. But even if we should arrest their top leaders, they would retain their tight underground organization, and that is one problem we still have to solve."

There is a great deal of private debate, among both Vietnamese and Americans, over precisely this problem, and nearly always the discussion gravitates toward the central issue of creating and administering an altogether new government mechanism that would be both strong and effective. Can a tightly coördinated system be devised that will adjust itself to Vietnamese institutions and traditions and retain popular support even though the government manipulates it for political purposes? It is generally agreed that there should be political parties in Vietnam, but many Vietnamese believe that the elected government must have enough freedom of maneuver to guide and control mass movements and to direct and coördinate the operation of trained workers of its own. What is needed, the critics say, is an altogether new approach, based on a combination of Communist and Diemist methods and tactics. Though this may sound intolerably autocratic, they say, only such a plan, carefully conceived and carried out, can withstand the Communist political onslaught and construct a democratic base capable of resisting both dictatorship and disintegration.

"In all underdeveloped countries, there is an essential contradiction between centralization and decentralization," says a Vietnamese who played a prominent role under Diem and later helped mount the coup against him. "Too much central control creates problems and delays, and if you disperse power too widely it is abused. What is required is central political control and decentralized administration. The control should be exercised as the Communists exercise it—through trained and disciplined political workers. A good leader must, above all, be open-minded and know how to attract good young people to his cause. He must also know what good organization is, or he will operate sentimentally, on a basis of favoritism—which is something the Vietnamese have always done, and which accounts for the fact that once a man is in office in South Vietnam he invariably turns out to be a disaster. What we have to do today is to reorganize our entire military machine, and find new ways to improve the mechanics of government by improving the quality of leadership. To do this, we don't need an ideology or even a doctrine. What we do need is a rational concept of what we're doing—a reasonable explanation of our policy and how we want to apply it in organizing and leading the masses."

The inhibiting factor in the past has been the lack of prestige that the successive governments since the early days of Diem have suffered from—and so far there is no reason to believe that the Thieu government is any more highly regarded. However, an imperative necessity now takes precedence over everything else in South Vietnam—survival. Moreover, in a number of ways the South Vietnamese have become more efficient in managing a government during the last several years, although their mutual suspicion and factional quarrels continue. Much of the friction between Thieu and Ky has been sustained by the men around them, and the elderly

Huong, though he is still personally popular, has been damaged by the inefficiency of his staff; he has also been undercut by Thieu's staff at Independence Palace. In this Chinese puzzle, it is surprising that anything has been accomplished. There has been added confusion of purpose in attempts to establish pro-government mass movements. After Tet, there were two separate and conflicting organizations—the Liberal Democratic bloc, set up in Thieu's behalf by his Secretary-General at the Palace, Nguyen Van Huong, and the Front for the Salvation of the People, organized by General Tran Van Don and containing many Ky partisans. On July 4th, they were finally welded into the Alliance for Social Revolution, which also included the Association of Workers and Peasants, headed by the country's foremost labor leader, Tran Quoc Buu. Thieu gave the group his blessing, and for a few months helped finance the Alliance with Presidential funds. Dissension soon broke out, however, and the organization made very little progress in rallying the people to an anti-Communist crusade.

If the Vietnamese are at all serious about initiating a thorough overhaul of their political and administrative system, American experts and advisers could still play an important role. A number of Vietnamese, including some of those who have been most critical of the American role here and have blamed us for seeking to "Americanize" the country's political system as well as its economy and its mores, now actually hope for a continuing, if diminishing, American presence. The South Vietnamese have become aware, as perhaps never before, of their powers and prerogatives—the dispute over going to Paris was a significant element in this—but what they still lack is something that the Communists have always possessed; namely, a driving urge to get things done for the good of the country. Now that the real political battle with the Communists is about to be joined, one can only wait and see whether the Saigon government and its representatives in the provinces will be able to shed their partisanship and their urge for self-aggrandizement and devote themselves to the cause of the people they have heretofore only pretended to represent.

Despite the hamlet and village elections in the spring of 1967, there is still little sense of local participation either in the war or in the Saigon government. The Communists, whatever else they have done, have managed, by force or persuasion, to create and maintain a going organization in the settlements they control. They are currently exhorting their partisans to special, heroic efforts to further what are invariably described as "the death throes of the American imperialists and their puppets." By well-tried formulas of agitation and propaganda, they have got villagers to elect (or, when necessary, accept the appointment of) representatives of various elements—youth, women, farmers, and so on—who then theoretically choose the members of the hamlet or village councils and committees. "In scientific terms, the indirect method, in contrast to the more direct Western one, can be compared to atomic fission," a Vietnamese political scientist says, and he adds bluntly, "We should emulate it."

In what is shaping up as an increasingly close race to control the countryside, the government's Accelerated Pacification Campaign, which is working to establish a presence in eleven hundred hamlets between November 1st and February 1st, has already succeeded in doing so in more than eight hundred and fifty. In order to speed up this process of getting to more places with more men than the Communists, some of the fifty-nine-man Revolutionary Development Teams have been split into three smaller units and spread out among three hamlets, and each of these hamlets is supposed to be protected by a platoon of local Popular Forces. The Americans— most notably Deputy Ambassador William Colby, who is now our official in charge of pacification—are fully aware of the continuing need to encourage self-help, self-defense, and self-government among the Vietnamese, and to work as quickly as possible. The question remains: In the race against time, is quality being sacrificed for quantity? In the attempts to reorganize the government's clumsy bureaucracy, a number of plans have been suggested for consolidating the training and organization of all types of workers, not only Revolutionary Development people and village chiefs but also those responsible for organizing women and young people, for health programs, and so on—in short, everyone who has any contact with the village population under any government program. This would undoubtedly make more sense than the present scattered training system, which lacks cohesion and common purpose.

The ineffective use of manpower, especially of qualified young people, remains one of Vietnam's greatest weaknesses, and one to which the Americans in all their years here have devoted little attention, perhaps because they were devoting so much to firepower. The American Army set out from the beginning to create a conventional force in Vietnam—a type of force ill-geared to fighting the Communists' unconventional type of warfare. American bombers, guns, and helicopters have spelled the difference on the battlefields, but there is still nothing resembling a guerrilla force among the South Vietnamese, and in this respect our whole effort here may be compared to giving a number of blood transfusions without any attempt to seek the source of the disease. Once more, there is talk of the kind of military reorganization that is so obviously needed—the kind that would bring about the creation of regional, mobile battle groups up to brigade size and of battalions and companies operating at the provincial and district level, with village self-defense elements protecting their own communities. Most thoughtful young Vietnamese lieutenants and captains, and some higher-ranking officers as well, are aware of the importance of overhauling the entire military structure, but, like the university graduates, they are lost in the shuffle; if they speak their minds, they are invariably regarded as upstarts or troublemakers, and demoted. A year ago, when President Thieu took office, he promised to devote himself to reorganizing both the administrative and the military machinery. So far, however, almost nothing has been done.

In the light of the uncertainty and confusion of purpose in Saigon, it is not surprising that the South Vietnamese have gone to Paris without a firm plan for peace—not that the Americans seem to have one, either. Before the American elections, the South Vietnamese stalled for time partly in the hope that Nixon would not rush them into talks, as Johnson was doing. This hope, however, has now been dissipated, and about all that is expected is a period of grace before and immediately after Nixon sends his own team to the conference. Despite Ky's proposal that he talk to the insurgents in South Vietnam—which may have been prompted simply by American accusations of South Vietnamese dilatoriness—there is a deep division of opinion here over the advisability of opening the door to any such conversations. At this moment, one can hear almost any prediction in Saigon. The consensus, though, is that there will be at least one more round of serious fighting, initiated by the North Vietnamese, before the negotiators get down to business. In any event, a satisfactory solution in Paris seems to be a long way off—as does peace in Vietnam.

19. Saigon

~~~~~~

April 12, 1969

In these past two months, the war in Vietnam has entered a new and extremely complex military and political phase, which in all probability will go on, with increasing complexity and cost in lives, for the rest of this year. For the Saigon government, this stage brings a final opportunity to strengthen and consolidate itself to the point where, even with reduced American help, it can contain and assimilate the southern Communists so that Communist ambitions to reunify the two halves of Vietnam can be indefinitely delayed, as has happened in Korea and Germany. In the current period of what the Communists aptly describe as "fight-fight, talk-talk," regardless of who is saying exactly what to whom, they remain determined to complete their own tentative plans for the sort of accommodation and coalition they are now willing to accept as the first step to power. Historically, it makes small difference whether, in recent weeks, the Americans and the Saigon government "reëscalated" the war first, as the Communists charge and as some Americans acknowledge, or whether the Communists, by their troop movements threatening Saigon and their maneuvers in and around the Demilitarized Zone and elsewhere, provoked both the increase in

American bombing attacks and our more violent response on the ground. What has become clear by now—and was apparent earlier, though no one liked to admit it—is that tacit "understandings" reached in Paris last fall, leading to the halt in the bombing of North Vietnam on November 1st, were little more than semantic rationalizations that enabled both sides to claim concessions while keeping all of their choices intact. If there was some "agreement" regarding the supposed circumstances whereby a decrease in activity by the North Vietnamese around the D.M.Z. would bring about an end to the bombing and facilitate the participation of the National Liberation Front at the Paris talks, it was, at best, fuzzy on the question of Communist attacks on South Vietnamese cities. This is attested by the now admitted differences of opinion among high-ranking Americans of both the outgoing Johnson and the incoming Nixon administrations as to what cities were to be included in the moratorium, and also as to what really constituted an attack —rockets, sapper action and other forms of terror, or ground assaults.

Only immense good will on both sides immediately after the tenuous October talks could have prevented the resumption of serious fighting, and such good will was obviously not forthcoming; given the amount of mutual suspicion, no one could justifiably have expected it. Not only were Saigon and Washington at odds about the concessions made, and especially about the participation of the Front, but once that Allied quarrel was damped down, the long bickering between Hanoi and Washington about the shape of the conference table was an obvious and unavoidable prologue to any substantive deliberations. In this strained atmosphere, the Communists, to test their capacity and the Allied response—above all, President Nixon's response—were bound to try another offensive some time around this year's Tet holiday, or virtually admit their defeat to their own people and to the world. When the attacks finally began, on the night of February 22nd-23rd, after more than two months of jockeying for position by both sides, they were less intense than had been anticipated. Nevertheless, the Communists, by mounting repeated rocket and mortar barrages on more than a hundred towns, cities, and American installations, and by launching ground forays from the D.M.Z. to the Mekong Delta—mostly daring one-shot thrusts and ambushes accompanied by widespread terrorist attacks—have shown a flexibility that they lacked during the now historic offensives of 1968.

What they have been doing, among other things, with the help of new and advanced Soviet weapons, including tanks and rockets, is playing what could almost be called Russian roulette: they are risking, or conceivably inviting, a resumption of the bombing of North Vietnam, knowing that President Nixon is loath to order this for many reasons, the most compelling being that he knows he would be widely criticized around the world if he did. The fact that Communist rockets have killed some fifty Vietnamese civilians in Saigon alone, including more than a dozen children, indicates that the terrorist tactics are primarily designed to frighten the Vietnamese population into supporting the Communists. It is all but impossible to hit specific targets from the distance at which the rockets are launched—two to eight miles.

Whatever the strategy of the rocket assaults, the Communists are making it clear that they intend to go on fighting on the ground, in the belief that they can still reduce American resistance in Vietnam by increasing resistance to the war in the United States. In this sense, the start of their general spring offensive was certainly calculated to let President Nixon know that there was a strict time limit on his immunity from criticism over Vietnam. In the first four days of the February attack, some four hundred Americans and about six hundred South Vietnamese were killed, while the Communists lost six thousand men, mostly North Vietnamese. From the Communists' viewpoint, this ratio, which has since been fairly well maintained, is, although costly, much less so than that in last year's attacks. To put the figures in a different context, the new offensive has doubled the Communists' casualty rate of the previous several months but quadrupled the Allies'. Hanoi is still infiltrating some eight to ten thousand men a month into the South—less than half the average number they sent during the first months of 1968, but enough to compensate for losses and to sustain new hit-and-run offensives in the face of heavy Allied defensive pressure and, especially, truly devastating B-52 bombings. Some of the Communist troop replacements, such as those who have been engaged in the A Shau Valley, in the I Corps area near Laos and west of Danang, are tough, aggressive eighteen- and nineteen-year-olds who apparently have had at least three or four months' training, instead of the one or two that was usually the case a year ago. An Allied general told me, "These youngsters, many of them city boys off the streets of Hanoi and Haiphong, may never learn how to hide in canals and breathe through reeds, the way the old Vietcong guerrillas did, but they will fight until they drop."

Another development that has aroused a great deal of interest here is the Communists' dispatching, during the last few months, of boys in two separate age groups, from ten to fourteen and from fifteen to seventeen, from the South to the North. These youths, sons of veteran southern Communist cadre members, many of whom went north after the partitioning of Vietnam, in 1954, are receiving elementary indoctrination and training and, in the case of the older ones, specialized cadre training somewhere in North Vietnam. The eighty thousand so-called re-groupees who went north in 1954 became the nucleus of the supporting elements sent back south after 1959 to help the "stay-behind" guerrillas launch the present struggle. No one knows how many youths have now gone north to emulate their fathers, and it is not known whether Hanoi plans to train the older ones for fighting at once and use the younger ones to alleviate manpower shortages in the North, or whether the object is to prepare all of them for a new phase of the war to begin five or so years hence. The development, however, is especially significant in view of increasing internal troubles the North Vietnamese are experiencing. The evidence for this over the past few months includes—in addition to some remarkable admissions by the North Vietnamese themselves of mounting economic and political difficulties—the testimony of two recent prisoners, a journalist and a military political officer, to the effect that between two and three hundred prominent members of the Lao Dong Party have been purged in the last year and a half for favoring the pro-Russian line of modified military effort and more emphasis on a continuing political struggle in the South. The purge, said to be extensive, continued throughout the first half of 1968, and may still be going on. Such information would be treated skeptically were it not for a recent flood of broadcasts from North Vietnam decrying the counter-revolutionary sins of lax Party cadres. The alleged errors run the customary Communist gamut from "individualism" and "bureaucracy and commandism" to "corruption and decadence" and "lack of Party discipline." To all appearances, a "rectification campaign" comparable to that carried on in China in 1953 is currently under way in North Vietnam. "Radio Hanoi sounds just the way Radio Peking used to," one expert says.

The confusion of purpose that has marked the Lao Dong Party's leadership recently, in sharp contrast to its previous long years of unity and discipline, was initially commented upon in a scarcely noticed magazine article by Le Duc Tho, Politburo member and Party theoretician, published more than a year ago, in February, 1968. Tho, who is commuting these days between Paris and Hanoi via Moscow and Peking, as the chief adviser of the North Vietnamese peace delegation, alluded indirectly to the difference of approach between Le Duan, the tough, pragmatic architect of last year's Tet offensive, and Truong Chinh, who represents the pro-Chinese element in the Politburo and who favors a return to traditional ideology and protracted revolutionary warfare, with as much emphasis on political as on military measures. "There are at the present time a number of people among us who want the Party to follow the political line of this country or the political line of that country," Tho wrote, "or who, on seeing someone act in a certain way, want to follow that way. This is in no way compatible with Marxism-Leninism. . . . In the anti-United States national-salvation undertaking, we must constantly struggle against every manifestation of demoralization, accommodation, and the fear of difficulty and hardship."

A new article by Truong Chinh, released in another North Vietnamese publication only this past January, concerns "The Failure of the Coöperative System"; it decries misuse of private farm plots and general bad management methods, and offers fresh evidence of the economic difficulties caused by the war, which have been made worse by unexpectedly poor 1968 crop returns. Certainly all signs point to cracks in the heretofore near-monolithic North Vietnamese Communist structure. As one American student of Hanoi politics here has put it, "Given all the wartime troubles—above all, the bombing and the dislocation it has caused—it was inevitable that the end of the bombing would highlight some 'housekeeping' problems. What is particularly interesting is the admission that the bombing halt has not improved the economic situation but, in certain respects, has aggravated it." P. J. Honey, a British expert on North Vietnam, said in mid-March, "It is against [the] background of North Vietnamese Communist division, disarray, and internal conflict that the conduct of fighting in the South, and of the negotiations in Paris, must be assessed."

There is every sign that Hanoi is making such assessments very carefully. Sooner or later, the Communists will decide that talking can help them more than fighting—at least temporarily. In the meantime, however, they are convinced, with considerable logic, that the longer the present fighting lasts, the more they can continue to disrupt the Saigon government's administrative machinery and force acceptance of the idea that the Communists deserve and must be given some sort of political voice in South Vietnamese affairs. How strong that voice will be is the question at issue in the continuing struggle involving many areas of activity, on the government side as well as on the side of the Communists. One factor will be the state of the American-Soviet relationship and the degree of persuasion Moscow might exert on Hanoi. The ultimate political struggle in Vietnam that will follow whatever settlement is worked out may go on for years. It could produce a fresh outbreak of hostilities, including a new Communist-led guerrilla war, a resurgence of military rule, or a true nationalist rebellion opposing both the Communists and whatever Saigon government is in power. It could, finally, even produce peace.

The mood among official Americans remains, as usual, cautiously optimistic—what else could it be, after Washington's long, frustrating commitment?—while the South Vietnamese remain, as usual, more sharply divided in their opinions. In general, there are among them at least four main groups. President Nguyen Van Thieu and his immediate entourage have gained in self-confidence and self-righteousness to the point where most other Vietnamese consider them far removed from reality, even though it is widely agreed that their current programs are sounder in conception and in organization than their earlier ones. The trouble, as many outside the government see it, is that Thieu, despite his grasp of the problems besetting his country, is acting more and more like a latter-day incarnation of Ngo Dinh Diem, the autocratic head of the First Republic, who was murdered in 1963. Thieu's critics point out that he has recently even adopted a private imperial flag—two dragons gazing at a sparkling sun—and since he comes from central Vietnam, the seat of the old emperors, he is being accused of harboring ambitions to cling to power in traditional dynastic fashion. A second group of Vietnamese—including a number of leading political figures who favor a strong central government, with its power tempered by a reasonable amount of decentralization through the provinces, districts, villages, and hamlets—is willing to go along with Thieu, either in support or as a loyal opposition, but many of its members, too, are increasingly worried about some of his attitudes and tendencies. Members of a third group, including key military leaders, are maintaining their wary support of the President but still have their own ambitions and their own ideas of how the country should be run in a time of crisis. The appointment of General Tran Thien Khiem as Deputy Prime Minister in charge of pacification as well as Minister of the Interior, which makes him the second most powerful man in the country, has strengthened the military's hand. Khiem is being touted as the next Prime Minister. A fourth group, by far the largest—though also the least cohesive—remains openly critical of Thieu and of those around him. Seeing themselves as true nationalist spokesmen—protagonists of various religious, political, social, and professional elements—these Vietnamese run the gamut from coffeehouse malcontents to genuinely concerned political opponents of a regime they feel is hopelessly out of touch with public opinion and incapable of providing any inspiration or leadership to oppose the Communists. Some of them confess privately that in an either-or situation in a free election they might even vote for the Communists.

To comprehend the current political and military objectives of the Communists, it is useful to go back to last September, when the Communists' Central Office for South Vietnam (COSVN), which, under the direction of the Lao Dong, is charged with the over-all running of the war in the South, issued a policy statement known as Resolution Eight. This praised the Communist successes, but also noted the failures of last year's Tet drive and of the May and August attacks, and the inability to foster and exploit more mass support both in the cities and in the countryside. Essentially, the resolution justified the policy of renewing the attacks and maintaining "unremitting pressure." After four divisions operating north and northwest of Saigon were withdrawn last fall to Cambodia for replenishment, the high command in Hanoi and at COSVN ordered these troops back into South Vietnam and shifted additional regiments into the III Corps area surrounding Saigon. This gave the Communists a strike force of thirty to forty thousand men around the capital. New caches of food and ammunition were hidden underground in the jungle, and large numbers of mortars and new 122-millimetre rockets were cleverly emplaced within striking distance of the city. A significant innovation—a major result of the lack of coördination among attacking elements during the 1968 Tet assault on the capital—was the creation of five independent battalion-size forces, each known in Vietnamese as a *cum*, which were broken down into sixty- and ninety-man groups. These units, specially trained in street fighting, sabotage, and other harassment techniques, were to act as spearheads within Saigon and at the Bien Hoa air base and the Long Binh supply base nearby, and if they were successful in their attempts to cause disruption, and even "to blow up Saigon from within," a major attack on the capital would follow.

Beginning in September, the *cum* units crossed over from Bathu, in Cambodia, and started moving eastward toward Saigon, carrying AK-47 automatic rifles, *plastique* explosives, telecommunication sets, and other equipment. After approaching the capital by two infiltration routes, they were ordered to leave their supplies at secret caches and to proceed unarmed into the city; support units would bring their gear in to them. Early in January, by which time the Communists had twenty-two battalions of regulars—more than six thousand men—poised within twenty kilometres of Saigon, twenty-one members of one *cum* formation were captured in Hau Nghia Province, just west of the city, and they gave important information about the new attack plan. Although other *cum* elements probably did succeed in reaching Saigon, about a hundred and fifty were rounded up by the police and intelligence organizations. It was because of this, and because of the American success in keeping the battalions north of Saigon off balance, that the major Communist offensive planned for December and January did not materialize and the rocket and ambush attacks followed instead.

From the political standpoint, the new strategy, based partly on the *cum* spearheads, is doubly significant, for it seems to indicate that—for the time being, anyway—the Communists no longer believe so strongly in the possibility of spontaneous urban uprisings in support of general attacks on Saigon and other cities, as they did in last year's nationwide Tet assault. During November, December, and January, they did, to be sure, seek to instigate some demonstrations in Saigon, but they were disappointed with the response they got, especially when the government cracked down hard on would-be demonstrators, in line with Thieu's new, tough policy of not countenancing any activity judged to be a threat to the government's position—a policy that is getting tougher all the time. In mid-March, a ten-year sentence at hard labor was handed out to Thich Thien Minh, the Secretary-General of the militant An Quang Pagoda group of Buddhists, for harboring draft dodgers and deserters at his Buddhist Youth Center, not far from the pagoda, and for permitting pro-Communist activities to be conducted there. Most observers felt that although Thien Minh must have been aware of what was going on in the building, the sentence was unduly harsh and would simply serve to antagonize the militant Buddhists further.

The sentencing of Thien Minh, with whom I had a private talk in the Saigon suburbs the day before his arrest, late in February, is particularly significant in view of the recent attitude of the Communists toward the An Quang group of Buddhists. Following the American bombing halt last November, the Communists sought to take advantage of the friction between the Americans and the Thieu government over the seating of the National Liberation Front in Paris. In the words of one Communist document issued as a "guideline" at the time, "Johnson's clique remains very confused and brings pressure upon Thieu's clique owing to the imminent election of a U.S. President. Therefore, they can exert great pressure on Thieu by either using the political influence of the anti-Thieu Buddhist sect of An Quang or staging a *coup d'état* to overthrow Thieu if successful results cannot be immediately achieved." If the Americans should use the An Quang group against Thieu, the Communists suggested, "this would be a very favorable occasion for us to step up all aspects of our activities and rapidly stage the political struggle in towns and district seats." Regardless of such possibilities, the Catholic-oriented Thieu government has done nothing to improve its relations with the An Quang group, and it has, in fact, issued a charter to a group of opposition *bonzes,* or monks, headed by Thich Tam Chau, who has been ill or out of the country for most of the last three years and has had little influence.

The arrest and sentencing of Thien Minh could effectively make martyrs of him and his fellow-militants, as was done when the pagodas were raided in 1963. Thieu, who warned Thien Minh to cease his anti-government activities several weeks ago, when the monk made a particularly critical speech, is obviously aware of this possibility but chose to throw the book at him anyway, perhaps as an object lesson to others, and because he figured the An Quang group was too weak right now to react. Whatever happens, the Communists, who have been hoping for just such an issue to drive a wedge between the Americans and the Vietnamese, seem bound to benefit. The Americans at our Embassy, still extolling Thieu as the most "stable" of all the post-Diem Vietnamese leaders—as they earlier extolled Ky and several others before him—have had their own differences of opinion about the Buddhists. A minority has wanted to make a fresh approach to the An Quang group, while the majority has argued that the militant *bonzes*—as at best an untrustworthy, and at worst a pro-Communist, element—should be allowed to wither on the vine. It seems hard to believe that Thien Minh was naïve enough not to know that his Youth Center was being used as a Communist propaganda mill and a hideout for deserters, but at the same time both he and his fellow An Quang leader Thich Tri Quang, whom I also saw privately, a week after Thien Minh's arrest, have been seeking American support in their campaign to get Thieu to broaden his government and build a national union of religious and political forces.

Tri Quang, a far more cryptic and interesting personality than Thien Minh (at one moment he can be hard and remote, and the next warm and confiding, flashing a brilliant smile) maintained that the Americans had committed themselves to Vietnam, for good or for bad, and now they could not shirk their responsibility. "Political parties as such mean nothing," Tri Quang told me. "Only religions count in Vietnam, and President Nixon must readjust to that realization. What is important now is not just a 'peace Cabinet' but a decent new government that welcomes religious coöperation. A new approach and attitude are necessary whatever it is you want —peace, war, the defeat of the Communists by military or political means. But you cannot go on doing what you're doing and expect any results." The government of Thieu and Ky and Prime Minister Tran Van Huong was "a losing one," he added. "On the one hand, you cannot manipulate them, and, on the other hand, they are incapable of controlling the masses." Thieu's handling of the Thien Minh case was "infantile," he asserted—a defensive and repressive maneuver as fruitless as "beating the wind." There should be no question of martyrdom. "What is important is having a just cause," he said. "It is not a matter of one group or one religion against another. There is simply no justification for oppressing the Buddhists and preventing their full participation in the national life of the country. It is not too late, but there must be new ideas."

In South Vietnam today, there are some fifty registered political parties and nearly a hundred unregistered ones. Among them are many that are shopworn or outworn, despite their efforts to assume new guises. Some, their leaders motivated by opportunism, seek merely to capitalize on the present uncertainty and on the overwhelming desire for peace; a few represent bona-fide efforts to espouse new ideas and to confront the revolutionary challenges offered by the Communists with feasible alternatives, including ones that are equally authoritarian but perhaps may better fit the demands of contemporary Vietnamese society. Despite the dire need for a two- or three-party system, fragmentation, mistrust, ambition, and competition still run so deep in Vietnam that the efforts of the National Assembly to write a new political law that would limit the number of parties have so far proved fruitless. Legal niceties and definitions alone won't work anyway, for what is needed, and is so obviously lacking, is the willingness of political leaders, movements, and groups to work together instead of against each other. A Vietnamese politician I have known for many years told me, "The great danger is that when we do come down to a system of one man, one vote, as we undoubtedly must, there will still be so much division that we will totally defeat ourselves. The non-Communists may represent a majority, but the Communists, as a well-organized minority, may win by default. It won't matter whether they call themselves the National Liberation Front or the Saigon Soccer Association."

So many parties, movements, forces, and blocs are competing with each other today that it is virtually impossible to sort them all out. Within the religious groups, the three-way split among the militant clerics, the more conservative clerics, and the lay Buddhists continues to immobilize the Buddhists as a political force. The two clerical factions together probably still control about a million votes, and while the lay Buddhist group shows some signs of becoming stronger and of drawing support from the two quarrelling religious bodies, it lacks dynamic leadership and faces a reluctance on the part of the average Buddhist, whether he practices the religion or simply goes along nominally, to offend the *bonzes.* The Hoa Hao, an offshoot Buddhist sect with about a million and a half members, mostly in the Delta, is also badly divided. In the western part of the Delta, notably in An Giang and Chau Doc Provinces, the Hoa Hao villages have effectively organized and armed themselves and either fended off the Communists or made accommodations with them that could have some interesting results when peace finally comes. The other principal sect, the Cao Dai, an eclectic organization, whose ample pantheon houses Christ, Buddha, Victor Hugo, and Winston Churchill, and which is guided by a hierarchy composed of cardinals and "zodiacal lords," claims about two and a half million members. Primarily active in Tay Ninh Province on the Cambodian border and, to a lesser extent, in ten other provinces, the Cao Dai is split today into no less than a dozen factions, with the result that its political influence is less than the Hoa Hao's, though each is credited with controlling six or seven hundred thousand voters. About fifty thousand Cao Dai are close to the Communists, and in a showdown more might go along with them. Without some outside guidance, it seems doubtful whether the religious groups will ever consolidate themselves and play the important role in South Vietnam that their collective following warrants. If anything makes it easier for the Communists to dominate the future, it will be this failure to rally the scattered religious forces.

It seems highly doubtful if Thieu will make the compromises and adjustments required to heal the wounds. As a converted Catholic with a Catholic wife, he represents a minority element, just as Diem and his family did. He has appointed a preponderant number of Catholics as province chiefs and to other important posts, both military and civilian. The Church hierarchy, organized into two archdioceses, eleven dioceses, and eight hundred parishes, wields a political influence transcending its numerical strength—a million and a half communicants among the seventeen million in South Vietnam—and the hierarchy, as it did under Diem, appears to have considerable influence in the Presidential Palace. Almost half the Senate and about a third of the House are Catholic; Archbishop

Nguyen Van Binh, of Saigon, the most important Catholic prelate in the country, has so far remained aloof from any Catholic political movement or legislative bloc, and has even discouraged such activity. However, there are signs that both he and Thieu are willing to lend their approval, if not their support, to a new Catholic-led —although not exclusively Catholic—organization, the Nhan Xa, or Revolutionary Social Humanist, Party.

Legally registered in October, 1967, the Nhan Xa was quietly started two years earlier by a mixed group of prominent clerical and professional leaders who were mostly Catholics, and many of whom, as former Diemist officials or supporters, had been members of the old Can Lao movement, organized by Diem and his brother Ngo Dinh Nhu. The Can Lao, which began as a benevolent workers' association, evolved into a combined political party and secret society that wielded considerable power over the entire Diem-Nhu administration. The Nhan Xa, while admittedly borrowing some of Nhu's mystical thoughts, professes to be far more practical in its aims. Referring to the "unitarian characteristics" of Vietnam, it opposes both "excessive decentralization" and "excessive centralization." Between these two extremes, it favors an administrative policy of "deconcentration" that will enable "the people at various levels to participate in the management of their localities through direct election of their representatives to administer villages and hamlets . . . and to counsel the government authorities and civil servants at provincial and district levels." Strongly against any form of coalition government, the Nhan Xa seeks an independent South Vietnam that will reëstablish relations gradually with the North. In basing its immediate program on what it calls the "preparatory stage of the struggle for peace," the Nhan Xa favors the "Vietnamization of the war," with a gradual reduction in American military strength but with the Allies continuing joint search-and-destroy operations until these are no longer necessary.

The best-known leaders of the Party are Truong Vong Cuu, a former Cabinet minister under Diem, and Bishop Nguyen Van Thuan, whose mother is Diem's sister. A Buddhist lawyer from Saigon named Le Truong Quat, who served in Diem's National Assembly, is one of the Party's chief organizers and spokesmen. According to Quat, the Nhan Xa seeks to maintain "an independent stand" but is ready to support Thieu "if the President is sincere, clarifies the ambiguous relationship between himself and the

Prime Minister, and gives a greater voice to Cabinet ministers who will represent a wider variety of political and religious views." Whereas, during the Diemist days, the Can Lao increasingly isolated itself, the Nhan Xa is openly seeking the collaboration of other parties, including the religious groups. Neither the Cao Dai nor the Hoa Hao have shown much interest so far, nor have the militant Buddhists. On the other hand, a number of other parties and movements seem willing to collaborate but are waiting to see what kind of mass strength the new group develops. These include the Tan Dai Viet and the Revolutionary Dai Viet, the two main branches of an old nationalist party. Since Thieu is close to the Dai Viet, coöperation between its members and the Catholic-dominated regime has tended to increase, and the Nhan Xa could serve as an ultimate bridge.

While the Nhan Xa's importance at this point should not be exaggerated, it stands out in the murky Vietnamese political scene chiefly because it is better organized and has more of a sense of purpose and direction than most other parties or movements. Another old-line nationalist party, for instance, the Vietnam Quoc Dan Dang, is split into three main and several minor factions, and recent attempts to consolidate them have failed. Both this party and the Dai Viet seem primarily interested in their own survival, and though both have some representatives in the National Assembly and have taken part in local elections, neither has come up with anything resembling a dynamic program. The political scene is further confused today as a result of shifting alliances in the National Assembly, and especially in the Senate, where six different tickets of ten members each were elected in 1967. The Senate is now divided into a number of new "working blocs" that may or may not evolve into political parties. One of these calls itself the Civil Rights bloc and has about fifteen members, and another, claiming twenty-two senators, is the Social Democratic bloc. Just to confuse matters more, there is also a Democratic Socialist bloc. Thieu, whose relations with the National Assembly, and especially with the Senate, reached a low point last month in a petty fight over a small budget cut, has tried, so far with little success, to mend his political fences with the legislative branch through the medium of the Liberal Democratic Force, another bloc aspiring to be a party. All in all, the political picture in South Vietnam remains confused to the point of chaos.

The Communists, with their strategy of constant harassment, will probably try to capture a provincial capital or two, and some district capitals, and raise the Vietcong flag there for a few days. In the words of one of their recent manifestos, they intend to "wipe out the enemy administration at the lowest levels in cities and towns and, if possible, occupy them," seek to "disintegrate" the Vietnamese armed forces through "military proselytizing," conduct "small but harmful attacks on U.S. troops, especially their depots and airfields," "sabotage and occupy sensitive communications axes," and "intensify attacks by special action and secret self-defense forces in cities and towns." The recent increase throughout the country in terrorism, kidnapping, and assassination has confirmed this intent. In Saigon alone within the past several weeks, a Minister of Education and a university professor who might have succeeded him in his post were killed in the streets, while one of Thieu's top military advisers and Prime Minister Huong narrowly escaped after attempts on their lives.

The Communists are also concentrating on their own apparatus in the countryside. Out of twenty-five hundred villages in South Vietnam, they now claim to have established new Revolutionary Village Committees in fifteen hundred, though they have only identified about half of them by name, and they may have reached a peak in what they can accomplish at the moment. In many cases, these committees exist only on a shadow basis, with perhaps an undercover cadreman or two in charge, while in other cases the committees are governments-in-exile—that is, their members are somewhere off in the jungle or are hiding out in nearby towns. The five- to nine-man committees, supposedly appointed by larger, elected Revolutionary Councils—which often don't exist—are at least half composed of members of the People's Revolutionary Party, and these hard-core Communist cadremen hold the key jobs as heads of the military and security, financial and economic, and propaganda and cultural subcommittees. In certain cases, the P.R.P. members may go completely underground and delegate the work of the committees to semi-overt agents, an increasing number of whom are women. While women are hard workers, the Communists acknowledge that "they are credulous and cannot resist love" and need "special indoctrination on revolutionary concepts toward sex relations." As so-called "commo-liaison" agents—couriers and spies—young girls and boys, some no more than ten years old, are also being drafted.

Early in March, after several months of silence, a new declaration was issued by the Alliance of National, Democratic, and Peace Forces, which was formed as a new front group after the 1968 Tet offensive. The Alliance, the statement said, was "ready to coördinate its activities with those of the patriotic forces and individuals, regardless of their political tendencies and religions, including members of the puppet administration and armed forces, who oppose the U.S. aggressive war and approve [our] struggle slogans." The reappearance of the Alliance, with its new coalition line, suggests that the Communists still intend to introduce it in Paris as a middleman group to serve as a bridge between the Saigon government and the National Liberation Front. Such maneuvers are likely to increase as the negotiations move along. Afterward, when an open political contest starts in South Vietnam, the Alliance or something like it will be the popular instrument through which the Communists hope to defeat the government and gain power. Thus, if the covert People's Revolutionary Party apparatus remains the tough bedrock, the Alliance is the soft turf on top.

Saigon's newly expressed willingness to deal "realistically" with the National Liberation Front still leaves the government without any discernible strategy for peace. While the Communists are adjusting their apparatus to meet the possible contingencies of more fighting, less fighting, or no fighting, the government, in the words of one senator, remains "mentally unarmed." Both in the cities and in the countryside, I have lately found a growing curiosity on the part of many people about what is happening in Paris, about dealing with the Front, and about a number of other matters, including the long-delayed and now newly promised implementation of a land-reform program. In some places, there is a new spirit of community responsibility, evidenced by the spontaneous growth of local self-defense forces, and people seem more aware of the need to solve their own problems and settle their own fate than at any time since the fall of Diem. On the other hand, the issue of creating real village and hamlet autonomy, of giving communities control over locally collected taxes and over the distribution of outside aid without interference, is still unclarified and is a source of continuing dissatisfaction. "This remains a war of oppressed people, and pacification alone is not enough," one veteran nationalist who is also a senator told me. "There can be no democracy through militarization. Unless the dignity of the individual is realized, everything will fall apart even if the Communists leave." The pacification programs, while more consolidated, are still based too much on statistics and too little on political motivation—the very area in which the Communists excel. In the cities, where more than half the country's population is now congregated, hardly anything has been done by the government to come to grips with serious problems of social welfare, slum clearance, and public housing, and the mounting urban crisis is becoming a major threat here, as elsewhere in the world. "The streets are cleaner than they were last year in Saigon," a friend of mine said, "but there is still a lot of garbage in people's heads." In the cities and in the countryside, officials are being constantly changed and are often afraid to act on their own, or else they act too overbearingly and injudiciously. There is a strange over-all sense of irresolution, notwithstanding all the reiterated resolve. One is constantly reminded of the old saying, "The operation was successful, but the patient died."

Everywhere I went on a recent trip, in Thua Thien and Quang Tri Provinces in the north, in Tay Ninh in the center, and in the Delta, I heard encouraging reports about such things as the increase in Chieu Hoi returnees and the progress being made by the Phoenix Program, the combined American-Vietnamese intelligence effort that is now rounding up about two thousand members a month of the V.C.I. Yet except for using some of the Chieu Hoi defectors as "Kit Carson" scouts—guides on military attacks or patrols—very little is being done to reincorporate these people into the social and economic order, and they are in effect second-class citizens, languishing in camps or kept under surveillance as "parolees." Most of the V.C.I. being captured are low-level operatives and appear to be replaceable, though there are continuing signs that a shortage of cadremen is forcing higher-level Communists to take over several jobs simultaneously. This could, in due time, seriously affect their political plans, but the Phoenix Program remains essentially a defensive one, as does the Provincial Reconnaissance Unit Program, which involves small armed forays against known or suspected Communists. Neither program is a substitute for positive political action. They are counter-terrorist but not counter-insurgency programs, if by "counter-insurgency" one means offering people alternatives that will convince them, beyond fear of reprisal, that they have more to gain than to lose by siding with the government.

In spite of the apparent success of the three-month Accelerated Pacification Campaign that ended on January 31st, and which, according to official figures, brought "relative security" to some twelve hundred hamlets heretofore regarded as "contested" or "insecure," and in spite of plans designed to bring ninety per cent of the population under the protection of the government by the end of this year, far too many Vietnamese in too many places are still reserving decision about backing Saigon's programs. This hesitation is expressed in ways ranging from reluctance to run for office in local hamlets or villages, for fear of being killed by the Communists, to simple peasant belief in keeping options open to accommodate whatever side ultimately seems to be winning. In the words of Lieutenant Colonel Nguyen Be, who heads the training program for Revolutionary Development cadres, "Restoration of adequate governing powers for the village means that elected village officials are vested with *actual* and not just theoretical powers. They must in fact as well as theory lead their village. This means that both the Village People's Council and the Village Administrative Committee must employ and effectively deploy those armed units, those political cadres, and those permanent administrative units belonging to the village."

Be, who, as an ex-Vietminh leader, remains one of the most imaginative government officials, points out that "the old concept of [village] support made people slaves to technology and made the leadership slaves to the specialist class," he says. "The villages and hamlets have not been self-sufficient units but have been tied to a long logistical system running from top to bottom instead of having an acceptable degree of self-sufficiency on the *lower* levels. . . . Notwithstanding the fact that foreign technical advisers really desire to help us, the fact remains that we have delivered ourselves into slavery to foreign technical advisers through the *de-facto* political power wielded by our domestic technicians."

I reflected on what Be had said during a visit to a number of villages and hamlets in Quang Tri and Thua Thien, in the upper tier of the northern I Corps area, where, especially in the eastern coastal regions, large numbers of refugees, who previously fled into hastily assembled camps or into district towns and into Hué and Quang Tri City, are voluntarily returning, or being returned, to their native homes in the now cleared regions. Others are creating new communities, many of which are fishing villages. The government, with the Americans' help, is giving the returning refugees aluminum sheeting for the roofs of houses destroyed during last year's Tet and May offensives, small gasoline-engine rotary plows to replace their dead water buffaloes, and fertilizer, seeds of newly developed high-yield rice, and various other forms of aid, including guns for local self-defense forces. The extent of this rehabilitation and the emergence of thriving new communities is impressive, and for the first time in a number of years there seems to be a new spirit of hope, borne out by the zeal of the new self-defense elements—composed of local men (and some women) between the ages of eighteen and forty-five—and by the sustained improvement of the Regional and Popular Forces, which bolster provincial and local defenses and conduct some offensive operations. Nevertheless, as I walked through half a dozen communities and observed from a helicopter a score of others, including some that were still empty and barren, I wondered whether it was a question not only, in some places, of too little too late but also, in others, of too much too soon. Too much of what I saw either had an American W.P.A. air about it or smacked of precipitate action, undertaken without sufficient preparation and organization. There was something missing in most of these rejuvenated hamlets and villages, something that marred the obvious satisfaction of those who had come home again to their native soil and their ancestors' graves. What was lacking was a feeling of permanence, of belief that things would *stay* good, of assurance that after the first harvest it would be worth plowing again and planting a new crop. Too many times, through the long years in Vietnam, I have been to places like these that have changed hands over and over again, to the point where firepower can no longer sustain faith. Would it be any different now—or five years hence?

The question arose even more sharply farther south, in Quang Nam and Quang Ngai Provinces, large parts of which are still held by the Communists. A number of what are called "soft-cordon" or "long-cordon" operations have been under way in this part of the I Corps area for several months. The basic principle of all these campaigns is military saturation plus long-term development. Battalions of American and South Vietnamese troops are dropped in or around a Communist-held region. The population, having been forewarned, is brought out to nearby temporary camps, and, over a period of weeks, the region is carefully combed. Eight- or ten-foot metal probes are used to seek out underground hideouts. Lists of known Communists are carefully checked, and every person brought out of the area, or encountered still in it, is fingerprinted. On the Batangan Peninsula, for example, an old Vietcong stronghold, twelve thousand five hundred people were taken to a "holding and interrogation center" near Quang Ngai City while the peninsula was gone over, and some two hundred Vietcong were killed and two hundred and fifty V.C.I. were apprehended. The operation, which began in mid-January and is still going on, was described to me by a colonel as "the most complicated and enlightened one I've ever seen in Vietnam." As the cordon was closed, the people were gradually shifted back into their hamlets and the pacification parts of the plan, including the organization of self-defense units, were stepped up. Compared to operations of a similar nature that were conducted earlier in the war with far less expertise and far less regard for people, the Batangan performance was a commendable one, but, again, I could not help but recall that three years ago, on the upper part of the same peninsula, a large area had been similarly "cleansed" by the American Marines and a few months later the Vietcong were back as strong as ever. It may be that this time there will be sufficient inspiration for the returned villagers to decide that the area will be protected and supported by the government long enough for them to organize and defend their own communities, but I wouldn't want to bet on it. The Communists will not easily give up such a valuable piece of ground, and sooner or later, cease-fire or no cease-fire, they will filter back into Batangan. The villagers will be in a better position than before, perhaps, to protect themselves and their new plows and all the other new forms of assistance they have received, but whether they do so or not will depend on those intangible factors—self-help, self-determination, self-rule, and, in the final analysis, self-respect.*

---

*It is worth noting here that the infamous My Lai massacre of March, 1968, took place in this area and that the Vietnamese who were murdered included people originally from the Batangan Peninsula.

Everywhere in Vietnam, the pattern remains so uneven that it is both dangerous and difficult to make snap judgments about what will or will not happen during this phase. In Hué, for example, which I saw in ruins and despair at the end of the Tet offensive last year, the physical recovery and the rejuvenated spirit of the people are remarkable. During the Communist attacks in 1968, when North Vietnamese and Vietcong troops held the city for three weeks, three-quarters of the beautiful old imperial capital was damaged, and afterward nearly a hundred and fifteen thousand of the city's hundred and sixty thousand population required relief, nearly fifty thousand being homeless. More than a million and a half dollars of reconstruction aid was poured into Hué, including two hundred and sixty thousand aluminum sheets for roofing and a hundred thousand bags of cement. Except for the old Citadel, which will never be completely restored, most of the city has now been rebuilt. All the rubble has been cleared away, and the street-side and garden graves of the several thousand citizens who were killed in the big attack have been refurbished; during Tet this year, I saw silent mourners strewing fresh flowers on them. The Communists, who lost five thousand men in the Hué attack, caused so much terror and destruction before they gave up that—despite the damage the Americans and the South Vietnamese did—it is now apparent that the North Vietnamese lost more than they gained by their display of power. The citizens of Hué have traditionally been highly independent and, if anything, anti-government, but they now seem determined to protect themselves against any new attack.

Much of the credit for Hué's recovery belongs to Colonel Le Van Than, who was appointed its mayor as well as province chief in March, 1968. Than, a Catholic in a predominantly Buddhist community, has done such an exemplary job of organizing both city and provincial forces and of getting all political and religious groups to work together that he has won the affection and respect of almost everyone. I spent a day with him in Hué and travelling by jeep and helicopter to other hamlets and villages in the province. One of the places we visited was Lai Chu, a village just outside Hué, to which six thousand of its eight thousand former inhabitants have now returned. Lai Chu is blessed with fine soil, and the residents were busily cultivating their rice fields and picking vegetables, which they had recently begun to plant for sale to American troops. The day before, I had driven through Lai Chu with Colonel Tom Bowen, the American senior provincial adviser, who told me that in the previous two months there had been only two small contacts with the Communists from the nearby western hills. That same night, however, a Vietcong platoon came down out of the mountains, apparently to collect food in Lai Chu and to visit relatives. Four members of the platoon, who had cousins in the village, were shot and killed. When I went out there early the next morning with Colonel Than, the four bodies were lying in a sunlit field, with four AK-47 rifles, ammunition belts, and some documents stacked up next to them. The villagers were gathered on the side of the field, and the Colonel spoke to them. He told them there was no need for their "cousins" to have been killed, that the men's lives would have been saved if the villagers had been able to persuade them to come over to the government side. Than's whole tone was neither bitter nor recriminatory, and he spoke with a sense of the long war's tragedy. The villagers seemed deeply impressed by what was obviously more than the usual pep talk, and I left Lai Chu with the feeling that this was one place where the people now had a sense that their destiny was in their own hands.

Vietnam, Vietnam . . . There are no sure answers. Many valid criticisms can continue to be made of the Thieu government. By and large, there is no doubt that the regime is neither popular nor progressive. It moves at its own pace, for its own purposes, and despite its frequent promises of reform it has actually accomplished very little during almost a year and a half in power, beyond recovery from last year's Tet disaster. To my mind, it lacks direction and conviction and has never been in touch with the Vietnamese people. It is at best a stopgap, and at worst it will veer more toward authoritarianism. Consequently, during the current military-political phase of the war, and possibly during at least part of the next phase, when the real Paris showdown starts, South Vietnam's ability to create a dynamic alternative to the solutions offered by the Communists—whose declining popularity is revealed by their increasing use of indiscriminate terror—will depend on men in the field like Colonel Than and Colonel Be and the support they can obtain. There is always the danger, as there always has been before, that if such men become too successful and too popular, if they push their ideas of reform too far, they will be quietly removed from office. But a latent nationalism, based on local and regional pride, is still a force in the country, and it must be given a voice, while at the same time some effort must be made—if not through Thieu, through some other political leadership—to inspire an effective national consensus.

The Vietnamese are not yet ready to take over most of the military and civilian programs fostered and guided by the United States. That they are not is the fault of the Americans, who permitted and even encouraged the Vietnamese to become overdependent. This is now beginning to change, but things are not changing fast enough. Nothing, therefore, it seems to me, would make the Vietnamese more aware of the imperative need to stand on their own feet than the withdrawal from South Vietnam this year of at least a hundred thousand American soldiers, including some combatants, and as much as half of the cumbersome and ineffectual American bureaucracy.

20.   **Paris**

~~~~~~

July 12,   1969

As the Vietnam situation has unfolded in the last few weeks, several important events have taken place, in an inexorable sequence that suggests both Greek drama and a peculiarly American tragic dénouement. However quickly or slowly things move henceforth in Paris and in Vietnam, they must approach a resolution, whose outlines are beginning to become apparent, and, regardless of its exact form, it seems likely to recall both the pitiless harshness and the moral ambiguity of a Dreiser novel. No matter what we learn from our Vietnam experience about dealing with revolutionary and nationalist situations, and this may be very little, either substantively or psychologically, our whole future relationship with Asia can be seriously and permanently damaged—a fear that is probably reflected in the President's recently announced plan to go there this summer.

The chief event that has drastically altered the situation is, of course, President Nixon's decision, or at least his firmly stated resolve, or hope, as expressed at his press conference on June 19th, to remove all American combat forces from Vietnam by the end of 1970, leaving behind only enough men—perhaps two hundred thousand to two hundred and fifty thousand—to give the refurbished

South Vietnamese forces logistical support. The second important event originated in Hanoi, which, while persisting in its demand for the immediate withdrawal of *all* American forces and matériel, now has made an explicit, if probably temporary, political decision to allow the South Vietnamese Communists to travel their own revolutionary path—albeit under the sharp, experienced eyes of the hard men of the Communist North. What this means is that, for reasons of their own, the North Vietnamese have decided, in lieu of making further attempts at military conquest, now apparently unattainable, they will seek to "Vietminhize" the South—to follow the precedent of the broad coalition front, called the Vietminh, that the Communists created in the northern jungles during the Second World War and then successfully used in establishing their new government in Hanoi in 1945. (A similar but short-lived Vietminh-style effort in Saigon, called the Committee of the South, was quashed by British occupation troops that same year, before French troops and the French colonial administration returned.)

The Vietminh formula permits a large number of non-Communist, and even apolitical and primarily religious, elements to take part in the government during its initial period, devoted to building mass strength, after which the non-Communists undoubtedly will be eliminated by whatever means are handiest. Hanoi's decision to attempt this seems to derive from a decision, probably a very reluctant one, to take full control of the South more slowly than it had originally hoped to do, and to unite Vietnam later—perhaps five or ten years from now. This change of approach was signalled chiefly by the creation, in early June, of a new Provisional Revolutionary Government by the National Liberation Front and its fellow-travelling South Vietnamese adjunct, the Alliance of National, Democratic, and Peace Forces. The new P.R.G.—which, like the Front, has its headquarters somewhere in the South Vietnamese jungle near Cambodia, and which has already been given diplomatic recognition by twenty-three nations—has twenty-five members, of whom at least nine, including three generals of the North Vietnamese Army, are said to belong to the Lao Dong Party.

A third, and most uncertain, element at present is the manner in which the South Vietnamese regime of President Nguyen Van Thieu will try to avoid accepting the coalition government sought by the Communists and will propose an alternative formula for holding free elections in which the Communists can take part. Such elections would probably limit the Communists' strength to twenty or twenty-five per cent of the total, and so far, not unexpectedly, they have refused to accept, even in principle, any election scheme that does not provide for the replacement of the Thieu government by a provisional coalition in which they would automatically be given a prominent role—an evolution much more likely to assure their ultimate dominance.

While the Americans and the North Vietnamese continue to spar over the question of a mutual withdrawal or a mutual reduction of forces—ultimately, of course, Washington may go ahead and withdraw unilaterally anyway—the Vietnamese in the South will go on trying to work out some compromise on the coalition-vs.-elections issue. If this proves impossible, the war will drag on, although probably less fiercely as the year passes and as Hanoi responds to American withdrawals with unannounced ones of its own, or at least with a decrease of its infiltration rate. Thus, the over-all reduction of violence advocated by, among others, Averell Harriman, who was President Johnson's chief negotiator in Paris, should gradually occur, though far more slowly than most Americans and most of the rest of the world would like. The process might be accompanied by formal or informal agreements on local and regional cease-fires in Vietnam, and perhaps in Laos, too—or, at least, on reductions in the level of American air operations against the infiltration of North Vietnamese troops along the Ho Chi Minh Trail. These agreements might be supervised by some sort of international body—an idea that the Communists have not actually rejected, though they have refused to consider any international supervision of election procedures in advance of a coalition government's being established in the South.

In any event, as one looks at the many possibilities and the many imponderables, two points stand out: First, President Nixon has made it clear that he wishes to reduce the American role in Vietnam in the shortest possible time, and apparently hopes he can do this without leaving the Thieu government, or any successor Saigon regime with similar aims, in the lurch. Second, the chances of the Communists' winning politically what the Americans have kept them from winning militarily are better than they were before, not simply because the Communists are better organized for political victory (they always have been) but because the internal differences within the Saigon government continue unabated. For this, Saigon itself is chiefly to blame, though Washington certainly bears a heavy responsibility for the failure to inspire a more successful consolidation of anti-Communist forces in the fifteen years since the beginning of the American commitment.

The obdurate line that the Communists in Paris are currently following, designed to achieve their dual aim of hastening the American decision to withdraw and either overthrowing or weakening the Thieu government and replacing it with a "peace Cabinet," has been repeatedly spelled out here, both at the weekly meetings of the peace conference and during interviews, formal and informal, between Western correspondents and Communist officials. Among the officials, it is generally agreed, the most forceful and impressive has been Le Duc Tho, who is one of the leading theoreticians among the North Vietnamese Communists, and who is generally ranked No. 4 or 5 in Hanoi's Politburo. Tho, a tall, imposing man with an air of supreme confidence, is the "chief adviser" to the North Vietnamese delegation, and, as such, travels back and forth between Hanoi and Paris, making occasional stopovers at Moscow and Peking. During an impromptu conversation I had with him at a cocktail party in June, Tho smilingly and patiently declared over and over again that there could be no compromise with the Thieu government. "Thieu, Ky, and Premier Tran Van Huong must go—all three must go," he said. He also reiterated, with equal firmness, that a coalition in South Vietnam had to precede any election agreement. It is worth noting that these strong assertions came not from a representative of the newly created P.R.G.—such as Tran Buu Kiem, the erstwhile head of the Front's Paris delegation, or Mme. Nguyen Thi Binh, who, as Foreign Minister of the P.R.G., again heads that delegation here, as she did at first —but from "the big man from Hanoi." If there had been any additional need to demonstrate who calls the tune in the South, he provided it. And, in a long interview two days later with Murrey Marder, of the Washington *Post,* Tho went further; in the face of Nixon's latest comments on large-scale withdrawal of troops, he castigated the President's "warlike nature," described his "maneuvers" as comparable to "building castles in the air," and accused him of wanting to prolong the war by strengthening the South Vietnamese forces until they could become, in effect, American mercenaries. As Marder summed it up, "The thrust of Mr. Tho's remarks was intended to show no ray of hope, no way around yielding to the demands of the Communist side."

This apparently implacable Communist opposition to the present Saigon government gives rise to such questions as what the Communists hope to achieve by it, how long they are likely to maintain it, and whether their obduracy has its origin in weakness or in strength. Any attempt to answer the questions involves consideration of the situation in North Vietnam, insofar as outsiders or occasional visitors can gauge it. The North Vietnamese have shown a remarkable strength and determination, a truly astonishing endurance, having been afflicted over the last two years with severe manpower shortages, crop failures, widespread industrial destruction, and an over-all decline in production. Though the Communist delegates in Paris have been stressing with renewed vigor the goal of "total victory," the northern leaders—most recently Ho Chi Minh himself, in a talk to high-ranking Army cadres in May—have been emphasizing the need to "economize human and material resources and insure a satisfactory maintenance of weapons and equipment" and, in every way possible, "protect the Socialist North." Instead of blaming the weather for crop failures—though the weather last year was bad—the leadership is blaming "backward habits and traditions," and "corruption, waste, and luxury" on the part of certain cadres. According to a recent editorial in the Hanoi daily paper *Nhan Dan,* "The present danger originated within ourselves, and not from without," and the greatest single sin is "individualism," for it covers a multitude of other sins. None of this implies that the Communists feel themselves to be in a position that could cost them the war, but their huge manpower losses have surely been a major handicap to them in their effort to reduce the war to "manageable" proportions—which means primarily getting rid of American manpower and firepower. This, obviously, is what accounts for their obstinate stand at present, and it represents a valid gamble on their part to use stubbornness to force Washington and Saigon to deal on their terms. It may also indicate another reason why Hanoi has decided to rebuild its own Communist state before taking over the South. And since Saigon, despite its weaknesses, has sufficient political leverage—combined with that of other nationalist and reli gious groups in the South—to make an election too much of a gamble, the Communist goal, at least for momentary bargaining purposes, and perhaps for months to come, must be coalition.

It is true that, as a number of French experts maintain, the prosecution of the revolution in the South, in its own right, has been the principal aim of Hanoi since the Geneva Conference of 1954, and particularly so after the failure to hold the scheduled referendum on reunification in 1956. But it is also true that political conditions in the South have always been different from those in the North, going back to the nineteen-thirties and forties and even before that; and that the influences of various international revolutionary and evolutionary movements—Communism, Trotskyism, Socialism— were felt there before they were felt in the North. Standard Communist assertions to the contrary, Vietnam, in its two-thousand-year history, has not, except at rare and relatively short intervals, been "one and indivisible." Nevertheless, when the Vietminh succeeded in consolidating its Communist regime in Hanoi after the defeat of the French, its hope was to bring the South rapidly under its control, either by referendum or by force. When that failed to happen, chiefly because of the American support of the Ngo Dinh Diem regime, the North, in 1960, created the National Liberation Front (actually, the N.L.F. flag had been seen two years earlier in the Vietminh-dominated areas of the South), and in 1962 it set up the People's Revolutionary Party, a southern adjunct of the northern Lao Dong Party. The latter development denoted a true turning point, the action being taken for two main reasons—to resist separatist tendencies on the part of some of the southern revolutionaries, and to strengthen the Communist apparatus in the South, which had become weak. It may thus be said that the setting up of the P.R.P. marked the inception of the idea of eventually creating some sort of formal revolutionary government in the South as a prelude to the region's incorporation with the North, even though Hanoi retained hopes of taking over the South by force, if possible.

By the end of 1967, however, a serious debate had begun in Hanoi's Politburo over continued military prosecution of the war vs. toning down the North's commitment and thinking seriously about negotiations. The argument at that time was won by the do-or-die group, headed by Le Duan, which mounted the Tet offensive in South Vietnam at the beginning of 1968. As everyone now knows, the Tet offensive, and the offensive that followed it that May, resulted in huge military losses for the Vietcong and North Vietnamese troops but had considerable success politically and psychologically. Beyond disrupting the South Vietnamese government's schemes for pacification and administrative reorganization, it achieved the even greater feat of disillusioning such men as Robert McNamara and Clark Clifford and influencing President Johnson's decisions to end the bombing of the North and not to run for reëlection. The military stalemate that followed coincided with the start of the Paris peace talks. It remains to be proved whether, as Harriman maintains, Hanoi really was serious about diminishing the scope of the conflict when it withdrew many of its forces into Laos last year or whether the withdrawal was made simply because those forces needed to be rested and reëquipped; another contention of Harriman's that remains to be proved is whether Saigon's initial reluctance to come to Paris and the shifting of American troops from the Demilitarized Zone to the scene of fresh fighting along the Cambodian border also helped to prevent serious negotiations at that time. At any rate, Hanoi decided to return to a "theory of protracted conflict," in the words of Truong Chinh, who is one of Le Duan's rivals to succeed Ho. Rocket attacks against South Vietnamese cities, including Saigon, increased, the war continued to wax and wane—waxing especially during this year's Tet period—and the negotiations dragged on without progress. In this context, the creation of the Provisional Revolutionary Government must be regarded as an extension of Truong Chinh's "protracted-conflict" line, which is based on the conviction that the Americans have grown increasingly tired of the war and now want to get out under almost any circumstances, and that the Saigon government, with or without American support, cannot survive very long.

The evidence is that the plans to launch the P.R.G. were set in motion at least a year ago. When the Alliance of National, Democratic, and Peace Forces was created after the 1968 Tet offensive, as a group to rally urban intellectuals and proletariat elements, its purpose, based on the hope that the offensive would lead to the collapse of the Saigon government, was to set up a new government in Saigon, which would negotiate for peace first with the National Liberation Front and then with the Americans. When the Tet offensive failed, the Alliance quickly changed its attitude of independence from the Front—toward which its political manner for a time had been calculatedly patronizing. It had now been ordered by Hanoi to ally itself openly with the Front, which then reassumed its unchallenged role of leadership. On May 8th of this year, the Front issued its ten-point peace proposal in Paris. On May 23rd, representatives of the Front and the Alliance met in the jungle near Cambodia for a preliminary discussion of the formation of the P.R.G. On May 30th, an impressive group of Front and Alliance representatives and intellectuals met in "a liberated area near Saigon," and Huynh Tan Phat, who was soon to be named the Chairman of the P.R.G., read a report described as "a review of the southern revolutionary movement." He stressed the fact that the movement had steadily broadened, winning the sympathy and support of many "puppet" troops, police agents, officers, and administrative personnel in Saigon. Between June 6th and June 8th—just before the Midway meeting of Nixon and Thieu—what was described as the Congress of Delegates of South Vietnam held a major meeting, attended by eighty-eight delegates and seventy-two "guests," representing, according to the Front's Liberation Radio, "political parties, nationalities, religious groups, people's groups, various strata of the people, the People's Liberation Armed Forces [the Vietcong], and the shock youth troops from all over Vietnam." The presidium was composed of leading members of the Front and of the Alliance and representatives of various religious groups, youth groups, labor groups, and women's groups. Front and Alliance members made the keynote speeches and were allowed to guide the conference proceedings, after which a new "Republic of South Vietnam" was declared, on the basis of fourteen articles, the first of which adopted the national anthem and the flag of the Front, rather than of the Alliance. (Saigon, incidentally, was renamed Ho Chi Minh City.) Some of the other articles more or less repeated the 1967 program of the Front. "Vietnam is one, Vietnam is indivisible," Article 4 declared. Article 9 said, "The revolutionary administration in South Vietnam will be organized according to the principle of democratic centralism from central level to basic units." Universal suffrage was to be the means of electing People's Revolutionary Councils, which would designate the People's Revolutionary Committees.

It is significant that Huynh Tan Phat was named Chairman of the new P.R.G. Phat, an architect by profession, is a high-ranking member of the National Liberation Front and the head of the Democratic Party, which was one of the fringe groups of the early Vietminh and was also affiliated with the Committee of the South in 1945, during the brief seizure of Saigon by the revolutionary forces. Although South Vietnamese intelligence sources say he has secretly been a member of the Lao Dong Party since 1956, he was a logical choice because he has no *official* Communist position, because he is a southerner with many personal links to the area (he is said to have made several clandestine visits to Saigon in the last few years), and, finally, because he is a man of attractive, warm personality. It is equally significant that Kiem, who had been heading the Front's Paris delegation, was named Minister to the Chairman's Office; most observers believe that Kiem, a hard-liner and definitely a Lao Dong member, will be the dominant figure in the new government—the man at the southern end of the political strings that tie the new regime to the North. Tran Nam Trung, named as Defense Minister, does not exist; the name is an alias for whichever of several North Vietnamese officers is, at a given time, the commanding general in the South. Since late 1967, the top North Vietnamese director of both military and political affairs in South Vietnam has been Pham Hung, a Politburo member. Five members of the P.R.G., including Kiem and Phat, are members of the presidium of the National Liberation Front's Central Committee. Seven members belong to the Alliance of National, Democratic, and Peace Forces. Although almost all the ministers and deputy ministers came originally from the South or the central provinces, many have held important jobs in Hanoi, or have been in the North for varying periods. Significantly, Nguyen Huu Tho, the Front Chairman, and Trinh Dinh Thao, the Chairman of the Alliance, have been accorded the two top positions in an apparently ineffectual council—a pair of appointments that should leave no one in doubt about Hanoi's intention of running the P.R.G.

Both Radio Hanoi and Liberation Radio lost no time in emphasizing the importance of the P.R.G. Hanoi has made a special point of stressing the growth in the number of village, district, and provincial Revolutionary Committees set up in the South. The Communists now claim that there are about thirteen hundred village committees, a hundred and twenty district committees and twenty-three committees in towns and cities. Obviously, the P.R.G. is the new roof over these committees, giving them further "legal" governmental status in opposition to Saigon. Hanoi also particularly mentioned the continuing distribution of land to the peasants in Vietcong-controlled areas—perhaps to counteract the Thieu government's recently renewed promises of a truly effective land-reform program. And, naturally, the Communists, both in Hanoi and here in Paris, have placed great stress on the number of governments throughout the world that quickly gave diplomatic recognition to the P.R.G.—six more than have recognized the National Liberation Front in the nine years since its creation. It was also interesting that the Soviet Union, Yugoslavia, and China all quickly recognized the P.R.G., for Hanoi has had a hard job maintaining a balanced position in relation to these three nations—two of which, China and Russia, have rendered it extensive military assistance. As some Americans here have pointed out, when the delegates of Hanoi and the Front demand an end to American logistical support of the Saigon regime, the question might well be asked: What about the logistical support given to the North Vietnamese and the Vietcong by Moscow and Peking? When, if ever, will that cease?

Meanwhile, the Thieu government, as it faces the new challenge of the P.R.G., is as badly beset as ever by old internal conflicts. Since its election in 1967, the government has certainly never been as stable as the Americans have claimed. The ultimate "victory" of Thieu in his long internecine struggle with Vice-President Ky and his group did not solve any of the government's basic problems, which included bad relations between the Executive and the National Assembly, and mistrust of Thieu by many Vietnamese officials, both civilian and military. The last of these problems derived from a number of past antipathies and suspicions, and from Thieu's own exceptionally suspicious nature, which has been evidenced by an inability to trust anyone for very long and by a predilection for manipulation and maneuver with the assistance of a small personal palace guard. This group has included a wealthy pharmacist, Nguyen Cao Thang, who has sought, with some success, to improve Thieu's relations with members of the Assembly, and whom Thieu sent secretly to Paris a few months ago to talk with some of the exiled or expatriate leaders here about their returning to Saigon. Among these leaders was Au Truong Thanh, a former Finance and

Economics Minister, who was not allowed to run for President in 1967 because of alleged neutralist leanings, and who had been under house arrest in Saigon until last year, when he came to Paris. From time to time over the past year or so, Thieu has made efforts to establish contact, through his agents, with members of the National Liberation Front, ostensibly to determine what sort of deal they might be willing to make. There are those who maintain that instead of privately searching, as his supporters have claimed, for an "honest formula" under which individual members of the Front could be brought into the Saigon regime, he had a more personal motive; namely, to find out whether he would be acceptable to the Front as President under some sort of compromise. There is reason to believe, on the basis of private information from Hanoi, that the Communists, who will not deal with Ky, might, despite their anti-Thieu invective, make at least a temporary deal with the President.

During this period, too, the attempt to form new political parties or blocs in Saigon—to work out some common political front against the Communists—has continued to flounder, and many, if not most, Vietnamese, together with many Americans and neutral observers, have blamed Thieu for this. After the 1968 Tet offensive, there was an effort to rally a so-called National Salvation Front, but this did not amount to much. Then came an effort to combine that Front with two other groups—the Worker-Peasant Alliance, led by labor leader Tran Quoc Buu, and a group representing Thieu and the government, headed by Nguyen Van Huong, one of the members of Thieu's palace guard. Largely because Huong was extremely unpopular and overly ambitious, this effort also failed. Thieu next determined to take the lead himself in the creation of a political alliance, and on May 25th—at just about the time the Communists were setting in motion the machinery for the establishment of the P.R.G., of which Thieu undoubtedly had advance knowledge—he formed the National Social-Democratic Front, which he described as "the first concrete step in unifying the political factions in South Vietnam for the coming political struggle with the Communists." Defensively, he told some two thousand delegates to the opening convention that the new Front would not be "totalitarian or despotic," and said, "We shall do everything to prevent a hasty peace solution in Paris and to prevent the country from falling into the hands of the Communists." The new organization is composed of six essentially conservative bodies or parties: northern Catholic refugees from the 1954 period; a branch of the old Revolutionary Dai Viet Party; one of many factions of the Hoa Hao religious sect; part of the equally fragmented Vietnamese Kuomintang, a nationalist party formed in the twenties and modelled on the Chinese Kuomintang; some remnants of Buu's Worker-Peasant Alliance; and—perhaps the most interesting of the new groups—the Nhan Xa, or Revolutionary Social Humanist, Party, which includes some of the more enlightened young Catholic leaders of the old Can Lao Party, of the Diem era. Many other political forces and factions were not represented, either because they refused to join or because they were not invited—the most notable being the militant Buddhists of the An Quang Pagoda. At best, the National Social-Democratic Front can be considered the first serious effort to form a government party. At worst—and this view is more realistic—it can be considered doomed for not including the anti- and non-Communist forces in the country who for one reason or another refuse to support Thieu. All it has done is to combine a few of the fragments that have been strewn about the South Vietnamese political landscape for years.

A number of things happened following the creation of the National Social-Democratic Front. A Progressive Nationalist Movement, a potential "loyal opposition," was formed by Nguyen Ngoc Huy, one of the most respected members of the Paris peace delegation. Then, on June 4th, in Saigon, a Committee for the Establishment of a National Progressive Force, representing left-of-center students, intellectuals, and professional people seeking "a government of reconciliation," was formed. It was led by a lawyer named Tran Ngoc Lieng, who had defended Truong Dinh Dzu, the man who finished second in the 1967 Presidential election and was subsequently brought into court on some old charges of financial peculation and is now in jail, mostly because he advocates a coalition government that would include the Communists. On June 17th, Thieu ordered the arrest of a number of suspected Communists or neutralists who advocate coalition. At about the same time, he issued a warning, despite earlier governmental promise of a free press, that any newspaper distorting the news in order to "demoralize" the nation would be shut down, and that publication of the English-language Saigon *Daily News,* whose editor had just been jailed for establishing contact with a Communist, was suspended. About a dozen other papers, Vietnamese, Chinese, and French, have also been shut down or suspended from publishing in the past few months.

Thieu had by this time returned from his Midway conference with President Nixon—a conference, incidentally, that was arranged in a hurry, without much planning, after Thieu refused a less formal invitation from Nixon to come to California. Back in Saigon, Thieu was obviously jittery at not having received any firm pledges from Nixon, and he was made more so by Nixon's announcement from Washington about American troop withdrawals in considerable excess of the twenty-five thousand mentioned at Midway. Whatever Nixon had said publicly about doing nothing to impose a coalition government, Thieu was well aware of the implications of Nixon's disclaimer about being "wedded" to the Thieu government. Thieu, then, was in trouble and knew it, and the Communists' creation of the Provisional Revolutionary Government hardly diminished his worries. He was faced with a renewal of what the Communists call a "special war," between Communist forces relying on the Russians and the Chinese for their supplies and South Vietnamese forces relying on the Americans—the kind of war that preceded the major American commitment in 1965— and he still had no firm political base to speak of. In fact, opposition was growing on both the right and the left. The fence-sitters in Saigon, the traditional *attentistes,* began to talk of buying exit visas. Moreover, the pace of the war had picked up again, and although the South Vietnamese troops fighting on their own did well in a few battles, for the most part their performance was poor or less than adequate. Desertion rates were still high, the morale of soldiers in the ranks remained generally low, and, all told, the rate of improvement in the fighting capability of the eleven South Vietnamese divisions and of the Regional and Popular Forces was judged by American experts to be much too slow.

Thus, the race against time, on which both sides are now gambling, entered a new phase. Though there were signs that the Communists had stopped sending fresh reinforcements from North Vietnam, they still had plenty of troops making their way south along the Ho Chi Minh Trail, and plenty of strength to continue the "special war." They were also efficiently organized to continue their political offensive against the government both in the countryside and in the urban areas, which they were now again stressing as the key to the struggle. Obviously, the Communists remained convinced that they could keep both the Americans and the South Vietnamese on the run. They may be right, but there is certainly some question how long they themselves can endure a renewal of the "special war" under conditions of fatigue and declining morale, and also some question whether they can really outmaneuver and overthrow the Thieu government, as they still insist they will do before discussing elections.

What Thieu has not done but, in the opinion of many Vietnamese and some Americans, can still do is really reorganize his government, instead of making ineffectual efforts to create political "solidarity" by setting up new fronts and cautiously encouraging ineffectual counter-fronts while barring groups he suspects or fears. The Communists, still insisting on a new "peace Cabinet" in Saigon that would exclude Thieu, Ky, and Huong, might be put on the defensive if Thieu created something akin to a moderate peace Cabinet—a new body, set up expressly to conduct negotiations, representing a true cross-section of political opinion. Such a body could run the gamut from conservatives to far-leftists, and it should be able to lay the groundwork for the sort of southern solidarity that, in the moment of crisis, would be capable of preventing the ultimate "Vietminhization" of the South. There are not only southern conservatives but southern Communists and southern liberals who firmly believe in southern independence and could, if they were given some backing, work together to block a northern takeover.

The problem of revising the South Vietnamese constitution so that the Communists can legally take part in elections is one aspect of the current stalemate, but it is one that can be solved if it is handled delicately. So can the problem of creating election formulas and procedures on which the Communists, despite their present denials, might be willing to negotiate if they thought it would suit their purposes. But even if American withdrawal is carried out in an orderly manner, and not as a result of unfortunate episodes like Nixon's apparent public attempt to rebut Clark Clifford, Thieu must act to save his own side. The sort of reorganization that is necessary must bring into the government men like General Duong

Van Minh (Big Minh), who headed the junta that overthrew Diem; he could rally important Buddhist support, and he is now standing by in Saigon. Minh also has close ties with the Hoa Hao and Cao Dai religious sects and with other minority elements in South Vietnam, and, more important, he and Senator Tran Van Don, who, as a general, did most of the organizing of the 1963 coup against Diem, are the only men who could perhaps obtain the support of the many disillusioned, fatigued, and potentially rebellious junior officers and soldiers all over South Vietnam. Most of these men are tired of fighting, tired of facing death, and ashamed of the stealing they do from the peasants. To succeed, Minh and Don would have to obtain the coöperation of these remorseful, quasi-rebellious, often still idealistic men, some of whom are already thinking in terms of a new "resistance" that is far from the sort Thieu has in mind.

Many of the non-Communist exiles in Paris are sporadically being wooed or cajoled by both sides. Some of them could play a part in providing a southern revolutionary alternative to the Vietminh formula. Countless such bona-fide nationalists are to be found all over South Vietnam, too, and if Thieu is to survive he must create, from the whole spectrum of southern religious, political, professional, and military elements, a new representative body—a negotiating council, consisting of perhaps forty or fifty men. The Communists would undoubtedly label such a group "neo-colonialist" and the like, but, being hardheaded realists, if they were convinced that there was a functioning alternative to Saigon's political disintegration they would have to reconsider the gamble they are now taking. In my own opinion, if Thieu does not do something like this, he is in grave danger of letting the disaffected military officers and their supporters take the situation out of his hands anyway— a change that would either play more directly into the Communists' hands or lead to a new fratricidal war, which would complete the ravage of South Vietnam. Although Thieu seems to have been persuaded at Midway to come up with new election proposals of some sort, the Americans apparently failed—not for the first time—to persuade him to confront the far greater challenge of thoroughly reorganizing his rickety regime. This may prove to be the ultimate American failure in Vietnam, and the phrase, tying the past to the present, "Sink or swim with Ngo Dinh Diem" and now "See it through with Nguyen Van Thieu" may constitute the dual epitaph of the long, tragically undirected American involvement.

In the past month, I have attended three of the briefings that follow the weekly peace conference sessions, and I have talked with a score or more of the people connected with them, including Le Duc Tho, members of the Saigon delegation, and various Frenchmen, Americans, and Vietnamese exiles. Taken together, the official statements made at the conference sessions and at the ensuing press briefings by the four participating parties present a strange verbal caricature of what is really going on in Vietnam, in Washington, and in Hanoi. The spokesmen for Hanoi and the National Liberation Front endlessly repeat that mutual withdrawal of troops, as demanded by the Americans, is "absurd" and a "farce," and continue to deny that there are any North Vietnamese troops in South Vietnam. President Nixon is accused of wanting only to intensify "the war of aggression" through continued "neo-colonialist" support of the Saigon regime. The South Vietnamese say that "the task of developing armed forces capable of defending one's country is an ordinary task of any sovereign nation." Though the South Vietnamese realize the advantage that the Communists won by forming the P.R.G., they maintain that it represents "nothing new" but "simply a combination of the Front and the Alliance under a new guise." The Americans, insisting over and over again that "we will not accept a one-sided withdrawal from South Vietnam," keep pleading with the Communists to negotiate openly and honestly on mutual troop withdrawals or reductions and to join in free elections with the Saigon regime. And so it goes, *ad infinitum, ad nauseam*—a dialogue of the deaf.

For some months now, there have not even been any multinational tea breaks in the weekly meetings at the Majestic Hotel conference hall. Earlier, the representatives of the four sides would get together in informal groups during such breaks and exchange pleasantries, or even ideas that would lead to secret meetings around town between the opposing delegates. Some such meetings are still taking place, apparently, but they are being held far less frequently than before, and they have not yet produced any results comparable to those that led to the agreement on seating arrangements last winter, or to the more important, though merely tacit, agreement to halt hostilities around the Demilitarized Zone. According to Harriman, it was this agreement that induced the North

Vietnamese to withdraw for a time into Laos—a move that the Americans failed to accept as an honest indication of the Communists' willingness to reduce the level of violence. The Russians and the French, who worked behind the scenes during that period to bring about some of the compromises, are quietly trying to find some formulas for further progress but privately admit that they are getting practically nowhere.

Difficult though things look, with each side determined to outsit the other "until the chairs rot," in the words of a Communist spokesman, there has undeniably been progress in the year since these peace talks began—more progress, in fact, than was made during the first year of talks at Panmunjom to end the Korean war. The creation of the P.R.G. admittedly did polarize the situation, to the Communists' initial advantage. So far, however, many observers feel, the Communists are not nearly as strongly entrenched in the South as they say. It is true that they would be defeated in a fair vote, if only South Vietnam could disprove the Humpty-Dumpty thesis and put itself together again. The history of the fragmentation of the South over the last fifteen years would seem to indicate otherwise, but the human resources needed to "southernize" the government remain.

Some experts here believe that the creation of the P.R.G. was timed to coincide with the conference of Communist nations called by the Russians, and that the Russians suggested it. Others are convinced that Peking inspired the National Liberation Front to make the move because the Chinese Communists wanted to renew the "special war" in South Vietnam. Both theories may contain some truth, for both would fit into the framework of the Peking-Moscow feud. In addition, some Americans point to the recent increase in Russian activity in Southeast Asia, and especially in Laos, where their top diplomats have been talking to all sides—the government, the neutralists, and the Communists—in what could signify an attempt to end hostilities there before they end in Vietnam, and to reëstablish the tripartite Laotian government set up under the Geneva agreement of 1962. The Russians, these Americans say, may now be willing to guarantee the existence of such a government even though they were not willing to do so earlier, and consequently this may be the time to attempt to bring about a Russian-American détente in Southeast Asia, embracing all the for-

mer Indo-China states, and perhaps even a wider area. Such a détente could lead to a reduction of arms support for both sides in
Vietnam—although the Chinese would probably continue to give
such support to Hanoi, which would subject Hanoi to almost total
dependence on Peking, something that the North Vietnamese do
not want at all. In any event, a reduction of violence could occur,
as Harriman hopes, and then the peace talks here could get down
to the essential question of mutual withdrawals, with political discussions of elections—local, regional, and national—perhaps coin-
ciding with arrangements for a cease-fire. Determined as the
Communists are to capture South Vietnam, and good as their
chances of doing so appear to be, they, like everyone else, would like
to see the bloody phase of the war end. If how to do this "honorably"
is the Americans' predicament, how to do it with or without honor
and get away with it is the Communists'.

21. Saigon

~·

September 21, 1969

Over the last two months, an unduly prolonged Cabinet crisis and other political and psychological shock waves have further threatened what remains of this weary capital's equilibrium. Most important, there has been a sudden realization that the Americans are indeed determined to pull out a large number of troops as soon as possible, and that, although Washington will try to fulfill its pledges of continued military and economic aid, the burden of carrying on the war will fall more rapidly than had been expected on the still —and, it seems, perpetually—unprepared South Vietnamese. Unfortunately, as indicated once again by the failure to broaden the base of the government, they remain as sharply divided and as suspicious of each other as they have always been, and it seems quite possible that they will end by figuratively throwing themselves into the sea like lemmings. This potential for self-destruction must be taken seriously, despite the existence of a number of countervailing factors, including the increasing difficulties that the Communists have admitted experiencing. These difficulties may now be exacerbated by the passing of the illustrious and irreplaceable Ho Chi Minh, for a serious power struggle could take place in the North—though such a struggle does not seem likely to take place in the immediate future, and the probability is that Ho's memory will be resoundingly invoked as a rallying cry for victory.

The difference between the two sides all along has been that the Communists have usually known what ailed them and done their best to cure it—as they are currently trying to do with the agricultural ills in the North while initiating in the South a new strategy of "great victories with limited strength," in the phrase of their Defense Minister and Commander-in-Chief, General Vo Nguyen Giap. Saigon, by contrast, is still flailing around ineffectively in dealing with most of its problems. Everything seems to hinge on organization and conviction. Even though there is evidence that the Communists' mass support has diminished in South Vietnam and is under severe strain in the North, the disciplined Communist leaders have managed to keep most of their followers convinced that their side is ultimately bound to win the war, throw the "neo-colonialists" out, and unite the two halves of Vietnam, whereas the disorganized and disgruntled leaders in the South, lacking any widespread backing beyond their own and the American bureaucracy, continue to rely on words and formulas as substitutes for true conviction. The new magic word is "Vietnamization," which may be defined as a process surrounded by difficulties comparable to those of carrying out a successful heart transplant. In a sense, the Americans, having failed in what once seemed a revivifying infusion of new strength, are now being rejected by the Vietnamese body politic, and it may be that the main thing we have succeeded in doing in Vietnam over the past fifteen years—or, anyway, the past ten—has been to inhibit a natural revolutionary development that might have evolved on its own to its own success or failure irrespective of the pressures from the North.

What seems almost inevitable is that the war in Vietnam will continue, one way or another, and that, as Ignazio Silone once forecast in another context, the final conflict will pit the Communists against the ex-Communists. Perhaps, as Asians, the Vietnamese, North and South, will make special, Asian-style accommodations with the inevitable and live happily—or else unhappily—ever after, but one somehow begins to doubt whether accommodation itself will be more than a phase. It is true that the average Vietnamese peasant traditionally wants only to be left alone to till his fields, but by now, in the North at least as much as in the South, he has been kicked around and shunted back and forth for so long that he has become a political person whether he wants to be or not, having been forced to form some definite ideas about social justice and about what his prerogatives are or ought to be. Over the years, I have talked to peasants and peasant-soldiers, including North Vietnamese prisoners, and their political convictions, whether pro- or anti-Communist, are quite strongly defined. One certainly also finds this to be true among the scattered religious elements in the South—the Buddhists, the Catholics, the Cao Dai sect and the Hoa Hao sect—and among the Montagnards as well, and these groups account for most of the population of South Vietnam. Deep-rooted political convictions also move people like Vice-President Nguyen Cao Ky, a French-trained but fiercely patriotic and xenophobic Vietnamese (who has said that if he had had the choice over again he might have sided with Ho Chi Minh), and many members of the earlier resistance—those who fought against the French in the Communist-dominated Vietminh between 1946 and 1954. Some of the former Vietminh leaders I know are northerners, as Ky is, or come from central Vietnam, and they claim, as Ky does, that they could raise a guerrilla division in North Vietnam right now. They may simply be boasting, and if so, and if the South does become "Vietminhized," these ex-Vietminh types will probably be the first to be eliminated; but if they are right, a new resistance in the South, opposed both to Communism and to a sellout peace, could spread to the already beleaguered and economically shackled North. No longer inspired by the organizing genius of Ho, faced with an apathetic and latently hostile population kept in line by carrot-and-stick measures, and held together politically by Ho's companions in the Politburo and by a still powerful Army, North Vietnam today is probably confronting its greatest challenge in its two and a half decades under Communism.

The events of the last two months here, seen against the backdrop of the talks in Paris, where I spent the month of June, have certainly seemed to offer scant hope that peace is any closer. The six-point invitation to the National Liberation Front to take part in elections, which President Nguyen Van Thieu issued on July 11th, was quickly denounced by the Communists as more "perfidious trickery," and both sides have since remained adamant. "We have gone as far as we can or should go in opening the door to peace, and now it is time for the other side to respond," President Nixon said on July 30th as he stood on the steps of Independence Palace in Saigon. Two weeks before that, Vice-President Ky had told a group of officers at the National War College that "to retreat one more inch would amount to unconditional surrender," and added that, in view of the Communists' intransigence, "I should think there is no more reason for us to maintain and prolong the Paris talks." This was, of course, part of the propaganda war between Saigon and Hanoi that is fought weekly in Paris; although neither side is ready yet to talk seriously about making peace, neither side has any desire to break off the negotiations. Some progress could still come late this year, but it now seems far more likely that the conflict, both military and political, will continue through at least part of 1970— at a reduced level of violence but at a higher and more critical level on the political front. The offers and counter-offers made so far will meanwhile sit on the shelf, not altogether ornamental but not yet the useful instruments they could become. They do, in fact, contain the shape, if not the substance, of ultimate accommodation and agrreement, and so what has happened here and in Paris in the past few months cannot be dismissed as utterly futile. The Communists, taking a more consistent approach, have moved ahead logically in their declarations over a longer period. The South Vietnamese and American strategy has been wobbly and, for the most part, defensive. Thieu's July 11th election offer—which the day before he had told a group of Saigon legislators he was submitting at the behest of the Americans—was a maneuver he obviously knew would be rejected, yet he ran a real risk in making it. The risk lay in the effect it would have on South Vietnamese morale, and particularly the morale of soldiers in the field, for in one breath he was talking peace and in the next exhorting them to go on fighting. For this reason, many Vietnamese I have spoken with believe that the Americans gave Thieu poor advice, and that in this case he should have exhibited his characteristic caution—above all, by discussing his peace plan behind the scenes with some of his compatriots before publicizing it.

The offer did have the predicted effect on the South Vietnamese soldiers—most notably, the younger officers. Why, they asked themselves, should they go on fighting and dying and urging their men to do the same if tomorrow the shooting might stop and their Vietcong opponents might emerge among them as "brothers"—and perhaps more praiseworthy ones in the people's eyes, because of their long absence from villages where the South Vietnamese have made themselves unpopular by stealing chickens and pigs? The question was a valid one. What was required as a prelude to any peace offer, many South Vietnamese feel, was a series of moves to reorganize the armed forces, to reëducate them, and to motivate them to continue fighting, and an effort to balance such a reorganization with reforms in the central government, so that it would cover a broader spectrum of the important religious and political forces, and there should also have been a more decisive move toward decentralization at the lower administrative levels, which has now just begun. Thieu himself, once he had made his offer, was aware of the trouble it might cause. When I saw him late in August, he was exuding confidence that the crisis was past, but he admitted, "The atmosphere for two weeks after July 11th was very heavy."

Just how heavy it was became apparent on July 22nd, when a group of nineteen retired general officers held a three-and-a-half-hour luncheon meeting at the home of Senator Tran Van Don, the key figure in planning the 1963 coup that overthrew Diem. A number of other heroes of the coup were at the meeting, including General Duong Van Minh, a still popular man who has been frequently mentioned as the logical choice to head a special advisory body that could create the broader consensus everyone admits is needed. The guest of honor was Ky. During the discussion, Ky repeatedly voiced contempt for the Americans. He referred to Ambassador Ellsworth Bunker as "Governor General Bunker" (the French administration in Indo-China was headed by a governor general), and said that the Americans had all along been "wrong in their evaluation of the abilities and capacities of the Vietnamese people" and wrong in their belief that within the limits they had set they could bomb the North into submission. He charged that "the Americans have threatened us many times, saying that if we did not accept their conditions they would reëxamine the matter of military aid to us," and he also charged that the United States had supplied the South Vietnamese with, among other things, "disgracefully ancient aircraft." At another point, he said, "According to reports by American advisers, a number of Vietnamese units are ineffective, and it will be difficult for them to replace American units. But I told the advisers that when there is a possibility of our doing the job they should let us do it, so we can win the respect of the people." If not enough aid is received soon enough, "the only thing to do is to try to separate ourselves from that influence, even though we are poor and starving," Ky said, and he continued, "We must strive to become self-sufficient, and to greatly reduce the influence of the Americans—the sooner the better." Although he stressed the need for a unified national policy and his own willingness to support Thieu and work with him, he also expressed fear of a coup by company-grade officers and soldiers, and toward the end of the session he declared, somewhat cryptically, that he had enough support to lead a coup himself, "because the people are confused and the government does not follow a clear policy line."

Although most Vietnamese and most Americans here doubt that Ky is strong enough or rash enough to try any such thing, he represents a viewpoint, typified by many of the country's dispirited junior officers, that has to be taken into account. Ky, who in recent months has either languished in idleness or halfheartedly carried out occasional tasks, including his "supervision" of the Paris peace talks, is playing what he calls "the waiting game," and it's the game that a number of ignored, discontented elements in the country today, including the Buddhists and various other religious and political groups, are also playing. The Americans have taken to pointing out to their Vietnamese friends that a lot of people in the United States didn't like Franklin D. Roosevelt at the start of the Second World War but supported him anyway in a time of national crisis, and that the Vietnamese ought to do the same with President Thieu. But the Vietnamese don't think that way, and it is a misreading of the Vietnamese mind to suppose that they could or would.

The thirty-one-man Cabinet that President Thieu recently selected—to replace a twenty-three-man Cabinet headed by the civilian Prime Minister Tran Van Huong—is led by Tran Thien Khiem, who, like Thieu, is a former general, and who has retained the important post of Minister of the Interior, which he held in the previous Cabinet. Although Khiem has played an increasingly important administrative role over the past year, Thieu is expected to dominate the new Cabinet, a mixture of politicians and technicians, as he did the old. Despite his comradeship-in-arms with Khiem (actually, Khiem outranked the President militarily, four stars to three), the two men have some long-standing differences, involving earlier political rivalries and loyalties, and the Vietnamese, who tend to remember such things, and who think along divisive lines anyway, are already envisaging a new power struggle. This does not seem likely to occur immediately, but it may come about in time, depending on how pliant Khiem proves to be as Prime Minister—a position that, under the constitution, makes him, in effect, only the executor of the President's policies.

In announcing the formation of the new Cabinet, Thieu declared that the step had three objectives: to enlarge the Cabinet, thereby increasing political representation; to make it more efficient; and to improve relations between the executive and legislative branches. It promises to be more efficient in some respects—particularly in the areas of finance and economy, where two men regarded as experts in their fields, plus two able new under-secretaries, have been named, and in foreign affairs, where Senator Tran Van Lam, a wealthy southerner with previous diplomatic experience, replaces Tran Chanh Thanh, who was neither very effective nor very popular. In what is largely a pro-Thieu lineup, with strong overtones of the former Diem regime, there is a small sprinkling of men with a liberal outlook, but their positions are unimportant and it seems doubtful that they will provide much more than window dressing. As for Thieu's desire to better his relations with the National Assembly, relations between the executive branch and the legislature were until recently downright bad, and while they have begun to improve, they are still far from good. At Thieu's behest, an attempt to form a majority bloc in both houses of the Assembly is being made by Senator Dang Van Sung, a newspaper publisher and veteran politician, but it has so far failed, chiefly because Sung has run into trouble among Thieu's own friends in the House, and because he himself and some other senators are skeptical about Thieu's willingness to coöperate on a practical give-and-take basis.

The word one hears most often nowadays in Vietnam is "sincerity," and it is used mostly about Thieu. Many politicians, whether in or out of office, and a number of prominent independent men, like General Minh, feel that Thieu's main purpose at present is to guarantee his reëlection as President in 1971 (assuming that there isn't an election sooner, under a different dispensation, as a result of some sort of compromise with the Communists). Such people almost unanimously mistrust Thieu's advances to them as being hedged by his wanting, in effect, to sign them up as part of his "team" without either explaining his program or making it clear whether they will be allowed to retain their own independent voices. Thieu has done this, inadvertently or purposely, even with members of the National Social-Democratic Front, which is a six-party group he created as a pro-government force, and which has so far proved ineffective, as Thieu himself admits, because of rivalries and jealousies among the six party leaders—rivalries that he himself could resolve if he really wanted to. One American observer said recently, "Thieu has developed the clay-pigeon technique to a fine art—he makes a public show of dealing with men whose coöperation he says he wants but of whom he is basically afraid, and he shoots them down by arousing their skepticism and then putting out rumors of their unwillingness to coöperate." This happened a few weeks ago with General Minh. The Palace let it be known that Minh had come to see Thieu, whereas Thieu had actually paid Minh a visit at the latter's home in Saigon, at which time Minh's participation in the possible advisory council was reportedly discussed. In reality, Minh later revealed that Thieu did not say a word about such a job, and the two men did little more than exchange amenities for three-quarters of an hour. It may be that Thieu—who, it should be said, has just as much right to mistrust the sincerity of others as they have to mistrust his—was testing Minh's willingness to work with him, and it may indeed be that he was "clay-pigeoning" Minh by floating reports that would inevitably place Minh in an embarrassing position. It is still possible that Minh may play some sort of role in the government, but, like several other Vietnamese I have talked with who are willing to work with Thieu, he is reluctant to take on some ill-defined assignment unless Thieu is serious about listening to advice concerning the strategy for peace and other matters. "If he is simply looking for yes-men, whom he can listen to or ignore at will, then I want no part of it," one of these men has said.

When I spoke with Thieu at the end of August, a few days before he announced the formation of the new Cabinet, he seemed much more self-confident and open in his attitude than the last time I had seen him alone—in January, 1968, not long after he took office. The President is a man who at best is difficult to read, but then so are most Vietnamese, who carry their mutual suspicions to a point beyond the comprehension of Westerners. I observed that if he wished to win the confidence of the American public and also of more of the Vietnamese, it seemed apparent that he would need to broaden the base of his government, including in it representatives of as many different religious and political groups as possible, and especially groups like the Buddhists, who had mass support. Thieu agreed. He also agreed that it was important to move quickly to improve his relations with the National Assembly, and to create an advisory council for negotiations which would include some American advisers, so that a consistent policy for peace could be devised. He planned to do this "as soon as possible," he said. The trouble was, he explained, that he had to be convinced of other people's "good intentions." We spoke specifically of the Buddhists of the An Quang Pagoda, whose political leader, Thich Thien Minh, had been jailed by Thieu's police for harboring deserters and pro-Vietcong elements in his Buddhist Youth Center, and whose spiritual leader, Thich Tri Quang, I had spoken with a few days earlier.

Tri Quang had made it clear to me, in a characteristically elliptical fashion, that the Buddhists of the An Quang group had no intention of collaborating with the Thieu government under any circumstances—whether Thich Thien Minh was released or not, or whether Thieu gave An Quang a charter of its own under which to operate, or met any of its other conditions, such as a Cabinet post for a man designated as a friend of the pagoda. "You Americans simply do not understand," Tri Quang had told me. "It is a matter of lack of trust, of our having no hope of anything from this government. It is not a matter of making conditions. After all the money you have spent, and all the men you have had killed and wounded here in Vietnam, you still fail to realize that Thieu and his people are removed from the masses, that you have lost the revolution you thought you were helping win for us in 1963."

President Thieu, as I spoke with him about the An Quang problem, seemed willing to release Thich Thien Minh from prison if the An Quang *bonzes* were "sincere," and he intimated that he would even free Truong Dinh Dzu, who had been in jail for more than a year because he recommended a coalition government. Dzu, who has become at least as much of a *cause célèbre* in America as he is in Vietnam, could go free, Thieu indicated, if he would write a letter of "clarification"—by which he obviously meant "apology," since the word "coalition" is still taboo in South Vietnam, and any newspaper that uses it can be banned and any person advocating it can be jailed. I left Thieu with the word "sincere" ringing in my ears.

The official American establishment in Vietnam, which was more responsible than the Vietnamese themselves for what many consider the premature creation of the "legal," constitutional Second Republic in 1966–67, feels that Thieu has come a remarkably long way since he took office, and it is reluctant to push him hard now. "If you demand too many things too quickly, he just backs away and moves more slowly," one high-ranking American says. Other Americans, and a great many Vietnamese as well, firmly believe that at this eleventh hour the United States should take the utmost advantage of its leverage—threats of faster troop withdrawals, promises of future aid—to force Thieu to do things that are necessary. They feel that since he lacks both a firm policy and a strategy for negotiations, and has not succeeded in establishing anything remotely resembling a national consensus, he must at least be persuaded to let others help him achieve these things, or let them make the effort on their own, under his supervision. A Vietnamese senator who is both consistently critical of us and deeply pro-American said to me the other day, "The trouble with you Americans is that you have confused legality with legitimacy. These are two different things, and it's something the Communists know much better than either of us. Legality is simply a form. Legitimacy is based on the formulation of a sound national policy —which we lack—and the ability to get it approved. We have produced some ideas and many plans and projects—for pacification, for land reform, for village autonomy, and so on—and some of them have begun to work, on a limited scale. But we still have no philosophy of government, no fundamental sense of the direction in which we are going, and, above all, no system of political organization, which must inevitably begin at the bottom."

The Americans have tended to compound the problem with their computers, grinding out data on how many hamlets and villages are in what category of combined security and development. Thus, it is officially proclaimed today by both the South Vietnamese government and the Americans that nearly eighty-five per cent of the country's population is under either complete or partial government control, and it is true that in the last few months increasing numbers of people have left Communist-dominated areas and—for whatever combination of reasons, which may include higher Communist taxation, insufficient food, and the conscription of young people into Communist military or labor ranks—moved into regions that are more or less controlled by the government, or where there is at least some government presence. It is also true that the roles of the chiefs of nineteen hundred villages (out of some twenty-five hundred in the country) where elections have now been held are enhanced to the point where these chiefs and their councils operate locally with near autonomy; they have their own locally elected development teams and have been given control over those trained and sent in from outside, such as rural-development workers, and over the so-called Popular Forces. By and large, despite the difficulty of getting enough qualified men to run for local office because of fear of Vietcong reprisals, the new degree of spontaneous political participation has proved that such measures should have been taken long ago.

Yet all this does not work well enough, because not enough else has been done.

As Yeats wrote,

> Things fall apart; the centre cannot hold;
> Mere anarchy is loosed upon the world.

The district chiefs—the echelon between village and province chiefs—are extremely jealous of the new prerogatives given to the village officials, and, furthermore, the district chiefs, who used to be the local bosses, as well as the province chiefs, are all still under the thumbs of the cumbersome Saigon bureaucracy or of the generals in their areas. These difficulties were compounded by the too hastily arranged 1967 national elections; neither the sixty senators, chosen on separate slates-at-large, nor the hundred and thirty-seven representatives, who theoretically represent certain areas but mostly paid for their votes at the provincial or district level, have had any sense of responsibility toward specific constituencies. The legitimate questions, then, are: What price the political parties and blocs in Saigon, which are essentially urban intellectual or bourgeois salon organizations, and what price constant Cabinet reshuffles involving faceless men who may have some good ideas but represent no one except themselves and their small circles of friends? Whatever the weaknesses of the Communists, and however true it may be that in a national election today they would garner only twenty or twenty-five per cent of the total vote, their organizational advantage and their ideological appeal might enable them to win many of the old or new and still uncommitted voters, since they have been forced to remain in a political no man's land. Even after Ho's death, many of these people might still prefer to vote for him—or his heirs—out of respect rather than for Nguyen Van Thieu out of apathy.

Belatedly, but perhaps not too belatedly, some Vietnamese and a handful of Americans are trying to build up new popular mass movements in various ways, with modest degrees of success. After long deliberation, Tran Quoc Buu, the head of the Confederation of Vietnamese Laborers, has determined to launch a peasants'-and-workers' party. There are a hundred and eighty-five thousand members of Buu's Tenant Farmers' Union, which is the largest of a number of federations that make up the parent body, and there are several hundred experienced organizers among the peasants, who could furnish the nucleus of a solid new political organization at the hamlet and village level. Buu is one of those national leaders who have been willing to coöperate with Thieu, but, like so many of the others who have regularly visited the Palace, he has felt his relationship with Thieu to be restricted by the members of the President's inner entourage, a group of half a dozen men who have been accused of creating a "fogbank" between Thieu and the many Vietnamese leaders who are more ready to help him than he imagines.

Buu is not the only man who is trying to get a popular movement or party started. Senator Don, who is one of the heads of the Free Veterans' Association, has decided to turn his National Salvation Front, established after the 1968 Communist Tet offensive, into a political party. He is currently visiting the United States in his capacity as head of the Senate's Defense Committee, and meanwhile he has been trying to set up chapters of his organization in as many provinces as possible. The importance of the veterans, of whom there are now some four hundred thousand, is bound to increase in the postwar period of accommodation, and Senator Don has taken a special interest in trying to work out programs to obtain housing, rice, and schooling for their families and some assurance of economic survival for their widows.

A problem that plagues South and North Vietnam equally, if in different ways, is agriculture. Last February, after years of procrastination, far-ranging land-reform measures were finally introduced, largely at the urging of Americans, in Saigon's National Assembly, but the landlords are fighting back to keep the limits of acreage retention at a fairly high level. Even if and when a decent bill is passed, it will take a long time to unravel the bureaucratic red tape involved in handing over titles to tenants and compensating landlords with a combination of cash and government bonds. Many experts feel that more important than ownership for the farmer-tiller at this juncture is an enforced system of rent reductions, as a first step to full reform. In contrast, in the North, where full-scale agrarian reforms based on the Chinese system of collectivization led to the killing of many thousands of rebellious peasants in the early and middle nineteen-fifties, a new program to spur agricultural production through the establishment of revived coöperatives has run into multiple snags, and these are causing the North Vietnamese rulers their greatest headache at the moment. The agricultural crisis in North Vietnam is exacerbated by the fact that, owing to bad weather, the last really good harvest was a decade ago. Other important factors are the lack of trained administrative personnel, the deterioration of irrigation systems, and a drastic shortage of equipment. The North Vietnamese press and radio have not hesitated to admit, with astonishing frankness, the existence of the worsening problems and shortcomings. A recent editorial in the official Party newspaper, *Nhan Dan,* for example, acknowledged that "the technical revolution has not been properly and comprehensively developed, little improvement has been achieved in management tasks, no great results have been obtained from capital investments, the collective economy has not been properly strengthened, and democratic activities have not been duly developed." Despite the fact that almost all local industry, and some centralized industry in the Hanoi area as well, has been diverted to the manufacture of agricultural equipment, agricultural production has continued to lag, and, for that matter, industrial production has made such small gains as to be negligible, especially when the inflation plaguing the North as well as the South is taken into account.

In the South, the whole agricultural crisis has come to a head at the very time that the price of rice in Saigon has soared to an unprecedented high of as much as six thousand piastres per hundred kilos of the most commonly used variety. (At the official rate, the piastre is worth a hundred and eighteen to the dollar, but the black-market rate is currently about two hundred and twenty to the dollar, and it is still soaring.) The latest price rise has been due chiefly to a shortage of rice, which, in turn, was due to mismanagement and bad warehouse practices. Actually, the price of rice, as of other commodities, began rising sharply three years ago, and last year the Americans began removing their subsidies on imports in an effort to stimulate agricultural production in Vietnam and to do away with the false consumer-goods economy that Washington had earlier supported in an effort to sop up piastres—most notably the huge wartime profits that were being made as a result of large American expenditures in Vietnam. In that earlier period, it had been felt that the best way to keep the inflation from getting out of hand was to let the Vietnamese buy all the Hondas and TV sets they wanted, but this, it turned out, simply encouraged the rich to buy more and kept the poor from having enough money to buy anything. The Vietnamese are still annually importing goods worth eight hundred million dollars, about two-thirds of them consumer products. The government has considerable foreign-exchange reserves, amounting to some two hundred and seventy-five million dollars, and has been loath to use them as long as it could make money off the Americans. Now the subsidies are being cut further, as part of the Vietnamization process, and the word has gone out that, as one high-ranking American put it, "the Vietnamese have to become convinced that they can't go on living off the fat of the land."

The Vietnamese who are in charge of trying to straighten out the economy are resentful because, as one of them said to me, "You created an economic Frankenstein monster here by making this a big war, and now you are telling us that we have to learn almost overnight to be austere and to take care of ourselves, when we all know this is a long process and that there is no such thing as instant Vietnamization." He went on, "Instead of trying to understand our economy and help us plan rationally, you kept giving us temporary, stopgap panaceas. The situation was bound to get out of hand, to the detriment mostly of the poor and the middle classes. After the shock of the 1968 Tet offensive, we tried to let supply and demand guide the situation. There was still a lot of mismanagement and corruption, and prices kept rising, but instead of helping us deal with our fundamental need to improve our bureaucracy and our management techniques you remained solely interested in winning the war. So the bureaucracy became swollen, engineers became politicians, and austerity became a mere catchword. It's fine to talk about long-term plans for agricultural production, forestry, fishing, and so on, but we're in trouble right now. You've never thought of really teaching us instead of just building things, and in that respect you've done us as much harm as the French did."

The sudden bitterness expressed by this man, who is ordinarily mild and pro-American in his sympathies, may convey some idea of the near schizophrenia that is developing among the Vietnamese today as the Americans begin to leave. Since we have failed, for so many years, to help build a functioning political system or an efficient army in Vietnam, there is considerable reason to doubt that the transplantation process called Vietnamization can now be accomplished in a short time span. Militarily, the Vietnamese have already received most of their "legitimate requirements," as the Americans put it. Modern M-16 rifles, for example, are now in the hands of all regular South Vietnamese Army troops—officially, more than four hundred thousand men, but actually, given the still high desertion rate and battle losses, considerably less than that. By the end of this year, the two hundred and fifty thousand members of the improved Regional Forces will also have them; most, if not all, of the hundred and eighty thousand members of the Popular Forces will get their rifles by the middle of 1970. Of the more than a million local self-defense forces in the hamlets, villages, and towns, two-thirds have received brief training courses, and three hundred thousand now have arms—mostly carbines. Other essentials, such as mortars, light artillery, and transportation equipment, have recently been turned over to the regular armed forces, as have the first of several hundred helicopters and some modern jet fighter-bombers. The real nub of Vietnamization, however, is the time needed for training and indoctrination. The Communists, in debating their own strategy, undoubtedly realize that an early settlement of the war, leading to an accelerated withdrawal of American forces, would shorten the time in which Americans could train South Vietnamese to use such intricate machinery as radar networks, electronic devices, and communications equipment, or even to see to the upkeep of modern diesel vehicles and of the patrol boats that have vastly strengthened the riverine forces in the Delta.

The prospects for successful Vietnamization of the armed forces vary greatly from one part of the country to another. In the north —the I Corps area—where the United States Marines have stressed combined American-Vietnamese operations almost from the outset of their tour in Vietnam, considerable progress has been made in teaching the Vietnamese both how to use American equipment and how to plan operations of their own, including the coördination of fire support, ground-to-air facilities, and inter-unit maneuvers. There has been progress elsewhere, too. In the III Corps area, above and around Saigon, General Do Cao Tri, considered by many to be the best South Vietnamese general, told me the other day that now that two of his poorest division commanders have finally been replaced (they were friends of Thieu's, and it took a year of American prodding to get Thieu to remove them), he thinks he can accomplish a full takeover from the Americans in a year and a half. Lieutenant General Nguyen Van Vy, the Minister of Defense, who is one of the holdovers from the previous Cabinet, hopes by the end of this year to give each Regular Army regiment its own independent artillery and tank support. But there are still many weak spots, the most serious being poor leadership in the officer corps, from generals down through captains and lieutenants to noncoms. And although the Americans have begun to teach the Vietnamese the techniques of battlefield coördination, the question remains: What will happen when the American officers in the field who are still pressing the buttons and calling the shots in combined operations leave Vietnam? One top-ranking American commander remarked to me, "The shift from coöperation to liaison on our part is still some years away."

General Creighton W. Abrams, the American military commander in Vietnam, has attained near perfection in the development of his strategy and tactics of maximum pressure and quick response to any Communist action, and his large deployments of artillery and B-52 bombers have annihilated the enemy in virtually all large- or medium-scale engagements. Long-range and nighttime patrolling by the Americans—tactics that the Vietnamese have only just begun to adopt, and not yet very satisfactorily—have led to some improvement in the gathering of intelligence, and by keeping the Communists on the run have interfered with their battlefield preparations, so that when they have chosen to stand and fight, or have made suicidal assaults, they have suffered severely. But Abrams' way of fighting the war is still essentially orthodox, and what will happen when some of that heavy artillery and most or all of those heavy bombers are removed is at the moment unknown.

The Vietnamization of the war nevertheless worries Hanoi—a fact that is being sharply revealed in propaganda both mocking and condemning it. Speaking on September 1st at a ceremony commemorating the twenty-fourth anniversary of the founding of the Democratic Republic of North Vietnam in Hanoi, Premier Pham Van Dong described Vietnamization as "puppetization" of the war, which, he said, was "a return to the special war defeated long ago," meaning by "special war" the war as it was fought prior to 1965. He went on to say, "It is nothing but hackneyed juggling. To use Vietnamese to fight Vietnamese is indeed an attractive policy for the United States! When one has money and guns, can there be a better way to reach one's aims than simply to distribute money and guns? Unfortunately, in the present epoch, such a parodoxical move is flatly impossible. . . . Certainly there is no means, no magic way, to 'ize' the war into something other than the most atrocious and most abominable colonial war in history."

The Politburo in Hanoi, in determining its military strategy and relating this to the two other prongs of its offensive—its political and diplomatic strategy in South Vietnam and in Paris—is engaged today in something very much like a poker game for huge stakes. Hanoi's main interest lies in getting as many American troops as possible out of Vietnam as quickly as possible. The easiest way to achieve the rapid troop reduction would be for Hanoi to reduce the level of activity in South Vietnam and simultaneously reduce the number of replacements infiltrated into the South from the North. Hanoi has repeatedly been told by Washington that this would hasten the pace of American withdrawals and would be considered a basis for agreement. However one wants to interpret the recent eight-week lull, its ending in mid-August, followed by heavy rocket and mortar assaults on Danang two days after Ho Chi Minh's death, showed that the Communists believed that they could not afford to do nothing for very long. Furthermore, since the Communists are not certain what President Nixon wants to do—whether he has made up his mind, as some observers believe he has, to withdraw virtually all American forces from Vietnam by the end of 1970 whatever the circumstances, or is planning to move more slowly and gauge the withdrawals to the moves made by the Communists —they are still thinking in terms of killing between a hundred and fifty and two hundred Americans a week. They figure that this will force Nixon's hand politically at home so that the option of gradual withdrawal will be denied him.

The Communists are obviously eager as soon as possible to score some resounding victories in key battles with the South Vietnamese forces fighting on their own, so as to prove to the South Vietnamese people that their troops have no chance against the North Vietnamese and the Vietcong. What the Communists do not want, despite the fact that they are preparing themselves for it, is a return to the special, or pre-1965, war. Their own weakened situation, in both the North and the South, renders that a hazardous undertaking. They would undoubtedly rather try to Vietminhize, or Communize, the South politically than take chances on draining their own resources any longer in a protracted conflict. For that reason, if they decide that their situation in the North is too shaky to let them continue to sustain the major burden of the war in the South, they may settle for a series of regional cease-fires under some system of international supervision, followed by regional or provincial elections and then by a national election. This would presumably give them control over a number of areas—mostly sparsely populated ones along the Laotian and Cambodian borders, and some of the more populated places in the Delta and in the central plateau region. Such a compromise would make sense to them, not only because of their war-weariness and their dwindling manpower but because of their current military and political campaign in Laos, which is proving successful. In effect, though Washington doesn't like the term, this would mean a *de-facto* partitioning of South Vietnam, at least temporarily, as a prelude to an eventual election there.

Unless the South Vietnamese government is really strong enough politically and militarily to resist such an offer, Saigon would find it difficult, in the face of American and world opinion, to reject it.

A number of American experts who believe that Saigon is neither sufficiently strong nor sufficiently aware of the dangers it faces are urging a far faster rate of political preparation for potential regional contests. This would entail some knocking together of South Vietnamese heads. For example, in a specific area where the Hoa Hao or the Cao Dai or the southern Buddhists or the peasant-labor forces or the old nationalist parties are the strongest single community force, that group would have the best chance of commanding regional or local respect and should be given the go-ahead. As for the cities, where the degree of political divisiveness is worse than in the countryside, some serious effort should be made to unite all the contending forces. Ultimately, there would have to be a trade-off of some degree of rural control by the Communists for government control over the more populous areas, in order to avoid handing the Communists the sort of coalition deal they want on a silver platter.

Saigon remains the No. 1 objective of the Communists, and any temporary deals they may make in Paris and Vietnam won't change that situation. It was not recently renamed Ho Chi Minh City in their propaganda for nothing. Bad planning and bad execution of plans lost them their chance of capturing it during the Tet offensive in 1968, and today their chances of taking it either by force or through subversion have dwindled. Having infiltrated only half as many men into South Vietnam so far this year as they had up to this date last year, and having suffered almost as many casualties as they had up to this date in 1968, they are facing a serious problem of attrition, which has forced them to make some cold recalculations. The new Communist military methods, as enunciated a few weeks ago by General Giap, call not for "offensives" in the old sense but for "campaigns," each one of which is a fairly fluid affair consisting of "low" and "high" points. Because the Communists have had an attrition rate—that is, losses exceeding replacements from the North—for the last half year of five thousand men a month, no sustained attack is now anticipated unless Hanoi puts more men into South Vietnam. Between engagements, the main Communist forces have followed their custom of moving across the Cambodian border to jungle sanctuaries. In Paris, the Americans have made it clear that if Hanoi wants to offer any serious signal of an intention to cut the total of its forces, it will have to withdraw some of them northward from base areas in both Cambodia and Laos as well as continue to decrease the rate of infiltration.

To the best of their ability, which is still considerable, the enemy forces have made the necessary adjustments. The foundation of their new order of battle is the small sapper unit, consisting of regular assault troops specially trained for demolition and sabotage and of special-action teams, which are paramilitary organizations used for assaults on urban areas. The latter most often wear civilian clothes and concentrate on terrorist activity, setting off satchel charges and other explosives at police stations, military installations, and so forth, and throwing grenades from vehicles. For planned major attacks on Saigon, which they haven't been able to carry out, the Communists last April set up special-action teams called *cac cum,* which are broken down into companies, squads, and, in some cases, three-man cells. Some of these units were ordered into the capital in June, but only a limited number—about a hundred men—succeeded in penetrating the city. Since then, with the assistance of teen-age terrorists who live here, they have been responsible for the series of explosions that have occurred over the past weeks. Other *cum* units, hiding in the suburbs or farther out, presumably will be the spearheads of the action following the next lull. This new offensive tactic is based on following up a sapper thrust, if it is initially successful, with larger reinforcements. In Vietnamese, the tactic is known as *mui* (nose) *nhon* (pointed) *duoi* (tail)—the pointed nose of the sapper unit or special-action team being supported by the spreading peacock tail of a battalion or a regiment.

As if Saigon had not had enough problems and perplexities over the past weeks, it has had to live through the embarrassment of two major espionage scandals, one involving the American Special Forces, or Green Berets, and the other involving a spy ring that reached right into the Presidential Palace. The Green Beret case arose from the murder of an alleged Vietnamese double agent named Thai Khac Chuyen, who was working for the Special Forces. The case broke when a sergeant in the Green Beret group involved sought the help of the Central Intelligence Agency, which had advised against killing Chuyen; the sergeant, who had also advised against the murder, felt his own life was endangered. Whether Chuyen was a double agent or not, if he was murdered it was a mistake, whatever the exigencies of the wartime situation, and an inexcusable one, as almost all Americans here seem to agree.*

The other spy case involves the largest espionage ring uncovered in ten years. This organization was under investigation for seven months before the first arrests were disclosed, in July, and since then about a hundred persons, including perhaps a score of women, have been taken into custody by the Vietnamese Special Police, and at least two-thirds of these are still in jail. The C.I.A. collaborated closely with the Vietnamese in breaking the spy network, and is said to have opened up the first leads. Operating within several ministries as well as within the Presidential Palace, the ring reported directly to the Strategic Intelligence Branch of the Central Office for South Vietnam (COSVN), the top Communist echelon in South Vietnam. This branch is known as B-22 and is run by one of Hanoi's main agents in South Vietnam. He is Dang Van Huong, alias Mat Ro, and he has not been apprehended. The Saigon network was handled by Vu Ngoc Nha, a Catholic, who was sent south by Hanoi in 1955, and who had close Palace connections as a result of being introduced there by some unwitting priests. Nha's principal agent at the Palace was one of President Thieu's assistants for political affairs, Huynh Van Trong. Trong is said to be a former French agent who pretended to work for the late Ngo Dinh Diem. Thieu is said to have been told about the existence of the spy ring early this year, and to have instructed the police to continue their investigation and uncover further ramifications of the case. The ring is said to have done considerable damage, especially in reporting to Hanoi on the progress of pacification programs and on the political activities of various religious groups in the South.

In the midst of these turbulent events, Saigon has been besieged by more than the usual number of visiting firemen from America —a state of affairs that has scarcely made life easier for harassed Allied officials. Among the visitors was a delegation of the Citizens Committee for Peace with Freedom in Vietnam, which is a group of a hundred and thirty distinguished Americans that former Senator Paul Douglas, of Illinois, organized in October, 1967, and whose founding honorary chairmen were former President Harry Truman and the late President Dwight Eisenhower. The committee is in

---

*Ultimately, the court-martial case against all eight defendants, including the commander of the Special Forces in Vietnam, was dropped by the Army.

favor of obtaining a peace in Vietnam that will not lead to what they consider a sellout to the Communists and will guarantee the South Vietnamese the right to determine their own future through safeguarded elections. Next came a delegation of the National Committee for a Political Settlement in Vietnam, which seeks an immediate, standstill cease-fire, supported by an international peace-keeping force to supervise withdrawal of all troops; prompt free elections, under the supervision of a joint electoral commission; complete land reform; and extensive postwar economic aid, under the auspices of the United Nations. Before, between, and after these committee visits, there was a stream of members of Congress. All these visitors went through the customary top-level briefings and tried to see as many Vietnamese as they could during their stays, which varied from a day or two to two weeks, and all of them left apparently as bewildered as or more bewildered than they were when they arrived. The trouble seems to be that too many such Americans, thoroughly concerned though they are, are seeking answers without knowing the right questions. Perhaps this has been our trouble in Vietnam all along.

22. Saigon

~*

January 31, 1970

On February 6th, another Tet holiday will usher in the Year of the Dog, and while there are as many opinions about what will happen in Vietnam in 1970 as there are breeds of dog, there is universal agreement that it will be the most critical year since this misbegotten war began a decade ago. If President Nixon, backed by his silent majority, sticks to his tentative timetable, it will almost surely be the last year of major American combat involvement. This does not mean that a year from now American troops of all sorts will not be engaged in some fighting, or that the American death toll of just over forty thousand could not eventually rise to fifty thousand or more. Under the present withdrawal plan, between twenty and forty thousand American military advisers and technicians will be left here as late as the end of 1972, and the lower figure will still be about three times the number that were in the country in 1962. Those Americans who are known here as 'the new optimists"— people who believe that the process of Vietnamization is really beginning to work—acclaim the Nixon program as the only sensible course. Others who are more skeptical believe that if Vietnamization is to have any success, five years or more will be needed. And still others remain convinced that no amount of time will enable our Allies to master the complex weapons systems that the Americans themselves have had only limited success in using conventionally in this unconventional war.

Apart from the military arguments, even those Americans here who are most strongly opposed to the war and want to get out quickly are forced to admit that a further acceleration of the American withdrawal, in the absence of sudden concessions by Hanoi, would endanger the vulnerable social and economic reconstruction programs and perhaps provoke the collapse of the present Saigon government. However, more and more people are beginning to wonder whether another government might not be able to end the war sooner and still preserve an independent, non-Communist South Vietnam, and perhaps a stronger and sounder one as well. The constitutional "legality" of the present administration, which was elected for a four-year term that will end in the fall of 1971, is still acknowledged, but such legality is not held to be as sacrosanct as it was a few months ago. The doubts that are arising about both the intentions and the political efficacy of the Thieu regime could therefore prove to be more important than all the complicated technical and administrative machinery of Vietnamization, and their consequences could unhinge Nixon's whole scheme.

However justified or unjustified the skepticism may be concerning Nixon's silent majority in the United States, a silent majority unquestionably exists among the seventeen million South Vietnamese, and although this majority opposes the Communists, only a relatively small portion of it is really behind Thieu. This much is admitted by Thieu's most enthusiastic American supporters, who have nursed him along through uncertainty and self-doubt to his current euphoric overconfidence, which bears an ever-growing resemblance to the overweening, self-destructive assurance shown by the late President Ngo Dinh Diem at the end of the nineteen-fifties. Nixon and Thieu, who are alike in many ways, will most likely do their best not to upset each other's plans, which are carefully calculated to bring about their respective reëlections. Whatever Nixon may privately think of Thieu—and it is hard to imagine that he could actually believe the Vietnamese President to be, as he has called him, "one of the four or five best political leaders in the world"—he will almost surely go to any lengths to avoid an upheaval in Saigon that might affect his twofold aim of getting out

of Vietnam as gracefully and quickly as possible and keeping himself in the White House until 1976. Like pilot and co-pilot on a
takeoff, they have reached a point of no return, and now they must
fly on together toward their common destination. It will be ironic
for Nixon if the flight is hijacked by some of Thieu's more fractious
passengers.

Obviously, this is one of the eventualities the Communists are
hoping for; in fact, their present strategy and tactics are geared to
it. Last year and the year before, Hanoi's plan was to keep American
casualties at a high enough level to stir up strong sentiment against
the war in the United States, as a way of achieving its ultimate aim
of American withdrawal and a favorable political solution through
the forced establishment of a coalition government. Their 1970 plan
is apparently designed to achieve the same aim by subtler means;
namely, by attacking the Vietnamization program on all levels
through increased terrorism, and by further denigrating and dividing the by no means popular Thieu administration. Naturally, the
Communists' official line is that Vietnamization cannot work, but
at the same time they appear to worry that it might; at least, this
would account for what seems to be a strong difference of opinion
in Hanoi about how the war in the South should now be fought.
Some observers, citing manpower and production problems that the
North Vietnamese themselves have admitted to, believe that a
power struggle is beginning. After the death of Ho Chi Minh last
September 3rd, the triumvirate of Premier Pham Van Dong; Le
Duan, the First Secretary of the Lao Dong Party; and Truong Chinh,
the chairman of the National Assembly Standing Committee,
seemed to be taking over smoothly and swiftly. Now, however,
there are some signs that Dong, who might be said to occupy the
driver's seat, is being subjected to more and more back-seat driving
from Chinh and Duan, who differ with him and each other about
priorities at home, especially in the vital areas of agricultural production and Party reorganization and discipline. While Duan, as the
chief Party leader, is working closely with Dong to keep the government running properly and to maintain a balance between Moscow
and Peking, he appears to believe that Hanoi can win the war in the
South, or at least achieve a stalemate, in a relatively short time, and
will then be in a position to pay more attention to domestic difficulties. Chinh, the chief Party ideologist, who has recently been ap-

pearing in public almost weekly and who follows a more pro-Peking line, wants to shore up the North's economy first, and accepts the inevitability of a protracted challenge in the South. In a succession of statements and speeches, which have covered everything from the effects of floods and droughts on food production to revisionist trends in art and the need to revitalize "mass leadership," Chinh has sounded increasingly like a scolding leader of the Cultural Revolution in China. Duan, on the other hand, has so far appeared in public only rarely, and, when he did so late in October, declared pragmatically, "Solidarity does not mean that differing views are impossible between two comrades in the Party [but] the collective system must be firmly maintained. It is inadvisable to adopt the opinion of one person and force all others to follow it [but] we must, at all costs, achieve solidarity."

Even if the differences of opinion and of approach in North Vietnam are not yet serious enough to amount to a power struggle, and I don't think they are, they do convey some idea of the complicated situation in that country. The statements being made by both sides in this long and brutal war are, in fact, increasingly shrill and confused. The Vietnamese opponents have come to seem like two punch-drunk prizefighters in an old-time bare-knuckle brawl that has lasted more rounds than either can remember. Both are wobbly and can hardly stand but are kept going by their seconds, who between rounds clean them up, fix their cuts, and give them smelling salts, then send them out again when the bell rings. Sooner or later, one of the weary battlers may simply collapse and drop to the canvas. Or the fight may go on and on, with the spectators helpless. It is easy to say that if the seconds would just pack up and go home it would all be over, but the seconds can't; neither the American moral predicament nor Communist revolutionary dialectics and objectives will permit it.

The most important Communist statements made recently on the military and political direction of the war are contained in a seven-part article by General Vo Nguyen Giap, North Vietnam's Defense Minister, that appeared in two Hanoi newspapers in mid-December, and in copies of a number of directives that were captured in South Vietnam—notably a pair called "cosvn Resolution Nine" and "cosvn Resolution Ten." Though the veracity of captured documents has often been questioned, I have seen the Vietnamese originals of the ones I am referring to, and am sure that they are authentic. COSVN, the Central Office for South Vietnam, is the headquarters that, under Hanoi's direction, runs the war in the South; it is at present situated in Cambodia, just across the western border of Tay Ninh Province, northwest of Saigon, and has a forward headquarters in Tay Ninh itself. There have been ten resolutions since COSVN was established, at the end of 1961, or about a year after the creation of the National Liberation Front in the South. These resolutions are, in effect, orders and interpretations of orders for Party workers and followers in South Vietnam, and are based on prior Lao Dong resolutions, handed down from Hanoi. For example, Resolution Nine, which was issued last July, was based on a Lao Dong resolution issued by the Politburo in Hanoi in April. Resolution Nine was captured here when a Communist courier was ambushed and killed by members of an American brigade north of Saigon in October. It was the first complete resolution ever obtained, and it is considered especially significant because it contains a lengthy and detailed analysis of the war. It was presumably written by Pham Hung, the fourth-ranking member of the Hanoi Politburo and the highest-ranking Communist in the South, who directs both the military and the political war effort, and one sign of its importance is that Party workers are ordered to study it for "fifty hours."

Often defensive and even bitter in tone, and replete with harsh criticisms of past shortcomings, Resolution Nine charts a complicated, sometimes seemingly contradictory, course for "achieving a decisive victory within a relatively short period of time" while "firmly grasping the precept of protractedness" in order to "defeat the enemy in case they try to prolong the war." Hopes for rapid American deëscalation and for the failure of Vietnamization are repeatedly expressed, as is the hope that the Americans will be "forced to seek an early end to the war through a political solution that they cannot refuse"; namely, a cease-fire followed by the establishment of a coalition government. But even after that, the document says, "our struggle against the enemy will go on with extreme complexity" until the "ultimate victory"—reunification of the North and South—is achieved. While accepting the fact that "the Saigon area is our major battlefield for the whole of South Vietnam," Resolution Nine appears to acknowledge the difficulty of again laying siege to Saigon and other major cities in the manner of the 1968 Tet offensive. One phrase that is constantly reiterated is "especially in the Delta," and it is there in particular—the rich rice region south of Saigon—that Communist troops are supposed to grab the initiative and "liberate and control the major part of the rural area, liberate . . . a number of towns and municipalities, and build the liberated areas into perfect revolutionary bases to serve as the firm, direct rear of the resistance." It is in the Mekong Delta, however, where guerrilla activity back in 1959 touched off the present war, that the South Vietnamese government has made the most progress in the last year. Largely on the basis of advances in this area, President Thieu has claimed that his government now "controls" ninety-five per cent of the total population of South Vietnam—a claim that even optimistic Americans privately acknowledge to be exaggerated by at least fifteen per cent by night, and in some places by day.

There is no doubt that improvements have taken place. Many roads that had been closed to traffic for years are open again. Rice and other produce are moving, a number of former contested areas have now been brought under either partial or nearly complete government control, and thousands of the people who had been living in Communist villages and hamlets have crossed over into safer zones. It is in the Delta, too, that the biggest improvement has been made in the use of Regional and Popular Forces, which together now number almost half a million men and are being supplied with more and more American M-16 rifles. With American help—and our air and artillery support particularly are still vital—the South Vietnamese have managed to set up outposts in the two long-established Vietcong base areas in the Delta—the U Minh Forest and Base Area 470—close to the Cambodian border. That the Communists are now feverishly concerned about the Delta is therefore no surprise.

Late last year, the Vietcong's 273rd Regiment moved into the area, and since more than half of this unit is now composed of North Vietnamese "filler" troops, the move marked the first time that Hanoi elements had come that far south. With the withdrawal of the American 9th Division—a unit that established a tremendously high, and quite possibly exaggerated, ratio of combat losses to enemy casualties, and left as many enemies as friends among the South Vietnamese—the North Vietnamese shifted more forces

south. Today, there are elements of four identified North Vietnamese regiments in the Delta, and also countless additional
"fillers" sent in as replacements for depleted main-force Vietcong
units, some of which are now eighty per cent North Vietnamese. All
in all, there are probably at least ten thousand North Vietnamese
soldiers in the area, and, counting political workers, main-force
Vietcong, local guerrillas, and men, women, and children handling
supplies and acting as communications and liaison personnel, a
total of between fifty and sixty thousand Communists are active
there. Although the rate of infiltration from North Vietnam at any
given time is extremely difficult to determine until months later,
when certain elements in the South may be identified, the best
available intelligence indicates that four or five thousand North
Vietnamese came south during November and somewhat fewer in
December. These figures, if they are right, are in keeping with the
over-all Hanoi plan to fight the war in the South in 1970 by using
highly trained, fast-striking small units to attack larger American
and South Vietnamese units whenever an opportunity arises and
continuing to attack such important targets as government administrative centers.

Obviously, the Communists are getting ready for something in
the Delta, but no one knows what. The best guess is that, in conjunction with forces that they are maintaining in the central highlands
to the north, and also still farther north, adjacent to Laos, they are
doing two things: slowly establishing a new system of linked base
areas reaching all the way from North Vietnam to the tip of the
Delta, and getting ready to sweep eastward from these bases to
attack district capitals, and perhaps some provincial capitals as
well—one of which, either in the highlands or in a remote section
of the Delta, might be proclaimed the capital of the Provisional
Revolutionary Government that COSVN and Hanoi established last
June. Such a widespread campaign, aimed at seizing specific places
and simultaneously disrupting the pacification and Vietnamization
programs, could pave the way for a cease-fire and political talks.
What Hanoi may increasingly have in mind is the consolidation of
a wide belt of territory embracing all of western Vietnam and all
of eastern Laos, including, in Laos, part of the Plaine des Jarres,
which the Communists lost last fall. Together, these areas would
constitute a "liberated" system of interlocking zones, which, except

for some of the Delta regions, are largely uninhabited. What would follow if this happens might lead, according to what is called by American officials the "leopard-spot theory," to regional cease-fires accompanied by political accommodation and followed by local and regional elections, the end result being the division of both Vietnam and Laos into Communist and non-Communist areas. Although such a partition could become a permanent or semi-permanent solution in Laos, it probably couldn't in Vietnam, for political and guerrilla warfare would undoubtedly continue regardless of cease-fires. There is no doubt that Hanoi is likely to persist in its reunification aim even if it takes five, ten, or twenty years longer.

A number of references in Resolution Nine to completing Party organizational work by "June, 1970," indicate both that the task is urgent and that if a "decisive victory" can be attained by that date a cease-fire may end the major fighting, at least temporarily, and the political struggle may be stepped up. Progress has been far too slow, the Resolution says, in building "party chapters, youth group chapters and masses' organizations." More women, teen-agers, and "ethnic minorities, especially Buddhists," must be recruited as part of "a broad political high tide," which, with the help of "fifth columnists, will cause permanent political unrest in the urban areas and help develop the guerrilla warfare movement." Portions of Resolution Ten and other documents exploit the cease-fire theme further. There are frequent references to "the situation developing quickly," possibly because, as one document admits, confidence in total victory at this stage "has been considerably lessened since Ho Chi Minh's death." According to a notebook taken from the body of a high-ranking officer killed southeast of Saigon in November, the Communists, in order to expedite American withdrawal and "frustrate de-Americanization," can create "an unfavorable situation for the Americans and the Saigon government when a cease-fire is stipulated" if "we capitalize on the opportunity by planting our personnel in government-controlled areas to take advantage of any changes"—possibly a reference to an anti-Thieu coup. This notebook adds, "In the immediate future, we will accept a cease-fire. Whenever the cease-fire is promulgated by us, our troops will continue to attack and overrun government Army posts. We will not make prisoners of puppet soldiers. Rather, we will educate them and release them on the spot. But we have to capture as many [enemy] soldiers as possible in preparation for a political settlement." Another document, belived to be a section of Resolution Ten, speaks of an increase in military proselytizing among both government and Allied forces and of supporting "a fifth column in place" within Allied units to erode morale, instead of simply encouraging deserters. A new organization, the People's Democratic Peace Front, is mentioned, which would replace the Provisional Revolutionary Government after a cease-fire and would subsequently control the provisional coalition as the People's Democratic Peace Alliance.

There has been considerable discussion of whether the Communists, if they took over South Vietnam, would kill their political enemies, as they did in North Vietnam in 1945-46, and again in the mid-fifties, when there was a peasant rebellion against enforced collectivization; between fifty thousand and a hundred thousand people were killed during each period. Predictions about such matters are hazardous, but although the Communists have joined the rest of the world in condemning the American massacre at My Lai —or, to give it its correct Vietnamese geographical designation, Tu Cong—in March, 1968, they have also, according to scores of documents I have just read, given orders to "kill tyrants and traitors" throughout the country now and also when uprisings take place just before and just after a cease-fire is declared. The rate of terrorism, including the assassination of village and hamlet officials, especially those engaged in pacification and self-defense, rose at the end of 1969 quite sharply, having averaged slightly less per month during the rest of the year than in 1968, when during the Tet offensive in Hué the Communists appear, on the evidence of mass graves still being uncovered, to have murdered close to five thousand people— government functionaries, anti-Communist politicians, pro-government intellectuals, religious leaders, and so on. The documents captured during 1969 also included orders to "annihilate" opposition elements by categories, much as was initially done in Hué. Several of the documents gave orders for the "annihilation" of a specific number of people in each of various villages in central Vietnam; for one province, the number ranged from five to forty per village. Instructions issued in mid-1969 to Party committees of two Delta provinces ordered rosters to be prepared of "wicked village delegates, policemen, hamlet chiefs and assistant hamlet chiefs, intelligence agents, spies, and betrayers who have committed a blood debt against our people." One document advocated careful procedures, saying, "We should not take advantage of the situation to terrorize, assassinate, and torture indiscriminately. We should fully understand the policy of using violence and implement it correctly and democratically." Another document was more blunt. "Each comrade must kill one reactionary," it said.

A distinction should be made between captured enemy documents, usually sent out for official Communist guidance, and public speeches or articles, such as the seven-part article by General Giap. The importance of Giap's article lies in the imprimatur it gives to the earlier COSVN resolutions and documents and in the corroboration it offers of the kind of war the Communists are now preparing to fight—one emphasizing "the art of using a small force to fight a big force." In his current article, Giap, sounding far less positive and confident than he did when he wrote his famous guerrilla textbook *People's War, People's Army,* in the fifties, speaks of "the great imbalance of numerical strength and population, and also a great imbalance of technical equipment," and of the need for enough time "to gradually exterminate and weaken the enemy's forces, to restrict their strength and aggravate their weaknesses, to gradually strengthen and develop our forces and overcome our deficiencies." Giap adds, "We should not apply old experiences mechanically, or reapply outmoded forms of warfare." The theme throughout is to make economical use of the forces that the Communists have at their command, which are now estimated to include a hundred and thirty thousand North Vietnamese fighting men in the South (or in rest camps in Cambodia), in a total combined force—among which are Vietcong main-force units, guerrillas, political workers, supply troops, and so on—of three hundred and thirty thousand.

A recent study, based partly on interviews with some of the six thousand North Vietnamese battlefield prisoners being held in South Vietnam, reaches the conclusion that the North Vietnamese are still deeply dedicated to their cause of the "liberation" of the South and hold a continuing staunch belief in the advantages of Communism in the North. This belief, which, it has been found, is held even by sons of some former landowners who were killed in the mid-fifties' purge, entails acceptance of the harsh regimen and strict security measures imposed on the North by the war, and a conviction that the war in the South has been a legitimate drive for "national salvation"—a natural and logical sequel to the struggle against the French that began in 1945. Thus, although the North Vietnamese soldiers regard their three-to-six month trip to the South as a painful experience, and although many of them acknowledge, with a kind of Buddhist or Taoist fatalism, that they may never return to their homes and families again, they tend to accept their role as a totally unavoidable commitment, a responsibility from which there is no escape. The attitude of these North Vietnamese soldiers is in considerable contrast to the feelings of many South Vietnamese Vietcong *hoi chanh* (returnees), who have averaged twenty-five thousand a year over the last four years, compared to a total of some two hundred North Vietnamese who have defected without being forced to surrender on the battlefield since the war began. There are many dedicated Vietcong soldiers, but there are just as many who, after joining the Communists either voluntarily or by impressment— and in the last two years the latter has been the case more and more often—have revealed a negative attitude. A large number of the *hoi chanh* who volunteered have said that they did so because they were against the government for one reason or another—lack of faith in the successive Saigon regimes, anger over specific cruel or discriminatory actions by local officials. Those who had fought the hardest for the Vietcong did so because they related their actions directly to what they felt for the South Vietnamese "homeland," and they showed no strong convictions about reunification with the North. Until recently—and even now, to a lesser extent—they were also motivated by the belief that they were fighting on the winning side. Something that is new in the past year, according to the study, is a decline in morale, owing to physical and economic hardship—the result, in large part, of the devastating B-52 raids. The drop in morale has also been due in part to the diminishing number of zealous and well-trained political workers. Today, there is less expounding of revolutionary ideology, less careful indoctrination, and more direct preaching about anti-Americanism and survival, together with vague allusions to promotion and status once the war is won. The Communists are still recruiting people at a rate of at least five thousand a month, but most of the new recruits are boys of eleven or twelve, women, and old men. Despite all this, and despite growing friction between the dedicated northerners and the southerners who dream more simply of peace, interrogations indicate that the average Communist political worker in the South still has stronger motivation than his counterpart on the government side.

Because what is now South Vietnam has, historically, been more often divided than united, and because it has been subject to more divisive foreign influences than the North, the South Vietnamese inevitably lack the solidarity and the sustained revolutionary ardor of their northern brethren, and are today bewildered and uncertain about their own capacity to hold together and to restore their broken nationalist roots under the harsh imperatives of time and of such essentially artificial programs as "Vietnamization" and "pacification." To be "Vietnamized" or "pacified" or "reconstructed"—words that Aldous Huxley or George Orwell would have relished—without being given time or opportunity to rediscover a southern consciousness, which exists but lies deeply submerged, is apt to be meaningless. This is the fundamental problem in South Vietnam today, and nothing makes this fact clearer than a trip, such as one I made last month, through the provinces of the seething Delta.

In certain respects, the journey is comparable to a tour of New York City that includes the ugly, violent slums of Harlem and Williamsburg, the bland middle-class sections of Queens and the Bronx, and the insulated wealthy blocks of upper Fifth and Park Avenues. It may be no accident that the two terms one hears used most often by the Americans in Vietnam these days are "social mobility" and "decentralization." The first has to do with the involvement of many more people in the Revolutionary Development Program and in the complex bureaucratic social structure of the provinces. There are now hundreds of new "experts." Seventeen different types, including village chiefs, are being trained at Vung Tau, on the coast near Saigon, for rural-development work of one sort or another; district and province chiefs are being specially trained elsewhere. Ordinary villagers are getting short courses designed to encourage building up useful relationships among themselves and among neighboring communities. The Americans hope that when elections are held for provincial councils, sometime this spring or summer (the forty-four province chiefs will continue to be appointed), social mobility will increase, especially if, as is anticipated, each candidate is required to run from the district in which he lives. As for decentralization, it is a concomitant of social mobility. It refers to the reëstablishment of traditional local autonomy through the election of hamlet and village chiefs and councils. On the average, four to six hamlets make up a village, and, according to the latest American figures, there are 2,157 villages and 10,731 hamlets in South Vietnam. Ninety-two per cent of the villages have chiefs, assistant chiefs, and councils, most of them locally elected, and the fact of their having been elected entitles them to government funds of a million piastres (about eight thousand dollars at the official rate, but less than three thousand at the current black-market rate) for development projects of their own choosing; villages whose officials are still appointed, because they are not secure enough to hold elections, get only four hundred thousand piastres. When the provincial councils are set up, they will also have their own development funds, and it is hoped that these councils will encourage social mobility further by dealing directly with their village counterparts in promoting development projects.

It might work, but, given the subtle, often intractable ways of the Orient, it is too pat, too "Western" a concept. There has always been a tendency among the statistics-minded, reform-minded Americans here to play numbers games, and by now the Vietnamese have caught the habit. Thus, when President Thieu claims to have ninety-five per cent of the population of the country under control, he is taking cognizance of the fact that about forty per cent of the people now live in or around cities, in contrast to just fifteen per cent before the war. In the Delta region, which has more than half the country's total population, the number of hamlets under Vietcong control, the Americans say, has been more than halved since a year ago—fourteen per cent of the population compared to thirty-five per cent. Undoubtedly, the government has improved its position a great deal by denying resources to the Communist area through military pressure—as one Vietcong village chief said after crossing over: "It was just getting too hard to see my wife." There are five hundred thousand more guns on the government side today than there were a year ago—about a hundred and fifty thousand of them new M-16 rifles that have been distributed to the Regional and Popular Forces, and the rest mostly carbines that have been given out to the Popular Self-Defense Forces—volunteer groups that patrol communities at night. As for economic improvements in the Delta, today one can see there thousands more Hondas, sewing machines, television and radio sets, and the like, than one could a year or so ago, and the current rice crop, amounting to more than five million tons, is the highest in several years.

In 1969, what was called the Accelerated Pacification Campaign was supposed to get as many people as possible into as many secure villages as possible before the Communists got there. The 1970 program is emphasizing consolidation—building up the new village governments and stimulating more information campaigns and development projects (bridges, schoolhouses, pig-raising centers, social halls, and so on). Two of the worst weak spots are the local police forces, which have been a problem ever since the time of Diem, and the Phoenix Program, a provincially coördinated plan for collecting intelligence on important local Communists and then arresting them. Another, over-all, weakness is a tendency to emphasize quantity at the expense of quality, and this is something that pervades the whole Vietnamization program, including the recruitment of paramilitary elements. But the greatest weakness of all, as I see it, remains the lack of political motivation from the bottom up. This is something that only the Vietnamese can ultimately provide, but the Americans have all along failed to stimulate such efforts, and the new heavy emphasis on rapid Vietnamization, with its manifold technical aspects, scarcely helps to focus attention on useful political developments. "Village democracy," beginning with the election of a chief—there often is only one candidate, frequently a reluctant one—continuing with a group decision whether to build a schoolhouse or a pig farm, and facilitated by an increase in administrative efficiency, may stimulate an emerging political consciousness. But these have proved to be material measures, and neither such efforts alone nor an improvement in military security—important as that is—nor a combination of the two will save Vietnam if more substantial political institutions are not established. Technology and bureaucracy are surely not enough when the Communists are still far from defeated—when, as one veteran American economic-development worker commented, "two Vietcong in a hamlet can still undo most of what we've accomplished." The Americans, after fighting the war themselves for too long, without equipping and training a mobile Vietnamese army, are now, as they hastily try to put American-style social-welfare and economic-improvement programs into effect, again doing the job themselves instead of letting the Vietnamese learn the hard way. As one American adviser says, "We're still holding hands with them across the paddies."

Most Americans consider Kien Hoa, a coastal province southeast of Saigon that has traditionally been a Communist stronghold and major recruitment center for the Vietcong, possibly the worst province in the country. Today, things there are not as bad as they once were. Some roads can now be driven over by day, and some long-closed markets and schools are open again. But more than two thousand Communists, or about twice as many as there were a year ago, are currently active in the province, and in the past few months the number of Vietcong incidents has increased four or five fold—to about a hundred and fifty a month. Most of these are acts of terrorism against and attacks on the Regional and Popular Forces, whose members still tend to hole up in outposts or, if they do patrol, to take the same routes over and over—an open invitation to attack. In one recent five-day period, the Vietcong killed three hamlet chiefs and seriously wounded a village chief and a school-teacher. The new government workers more often than not lack direction, whether because the district chiefs, who are usually Army captains, don't know how to assign them or because the village chiefs, who are now supposed to be in charge of the incoming Revolutionary Development workers and other specialists, are afraid to exercise their new authority or are harassed by their jealous district and provincial superiors. The situation is not made easier by the fact that some of the more experienced technical cadremen, with academic degrees from Saigon, are paid more than most provincial officials and twice as much as the village chiefs. Five-man Mobile Advisory Teams of Americans, who either work with the Regional Force companies or work on village development schemes, put in only thirty- or forty-day stints, in which they can seldom accomplish enough to make a lasting impression.

Neighboring Vinh Binh Province is another Communist backwater, with between two and three thousand main-force Vietcong and local guerrillas still active, but there the government has established some degree of control over twice as many hamlets as it could claim a year ago. Nevertheless, the Vietcong still hold several important areas—most notably Cang Long District, which has been an enemy base for many years. The American senior adviser told me that the Vietnamese Army commander in the Delta was willing to put two regular regiments into Cang Long for one month but that it would take six months to clear out the Vietcong. Police work in the province is poor, too, and there is a lack of coördination within the local Phoenix Program. Though some roads are now passable even at night, the Communists are still able to move between Vinh Binh and the neighboring provinces almost at will after dark, using an intricate system of canals and rivers as well as many of the roads. In Ba Xuyen Province, south of Vinh Binh, the situation has improved more substantially, with the estimated total of armed Vietcong and guerrillas having dropped in the past year from nearly four thousand to slightly more than two thousand. The Regional and Popular Forces there have done particularly well, the local senior adviser said. All but sixty thousand of two hundred and eighty thousand hectares of riceland are under government cultivation. As I moved on south to Thoi Binh District, in An Xuyen Province, at the far end of the Delta, which is another contender for the designation of the worst area in the country, I was given the latest evaluations on its hamlets, which, according to the Hamlet Evaluation System—an American system of rating hamlets from "A" down to "E" on the basis of their security and development, with "V" used to designate a hamlet still completely in Vietcong hands —had no "A"s, four "B"s, four "C"s, five "D"s, and seven "V"s. Here, the American advisers agreed, the Communists, if they choose to, can hit hard in the coming months.

I had now been in four bad provinces in a row. The next two were a sharp contrast. In Kien Giang, on the southwest coast, eighty-eight per cent of the population is living in hamlets rated "A," "B," or "C," and territory that was abandoned to the Communists is being rapidly reoccupied. The people of Kien Giang are not yet altogether pro-government, but they are becoming more openly anti-Communist; though they still retain their fear of reprisals, they are now willing to give information about Vietcong agents, possibly because they get paid for it. In Chau Thanh District of An Giang Province, just to the north, the situation is even better. A majority of the district's population are members of the Hoa Hao, one of the two major religious sects in the South, and its leaders in this region for years maintained a successful truce with the Communists. The improvement was also noticeable in Kien Van District of Kien Phong Province, our next stop, and markedly so at our last stop in Dien Tuong Province, a principal funnel route for Communist troops coming in from Cambodia. A sergeant in Giao Duc District there, who had been in the same village in 1965, recalled, "Back then I couldn't move thirty yards out of my compound without a platoon. Now the roads and canals are open for miles around."

In the Delta, as elsewhere in South Vietnam, many of the improvements are bound to prove transitory if they do not keep pace with the ability of the Communists to retaliate—and Hanoi still has the ability to do so. One high-ranking American civilian official with many years of experience here told me, "The Vietnamese are never going to be able to live happily ever after. A lot depends on their sticking to what they're doing right now. There are three curves—the curve of increasing Vietnamization, the curve of our declining direct support, and the curve of Communist action. If we can keep the first two curves ahead of the last, we'll be all right." Many Americans complain privately about the "thin veneer" of ability among Vietnamese officers, though they praise some individuals highly. More are now being trained in the United States and elsewhere abroad, and the training period in Vietnam is longer, too, but the question of quantity vs. quality remains a vital one. There also remain all sorts of other military difficulties, having to do with logistics and with strategy and tactics. For example, the job of training helicopter pilots and mechanics, which takes three years and should have been started long ago, was only recently begun. The tasks of running depot and maintenance facilities and of keeping proper inventories were carried on almost exclusively by the Americans for years, and when the Vietnamese—along with some Koreans—took parts of them over, pervasive laxity led to corruption. One lucrative source of corruption among Vietnamese officials today is scrap metal—steel, copper, and brass—which is secretly being shipped to Singapore and other places for high profits. Corruption and inflation go together, and Vietnam today, despite recently introduced austerity taxes—or, rather, partly because of them, since they caused immediate price increases—is undergoing a new period of inflation so severe that it may ultimately force devaluation of the piastre. An Army private with five children makes seven thousand piastres a month, but he cannot possibly get along on less than twice that amount. Officers and civil servants are similarly situated, and the obvious result is moonlighting, or corruption, or both.

There is also the tripartite question of military equipment—what the Vietnamese want, what they can use, and what the United States feels they should have. One Vietnamese general told me, "We're really three years behind now, because you've always been afraid of moving faster. Things would have been a lot different if you had started sooner, not only with your M-16 rifles but with other equipment, including jet fighters. Maybe we didn't know how to use all these things, and maybe we'd have had trouble learning quickly, but the effort at least should have been made. Suppose we lost a hundred thousand M-16s to the enemy in battle, or through smuggling or corruption. Look at the Russians and the way they supply the Egyptians. They don't like to see matériel and planes being lost to the Israelis, but that hasn't stopped them from giving more, has it?"

It may be true, as General William C. Westmoreland, the former commander-in-chief in Vietnam, is known to believe, that if the North had been more thoroughly bombed, or if we had invaded Laos and Cambodia to hit at the Communist sanctuaries, the war could have been "won." Such actions might have turned the tide significantly, yet it is doubtful whether the war would have been won permanently that way; in any case, it wouldn't have affected the complaint of the Vietnamese about why it took us so long to help them defend themselves adequately, which is what every President from Eisenhower through Nixon has professed our policy to be. The truth is that we were always more interested in doing the job *for* the Vietnamese. Whatever the initial opposition of the military to our getting involved in a major war on the Asian mainland, once we were in, the American military-industrial complex wanted to run the show, and it did.

That shortsighted policy also helps explain our poor political performance in Vietnam, which may yet undo Vietnamization and all that it seeks to accomplish. For four years after the Americans helped engineer the overthrow of President Diem and his brother Ngo Dinh Nhu in 1963, we did little or nothing to create new political institutions in Vietnam, and when we did interfere in Vietnamese politics it was with remarkable maladroitness. Having fostered the new constitutional government of the Second Republic, which led to the elections in the fall of 1967, we devoted inordinate care and attention to building up President Thieu as a national figure capable of leading the South Vietnamese from war to peace and of instituting a form of guided democracy that would combine a degree of benevolent authoritarianism with a system of decentralized government gradually established. The theory was a plausible one, but it hasn't worked. Thieu has turned out to be a military mandarin, and though decentralization had begun to take place, and could in time become politically productive, it was administratively imposed from the top, and has therefore become a factor in a possibly dangerous new polarization of political forces. This polarization is largely the result of the other Vietnamese leaders' mistrust of Thieu, owing to his devious methods, his mixture of pride, caution, and suspicion, his growing isolation, and his essential lack of popular appeal, and also owing to the natural tendency of Vietnamese politicians to mistrust each other and to pursue selfish ambitions, and to the general confusion and fear over what sort of compromise will ultimately be made with the Communists and who will then survive and who will fall.

It would be virtually impossible to take a public-opinion poll in Vietnam today, but if one could be taken I think it would show something like the following results: twenty per cent pro-Communist, twenty per cent pro-Thieu, twenty per cent anti-Thieu and anti-Communist and aligned with one of the dozen-odd political or religious parties or groups of some significance, and forty per cent undecided and confused but deeply desirous of peace and some form of new, preferably more locally representative self-expression. No American correspondent can visit the Communist areas in South Vietnam, so it is impossible to obtain a clear picture of what the popular feeling there is. But then it is also impossible to ascertain how many of the people living in government or contested areas are privately willing or prepared to go along with the Communists if a coalition is created. As for Thieu, he continues to rule the country from Independence Palace with an entourage that is small and tight but, even so, divided into several factions.

Thieu has continued to give formal support to the group known as the National Social-Democratic Front—now a five-party rather than a six-party group, since one of its original component parties, representing the Hoa Hao element, quit. He created this group last year, but it has gained little popular prestige or support. While its more opportunistic members vie for his attention and patronage, Thieu, in turn, uses them for his own protection and as a convenient sounding board, and that is about all. However, he has privately drawn closer to two of the parties in the Front—the Dai Doan-Ket, or Greater Solidarity Force, composed chiefly of northern Catholic refugees, and the Nhan Xa, or Revolutionary Social Humanist Party, which is primarily a central-Vietnamese Catholic organization. Thieu, himself a Catholic, has also encouraged the reëstablishment of the Can Lao, a quasi-secret Catholic party from the Diem period, of which Nguyen Cao Thang, for one, was a member, but so far it has gained little vitality. More important, Thieu is trying to create a national organization of his own based on his continuing control of the Army and the whole military bureaucracy, and of the national network of civilian workers involved in pacification and other administrative duties. It is upon this still loose and amorphous group, unofficially called the Cadre-Khaki Party, that he is basing his hopes for reëlection in 1971, and some people believe that if his hopes are realized he may try to make some sort of accommodation with the Communists, despite his present disclaimers about ever accepting a coalition government. A number of experienced Vietnamese politicians, including some whom Thieu fears or mistrusts deeply but who are willing to help him now in order to strengthen the still fragile Second Republic, are convinced that if he wins the Presidency in 1971 by a minority vote, as he did last time, it will mean that he has failed to create a strong enough organization to withstand the Communists and their potential allies among the opposition groups in the country.

These opposition groups are now compartmented, quarrelsome, and ineffectual. Thieu has helped keep them this way through divide-and-conquer tactics, at which he is adept, but this has not slowed the growing polarization of forces—pro-Thieu and anti-Thieu. His own increasing Diemist tendencies came to general notice last November 3rd, when he permitted the Catholic Nhan Xa members of his Cabinet—who control the Information Ministry and its eighty thousand workers, on whom he is depending to build up the Cadre-Khaki Party—to commemorate the murders of Diem and

Nhu. A ceremony at their unmarked graves in Saigon—the first to take place since their deaths—was attended by three thousand people, including Mme. Thieu and several members of the administration. That same week, two of the former generals who were leaders of the coup against Diem—Duong Van Minh and Tran Van Don— gave parties at their homes, and each of these gatherings, in typical Vietnamese fashion, began at a significant hour, Don's shortly after noon on October 30th, when, in 1963, the junta that plotted the coup held its final secret meeting, and Minh's at 1:30 P.M. on November 1st, the exact time the coup began six years before. The avowed purpose of these two gatherings was to "reinstill the spirit of the revolution of 1963," in which Thieu took part, somewhat reluctantly, as a division commander outranked by both Minh and Don. Resentment against Thieu had already been mounting, because harsh austerity taxes had been imposed a week before, and also because Thieu had pushed the taxes through by decree instead of obtaining a two-thirds vote in the House of Representatives, as the constitution prescribes. For several weeks after the tax decree was issued, a flurry of coup rumors circulated in Saigon. President Nixon's speech of November 3rd helped quiet them, but the opposition to Thieu has continued to grow.

Don, following a trip to the United States, during which he was impressed by the anti-war sentiment, made an effort to start a Third Force Movement, and, having failed to do this, he has now formally placed himself in opposition to Thieu by creating a new People's Bloc. Publicly, Don has taken a strong stand against Thieu on numerous issues, including that of the American massacre at Tu Cong, which he and some of his fellow-senators investigated on their own after the government had hastily declared that there had been no massacre. The Don group concluded that a massacre had indeed taken place, in which at least eighty persons, mostly women and children, were murdered in cold blood—a conclusion that the investigators arrived at after speaking with a number of survivors and with two Vietnamese interpreters who had accompanied the American platoon charged with the massacre. The Don investigation also uncovered evidence that other massacres have taken place around the country, mostly in the northern section but also in the Delta, and have involved Korean troops as well as Americans, and that at least four or five hundred Vietnamese lost their lives in these "incidents," which mostly grew out of abuses of the so-called "free-fire-zone" regulations, which permit Allied attacks on Communist areas by air, artillery, or direct assault without sufficient prior clearance from the Vietnamese, or without the government's knowledge. Though the Tu Cong massacre has aroused far less emotion here in Vietnam than in the United States and elsewhere, it has added to both the growing anti-Americanism and to the mounting anti-war sentiment.

Don, who is one of twenty-nine senators who have to run for reëlection next September, will undoubtedly take his case to the people and speak out even more strongly against Thieu. Unfortunately, though he is popular, he lacks political experience and astuteness, and tries to go off in several directions at once. As for former General Minh, who was Chief of State after the fall of Diem, he has reverted to silence after issuing a call early in November for a national referendum, which he never clearly defined, but which was designed to obtain approval or disapproval of the government's policies. Vice-President Nguyen Cao Ky, who is supposed to be still "supervising" the dormant Paris talks but hasn't attended them in many months, is in the position of an astronaut between space flights, waiting for the next countdown. He is currently testing his political strength by taking private surveys to see whether he has a chance to win the Presidency in 1971 as a staunch anti-Communist hawk. Prime Minister Tran Thien Khiem, who gets along with Thieu on the surface but has his own designs on the Presidency, might, if a showdown occurred, side with Don and Minh, and perhaps with Ky.

The "loyal opposition" is represented by two parties of some potential strength. One is the Progressive Nationalist Movement, headed jointly by Nguyen Van Bong, of the National Institute of Administration, and Nguyen Ngoc Huy, a member of the Paris delegation and a leader of the old Dai Viet nationalist party. The other is the new Farmers-Workers Party headed by Tran Quoc Buu, the nation's top labor leader, who has had a lifelong tendency to hover in the background as a political mastermind but may now finally be ready to come out into the open and lead a party personally. If he does so, it could be an important development, for he controls several hundred worker and peasant groups around the country.

As for the religious factions, the militant Buddhists, headed by the An Quang Pagoda group, of which Thich Tri Quang remains the dominant leader, are speaking out more loudly for peace, and are also taking soundings to determine if they should start a formal political party. Tri Quang himself is more moderate and less virulently anti-American than he once was, and has expressed himself in favor of a neutral South Vietnam that would be independent and apart from the North indefinitely. The Catholics remain strongly anti-Communist, but they are more sharply divided than they once were. One faction is willing to accept anything Thieu wants, a northern refugee element is in favor of peace but against Thieu on personal grounds, and a basically conservative southern element is beginning to think in terms of accommodation with both sides. The Hoa Hao and Cao Dai sects have recently made some efforts to heal internal factionalism, but both remain divided.

And so it goes—a kind of compulsive mutual-vivisection society, in which everyone wants to cut everyone else up to determine the cause of the national disease, which may be incurable. Vietnamization may prove unworkable because the weak body politic may not be able to withstand the treatment. Nevertheless, in due time Vietnamization will get the United States out of this desperate war, though I doubt it will happen as smoothly as President Nixon hopes. In all likelihood, the war will go on indefinitely between the Vietnamese themselves. It will end sometime, of course, as all wars do, and by then most of the Americans will have gone home, leaving behind what we started with—a handful of advisers assisting in an enterprise that very few of them will ever understand.

Postscript: Indo-China

June, 1970

The overthrow of Prince Norodom Sihanouk, Chief of State of Cambodia, on March 18th, 1970, by a pro-Western group of generals and politicians clearly altered the course of the Second Indo-China War. The coup took place as the North Vietnamese and Pathet Lao forces in Laos were mounting their strongest offensive since 1962 against the government of Prince Souvanna Phouma, who, like Sihanouk, had sought to keep his country neutral and out of the Vietnam maelstrom. The efforts of both princes had long been doomed to failure. In Laos, the North Vietnamese, having for years used the Ho Chi Minh Trail to funnel supplies into South Vietnam, had also pressed their drive to occupy more than half the country to substantiate their claim to control a new coalition government. In Cambodia, the North Vietnamese and the Vietcong had created a series of military sanctuaries, from which they were able to attack South Vietnam at will and into which they could periodically retreat for rest and resupply.

Where Sihanouk had sought to mollify the Communists, and had adopted, until close to the time of his ouster, a generally anti-American posture, Souvanna had veered as early as 1964 from left-wing to right-wing neutrality. He had accepted an increasing amount of low-level counter-insurgency help from the Americans —mostly C.I.A. supplies and advice to the Meo tribal leader Vang Pao and his troops, but also some American bombing aid—in order to keep his country from being overrun by the Communists. This "secret war" in Laos—never really so secret—became a *cause célèbre* in the spring of 1970 as a result of hearings held by the Senate Foreign Relations Committee, which served to heighten opposition in the United States to our whole Southeast Asian policy.

Six weeks after the coup against Sihanouk, a large combined American and South Vietnamese force did what the American military had wanted to do all along: it moved into Cambodia to deprive the Communists of their privileged sanctuaries. The bombing of the Ho Chi Minh Trail, which was still continuing, had never interdicted the North Vietnamese traffic southward enough to preclude Hanoi from sustaining and strengthening the Cambodian havens for the "protracted war" its leaders now said would be prosecuted after the departure of the Americans. However, the new Phnom Penh government of General Lon Nol had cut off the northward flow of supplies, at least temporarily, from the Gulf of Siam ports of Sihanoukville, Kep and Ream into the Mekong Delta of South Vietnam.

President Nixon's controversial decision to put troops into Cambodia, if only for six or eight weeks, was described as a necessary risk to protect the lives of American soldiers in Vietnam and to safeguard the process of Vietnamization. There was no guarantee, though, that South Vietnamese forces would not make continuing forays across the border, and that traditional Cambodian-Vietnamese antagonisms, already heightened as a result of the massacre of Vietnamese citizens in Cambodia, would not be further aggravated. It remained uncertain, moreover, whether the widening of the Indo-China battlefield would save the Lon Nol government; the North Vietnamese, the Vietcong, and the relative handful of native Khmer Rouge moved quickly to grab as much Cambodian territory as they could after the coup, and to rally as many people as possible to their new insurrectionary cause. The small and inexperienced Cambodian Army was no match for them, even with captured Communist weapons supplied by the South Vietnamese and the United States—under Sihanouk, the Cambodians had received or stolen similar weapons from the Communists as "tribute" for the unhampered use by Hanoi of Cambodian soil. Various political possibilities loomed. Lon Nol and Sirik Matak, the strong man of the new regime, might be able to consolidate themselves and survive. There might be more coups, as had happened in Vietnam after 1963. Or Sihanouk, still highly popular among the people, might ultimately return as head of a new revolutionary government proclaimed after a "summit conference" held in south China late in April, 1970, attended by Vietnamese, Lao, and Chinese Communist leaders. If he did, he would almost surely be the captive of the Chinese Communists, who took it upon themselves to appoint a number of key men to his "government in exile," including at least three he had described in 1967 as among his principal enemies.

The belated attempt to destroy or to damage the Cambodian sanctuaries obviously hurt the Communists; large quantities of arms and ammunition and other supplies were captured—enough, it was officially claimed, to set Hanoi back anywhere from six months to a year. This was possible but debatable, and in any event it was illusory to suppose that the Allied attack would deter Hanoi from its goal of conquering all of the former Indo-China area. In fact, the assault offered both Hanoi and Peking a whole new set of options and opportunities, and seemed to place the Chinese Communists in a stronger position to control the revolutionary apparatus throughout Southeast Asia than at any time since 1965, when the Vietcong were stopped by American troops from winning the Vietnamese war and when the Peking-backed coup failed in Indonesia. More than anything else, President Nixon's gamble, taken in spite of the strong anti-war feelings back home and considerable doubt about its wisdom within his own administration, brought into sharp focus the problem we had all along refused to confront in Vietnam—the unrealism of fighting an isolated war in one small country in the middle of a large racially mixed area without sufficient understanding of the over-all political or military consequences. The President's move also demonstrated the fallacies inherent in the doctrine he espoused at Guam in July, 1969, when he stated our intention henceforth to adopt "a low profile" and to limit our involvements in Southeast Asia, depending instead on Asian initiatives to deal with Communist threats of insurgency or invasion.

Notwithstanding the Cambodian coup, Nixon had rejected the advice of his generals and, on April 20th, had announced his intention to withdraw one hundred and fifty thousand more men from Vietnam in a year's time. He subsequently defended the move into Cambodia as a "decisive" one, in contrast to President Johnson's "step-by-step" actions, and as a response that served notice on the Communists that any new escalation by them, such as a fresh attack across the D.M.Z., would be met with "more force" by the Americans. Presumably this meant renewed heavy bombing of North Vietnam, which had already taken place sporadically in retaliation for North Vietnamese firing on our reconnaissance planes. It could also mean delays in the projected troop withdrawals, since nixon had several times hinted at such a possibility.

Over the years in Laos, during the alternate wet- and dry-season offensives of the government and Communists respectively, we had bought time but not space. Now the same appeared to be true in Cambodia. In Vietnam, on the other hand, still the key to the war, time had bought space and more population control for the government, though it was by no means yet certain that the Saigon regime would be able to fend for itself once most of the American combat troops were gone. The Cambodian venture appeared, if anything, to complicate the task. The severe economic crisis caused by the high cost of Vietnamization, by the soaring inflation, and by the discrepancies in income—"*doi*," or hunger, was what the low-paid Vietnamese troops were everywhere complaining about—threatened to undo other gains that had been made, both militarily and in the field of pacification. Neglected disabled veterans were demonstrating, as were students protesting against the government's highhanded methods of trying accused pro-Communists in military instead of civil courts. In a series of decisions handed down in the first few months of 1970, the Supreme Court, ruling against the government in a number of important cases, had suddenly emerged as the conscience of the foundering Second Republic; but there was no guarantee that the firm stand of the court would be sustained indefinitely. President Thieu seemed to be moving more and more toward a position politely described by his aides as "clear-sighted dictatorship." This might enable him, legally or illegally, to rule by decree in dealing, chiefly, with the economic situation, but many feared in handling other matters as well.

Vietnam was obviously going through another one of its periodic paroxysms that had shaken the country so often for so many years, and it was apparent that, politically, almost anything could happen before the next Presidential election in the fall of 1971. Religious groups and political movements and parties were as fragmented as ever, and this threatened to inhibit the ultimately inevitable process of accommodation and to enhance the prospects of the minority Communists. They, too, had their troubles as their guerrilla support dwindled, but at least they knew what ailed them and had taken corrective steps. If there was a crisis of leadership in Hanoi, as some observers thought, and an even deeper crisis of management in the strained economy, the North Vietnamese appeared to be coping better than the government in the South. It seemed increasingly apparent that the Americans had force-fed the South Vietnamese Western-style democracy too hastily, and had thereby impeded the subtle process of first organizing a strong and efficient body politic at the center, willing and capable of then delegating and decentralizing authority.

What was also apparent, unfortunately to everyone but Hanoi and Peking, was that negotiation was still the most sensible solution to the war. President Nixon hoped that his Cambodian move would convince "the other side" to negotiate seriously, but the odds seemed against it. At best, whether in Paris or at some new and larger forum, there would be a continuation of the Communists' policy of "fight-fight, talk-talk." The efforts of other Asian nations, led by Indonesia, to solve the Cambodian issue were at best an intimation that at some point in the future they might be able to work out their own solutions; for the time being, however, there seemed to be too many differences and suspicions among them, and it was doubtful that Japan, with its own resurgent ambitions, and its own desire to establish a new powerful if ambivalent role in Asia, could be a successful catalyst or mediator.

The developments in Cambodia could not be considered apart from developments and trends elsewhere in the world. Deeply worried about Russian intentions in the Middle East, President Nixon had made his Cambodian decision to emphasize America's determination not to "let down our friends" or be stampeded into isolation and withdrawal. There were indications that he also hoped to encourage the Russians to do more than occasionally hint that the grave Indo-China situation could best be dealt with in another Geneva-type conference. Worried about the expansion of Chinese influence in Southeast Asia, the Russians might eventually help out; but there was also the possibility that Moscow and Peking, while still bitter ideological enemies, might temporarily bargain to help the North Vietnamese sustain an insurrectionary thrust through the Indo-China peninsula and into Thailand as well. However, while Moscow could counter Peking diplomatically and commercially, there seemed little the Russians could actually do to stop the Chinese from assuming a more dominant revolutionary role in Asia.

If the Vietnam war, in all its deep ramifications, in the United States and abroad, now resembled "a bad trip," the problem remains of what we, as the most powerful nation in the world, will do in the future. What seems more than ever necessary is a total reëvaluation of the manner and method in which American foreign policy is conducted. This calls for something exceeding our customary predilection for recrimination and self-expiation. Beyond some overdue bureaucratic housecleaning, the long misbegotten Vietnam adventure, the result mainly of abysmal political miscalculations, has clearly demonstrated the need to define the confused and often contradictory roles played by numerous American agencies engaged in formulating and executing foreign policy. The President retains the responsibility of making most of the final and often painful decisions. But not only are the prerogatives of the Senate in rendering its "advice and consent" unclear, but the lines of authority among the State Department, the Pentagon, the C.I.A., and the National Security Council and other executive bodies are badly blurred. What relationship, for example, should exist between the State Department in fashioning and executing our basic policies abroad, and the more resilient capability of the C.I.A. in carrying out low-level counter-insurgency operations, and in seeking to build political parties and institutions in foreign countries? Much of the problem involves distinguishing between overt and covert operations, a distinction the Communists have always made but one which seems to go against the American historical grain.

Whatever happens in Vietnam, Cambodia, and Laos, and whatever course we chart in Asia in the years ahead, it remains axiomatic that we are going to have to deal with similar situations in the future, not only in Asia but elsewhere. And we must, for our own salvation, discover more about the significance of time and timing, about when to move swiftly or slowly, about when to use strong words and back them up, and when to speak softly or not at all. It is not enough if Vietnam has merely taught us that the road from war is far more difficult and painful to travel than the road to war; or that what at first represents a valid commitment can, if misunderstood and mishandled, lead to tragic results. We cannot, by ourselves, find the road to peace, and permanent peace remains as elusive as permanent love. Both are romantic dreams, and, given man's foibles and his capacity for self-destruction, neither dream is attainable, not even in the best of all possible computerized worlds. Hopefully, though, we can at least find a way to avoid the pitfalls and roadblocks that Vietnam imposed upon us, and that we imposed upon ourselves.

Index

Abrams, General Creighton W., 318-319
Accelerated Pacification Campaign, 260, 279, 338
Advance People's Action Groups, 38, 40
Agency for International Development (A.I.D.), 34
Agriculture, problems of, 315-316
Air Force, U.S., 93, 111, 112
Algeria, 232
Alliance for Social Revolution, 259
Alliance of National, Democratic, and Peace Forces of Vietnam, 201-202, 230-232, 239, 251-252
National Liberation Front and, 231, 251, 277, 291-292
Provisional Revolutionary Government created, 286, 292
An Giang Province, 36, 273, 340
An Lao Valley, 39, 138
Annam, 174
Anti-Americanism, 121-122
Buddhist, 66, 68, 72, 128
economic programs criticized, 316-317
elections and, 158
of Ky, 221, 307-308
in political crisis, 1966, 53, 55-58, 64
of Vietcong, 23
An Trach, 43-44
An Xuyen Province, 340
Armed Forces Council, Vietnam, 4, 15, 57
Army-Civilian Advisory Council, Vietnam, 85
A.R.V.N., see Vietnamese Armed Forces
A Shau Valley, 138, 211, 264
Association for Improved Relations between Vietnamese Classes, 226

Association for the Protection of the Personality of Vietnamese Women, 226
Association of Workers and Peasants, 259

Ba Long Valley, 96, 101-102
Ban Me Thuot, 192, 196
Bao Dai, Emperor, 7, 74, 210
Batangan Peninsula, 281
Ba Trau (Le Ngoc Lan), 225-226
Ba Xuyen Province, 340
Be, Lieutenant Colonel Nguyen, 36-37, 283
on Communist actions in ceasefire, 256
Revolutionary Development Program, plan for, 134-136
on village problems, 279
Bell, Lieutenant Colonel Van, 93-94, 108
Bench, Lieutenant Colonel Arnold E., 104-105, 107-108, 111, 113-115
Ben Hai River, 90, 97
Ben Tre, 192, 199
Berger, Samuel, 243
Bich, Colonel Nguyen Ngoc, 70
Binh, Mme. Nguyen Thi, 238, 288
Binh, Nguyen Van, Archbishop, 273-274
Binh, Pham Van, 210
Binh Dinh Province, 8, 12, 25, 120, 138, 179
rural construction programs, 36-40
Binh Xuyen sect, 190
Bong, Nguyen Van, 346
Bong Son, 39, 138
Bowen, Colonel Tom, 283
Bru tribe, 93, 101
Buchanan, Captain Buck, 98-99
Buddhist Church, Unified, 66, 71

Buddhist Institute for Secular Affairs, 54
Buddhist Youth Association, 70
Buddhist Youth Center, 270, 271. 311
Buddhists, 35, 48, 183, 244, 272-273, 305
American opinion of, 271
An Quang Pagoda group, 252, 270-271, 296, 311, 347
anti-Americanism, 66, 68, 72, 128
Committee of Force, 58
Communists and, 51, 55, 60, 66, 68, 77, 270-271, 273
in coup against Khanh, 6
elections boycotted, 75-76, 85
elections demanded, 61-62, 66-67
elections denounced, 153, 162
Ky defeats, 95, 127
Ky opposed by, 61-73
Mahayana, 71
objectives of, 6-7, 70-71
peace Cabinet demanded, 252
peace campaign, 4, 6-7, 346-347
political actions, 48-51, 54-58, 85-86, 149, 162
revolt against Diem, 71
sects, 71; *see also* Cao Dai sect; Hoa Hao sect
in Senate, 185
Struggle Force, *see* Struggle Force to Achieve the Revolution
Theravada, 71, 128
Thieu opposed by, 85, 162, 270, 272
Thieu's attitude toward, 311-312
Tri Quang's leadership revived, 128
Bunker, Ellsworth, 133, 165, 307
Thieu and, 184, 186, 242-243
Burchett, Wilfred, 202
Buttinger, Joseph, 173
Buu, Tran Quoc, 162-163, 295
as labor leader, 127, 161, 259, 314, 346
on local elections, 126

Cadre-Khaki Party, 344
Ca Lu, 101
Ca Mau Peninsula, 141
Cambodia, 348-352
American troops in, 342, 349-352
Central Office for South Vietnam in, 329
Communist forces in, 241, 253, 268, 269, 321-322, 349
National Liberation Front in, 250

Cambodia (*cont'd*)
supplies for Communists sent through, 211, 349
Vietnamese citizens massacred, 349
Cam Lo, 97, 98, 101, 103, 114
Cam Lo River, 92
Cam Ne, 43
Camp Carroll, 137, 205, 214
Cang Long District, 340
Can Lao society, 160, 274, 275, 344
Can Tho, 69, 153
Cao Dai sect, 71, 76, 85, 162, 174, 183, 209, 221, 244, 275, 305, 321, 347
membership and influence, 273
Carroll, Captain J. J., 117-118
Catholic Relief Services, 43
Catholics, 7, 35, 85, 86, 183, 209, 244-245, 305, 347
with Buddhists, 71, 76
in coup against Khanh, 6
in National Social-Democratic Front, 296
in Nhan Xa Party, 274
political activities, 29, 56, 58-59, 186, 273-274
political parties, 274, 344
in Senate, 160, 162, 185-186
Cease-fire:
Communist plans for, 256, 320, 332
local and regional, 287, 320, 332
Census Grievance and Aspiration Teams, 41, 47, 181, 182
Central Intelligence Agency (C.I.A.), 29, 34, 38, 182, 322-323, 349, 353
Central Military Region, 45
Central Office for South Vietnam (cosvn), 142, 166, 229, 268-269
Resolution Eight, 268
Resolution Nine, 328-330, 332
Resolution Ten, 328-329, 332-333
Strategic Intelligence Branch, 323
Cereghino, Colonel Alexander, 113, 115
Cham people, 183
Chau Doc Province, 273
Chau Thanh District, 340
Chieu, General Pham Xuan, 56-57
Chieu Hoi (Open Arms) program, 80, 100, 142, 278
China:
American bases as threat to, 246
Cambodia influenced by, 350
Communist ideology in Vietnam, 167, 190

China (*cont'd*)
 entry into war possible, 27
 military strategy from, 194
 military supplies from, 12, 27, 97, 297
 and Paris peace talks, 246
 and Provisional Revolutionary Government, 294, 301
 role in Vietnam, 2, 26-27, 123, 178-179, 225, 246, 302, 350
 Russian friction with, 301, 352-353
Chinese citizens in Vietnam, 183
Chinh, Truong, 239, 240, 251, 266, 291, 327-328
Chinh Luan, newspaper, 161
Cholon, 127, 149, 183, 249
 reconstruction programs, 45-46
 Tet offensive against, 191, 200
Chuan, General Nguyen Van, 55, 56, 59, 68
Chu Lai, 72, 111
Chu Lai Peninsula, 24, 25
Chuyen, Colonel Le Xuan, defector from North Vietnam, 141-142
Chuyen, Thai Khac, Green Beret murder of, 322-323
Citizens Committee for Peace with Freedom in Vietnam (American), 323-324
Civil Affairs Team (C.A.T.), 37
Civil Operations and Revolutionary Development Support, 133-134
Clifford, Clark, 249, 291, 298
Co, General Nguyen Huu, 50, 87
 in political crisis of 1966, 55, 56
 removed from office, 125
Coalition government:
 alliances and fronts promoting, 227, 230-231
 Communist control of, 257
 as Communist objective, 168, 177, 190, 201-202, 224, 288, 290
 neutralists and, 210
 South Vietnamese attitude toward, 239, 257-258, 262, 296, 312
 South Vietnamese election formula, 286-287
 Vietminh formula, 286, 320
Coast Guard, U.S., 94
Cochin China, 174
Colby, William, 260
Combined Action Group, Marines and Popular Forces, 44
Committee for a Self-sufficient Economy, 226

Committee for the Establishment of a National Progressive Force, 296
Committee for the Protection of National Culture, 226
Committee of the South, 190, 286
Committee to Organize the People for the Safety of the Nation, 204, 209
Communist Party, 232, 240
Communists:
 attitude toward war, 48, 129, 141-145, 166-168, 327-330, 334-336
 Buddhists and, 51, 55, 60, 66, 68, 77, 270-271, 273
 cease-fire, plans for, 256, 320, 332
 coalition government, *see* Coalition government
 documents captured from, 142-143, 333
 in elections, 77-78, 158, 298
 friction among, 80-81, 265-267
 killing of political opponents, 333-334
 military strategy, 81-82, 89, 120, 136-138, 179-180, 188-189, 251, 253, 276, 321-322
 military strength, total, 141, 166
 organizations and fronts established by, 226-227, 230-232, 239-240, 251, 254-255, 276
 in Paris peace talks, *see* Paris peace talks
 partitioning of Vietnam, plans for, 320-321, 331-332
 political program, 48-49, 60, 167-169, 209-210, 217-218, 226-229, 251-252, 267
 Program Maximum, 223-224
 Program Medium, 224
 Program Minimum, 224
 in South Vietnam, 3, 13, 18, 35, 45-47, 174-177, 222-223, 233-234, 248-249, 313-314, 320, 343
 terrorism, 217-218, 255, 276, 333-334
 Tet offensive plans, 193-201
 in war, 80-81, 136-138, 216-217, 219, 262-265, 304-305
 see also National Liberation Front; North Vietnam; Vietcong
Confederation of Vietnamese laborers, 161, 221, 314
Confucianism, 71
Con Thien, 114-115, 137, 189, 205

COSVN, *see* Central Office for South Vietnam
Couve de Murville, 158
Cuba, 232
Cummings, Major Lawrence, 93
Cushman, Lieutenant General Robert E., Jr., 215
Cuu, Truong Vong, 274

Dai Doan-Ket (Greater Solidarity Force), 344
Dai Viet Party, 85, 184, 185, 275, 296
Dak To, 179, 189, 195, 211
Dalat, 55, 69-70
Dam Quan Valley, 39-40
Dan, Phan Quang, 85, 86
Danang, 12, 42, 50, 53, 61, 70, 89, 138, 179
  air base, 1, 65, 111, 112
  arrests in, 77
  attacks on, 319
  Buddhist activities in, 67, 68
  demonstrations in, 153
  Dinh in command, 69
  Ky orders troops to, 70
  Ky threatens attack on, 57-58, 62-63, 66
  pagodas, attacks on, 63, 70
  in political crisis, 54-55, 57-59
  rural construction programs near, 36, 41-42, 44
Death Volunteers Association, 67
Demilitarized Zone (D.M.Z.), 137, 138, 141, 262-263
  American and South Vietnamese invasion, 131-132
  halt of hostilities near, 300-301
  North Vietnamese invasion, 90-101, 109-112, 115, 118, 119
Democratic Party, North Vietnam, 293
Diem, Ngo Dinh, 3, 5, 68, 125, 134, 219, 223, 263, 274, 323, 326
  American support of, 290
  attitude toward, changing, 160-161
  Buddhist revolt against, 71
  as Catholic, 273
  commemoration of his death, 344-345
  elections under, 74
  end of regime, 247, 342, 345
  First Republic, 247-248
Dien Bien Phu, 172, 175, 205, 214, 215, 240
Dien Tuong Province, 341

Dier, Ormond W., 189-190
Dinh, General Ton That, 68-69
Dinh Bo Linh, 70
District Intelligence Operations Centers (DIOC), 233
Do, Tran, Major General, North Vietnamese, 143-144
Don, Tran Van, 299, 307
  Buddhist leader, 71-72
  Foreign Minister, 12, 150
  in National Salvation Front, 209, 245, 259, 314
  opposes Thieu, 345-346
  Senator, 160, 161
Dong, Pham Van, 155, 225, 240, 319, 327
Dong Ha, 93, 98, 100-101, 103, 111, 114, 137
Don Hau, Thich, 231-233, 252
Douglas, Paul, 323
Downey, Sergeant Arthur, 117
Duan, Le, 144, 222, 239, 251, 266, 290, 327-328
Duclos, Jacques, 222
Dulles, John Foster, 174
Dung, Van Tien, 82
Dzu, Truong Dinh, 155, 157-159, 296, 311-312

Eagle Flights, 10-11
Egypt, Russian support for, 342
Eisenhower, Dwight, 323, 342
Elections, 83-87, 151-153
  American role in, 76, 151, 158, 159, 162
  Buddhist boycott of, 75-76, 85
  Buddhist demands for, 61-62, 66-67, 72-73
  Communists in, 77-78, 158, 298
  in Diem regime, 74
  faults of, 313-314
  in hamlets, 78-79, 86, 125-126, 145-146, 337
  Ky's view of, 69
  of National Assembly, 124, 151-152, 160
  National Liberation Front in, 305, 306
  preparations for, 74-79, 82
  of President and Vice-President, 124, 130, 147-151, 157-158
  promised, 58, 61-62
  South Vietnamese alternative to coalition, 286-287
Electoral Council, 66, 69, 72, 77

English, General Lowell E., 103-106, 108-111, 115, 118
Espionage scandals, 322-323

Fake, hill, 117
Farmers-Workers Party, 346
Fatherland Front, 227
French:
  in Indo-China War, 170, 172, 240
  and Paris peace talks, 236, 241, 246, 301
  policy on Vietnam, 210
  in Vietnam, 88, 173-174, 210, 219, 223, 248
Fulbright, Senator J. W., 123
FULRO (Front Unifié de Lutte des Races (Opprimées)), 183

Geneva agreements, 90
Gia Dinh Province, 45
Giao Duc District, 341
Giap, General Vo Nguyen, 94, 143, 155, 175, 205, 304, 321
  newspaper article, 328, 334
  in Tet offensive, 194-195, 204, 239
Giau, Tran Van, 174
Gio Linh, 137, 189, 205
Golden Fleece campaigns, 96
Great Britain:
  and Paris peace talks, 246
  troops in Vietnam, 1945, 286
Greece, American advisers in, 17
Green Beret case, 322-323
Groucho Marx battle, 112-114
Guam Conference, 155

Haiphong, bombing of, 27, 131
Hamlets:
  Accelerated Pacification Campaign in, 260, 279, 338
  American influence in, 18-19, 42-45
  Communist power in, 223, 228-229, 259-260, 276-277, 293-294
  constitutional rights, 86
  construction and pacification programs in, 38-45, 47
  elections in, 78-79, 86, 125-126, 145-146, 337
  evacuation from battle areas, 281
  Evaluation System, 180-182, 340
  local government problems, 279
  number of, 337
  Revolutionary Development Program, evaluation of, 180-182
  Strategic Hamlet Program, 33, 134
  terrorism in, 217-218

Hamlets (cont'd)
  Vietcong control of, 47, 79-80, 126, 146, 181, 255-256, 337
  see also Revolutionary Development Program; Rural construction programs
Handrahan, Captain Robert, 117
Hanna, Captain John R., 112
Hanoi:
  bombing of, 27, 131
  Radio Hanoi, 201, 202, 227, 266, 293
Hanoi government, see North Vietnam
Hao, Le Van, 227-228
Harriman, Averell, 246, 287, 291, 301, 302
Hart, Lieutenant James, 109
Hate America Month, 23
Hau Nghia, 45
Hazelbacker, Major Wayne, 113
Helicopter Valley (Son Ngan Valley), 103, 105, 106, 108, 109, 115
Hickey, Gerald, 183
Hieu, Nguyen Van, 202-203, 238-239
Hill 400, 115-118
Hill 484, 115, 117-118
Hill 881, 138
Hoa, Duong Quynh, 232
Hoa Hao sect, 71, 76, 85, 162, 174, 183, 186, 209, 221, 244, 275, 296, 305, 321, 340-341, 344, 347
  membership and activities, 273
Hoai An, 39
Ho Chi Minh, 27, 136, 144, 170, 186, 245, 289, 305, 314, 319, 332
  death, 303
  Ky praises, 221, 305
  Ky ready to negotiate with, 122, 130
  objectives, 172-173
  Tet poem, 197
  in Vietminh, 175, 222
Ho Chi Minh Trail, 94-95, 141, 211, 287, 297, 348, 349
Honey, P. J., 266-267
Honolulu Conference, 32, 34, 50, 51, 94
Houa Phan Province, Laos, 224
Hué, 50, 55, 58, 70, 280
  arrests in, 77
  blockade of, 72
  Buddhist headquarters, 61, 66-68
  Communist murder of opponents in, 333

Hué *(cont'd)*
  corruption and inefficiency of government, 213-214
  demonstrations in, 56-57, 72, 153
  destruction of, 212-213
  reconstruction of, 282
  revolutionary groups in, 227-228
  Tet offensive against, 188-189, 191-192, 199, 202, 205, 210, 212-213
Humphrey, Hubert, 242, 245
Hung, Pham, 232, 293, 329
Huong, Dan Van (Mat Ro), 323
Huong, Nguyen Van, Secretary-General, 184, 209, 259, 295
Huong, Tran Van, 6, 226, 308
  Premiership offered to, 160
  Presidential candidate, 149-150, 157
  Prime Minister, 219-221, 233, 245, 252, 259
Huy, Nguyen Ngoc, 346

Ia Drang Valley, 95
Indo-China, 348-354
  Russian influence in, 301-302, 352-353
Indo-China War, 170, 175, 215, 247, 248
Indonesia, 27
Inflation in Vietnam, 21-22, 75, 89, 316, 341-342
Intelligence services, 182, 233-234, 254, 278
Iron Triangle, 128, 137

Johnson, Lyndon B., 12, 63, 76, 123, 133, 170, 215, 245, 249, 351
  bombing of North Vietnam halted, 235, 241-242, 291
  at Honolulu Conference, 32, 34, 50
  and Paris peace talks, 223, 225, 237-238, 241, 243-244, 261
  in peace negotiations, 129
Joint United States Public Affairs Office, 29

Kelly, Robert, 213
Khanh, General Nguyen, 4, 53, 58, 71
  Thao's attempted coup against, 4-6
Khe Sanh, 93, 101, 118, 189, 202, 204, 205
  attacks on, 137-138, 214-215
Khiem, Tran Thien, 4-6, 268
  Prime Minister, 308-309, 346
Khmer people, 183
Khmer Rouge, 349

Khoa, Phan Van, Mayor of Hué, 213-214
Kiem, Tran Buu, 238-239, 288
  in Provisional Revolutionary Government, 293
Kien Giang Province, 340
Kien Hoa Province, 339
Kien Phong Province, 341
Kien Van District, 341
Kieu, Nguyen Van, 209
Kim, Le Doan, 222
Kim, Le Trung, 221-222
Kim Chong-pil, 69
"Kit Carson" scouts, 278
Komer, Robert, 134, 181, 234
Kontum, 138, 179, 211
Kontum Province, 25, 119
Korea:
  American advisers in, 17
  forces in Vietnam, 37-38, 119, 167, 341, 345
Korean war, Panmunjom peace talks, 301
Kuomintang, Vietnamese, 296
Ky, Nguyen Cao, 16*n.*, 39, 49, 69, 75, 76, 88, 125, 163, 261
  anti-Americanism, 221, 307-308
  Buddhist opposition to, 61-73, 85
  Buddhists curbed by, 95, 127, 162
  coup by, suggested, 308
  government of, 27-29, 34-35, 50
  and neutralists, 221-222
  on Paris peace talks, 306
  peace negotiations, possible, 122, 130
  political convictions, 305
  in political crisis of 1966, 51-54, 56-59
  Presidential candidate, 130, 148-150, 155-158
  in Tet crisis, 203-204
  Thieu versus, 87, 148, 155-157, 159-160, 163, 258-259, 294
  Vice-President, 157, 159, 184, 209, 220, 243, 252, 346
Ky, Mme. Nguyen Cao, 34, 87
Ky, Ton That Duong, 232
Kyle, Major General Wood B., 103

Lai Chu, 282-283
Lam, Pham Dang, 238
Lam, Tran Van, 160, 309
Lam Son 29, 109-110
Lan, Le Ngoc, *see* Ba Tra
Land reform, 18-19, 277, 294, 315

Lansdale, Major General Edward G., 30, 31, 34
Lao Dong, Workers' Party of North Vietnam, 81, 142-143, 176, 210, 228, 268, 286, 293
purge of, 265-266
resolutions, 329
Laos, 287, 351
American aid to, 349
American invasion suggested, 342
communication and supply lines, 24, 94
Communist forces in, 241, 291, 301, 320, 322, 348-349
North Vietnamese claims for territory, 224
partitioning, Communist plan for, 331-332
Russian activity in, 301
Souvanna Phouma overthrown, 348-349
Lattre de Tassigny, Jean de, 135
Lee, Captain Howard V., 113
Lei Me, 42
Liberal Democratic Force, 275
Lieng, Tran Ngoc, 296
Lien Viet, 227
Lin Piao, 167
Loan, General Nguyen Ngoc, 77, 88, 157, 159, 185
deposed, 220
in Tet offensive, 196-197, 200
Loc, Nguyen Van, 160, 184, 203, 220
Loc, General Vinh, 36, 53, 87-88
Loc Ninh, 179, 195
Lodge, Henry Cabot, 30, 54, 63, 70, 155
Lon Nol, General, 349-350

McGinty, Sergeant John J., 106-107
McMahon, Captain Daniel K., Jr., 115
McNamara, Robert, 128, 291
Mai Den (Nguyen Thanh Tung), 185
Malik, Adam, 178
Man, Nguyen Van, Mayor of Danang, 56-58, 69
Mang Xim, 96
Mansfield, Senator Mike, 34, 132-133
Mao Tse-tung, 233
Marder, Murrey, 288-289
Marine Corps, U.S., 1, 12, 24, 92-93, 96, 100, 137, 166, 179, 195, 215, 281
in Combined Action Group with Popular Forces, 44

Marine Corps, U.S. (*cont'd*)
divisions, organization and equipment, 102-103
in Hué, 212-213
in Khe Sanh attack, 137-138
in Operation Hastings, 102-111
in Operation Prairie, 111-118
in pacification and reconstruction, 42-45
reconnaissance missions, 98-100
in Tet offensive, 192
Vietnamization progress, 318
Masterpool, Lieutenant Colonel William, 115-116
Mekong Delta, 24, 25, 94, 95, 140-141, 210-211, 253, 263, 278, 336-341
Communists in, 140-141, 330-331, 337, 339-340
Revolutionary Development Program, 336-337
South Vietnamese progress in, 330, 336-338
Mendès-France, Pierre, 225
Minh, General Duong Van (Big Minh), 4, 298-299, 307, 309-310, 345, 346
Minh, Ho Chi, *see* Ho Chi Minh
Minh, Van, columnist, 207, 208
Mission Council, U.S., 133
Mnong tribe, 192
Mobile Advisory Teams, 339
Modrzejewski, Captain Robert J., 104, 107, 117
Montagnards, 101, 139, 183, 192, 305
Movement for Student Autonomy, 226
Movement to Struggle for Peace, 251, 252
Mus, Paul, 70-71
My Lai (Tu Cong) massacre, 281*n.*, 333, 345-346
My Tho, 192, 243

National Committee for a Political Settlement in Vietnam (American), 324
National Congress for the People's Salvation, 245
National Democratic Peace Alliance Front (Hué), 202, 227, 231
National Leadership Committee, 185
National Liberation Front, 3, 27, 35, 78, 80-81, 159, 175-176, 190, 226-227, 239-240

National Liberation Front (*cont'd*)
  and Alliance of National, Democratic and Peace Forces, 231, 251, 277, 291-292
  in Cambodia, 250
  in coalition government, 257
  in elections, 305, 306
  establishment of, 175, 290
  and neutralists, 209-210
  North Vietnamese control of, 142-143, 178
  organizational groups, 228
  in Paris peace talks, *see* Paris peace talks
  in peace negotiations, 26-27, 59, 74, 122, 128, 170, 176, 222
  political programs, 167-168, 177, 201-202
  Provisional Revolutionary Government created, 286, 292
  radio, 23, 68, 227, 293
  self-criticism, 166, 175-176
  in Tet offensive, 197, 200-202
  Thieu's negotiations with, 295
National Recovery Committee (in Tet crisis), 203
National Salvation Front, 209, 245, 259, 295, 314
National Social-Democratic Front, 295-296, 310, 343-344
Navy, U.S., 94, 110
Neutralists, Vietnamese, 221-222, 297
  in government, 210
  in Paris, 209-210, 221-222
  in Phnom Penh, 209-210, 221
Newspapers, suspension of, 296-297
Nghiem, Thai Lang, 161
Nha, Vu Ngoc, spy, 323
Nhan Dan, newspaper, 289, 315
Nhan Xa Party, 274-275, 296, 344
Nhu, Ngo Dinh, 33, 68, 127, 160, 219, 248, 274, 342, 344-345
Nixon, Richard M., 238, 243, 245, 263, 271, 342, 345, 347, 352
  Midway meeting with Thieu, 292, 297
  North Vietnamese criticism of, 300
  and Paris peace talks, 261, 305-306
  policy on Vietnam, 244, 250, 264, 287, 350-351
  Thieu and, 326-327
  troops ordered to Cambodia, 349-352
  visit to Vietnam, 286, 306

Nixon, Richard M. (*cont'd*)
  withdrawal of forces from Vietnam, 286-288, 297, 298, 320, 325-327, 350-351
Nong Cong Binh (Farmers, Workers, Soldiers) Party, 161
North Vietnam:
  bombing of, 1-2, 27, 94-95, 131, 155, 166, 179, 342; as genocide, 146; halt, 123, 235, 236, 241-243, 266, 291; peace negotiations and, 171, 189, 223, 236, 241, 263; reduced, 223, 224; resumption, 241, 264, 351
  boys from South trained in, 265
  Communists kill political opponents, 333
  control of war, 142-143
  documents of, captured, 142-143, 333
  economic conditions, 193-194, 266, 289, 315
  government after Ho Chi Minh, 327-328
  infiltration from, 8, 12, 24, 94, 128-129, 141, 166, 217, 321, 331
  internal problems, 265-267
  neutralists and, 209-210, 222
  in Paris peace talks, *see* Paris peace talks
  in peace negotiations, *see* Peace negotiations
  Politburo, 142, 144, 194, 222, 266, 290, 319
  Tet offensive, *see* Tet offensive
  Vietminh formula for government, 286, 320
North Vietnamese Armed Forces (N.V.A.), 8, 80-82, 89, 95, 136-138, 210-211, 217
  attitude of soldiers, 334-336
  in Cambodia, 241, 253, 268, 269, 321-322, 349
  cum units, 269, 322
  in Demilitarized Zone, 90-101, 109-112, 118
  invasion of South Vietnam, 96-120; planned, 92, 94-96
  Khe Sanh attack, preparations for, 214-215
  losses in 1968, 250
  in Mekong Delta, 330-331
  Operations against, *see* Operation Hastings; Operation Prairie
  strength, 119, 137, 141, 211, 253, 334

North Vietnamese Armed Forces (*cont'd*)
in Tet offensive, 195, 204, 229
troop replacements, 264-265
winter-spring offensive, 1968, 229-230
withdrawal promised, 241

Office of Civil Operations, U.S., 133-134
Open Arms, *see* Chieu Hoi program
Operation Cedar Falls, 142
Operation Hastings, 101-110, 118-119
Operation Junction City, 142
Operation Oregon, 139
Operation Prairie, 111-119

Pacification programs, *see* Accelerated Pacification Campaign; Revolutionary Development Program; Rural construction programs
Panmunjom peace talks, 301
Pao, Vang, 349
Paris:
Vietnamese exiles in, 299
Vietnamese neutralists in, 209-210, 221-222
Paris peace talks, 216, 217, 223-225, 235-246, 291, 300-302, 305-306
National Liberation Front in, 223, 225, 232, 236-239, 241, 242, 251, 263, 270, 292
North Vietnam in, 223-225, 236-238, 241, 250, 288-289
United States in, 224-225, 236-238, 241, 246, 263
Vietnam Republic in, 224-225, 236-238, 242-245, 261, 263
Park, Chung Hee, 69
Pathet Lao, 348
Patriotic Armed Forces, 202
Peace negotiations:
Johnson in, 129
National Labor Front Resistance to, 176-177
North Vietnamese conditions for, 171
North Vietnamese plan, fighting and negotiating, 132, 144, 167, 178-179, 189-190, 224, 239
in Paris, *see* Paris peace talks
possibility of, 26, 59, 74, 128-130, 132, 144, 154-155, 170-173, 178-179, 352

Peace negotiations (*cont'd*)
Vietnamese attitude toward, 170-172
Vietnamese without Americans, 122-123
People's Action Teams (P.A.T.), 37-44, 78, 79
People's Democratic Peace Front (Alliance), 333
People's Movement for the Struggle for Democracy, 158
People's Revolutionary Committee, Thua Thien Province (Hué), 227, 231
People's Revolutionary Party (P.R.P.), 81, 142, 176-178, 228, 233-234, 238, 239, 276-277
committees, 254-255, 276, 292
founding of, 176, 290
Phat, Huynh Tan, 238-239
in Provisional Revolutionary Government, 292-293
Phnom Penh:
National Liberation Front in, 238
Vietnamese neutralists in, 209-210, 221
Phoenix Program, 182, 233, 254, 278, 338, 340
Phong Saly Province, Laos, 224
Phu Bai, 44, 103
Phu Cat, 10, 11
Phu My Valley, 138
Phu Quoc Island, 77
Phu Yen Province, 12, 24, 179
Pike, Douglas, 175, 176
Plaine des Jarres, Laos, 331
Pleiku, 11, 138, 211
Plei Me, 24
Police Field Force, 182
Popular Forces (local), 39, 40, 79, 119, 192, 253, 280, 297, 317, 330, 337, 339, 340
in Combined Action Group with Marines, 44
Revolutionary Development Program combined with, 135-136, 260
training program, 182
Popular Self-Defense Forces, 337-338
Porter, William J., 34, 133
Princeton, U.S.S., 106
Progressive Nationalist Movement, 296, 346
Propaganda and Maneuver Team, 37
Provincial Reconnaissance Units, 165, 182, 278

Provisional Revolutionary Government (P.R.G.), 286, 288, 297, 301, 331, 333
creation of, 291-294

Quang, General Dang Van, 53, 87-88, 125
Quang Nam Province, 280
Quang Ngai Province, 25, 280-281
Quang Tri, 102, 189, 199, 280
Quang Tri Province, 101, 202, 205, 224, 278
North Vietnamese invasion, 90, 92, 94-96, 99, 101-102, 114, 118
refugees in, 279-280
Quat, Le Truong, 274
Quat, Phan Huy, 4, 9, 12
Prime Minister, 7, 15
resignation, 16*n.*

Razorback Ridge, 102, 114, 115
Red River Delta, 27
Refugees:
aid to, 279-280
Vietcong use of, 8, 25
Regional Forces (provincial), 119, 135, 192, 253, 280, 297, 317, 330, 337, 339, 340
Re tribe, 139
Revolutionary Committees, *see* Village Liberation Committees
Revolutionary Development Program, 78-79, 123, 126, 132-136, 152, 155, 163
difficulties of, 164-165, 192-193, 234
evaluation of, 180-182
management reorganization, 133-134
in Mekong Delta, 336-337
Revolutionary Development Teams, 78-79, 134, 146, 164, 180, 192, 339
in Accelerated Pacification Campaign, 260
at Hué, 214
Rhade tribe, 192
Rice:
importation program, 21, 123-124
for North Vietnamese Army, 96-97
prices, 315-316
Richwine, Lieutenant David, 104
Rockpile, 99, 101-102, 108-109, 114, 119
Roosevelt, Franklin D., 308
Rosson, Lieutenant General William B., 139, 215

Rung Sat Special Zone, 45
Rural construction programs, 30, 32-33, 36-47, 123
see also Revolutionary Development Program
Rural Construction Units, 37, 38
Rusk, Dean, 63
Russia, *see* Soviet Union
Ryman, Captain Roger, 116-117

Saigon, 20-23, 88-89
American troops in, 122, 191
arrests in, 77
attack expected, 211-212
attacks on, 229-230, 243
bombardment of, 216-217, 264
Buddhist rebellion in, 70
Communist forces surrounding, 269
as Communist objective, 321
Communist terrorism in, 276, 322
demonstrations in, 56-58, 72, 153, 270
economic and social problems, 21-22
Ho Chi Minh City, Communist name for, 292, 321
neutralists in, 209-210
reconstruction programs, 36, 45-46
Tet offensive against, 188, 190-191, 196-201
Vietcong in and near, 45-47, 89, 137, 249
Vietminh government in 1945, 190
Saigon *Daily News,* 296
Saigon government, *see* Vietnam, Republic of
Saigon *Post,* 122
Sharp, Admiral Ulysses Grant, 100
Sihanouk, Prince Norodom, of Cambodia, 3, 178, 211, 349-350
overthrow of, 348
Silone, Ignazio, 304
Singapore, 341
Siri Matak, 350
Son Ngan River, 104-105
Son Ngan Valley, *see* Helicopter Valley
South Vietnam:
consolidation and accommodation, 183-187
as independent state, 3
invasion by North Vietnamese, 92, 94-120
see also Vietnam, Republic of
Souvanna Phouma, Prince, of Laos, overthrown, 348-349

Soviet Union:
  Chinese friction with, 301, 352-353
  in Egyptian-Israeli war, 342
  in Laos, 301
  military supplies from, 27, 97, 137, 214, 264, 297
  and Paris peace talks, 236, 241, 246, 301
  and Provisional Revolutionary Government, 294, 301
  role in Vietnam, 2, 225, 240, 267
  in Southeast Asia, 301-302, 352-353
  Vietnamese Communism influenced by, 174, 176
Special Forces:
  American, 93, 182, 322
  Vietnamese, 15, 139
Spy ring, 323
Strategic Hamlet Program, 33, 134
Struggle Force to Achieve the Revolution, 56, 61, 67-70, 76-77, 95, 162
Student demonstrations, 54-58, 153
Sung, Dang Van, 85, 161, 309
Suu, Phan Kac, 85, 149, 157, 158

Tactical Air Fuel-Dispensing System, 111
Tam Chau, Thich, 6, 149, 270
  moderate Buddhists led by, 56, 162
Task Force Delta, 103
Ta Vinh, execution of, 52
Taylor, Maxwell, 9
Tay Ninh Province, 119, 137, 273, 278, 329
Tenant Farmers' Union, 314
Terrebonne, Captain Terry, 98-99
Tet, 121, 189, 325
Tet, Lam Van, 233
Tet offensive, 188-205, 212-213, 239, 268, 269, 290-291
  casualties, military and civilian, 193
  Communist operations following, 204-205
  effects of, 206-207, 291
  plans and objectives, 193-201
  political programs for, 201-203
  second, 1969, 263-264, 291
  Vietnam government's response to, 203-204, 206-208
Than, Le Van, Mayor of Hué, 282-283
Thang, Nguyen Cao, 294, 344
Thang, Major General Nguyen Duc, 47, 163-165, 208

Thanh, Au Truong, 159, 294-295
Thanh, General Nguyen Chi, 142-145
Thanh, Tran Chanh, 309
Thao, Phnam Ngoc, 4-6, 16n.
Thao, Trinh Dinh, 230, 232, 293
Thi, General Nguyen Chanh, 4, 5, 7, 72
  Americanization opposed, 42
  with Buddhist forces, 68
  leader of power bloc, 29
  in pacification and construction, 42-44
  in political crisis of 1966, 52-56, 59, 65-66
Thien Minh, Thich, 162, 252
  in Buddhist Committee of Force, 58
  sentenced to hard labor, 270-272, 311
Thieu, Nguyen Van, 16n., 50, 55, 66, 72, 73, 75, 214, 318, 337
  ambition for power, 267-268
  American attitude toward, 299-300, 312, 343
  Buddhists oppose, 85, 162, 270, 272
  Bunker and, 184, 186, 242-243
  Cabinet, new, formed, 308-309
  Catholics and, 273-274
  government of, 184-185, 201, 208-209, 220, 247-248, 258-259, 267-268, 283, 294-295, 298-300, 343-347, 351-352
  interviews with, 148-149, 307, 310-312
  Ky versus, 87, 148, 155-157, 159-160, 163, 258-259, 294
  leader of power bloc, 29, 35
  Midway meeting with Nixon, 292, 297
  and National Assembly, 309
  and National Liberation Front, 295, 305, 306
  and National Social-Democratic Front, 295-296, 310, 343-344
  and neutralists, 221-222
  and Nixon, 326-327
  opposition to, 294-296, 344-346
  and Paris peace talks, 237, 242-244
  policy against anti-government activities, 270
  in political crisis of 1966, 55, 56
  and political parties, 274-275
  President, 153, 159, 161, 163, 261
  Presidential candidate, 130, 148-150, 155-157

Thieu, Nguyen Van (*cont'd*)
    public opinion of, 309-310, 326,
    343-344
    and spy ring, 323
    in Tet crisis, 203-204
Thieu, Mme. Nguyen Van, 156, 273,
    345
Tho, Le Duc, 266, 300
    interviews with, 288-289
Tho, Nguyen Huu, 159, 293
Thoi Binh District, 340
Tho Nghia, 40
Thon San Lam, 101
Thuan, Nguyen Van, 274
Thuan, Tran Quang, 72
Thua Thien Province, 202, 224, 278,
    279
    North Vietnamese invasion, 92, 95-
    96, 99
    People's Revolutionary Committee,
    227-228, 231
Ton, Buu, 67
Tri, Do Cao, 318
Trinh, Nguyen Duy, 171
Tri Quang, Thich, 6, 53, 78, 252, 347
    on Americans, 64, 66, 128, 162,
    271, 311
    hunger strike, 76, 86
    interviews with, 61-62, 64, 67-68,
    73, 271-272, 311
    Ky opposed by, 61-73
    political activities, 29, 50-51, 54-
    56, 60, 128, 149
    in seclusion or custody, 127, 209
    Thieu opposed by, 162
Trong, Huynh Van, spy, 323
Truman, Harry, 323
Trung, Tran Van, alias for North Vi-
    etnamese officers, 293
Tu Cong, *see* My Lai
Tung, Nguyen Thanh (Mai Den),
    185
Tuong, Colonel Le Truong, 36-37

United Nations, 240, 324
United States:
    economic aid program (USAID),
    219
    economic and social reform pro-
    grams, 32-34, 40-41, 316-317
    foreign policy in Asia, 178, 353-354
    government agencies in Vietnam,
    29-30, 34
    import subsidies, errors of, 316

United States (*cont'd*)
    military commitment in Vietnam,
    12-15
    in Paris peace talks, *see* Paris
    peace talks
    in politics of Vietnam, 49, 54, 63-
    66, 259-260, 342-343
    propaganda against, 23, 218
    refugee aid program, 280
    role in Vietnam, ix-xii, 3, 59, 62,
    82, 119-120, 123, 153-155, 165-
    166, 174, 177-178, 297, 299-300,
    342-343, 351-354
    training programs, 40-41, 47, 182
    in Vietnam elections, 76, 151, 158,
    159, 162
    Vietnamese attitude toward, 23, 64-
    65, 80, 121-122, 150, 153-155,
    171-172, 218-219, 249-250, 304,
    312, 342; *see also* Anti-Ameri-
    canism
    Vietnamese breach with, after Tet
    offensive, 207-208
    Vietnamese dependence on aid,
    146-147
    visitors to Vietnam, 323-324
United States Armed Forces:
    advisers with Vietnamese, 15-18,
    119, 134-135
    Air Force, 93, 111, 112
    bombing of North Vietnam, *see*
    North Vietnam, bombing of
    in Cambodia, 342, 349-352
    in Demilitarized Zone, 131-132
    intelligence services, *see* Intelli-
    gence services; Phoenix Program
    at Khe Sanh, 214-215
    Marines, *see* Marine Corps, U.S.
    massacre of civilians, 281*n*., 333,
    345-346
    military actions, 24-25, 80-81, 95,
    138-139, 142, 167, 194, 205, 216
    morale, 139-140
    Navy, 94, 110
    Operation Hastings, 101-110, 118-
    119
    Operation Oregon, 139
    Operation Prairie, 111-119
    in II Corps area, 138-139
    strength in Vietnam, 119, 140
    in Tet offensive, 189, 192, 193, 200,
    212-213
    withdrawal from Vietnam, 55, 172,
    178, 251, 284, 286-288, 303, 320;
    Nixon's plan, 286-288, 297, 298,
    325-327, 350-351; North Vietna-

United States Armed Forces (*cont'd*)
mese response to, 287, 300, 319-
320; in Paris peace talks, 223
United States Operations Mission, 29
U Thant, 228

Vale, Lieutenant Colonel S. A., 104,
108
Van, Tram Van, 85, 127
Vance, Cyrus, 246
Vien, Cao Van, 100, 156, 163
Vietcong, 2, 3, 6, 37, 248-249, 251
anti-American propaganda, 23
attitude of population toward, 80
attitude of soldiers toward war, 335
Buddhists aided by, 68
coercion and persuasion used, 180
commandos, 197-199
at Dong Ha, 93
in election, threats, 85
hamlets controlled by, 47, 79-80,
126, 146, 181, 255-256, 337
influence lessened, 183
infrastructure (V.C.I.), capture of,
254, 278, 281
at Lai Chu, 283
in Mekong Delta, 330-331, 339-340
military actions, 8, 23-26, 136-137,
166-167, 178-180, 194, 210-211
military plans, 11-12, 26, 89
military strength, 24-25, 119, 137,
140, 253-254, 334
in North Vietnamese invasion of
South, 96, 99, 118
North Vietnamese units with, 80-
81.
Operation Oregon against, 139
organizations directed by, 251
population controlled by, percentage, 180
recruitment decreasing, 166
refugees used by, 8, 25
rural construction programs
against, 37-39, 43-44
search for, in villages, 281
subversive tactics, 21-23, 45-47, 147
territory controlled by, near Saigon,
45-47, 89, 137
terrorism, 146, 199, 217-218, 255,
339
in Tet offensive, 189, 193, 195-200,
204
Vietminh, 37, 136, 137, 175, 183,
190, 222, 227, 240, 290, 305

Vietminh formula for government,
286, 320
Vietnam:
coalition government, *see* Coalition government
partitioning, possible, 320-321, 331-
332
revolutionary movements in, 173-
175, 290
unification of, 2-3, 172-173, 223
Vietnam, Republic of:
attitude of people toward government, 80, 121, 129, 218-219, 221,
258-259, 277-278, 303, 305, 308
Cabinet, 50, 184, 220, 303; new,
308-309; peace Cabinet, 251-252,
271, 288, 298
Constituent Assembly, 83-85, 87,
125; blocs and factions, 127;
candidates, 78; constitution
drafted, 84-87, 124-125; election,
83, 152
constitution: preparation of, 84-87,
124-125; revision of, 298
corruption increased by American
aid, 146-147, 341
democracy in, 152-153
Directory, 35, 48-49, 51-52, 57, 59,
75; Buddhist opposition to, 62, 65,
70; Constituent Assembly and, 84;
Constitution and, 124; in elections, 77; personal friction in, 87-
88
economic and social problems, 21-
23, 28, 146-147, 315-317, 351
elections, *see* Elections
government: Communist opposition to, 288-290; inadequacy of,
15-16, 207-209, 288, 303-304;
legality of, 326; military, 34-36,
125, 148; reorganization proposed, 258-260, 298, 299; under
Thieu, *see* Thieu, Nguyen Van
National Assembly, 124, 185-186,
203, 208, 247, 272, 275, 309;
election, 124, 151-152
in Paris peace talks, *see* Paris
peace talks
political conflicts, 48-60, 62-73,
294-296
political parties, 126-127, 161, 174,
258, 272, 274-275, 295-296, 314,
344, 346
population under government control, 312-314, 337

Vietnam, Republic of: (*cont'd*)
Premier, choice of, 159-160
public opinion on Communism and
Thieu, 343
reform programs, 32-34
Senate, 185-186, 275; election, 151-
153, 160-161
Supreme Court, 351
United States relations with, *see
under* United States
Vietnamese Armed Forces (A.R.V.N.):
American advisers with, 15-18, 119,
134-135
American aid to, 250, 260-261, 317
arrest of dissidents in, 77
Buddhists and, 68, 95
in Cambodia, 349-350
Danang attack, 57-58, 62-63, 66,
70
in Demilitarized Zone, 131-132
in elections, 75
inadequacy, causes of, 13-15
at Khe Sanh, 214
meeting of general officers, 156-
157
military actions, 24-26, 167, 195,
216
morale, 297, 299, 306-307
motivation and leadership, 14-15
Navy, 94
in North Vietnamese invasion, 92,
96, 99-100
in Operation Hastings, 102, 109-
110
in reconstruction programs, 30, 182
reorganization, possible, 135, 163,
261, 307
Revolutionary Development Teams
and, 134, 136, 164-165
strength, 13, 24, 119
in Tet offensive, 189, 192, 193, 200,
212
see also Vietnam war, Vietnamization
Vietnam Quoc Dan Dang Party, 85,
275
Vietnam war:
American attitude toward, 23, 132-
133, 166, 170-171
Communist attitude toward, 48,
129, 141-145, 166-168, 327-330,
334-336

Vietnam war: (*cont'd*)
escalation in spring of 1969, 262-
265
North Vietnamese control of, 142-
143
Vietnamese attitude toward, 132-
133, 150, 165-166, 170-172
Vietnamization (de-Americanization), 133, 303-304, 317-319, 315-
326, 338, 341-342, 347, 351; Communist attitude toward, 319, 327,
329; *see also* United States
Armed Forces, withdrawal from
Vietnam
Village Liberation Committees (Revolutionary Committees), 228-229,
254, 276
Village People's Liberation Councils,
229, 276
Villages:
consolidation program, 338
number of, 337
see also Hamlets; Revolutionary
Development Program; Rural
construction programs
Vinh, Lieutenant General Nguyen
Van, 143, 144
Vinh Binh Province, 339-340
Vinh Long, 192
Vung Tau training center, 38, 40, 47,
135, 256, 336
Vy, General Nguyen Van, 125, 318

Walt, General Lewis W., 42, 44
in North Vietnamese invasion, 92-
94, 98, 100-101, 103
Westmoreland, General William C.,
63, 81, 95, 120, 136, 165, 166,
215, 342
in North Vietnamese invasion, 92-
94, 97-98, 100, 103, 109, 112
responsibility for pacification programs, 133-135, 139-140
trip with author, 138-140
White Paper, American, 8
Wilson, Lieutenant Robert, 107
Worker-Peasant Alliance, 295, 296

Xuan, Mai Huu, 72

Yeats, William B., 313
Yew, Lee Kuan, 178
Yugoslavia, 294